BUILDING A CITY: WRITINGS
ON AGNON'S BUCZACZ
IN MEMORY OF ALAN MINTZ

BUILDING A CITY: WRITINGS ON AGNON'S BUCZACZ IN MEMORY OF ALAN MINTZ

Edited by Sheila E. Jelen, Jeffrey Saks, and Wendy Zierler

Indiana University Press

This book is a publication of

Indiana University Press
Office of Scholarly Publishing
Herman B Wells Library 350
1320 East 10th Street
Bloomington, Indiana 47405 USA

iupress.org

Manufactured in the United States of America

DOI: 10.2979/BuildingaCityWriting.0.0.00

Library of Congress Cataloging-in-Publication Data

Names: Mintz, Alan L. honouree. | Jelen, Sheila E., editor. | Zierler, Wendy, editor.
Title: Building a city : writings on Agnon's Buczacz in memory of Alan Mintz / edited by Sheila Jelen and Wendy Zierler.
Description: Bloomington, Indiana : Indiana University Press, [2023] | Includes bibliographical references and index. | Summary: "The fiction of Nobel Laureate Shmuel Yosef Agnon is the foundation of the array of scholarly essays as seen through the career of Alan Mintz, visionary scholar and professor of Jewish literature at the Jewish Theological Seminary of America. Mintz introduced Agnon's posthumously published *Ir Umeloah* (A City in Its Fullness)—a series of linked stories set in the 17th century and focused on Agnon's hometown, Buczacz, a town in what is currently western Ukraine—to an English reading audience, and argued that Agnon's unique treatment of Buczacz in *A City in its Fullness*, navigating the sometimes tenuous boundary of the modernist and the mythical, was a full-throated, self-conscious literary response to the Holocaust. This collection of essay is an extension of a memorial dedicated to Mintz's memory (who died suddenly in 2017) which combines selections of Alan's work from the beginning, middle and end of his career, with autobiographical tributes from older and younger scholars alike. The scholarly essays dealing with Agnon and Buczacz is an effort to remember the career of Alan Mintz and his contribution to the world of Jewish studies and within the world of Jewish communal life."
Identifiers: LCCN 2022039444 | ISBN 9780253065407 (paperback)
Subjects: LCSH: Agnon, Shmuel Yosef, 1887-1970—Criticism and interpretation. | Buchach/Buczacz (Ukraine)—In literature. | Mintz, Alan L. | LCGFT: Literary criticism. | Essays. | Festschriften.
Classification: LCC PJ5053.A4 Z5927 2023 | DDC 892.43/5—dc23/eng/20220926
LC record available at https://lccn.loc.gov/2022039444

First Printing 2022

Contents

BUILDING A CITY: WRITINGS
ON AGNON'S BUCZACZ
IN MEMORY OF ALAN MINTZ

Introduction

The Book Regained: S.Y. Agnon Comes Home

Sheila E. Jelen and Wendy Zierler

LITTLE DID WENDY know, when asked to speak at a book launch event for Alan Mintz's *Ancestral Tales: The Buczacz Stories of S.Y. Agnon*, that it would turn into a memorial evening, and that her preparation for a brief talk to take place on June 5, 2017 would become a three-year collaborative project of memorializing Alan and his work in a special double issue of *Prooftexts* and in this book. Little did she know, that her excursus into Alan's work on *'Ir umelo'ah*, Agnon's posthumously published collection of stories about his Diaspora home town of Buczacz, would culminate in the project of assembling together with Sheila, an array of scholarly essays that built on the work that his premature and sudden death on May 19, 2017, had cut so summarily short. Alan Mintz's loss continues to be felt intensely within the world of Jewish Studies and within the world of Jewish communal life. He was an activist in the progressive Jewish community since his student days and a major voice in Hebrew literary studies. Colleagues and students, friends and family, have worked to commemorate the significant scholarly and community legacy he left behind and to continue that legacy by picking up, to the best of our ability, where that work abruptly left off.

Looking back now over the arc of Alan Mintz's career reveals that the fiction of Nobel Laureate Shmuel Yosef Agnon—both its treatment of and relevance to Diaspora life—literally bracketed his scholarly life. To be sure, his was no one-note scholarly corpus. After making the shift from the Victorian novel to Hebrew and Jewish literature, Alan wrote about a wide array of subjects in Jewish and Israeli literature and culture, ranging from Jewish literary responses to catastrophe, to Hebrew autobiography, to American Hebrew poetry, to popular film and the Holocaust, and to contemporary Israeli fiction. But his interest in Agnon was a constant. His first published essay about Hebrew literature, a 1967 essay in *Response* magazine, written when he was still a Columbia undergraduate and which we have reproduced in this volume, was on the figure of Hananyah in Agnon's 1934 novella *Bilvav yamim* (In the Heart of Seas) as a model for the potential creative contributions of the younger generation to American Jewish life.[1] What was remarkable about that essay, aside from its precocity and eloquence, was its mix of

---

1. "Agnon on the Individual and the Community," *Response* (Summer 1967): 28–31.

exegesis and autobiography: the critic reading the writer and himself at the same time. Alan would return to this earlier essay in 2001 for a special issue of *Prooftexts* dedicated to re-readings of texts and would admit to his readers that he chose to contribute a "rereading" of *Bilvav yamim* "out of curiosity to catch a glimpse of who I was circa 1966."[2] And while he blushed at the seeming "ḥutzpah" of his younger self, as well as his brazen disregard for the centrality of Zion in Agnon's novella, he reaffirmed the core of his argument about Hananyah from that earlier piece. Rereading himself reading Agnon in the context of mid-century Diaspora Jewish life, he spoke of his ongoing commitment to going against the headlong Jewish American rush into the mainstream, even as he knew that he could not embrace the life of old world Orthodoxy. "Here," he said, "Agnon came to my aid,"[3] giving "through the reverie of reading what could not be given to me in life."[4]

Alan's interest in reading Agnon and Bucacz as a way of reading himself as a Diaspora Hebraist / cultural intellectual, persisted throughout his career and would ultimately be focused around his in-depth study of Agnon's Posthumously published *'Ir umelo'ah*, in his book *Ancestral Tales*. The seed of that later project, of course, had already been planted in the Introduction to *A Book that Was Lost*, the collection of Agnon stories that Alan co-edited with friend and colleague Anne Golomb Hoffman, insofar as the Introduction proudly foregrounded the inclusion of two previously untranslated stories from *'Ir umelo'ah*: "Buczacz" and "Mazal dagim" (Pisces). And the final line of that introductory essay specifically pointed to Agnon's fiction as a way of reading our own lives and times: "For Agnon, the past exists for the sake of the present, and its stories and symbols exist for the sake of what they offer to the construction of a fuller Jewish self-understanding in the modern world."[5]

If Alan Mintz began his career with an essay about an Agnon novella as a way of addressing the potential contributions of creative young people to American Jewish life, he spent his final years bringing several of the final works, and the final words, of the Nobel Laureate Prize Winning author S.Y. Agnon to an English reading audience. In an anthology of translations (*A City in Its Fullness*) published a year before Alan's death in 2016, and in his critical monograph *Ancestral Tales*, Alan introduced Agnon's posthumously published *'Ir umelo'ah* (A City in Its Fullness), a series of linked stories set in the 17th century and focused on Agnon's hometown, Buczacz, a town in what is currently Western Ukraine. Acknowledging and reversing his prior claims in his book *Hurban* that

2. Alan L. Mintz, "In The Seas of Youth," *Prooftexts*, vol. 21, no. 1 (Winter 2001), 60.
3. Mintz, "In the Seas of Youth," 69.
4. Mintz, "In the Seas of Youth," 69-70.
5. Anne Golomb Hoffman and Alan Mintz, "Introduction," S.Y. Agnon, *A Book That Was Lost: Thirty-Five Stories*, eds. Alan L. Mintz and Anne Golomb Hoffman, expanded edition (New Milford, CT: The Toby Press, 2008), 34.

Agnon did not treat the Holocaust in his literary oeuvre,[6] Mintz openly argued in this study that Agnon's unique treatment of Buczacz in *A City in its Fullness*, navigating the sometimes tenuous boundary of the modernist and the mythical, was a full-throated, self-conscious literary response to the Holocaust. This argument resonates meaningfully with Nitza Ben-Dov's reading that we have included in this volume of Agnon's story "Hasiman," which Alan dubbed the "Consecration Story" of *'Ir umelo'ah*.

The plan for Alan's last, unfinished project was an autobiographical, literary biography of Agnon, one that would include his own experience, his background in Worcester, MA and his journey to Hebraism, even as it tracked the life story of the great Nobel Laureate from Buczacz to Jerusalem.[7] We all regret that the plans for this work, still incipient, never came to full fruition. This collection of essays, however, an extension of a volume of *Prooftexts* (37:3, Spring 2019), dedicated to Alan's memory, which combines selections of Alan's work from the beginning, middle and end of his career, with autobiographical tributes from older and younger scholars alike, and scholarly essays dealing with Agnon and Buczacz, is our effort to compensate for the book by Alan Mintz that was lost to this world by his sudden passing.

When we invited colleagues to contribute to that volume, we received far more than we anticipated. So much was lost when Alan was taken from us unexpectedly. And so much was gained when he allowed so many people to share his life, who in turn felt called to commemorate his loss. Periodically, in the process of editing the *Prooftexts* memorial volume, when issues came up (as issues always do), several of Alan's close friends and colleagues said to us, "If only Alan were here, he would know how to approach this." Alan was a visionary with a heart. He fostered more careers and inspired more excitement and hope for the study of Hebrew literature and the remaking of modern Jewish experience, intellectual as well as spiritual, than we can capture in a single volume or introduction. But the publication of this additional memorial book speaks to an even deeper need than to make the most of the outpouring of grief and scholarship that accompanied our original call for papers. We are living in a moment when English speakers are attempting, yet again, to make sense of a world lost in the Holocaust, a moment that has seen *Fiddler on the Roof* produced in Yiddish on Broadway and with people enrolling in Yiddish classes in universities and community centers across the country.

Jeffrey Shandler has called this a "post-vernacular" moment, one in which the Yiddish language is certainly of relevance, but the culture surrounding the language—the idioms and the inflections, the images and the associations—of

6. See Alan Mintz, *Hurban* (New York: Columbia University Press, 1984), 159 and Alan Mintz, *Ancestral Tales* (Stanford: Stanford University Press, 2017), 12-13.
7. The first and only extant chapter of this study appeared this year in Alan Mintz, *American Hebraist: Essays on Agnon and Modern Jewish Literature*, Beverly Bailis and David Stern eds. (Penn State University Press, 2022

even greater interest. People are searching for the Yiddish that was first introduced in English in the 1950s with Elizabeth Herzog's and Mark *Zborowski's Life
is With People: The Culture of the Shtetl,* or Eliezer Greenberg's and Irving Howe's
Treasury of Yiddish Stories. Maurice Samuel, in *The World of Sholem Aleichem,*
published in 1943, before the end of World War II, articulated the impulse beautifully in his attempt to introduce East European Jewish experience to a second
generation audience of Americans through glosses of Sholem Aleichem's Tevye
stories and an accompanying, accessible, commentary. What does our moment
have in common with that moment, nearly half a century ago? And where do
Hebrew and Agnon fit in?

As Alan wrote in several autobiographical essays published over the course of
the last decade, his Hebrew education in the 1960s was the product of a Diaspora
Hebraism, a hold-over from the years before the State of Israel was established
and love of the Hebrew language could be separated from Zionist aspirations.
Later in the 20th century, he would write in his essay "Hebrew in America: A
Memoir,"

> Because Zionism became indissolubly identified with Israel, it's hard for us
> to imagine a time when the territorial dimension of Zionism was largely a
> romantic fantasy while its cultural dimension was real and revolutionary. As a
> vehicle for Jewish modernity, Hebrew had already been hard at work as a liter-
> ary language and a cultural program for over a hundred years. Hebrew, after
> all, was the portable component of the Jewish national idea, and that quality
> made it highly suitable for export in the shabby valises of passionate young
> men who arrived on these shores from the cultural centers of Eastern Europe.[8]

Mintz was educated in an afternoon Hebrew school in Worcester, Massachusetts that was not established in order to render its student body literate in
synagogue liturgy, as most synagogue affiliated religious schools are today. Neither was it reverently focused on identification with the State of Israel. Rather, his
school concentrated on Hebrew language literacy, on Hebrew culture, on Jewish
textuality, and on Hebraism as opposed to Zionism.

While Alan was educated Jewishly in an anachronistically pre-Zionist world populated by aging Hebraists, we are living now as Jewish Americans and academics in a
world where Hebraism has become so much the province of Israel as to be irrelevant
to American life. At the same time, Israel is so saturated with American culture and
English speakers that it has become a less than ideal place to learn and immerse one-
self in Hebrew. Sheila recently gave a lecture at a conference on Holocaust testimonies
in which she explored the idea that it might be easier to teach Hebrew culture today
from the vantage point of the Zionist youth activists involved in the ghetto uprisings

---

8. Alan L. Mintz, "Hebrew in America: A Memoir," in *What We Talk About When We Talk About
Hebrew (And What It Means for Americans)* (Seattle: University of Washington Press, 2018), 211.

than it is from the perspective of the current State of Israel. We all know, of course, that the end goal for all those Zionist youth activists in Akiva, Hashomer Hatsaʻir, Hapoʻel Hatsiyyoni, etc. who facilitated the ghetto uprisings, was emigration to Palestine and the establishment of a territorialized homeland. But as Alan Mintz indicated in his 1978 review of Hillel Halkin's *Letter to an American Friend*, American Jewish life and American Zionism, firmly rooted on American soil, are no mere passing phase. Agnon's Buczacz fiction, which trumpets the ideal of "Buczacz when it was Buczacz," even as it laments in certain stories Buczacz's eradication first by World War 1 and then by the Holocaust, gives unabashed voice to the notion of vibrant, multi-faceted Jewish life in the Diaspora with strong but increasingly complex ties with the State of Israel.

And so, while Agnon continues to be a mainstay of Israeli literary scholarship, with several major Israeli Agnon scholars represented in this book, Alan Mintz's work on Agnon, in collaboration with Toby Press, Agnon series editor (and co-editor of the present volume) Jeffrey Saks, has revealed the specific power and potential draw of Agnon and Buczacz for American / Diaspora readers today. Several of the contributors to this book, the editors of this volume included, were educated in the modern yeshiva movement, the day school system that taught us Hebrew as both a Zionist and a religious imperative. We read Agnon in high school and were surprised, as young adults spending significant amounts of time in Israel, to find that modern Israelis found Agnon inaccessible. Agnon, was, for us, eminently approachable, with his beautiful evocation of every stratum of traditional Hebrew, from the prayer-book liturgy through the Torah and the midrash as well, through his weaving together of themes that rendered tradition distinctly modern, and modernity distinctly traditional.

The elderly woman, Tehilla, with a small stool in tow which she used to sit and pray at the Western Wall, to whom we were first introduced in 11th grade, came back in a college syllabus on Gender and Jewish literature; the little boy who gave his mother's silk kerchief to a messiah-like beggar at the gates of his shtetl on the morning of his bar mitzvah; the goat who made its way through a cave to the Land of Israel with a parchment note tucked into his ear—all these and more have populated our imaginations since high school. They continue to accompany us through the halls of home and classroom, as we educate our children and university students alike.

The moment for Agnon has returned, we believe, in a world where the Yiddish post-vernacular is no longer a sufficient means of understanding the East European world that was destroyed in the Holocaust and that laid the foundation for the world we now inhabit. Something else has to inhabit that empty space. Reading Agnon in high quality English translation, but with thoughtful and careful glosses, interpretations, and contextualizations, enhances not only our understanding of Agnon, but ourselves. Over the last decade, the Toby Press, has made great strides in bringing high quality translations and annotations of Agnon to an English reading audience. Agnon's Buczacz stories could not have arrived in English too soon.

And what does the Buczacz oeuvre add to the mix that was not to be found before? The subtleties of Holocaust commemoration without the impulse toward terror, of memorialization without the impulse toward sentimentality, the impulse toward Eastern Europe without inappropriate nostalgia. Agnon's Buczacz is set in the pre-modern period. It is not Irving Howe's Lower East Side or Saul Bellow's West Side of Chicago. It is a weird place filled with visits to Hell, as described in Alan's lecture at UCLA, transcribed in this volume, or with ghostly encounters. What can this Buczacz afford today's English-reading audience? It can provide an encounter with a world that preceded the State of Israel, but was destroyed by the Holocaust; an encounter with allusions to the language and the traditions and the literary sensibilities that preceded modern nationalism and are in no way defined by it; an encounter with one of the greatest Hebrew minds of the modern era, a mind unashamed of the literary and cultural elements that constituted it; an encounter with a culture preserved in text not by theme but by allusion, nuance, gesture, reverence.

This is not to say that there aren't moments in *'Ir umelo'ah* where Agnon presents a seemingly idealized, overly rosy portrait of the *Kehillah Kedoshah* of Buczacz, a community structured around worship and sacred study. As Mintz shows, however, these moments are balanced throughout by other moments, where both the Jews and Gentiles alike fall hopelessly short of the ideal. One good illustration concerns the representation of Polish-Jewish relations in a remarkable story called "Hashutafim" (The Partners), which tells of how it came to be that a Jewish family and their descendants came to live in the cavernous basement of the Buczacz Town Hall. Alan featured this story prominently in the UCLA lecture transcribed here. In deference to the place of importance that he assigned the story in his Buczacz work, we have reprinted the story in this anthology too.

There is no reason to assume that the story told in "Hashutafim" is based on actual historical fact. But that doesn't mean that the story is not "true" in its own way. According to Mintz, "the permanent and irrevocable installation of a Jewish family in the basement of the grandest edifice in Buczacz stands for the place of the Jew in Polish society in general. True, the Jews are in the basement, but their right to be there has been secured,"[9] that is, until the twentieth century when that right is tragically taken away. Agnon adds here to the historical record by imagining what could or should have transpired between Jews and Poles, had the Poles recognized the Jews for "their constancy, sobriety, initiative, and good

---

9. Alan Mintz, *Ancestral Tales* (Stanford: Stanford University Press, 2017), 236

sense."[10] Lest we be misled by this imagined alternative history, *Ir umelo'ah* is filled with stories of Polish cruelty to the Jews and of Jewish cruelty to one another, distinctive and idiosyncratic stories that balance the record and that prevent an overly idealized picture. At the same time, the conclusion of "Hashutafim," which identifies the last remaining descendant of Nachum Zeev's family with Emmanuel Ringelblum, the curator of the Oyneg shabbes archives who was murdered in the Warsaw ghetto, returns this work of alternative history to the grim, limiting frame of Holocaust history. Agnon, as Alan so ably demonstrates had no interest "in giving us merely a flattened, objective and historically accurate Buczacz ... In these stories, Agnon makes no apology for giving us his version of Buczacz by recouping the city under the sign of study and worship, *torah ve'avodah*, and proceeding to organize his fictional universe around these two values. Yet as a great imaginative writer, Agnon also knows that the stuff of good stories lies not in the norms but in the deviations from the norms."[11]

Volume Overview

This volume is divided into four sections. "Alan Mintz on Agnon and Diaspora Hebraism" brings together three pieces by Alan that represent the beautiful osmosis between the personal, the communal, and the academic that was Alan's trademark. The first, as mentioned above, is an essay from *Response*, the journal Alan founded during his student days, in 1967. Titled "Agnon On the Individual and the Community," the article was an adapted version of a paper on Agnon's *Bilvav hayamim* (In the Heart of the Seas) written for a Jewish Theological Seminary class taught by Professor Avraham Holtz (one of the people to whom Alan dedicated *Ancestral Tales*). In 1967, the article served as a platform for a discussion of Alan's vision for Jewish community outside of the established, older-generation American institutions. A youthful indictment of the available spiritual resources for American Jews, Mintz turns to an analysis of the character "Hananya" (the inspiration, it seems for Amos Oz's Hananya *in A Perfect Peace*), who "is not governed by the conventions of society ... but seems to exist on a different level of reality, one free from the mundane prejudices and inhibitions of the communal faithful." Mintz draws inspiration from Hananya in this essay, for himself and for the community of young adults whom he believes have something to offer the Jewish American world, if only they will step forward and if only the institutions they must confront, in Mintz's view, will be attentive to them. In a rallying cry in both directions—directed toward his peers and toward the institutions in which he was raised—Mintz concludes his remarks on *In the Heart of the Seas* as follows:

10. Mintz, *Ancestral Tales*, 250.
11. Mintz, *Ancestral Tales*, 395.

Today there are people finishing school who have a vital and creative vision of Judaism to offer to the organized community. Whether they will try to contribute, whether the community will receive them, and whether they will have the courage to persevere in the face of disregard, all constitute questions not yet answered.

Mintz's deployment of Hebrew literature, and specifically Agnon's story, in service of the project of community building and spiritual inspiration, was something that he would do for the rest of his life. As David Roskies says in the tribute to Mintz that we have included in the second part of this volume, in which he describes the founding of *Prooftexts* in 1980, and his and Mintz's common cause both inside and outside the academy, "the decision to throw ourselves into Jewish literary studies was driven in part by the desire to foster the cultural renewal of the Jewish people." Mintz, Roskies asserts, "lived his personal drama inside the literary text."

This becomes evident in the second Mintz piece included in this volume, an essay he published in in the April 13, 2017 edition of *Mosaic* and which he expanded into a personal essay published in Naomi Sokoloff and Nancy Berg's *What We Talk About When We Talk About Hebrew* (Samuel and Althea Stroum Lectures in Jewish Studies, 2018). In this essay, Mintz reflects on his relationship with Hebraism within the context of his own Jewish synagogue and afterschool Judaic education in Worcester, MA and connects those early experiences with his later choice, after completing a PhD in English literature, to move into the study and teaching of Hebrew literature, not simply from an academic, but also from an American-Jewish cultural perspective. "What has happened to the study of Hebrew in America?" he asks. Like his friend and collaborator James Diamond in his essay, "Agnon's *Yamim Nora'im*: Then and Now," which is included in the third section of this volume, Mintz explores not only what American Jews knew of Hebrew or of Hebrew literature and culture, but how American Jews utilized it, drew from it, and were informed by it. In his essay, Diamond looks at Agnon's high holiday anthology *Yamim nora'im*, published in 1938, and asks, "Can Agnon's volume engage people today?" Tragically killed in a car accident in 2013, Diamond, former Hebrew literature scholar and director of Princeton's Center for Jewish Life, was in the midst of preparing with Mintz at the time of his death a critical edition of Agnon's *Hamashal vehanimshal* (The Parable and its Lesson) as well as an English translation and critical edition of *'Ir umelo'ah*. Mintz finished this work and dedicated it to the memory of his beloved colleague and friend, only to die himself before the publication of *Ancestral Tales,* his own study of *'Ir umelo'ah.*

One unexpected death after another. Indeed, from its very inception, with Agnon's writing of *'Ir umelo'ah* itself, we see a legacy of death-induced truncations. Agnon's ambitions of salvaging the glory days of Buczacz in *'Ir umelo'ah* were cut short by Agnon's death in 1970. (The book was published posthumously by Emuna Yaron, Agnon's daughter, in 1973.) The first part of Mintz's project took the form of a translated, edited volume of substantial sections from Agnon's *'Ir umelo'ah* , a project that had been initiated by James S. Diamond but was completed by Alan and Jeffrey Saks after Diamond's death. This volume, and the *Prooftexts* issue which inspired it, is our variation on Mintz's commitment to Diamond, and his commitment, as well, to situating Hebrew literature fully at the center of contemporary American Jewish experience and Diaspora Jewish experience writ large.

The third work by Mintz included here is the transcription and adaptation of a lecture delivered on February 12, 2015 at UCLA as the 14th in an annual series endowed in the name of pioneering Agnon scholar Arnold Band. In his introductory remarks, not included in the transcription, Alan mentions his debt to Band as the first American scholar to write a book-length analysis of Agnon's oeuvre, as well as acknowledging Band's role as a founding member of the Association of Jewish Studies and the Hebrew Literature Division there. (Mintz would go on to dedicate *Ancestral Tales* to Band, as well as to his first Hebrew literature professor, Avraham Holtz.) Valuing good citizenship was a trademark of Alan's and it comes out beautifully in his words about Dr. Band. Titled, "Late Agnon and the Reimagining of Galician Jewry," we chose to transcribe and include this lecture here because it captures Alan's accessible and engaging approach to what, in other hands, could have been an arcane subject. In addition to that, this lecture gives us a glimpse of the concerns and questions that underlie the final project of Mintz's career: What was Agnon's relationship to history? How did Agnon view his own role as a modernist conveying pre-modern subjects? What happened to the typical modern, literary, self-deprecating, psychologically self-conscious Agnonian narrator in this later work? We have included, at the end of this volume, one of the Agnon stories he discusses in this lecture ("Hashutafim" or "The Partners") as well as an excerpt of a second story he discusses in the lecture (*Hamashal vehani-mashal,* translated by Diamond as *The Parable and its Lesson*.) in order to reanimate the lecture, but also to share, in English, the experience of reading Agnon's Buczacz stories.

The second part of this book draws on several of the tributes shared by colleagues of Mintz's in our earlier *Prooftexts* memorial volume. David Roskies, mentioned earlier, Sidra Dekoven Ezrahi, and Anne Golomb Hoffman, all colleagues, friends, and collaborators of Mintz, address the trajectory of his career, their own feelings of gratitude to Mintz for his collegiality and respect, and their grief over his loss. Referring to her collaboration with Mintz on *A Book That Was Lost and Other Stories* (1995), a collection of Agnon's stories that were, to a large extent, previously not translated into English, Golomb Hoffman, quoting Agnon, says:

> A book that was lost: absence and presence. We wait together for a lost book to arrive. Agnon's words and Alan's, too, remind us not only of what we have lost, but also of what we have, and of what we may yet come to share.

With the loss of Alan, we may have lost the final part of his Agnon project, but many colleagues, scholars, and students, have stepped into the breach to continue what Alan began. Sidra Dekoven Ezrahi sums it up beautifully when she says of her friendship with Alan, "I would only have wished for one thing: more time...."

This book's third section introduces twelve critical essays on Agnon that serve as a continuation of the fruitful dialogue with Mintz's final Buczacz project that began in the *Prooftexts* memorial volume. Some of the essays are reprinted from *Prooftexts*, and some are being published for the first time here. These essays are divided into four categories: "Buczacz," "In His Generation," "Early and Late" and "A Revolutionary Traditionalist."

The essays in the first section, "Buczacz," specifically address Agnon's Buczacz stories, either in his posthumous *'Ir umelo'ah* or in his 1939 *Oreah natah lalun* (A Guest for the Night). Avidov Lipsker's "The Heavenly City: A Historiographic Paradigm in the Scholastic Cartography of S.Y. Agnon" advances a thesis that counters the dominant trend in Agnon scholarship, which sees *'Ir umelo'ah* as a work dedicated in its entirety to memorializing Buczacz. Instead, Lipsker observes that the majority of *'Ir umelo'ah* actually concerns the Torah scholars and rabbinic decisors in Kraków. Agnon looked to that 16th and 17th century urban Jewish community as the "Heavenly City," which contained "everything within it" (as hinted at in the city's Aramaic nickname: *Kraka dekula bei*). By contrast, Agnon sees Buczacz as the city destined for annihilation (as hinted at in the volume's title taken from the wrathful prophecy in Amos 43:8). Lipsker's "historiographic paradigm" of Galician cartography presents two contrasting cities, one idealized and "heavenly," and the other biographical, upon which Agnon mapped the Jewish world. This literary-philosophical structure also serves as a foundation for other Agnon novels, such as *In Mr. Lublin's Store* and *Only Yesterday*.

Another common thread between these three essays is their grappling with the question of how Agnon used his Buczacz stories as a means of addressing the Holocaust. Mintz's revised claim about Agnon's lack of engagement with the Holocaust, discussed above, is at the forefront of all the analyses presented here. In "Salvage Poetics: Agnon's 'Imaginary Real' in *A Guest for the Night*," Sheila Jelen asks how Agnon employs his "literary art to mobilize, improve upon, and preserve a culture that is in rapid decline." She explores how Agnon views "post-cataclysmic Jewry in light of Jewish texts" and argues that:

> modern Jewish texts frequently engage in a presentation of nineteenth-century East European Jewry as a world not simply devoted to texts, but constituted by them. Traditional Jewish texts within modern literary works thus represent traditional Jewish society metonymically and are read by popular audiences as an ethnographic précis of a culture.

Reading *Oreah natah lalun,* the most developed Buczacz-focused precursor to Agnon's *'Ir umelo'ah,* as an attempt, in part, to salvage the culture of the traditional House of Study or *Beit Midrash* in the aftermath of World War I, the novel would, she claims, serve as a model for the kinds of literary salvage efforts to be adopted by other texts within both an Israeli and an American context after the Holocaust. The final essay in the "Buczacz" section is "Divine Compassion From an Ironic Perspective: The Experience of the Shoah in Agnon's 'The Sign,'" by Nitza Ben-Dov. In this essay, Ben-Dov looks at "Hasiman" (The Sign), the story that Emuna Yaron placed at the conclusion of *'Ir umelo'ah* and which Alan Mintz placed at the beginning as an overture or consecration story, as an explicit response to the Holocaust, not just through its articulation of the narrator's having found out at the beginning of the story about the liquidation of Buczacz's Jewish inhabitants, but through its pervasive irony. This irony, Ben-Dov argues, butts against the purported piety expressed throughout the story. The story's "subtle but incisive irony" according to Ben-Dov constitutes the "protest it lodges against a God who did nothing to prevent this carnage."

The second section of critical essays, titled, "In his Generation," situates Agnon alongside other writers and public figures of his moment, and in some cases, from his hometown. The first essay, "Tales from Half-Asia: Small-Town Galicians Encounter the World," by Omer Bartov, considers Agnon within the context of "several individuals from Buczacz and its environs born between the mid-nineteenth century and World War I." Bartov, a historian says that his first encounter with Agnon's *'Ir umelo'ah* grew out of his research on a book about Buczacz. He realized, in working with it, says Bartov, that *'Ir umelo'ah* is not only a literary masterpiece. It is, he says, "at the same time a kind of biography of Buczacz and, by extension, of an entire vanished world." Wendy Zierler's "Rereading Flaubert's Madame Bovary and Agnon's *Sippur pashut* through Devorah Baron's 'Fradl,'" the second essay in this section, reads Agnon's *Sippur pashut* (1935) alongside Devorah Baron's corpus, theorizing an "intersexual dialogue" and considering each writer's fascination with Gustav Flaubert's *Madame Bovary*, with its depiction of small-twn provincial life, and the fate and aspirations of a married, female protagonist. The final essay in this section, "Last Translations: Gershom Scholem's Renditions of S.Y. Agnon's Polish Tales," by Maya Barzilai, looks at Gershon Scholem's translations into German of two of Agnon's stories, "Beit hakenesset haggadol," (The Great Synagogue) and "Ma'aseh Azriel Moshe shomer hasefarim," (The Story of Azriel Moshe, the Book Keeper). Barzilai reads Scholem's choice of stories as a "form of lamentation" and a "labor of mourning" for the Judaism in the face of German-Jewish assimilation. Through a series of close readings, Barzilai analyzes Scholem's translational choices and considers all that which remains "buried" in the German versions of the Hebrew stories.

"Early and Late," the third section of the critical essays, brings Agnon's stories into dialogue with one another. In his essay, " From "A City of the Dead" to *A City in Its Fullness*: Evolving Depictions of Buczacz in the Long Agnonian Arc," Jeffrey Saks finds precedent for Agnon's latest work in some of his earliest. Agnon's "'Ir hametim"

("The City of the Dead"), which appeared in the Lvov Hebrew newspaper, *Ha'et*, on March 14, 1907, preceded the publication of Agnon's signature story "'Agunot" by about a year, yet it contained all the ingredients of Agnon's later Buczacz projects. According to Saks,

> Agnon's long career can be traced as an arc from youthful, almost cynical focus on death and decay to a more mature and creative form of writing. With tragic irony, this later voice was surely informed by the knowledge of Buczacz's final destruction but was already formed prior to the Holocaust.

At the end of his essay, Saks includes the first and only extant English translation of " 'Ir hametim."

The concept of "early and late" in the arc of Agnon's career is also documented in Glenda Abramson's essay, "'Our Town': Mr. Stern and Buczacz In Mr. Lublin's Store." While *Beḥanuto shel Mar Lublin* (In Mr. Lublin's Store) was not published until late in Agnon's life, in 1964, it draws from the decades of Agnon's stay in Germany, from 1912 to 1924, anatomizing Jewish life in Germany and reflecting on Buczacz from a distance. Abramson points out that even though *Beḥanuto shel Mar Lublin* presents meditations on a modern Buczacz, and *'Ir umelo'ah* presents a pre-modern Buczacz,

> A City is a celebration of the richness of Jewish life in Buczacz in all its greatness and baseness, a reconstruction, consecration, and memorial, whereas *Mr. Lublin* is largely a lament.

With its final composition and publication closer to the Holocaust years themselves, *In Mr. Lublin's Store*, therefore appears to represent an earlier, more traumatized response to the war. By the time he had thrown himself fully into his Buczacz work, it seems, with *'Ir umelo'ah*, Agnon had worked out another way to commemorate the Holocaust and memorialize Buczacz—through a presentation of a city untouched by the multi-faceted destructive powers of modernity.

Michal Arbell, in *"A Simple Story*: Szybusz and the Crisis of Parenting," tracks Agnon's interest in the emotional and ethical aspects of matchmaking over the course of five decades of writing, before engaging in a close reading of this theme in *Sippur pashut*. Arbell revisits and critiques a reading that Mintz did of the theme of arranged marriage in the context of modernity, parenthood, and moral values in Agnon's story "In a Single Moment" (from *'Ir umelo'ah*) as it relates to the same theme in *A Simple Story*.

The final set of essays in this volume is organized under the heading of "A Revolutionary Traditionalist," based on Gershon Shaked's formulation of that appellation to explain Agnon's style. The first of these essays is by Haim Be'er. Titled, "'New Faces'—A Study of Agnon's Simple Story," Be'er's essay provides an intertextual study of Agnon's *A Simple Story* as a means of illustrating how the meeting of old texts with new texts underscores Agnon's dramatic skill at presenting a revolutionary modernism within a traditionalist frame. Ariel Hirschfeld's "The Source and the Depth of Oblivion: Story and Folktale in Two Stories by Agnon" extends this intertextual discussion in its treatment of Agnon's debt to folktales. He says:

> Between his own writings and the creations of the "folk," Agnon wove a complex web of tensions, paradoxes and uncertainties, to the point that his work appears at times intentionally to subvert the traditional story, to wreck its credibility or its basic notions of aesthetics and value, no less than it is sustained by the story's vitality and its ability to constitute an identity and a sense of the genuine.

The final essay in this volume, "Agnon's *Yamim Nora'im*: Then and Now" by James Diamond, already alluded to above, approaches this notion, presented by Gershon Shaked of Agnon as a "revolutionary traditionalist"[12] from yet another angle. In his discussion of Agnon's anthology on the high holidays, Diamond connects Agnon's focus on these holidays to the theme of Yom Kippur in the apostasy literature of modern Hebrew from the turn of the twentieth century. According to Diamond, Agnon's focus on this holiday (alongside Rosh ha-Shanah) did not just articulate a need to provide readers with an accessible guide to the texts of this holiday, it was also a way of expressing his understanding of the challenges of modernity.

The largest common denominator of all these essays is the focus on *'Ir umelo'ah* and *Sippur pashut*, it would seem. The latter, a modernist novel about modern dilemmas albeit set in a fictionalized version of early twentieth century Buczacz (renamed Szybusz), and the former, a series of loosely interconnected stories about a pre-modern Jewish city in a largely pre-modern form, demonstrate the breadth and depth of Agnon's artistry. Like Agnon, Alan Mintz had a long, illustrious and variegated career. Rounding it out with an exhaustive study of Agnon's *'Ir umelo'ah* was a homecoming of sorts for Alan, returning him to his first published essay on Hebrew literature, on a novella about a group of pilgrims to the Land of Israel who hail originally from Bucacz. But the homecoming Alan experienced in his final work on Agnon went deeper than writing about him again after 50 years. As Mintz was just beginning to write about his own Hebrew education in Worcester MA, he explored Agnon's homage to Buczacz, finding ways to revisit his own original sources of inspiration, alongside Agnon's.

12. See Gershon Shaked, *Shmuel Yosef Agnon: A Revolutionary Traditionalist*. Alan Mintz, "Review of 'Shmuel Yosef Agnon: A Revolutionary Traditionalist', by Gershon Shaked," *Hebrew Studies*, vol. 32 (1991): 61–66

SHEILA E. JELEN, is the Zantker Professor of Jewish Literature, Culture, and History at the University of Kentucky, and the director of the Program in Hebrew and Jewish Studies there. She is the author, most recently, of *Salvage Poetics: Post-Holocaust American Jewish Folk Ethnographies* (2020) and co-editor of *Reconstructing the Old Country: American Jewry in the Post-Holocaust Decades* (2017). Jelen's newest book, *Israeli Salvage Poetics* is forthcoming in 2023.

WENDY ZIERLER is Sigmund Falk Professor of Modern Jewish Literature and Feminist Studies at HUC-JIR in New York. She is the author of *Movies and Midrash: Popular Film and Jewish Religious Conversation* (SUNY Press, Finalist for the National Jewish Book Award in Modern Jewish Thought and Experience, 2017), *And Rachel Stole the Idols: The Emergence of Hebrew Women's Writing* (Wayne State UP, 2004) and co-editor with Carole Balin, of *To Tread on New Ground: Selected Writings of Hava Shapiro* (2014). In 2017 she became co-editor of *Prooftexts: A Journal of Jewish Literary History.* Together with Josh Garroway she is editor of *These Truths We Hold: Judaism in an Age of Truthiness* (HUC Press, 2022).

I. Alan L. Mintz on Agnon and Diaspora Hebraism

1   *Agnon on the Individual and the Community*

Alan Mintz

THE AWARD OF the Nobel Prize in Literature to S.Y. Agnon in October evoked very interesting critical reaction. The statement of the award made clear that Agnon was being recognized as the greatest living Hebrew author, and it implied that his achievement, with no disparagement intended, was located largely in a Jewish sphere. Reacting against this parochial limitation, American Jewish critics hastened to assert that Agnon's importance stood on his universality. He stages, they claim, the inner conflicts of modern man in an East European setting. To permit this controversy to create a tension between the universal and parochial interpretations of Agnon's work is a travesty and a waste of literary critical effort.

A recent reading of Agnon's important novella, *Bilvav yamim* (*In the Heart of Seas*), has shown the controversy to be misdirected and the tension to be artificial. On one hand, it is only common sense that a work has permanent worth only if it can be phrased in universal terms. On the other, a universal can be relevant only when it can be transposed into the parochial contexts in which we all live. In the case of *Bilvav yamim,* the author says something of paramount importance about the relationship between the individual and the community. This insight can have meaning, however, only after we liberate the characters from their particular predicaments and apply the knowledge to our own urgent, albeit parochial, problems.

The question of the relationship between the individual and the community is now so pressing because the last forty years have witnessed its almost complete disintegration in the American Jewish community. Until now, because Judaism has been misunderstood, and there have been few around to properly explain it, bright people growing, up in the Jewish community have become dissassodated from it. They have acknowledged Jewishness but rejected Judaism, and have reserved a special key on their typewriters for this syndrome: *Alienation.* Members of the generation coming of age now, however, find their connections with the organized community just as tenuous but for different reasons. They think they are on the verge of discovering the contemporary value of Judaism, but at the same time they are repulsed by the vulgarity and hostility to criticism and creativity that Judaism's organized forms display.

Let us look at the book. *Bilvav yamim* is the story of a group of Polish Jews who leave their *shtetl* and by wagon and boat finally make their way to Jerusalem. Although their occupations are different, they all make very real sacrifices in order "to go up." One leaves his ritual slaughtering knife behind, another his classroom,

Building a City: Writings on Agnon's Buczacz in Memory of Alan Mintz (2022): 017–019
DOI: 10.2979/BuildingaCityWriting.0.0.02

another his butcher shop; another his properties, and still another a wife divorced because she refused to accompany her husband. They are ordinary people who naturally are attached to their families and their *shtetl*. To give up this security and start on a dangerous extended journey is a serious undertaking requiring an equally serious sacrifice. The travel on land is smooth but the voyage on the sea and the lack of sustenance in Jerusalem immerse the Faithful in struggles and hardships.

If Agnon limited himself - to their story, his book would be less a novel and more a chronicle. Opposite the Faithful, however, he introduces an entirely fresh character: Hananya. Hananya is a Jew who has been wandering from town to town all his life carrying his belongings in a kerchief. He comes to the *shtetl* and asks to accompany them to the Holy Land. Since he is the tenth man and thus completes a *minyan*, they are happy to accept him. Through the story, we come to know him for his altruism and good deeds, and when the ship leaves for Palestine, he is detained on land, finding a woman whose husband's death was unknown to her but witnessed by him. He is not governed by the conventions of society, and is able to appreciate the righteousness and honesty of bandits who capture him.

Hananya is a very different character from the Faithful. They are householders and are making a serious material sacrifice by engaging in a communal effort which requires leaving a secure life and attempting such a journey. Hananya, on the other hand, has been going from place to place trying to go up to *Eretz Yisrael* all his life. They decide to give up their way of life; he never has to decide because he was always going up. Such is his nature. The contrast is drawn even more sharply, for they have difficulty in understanding Hananya, not to mention appreciating him. Because he is different, he is relegated to a lower status among them. He spends most of his time driving the woman's wagon and collecting wood and cooking. When the Faithful spend Shabbat in the town of Vaas, he is not called to the Torah with the rest of them. But Hananya shines above them as a totally free individual who exudes love and values men for their qualities, not their positions in society. He seems to exist on a different level of reality, one free from the mundane prejudices and inhibitions of the communal Faithful.

Agnon establishes this tension between the individual and the community, but, a consummate artist, he makes no explicit value judgment. We may, however, find one implicit by examining the structure of the book. In the beginning, Hananya accompanies them on land; in the middle, he is absent from the story; at the end, he is with them in Jerusalem. Parallel to this pattern, in the beginning, the Faithful are very successful in their journey on land; in the middle, after embarking without Hananya, they come close to drowning in a storm at sea; at the end, they are together with him in the Holy Land. The interlocking structure makes clear that with him they succeed and without him they almost die. When the Faithful set sail without him, they find that they are unable to praytogether because their *minyan* crumbles in his absence. Based on the artistic identity of structural form and content, we can say that without the inclusion of the free individual the effort of the community cannot succeed. If we think, moreover, that the individual seems to exist on a different plane of reality from the community, as in *Bilvav yamim,* we learn that these two levels must unite in order that the community can go up.

Agnon, however, limits the extent of this union by use of a symbolic device. The kerchief, in which Hananya' wraps all he owns, comes to represent his individuality. When he is stripped naked by the border guards at the beginning of the story, they leave him only his kerchief to cover himself with. The Faithful make fun of it because it is shabby and old, and offer him better bags for his belongings. But Hananya declines their offers and poignantly responds:

"אין...אני רשאי לזלזל בה"

"But I am not permitted to cheapen it so."

When the ship has sailed without him and he has no other means of travel, Hananya spreads his kerchief over the water, sits on it and skims the seas to *Eretz Yisrael.* The kerchief is a very delicate and beautiful metaphor for that which the individual cannot hand over to the community and still retain his uniqueness. That is the boundary, and the individual need contribute only on the condition that he can keep what has made him so.

Agnon's prescription is instructive but problematical. It bids the individual, especially the person who is free and creative, realize a responsibility to contribute to and participate in the community, for otherwise it cannot progress. But, at the same time, Agnon does not conceal the fact that such a person is unappreciated, disparaged and lured away from his principles. Clearly, the community-individual relationship is not one of self-help but rather requires unselfishness on the part of the individual. In the story, Hananya had love, freedom and singleness of purpose to offer the Faithful. Similarly, today there are people finishing school who have a vital and creative vision of Judaism to offer to the organized community. Whether they will try to contribute, whether the community will receive them, and whether they will have the courage to persevere in the face of disregard, all constitute questions not yet answered.

ALAN MINTZ (1948–2017) was Chana Kekst Professor of Jewish Literature at the Jewish Theological Seminary of America and co-founder and co-editor of *Prooftexts: A Journal of Jewish Literary History,* a publication that helped to establish the field of Jewish literary studies. Among his many books were *Hurban: Responses to Catastrophe in Hebrew Literature* (1984), *Banished From Their Father's Table: Loss of Faith and Hebrew Autobiography* (1989), *Sanctuary in the Wilderness: A Critical Introduction to American Hebrew Poetry* (2011), and *Ancestral Tales: Reading the Buczacz Stories of S.Y. Agnon* (2017).

2   Late Agnon and the Reimagining of Galician Jewry (14th Annual Band Lecture, UCLA, February 12, 2015)

Alan Mintz

Wʜᴀᴛ ɪ ᴡᴀɴᴛ to do this afternoon is to begin by retelling an Agnon story. When I am finished retelling it, I will look with you at the last few paragraphs of that story and then talk generally about Buczacz, and why Agnon devoted so much of his energy to writing a cycle of stories about this town, what its importance is within literary studies and Agnon studies, and then conclude with another story on a very different theme.

The first story is a story called *Hamashal vehanimshal* [The Parable and its Lesson], which came out in book form through Stanford University Press, translated by the late James Diamond, with an essay by myself. The story unfolds in the 17th Century, a generation after the Chmielnicki massacres which took place in 1648. It takes place in Buczacz. The city of Buczacz was not destroyed in the massacres, but most citizens of Buczacz, in the story, have lost someone if not in their immediate family, then in their extended family during the massacres. Buczacz, in the aftermath, is forced to reconstruct itself as a small community.

The story begins on one Sabbath morning. The beadle, the shamash, is on the *bimah* in the synagogue and he hears somebody talking during the Torah reading. Now apparently this was something that was not done at that time. The shamash tries to stop this chatter, first by giving very small verbal signals to the talker, raising his eyebrow, clicking his tongue, brandishing a finger. Nothing works. It turns out that the young man who is talking is the son-in-law of the richest man in town who has recently been, in a sense, acquired as a trophy and brought to Buczacz. He is whispering into the ear of a friend of his, something about the Torah reading. In other words, this is not about the stock market—this is about the Torah reading. But even this was not done back then. So the shamash descends from the dais and goes to the congregation, takes this young man by the elbow and escorts him out of the synagogue.

This is an extraordinary scandal in Buczacz because he is embarrassing somebody in public, which is a statutory sin, and not just anybody, but the man who funds the operation of the community—his son-in-law. So the following night, after the Sabbath is over, Sunday night, a *beit din* [a Jewish court] is convened to bring him up on charges, and in his defense, he tells a story that lasts for about 40 pages. It's a monologue within the narrative of the story as a whole.

Building a City: Writings on Agnon's Buczacz in Memory of Alan Mintz (2022): 020–031
DOI: 10.2979/BuildingaCityWriting.0.0.03

He says, "When I was a very young man, I was the assistant to Rabbi Moshe, the rabbi of the community at that time." (He is referring back to the generation right after the Chmielnick: massacres) "We were all recovering from this trauma." Rabbi Moshe had discovered only one relative from his whole extended family who had survived the massacre—it was a young girl named Zlata—and through serendipitous circumstances, he was able to find her, bring her into his home and raise her as his own daughter. Then he gave her in marriage to his most distinguished student, Aron. They were married, and then shortly after the marriage, Aron disappears. Nobody can find him. So this fifteen-year-old girl, the apple of Rav Moshe's eye, is rendered an 'agunah, a chained woman who can't remarry because you can't remarry unless you can document the death of the husband. Rav Moshe is bereft.

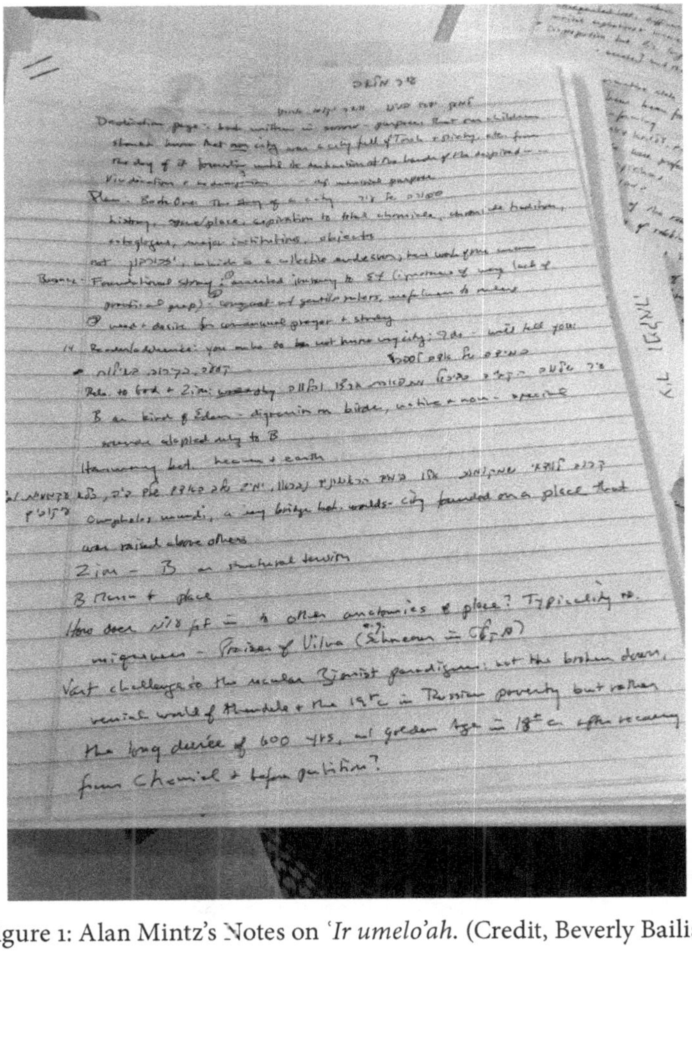

Figure 1: Alan Mintz's Notes on '*Ir umelo'ah*. (Credit, Beverly Bailis).

He consults with all the rabbis in the Polish/Lithuanian commonwealth, but there are no solutions. He reasons that if Aron were still alive, he would have somehow let Zlata know and release her. So Reb Moshe conceives of the idea of descending into the netherworld, into Gehinnom [hell], to look for Aron and to document the fact of his death. There so happens to be near Buczacz an entryway into Gehinnom that is very convenient. After Yom Kippur, before Sukkot, Rav Moshe and the *shamash* embark on a journey into Gehinnom. They enter, and soon enough they find Aron. (This is reminiscent of Dante's inferno, probably filtered through a translation by Emmanuel of Rome who wrote Hebrew poetry, a contemporary of Dante's). They find this young man, who is weeping and weeping, and he tells this story:

After the terrible massacres of the Chmilenicki era, this young very bright student could not reconcile the fact that God had allowed this to be done to his people. So he undertakes a search of Jewish philosophical literature to try to find answers to a problem of theodicy. Unsatisfied he learns Latin and he begins to borrow books from the local priest and to see if other religions have answers to this, and through this relationship with the local priest he is, in a sense, kidnapped, and dies of a broken heart. The reason why he can't leave the grave and inform Zlata of the fact that he is dead is because there is a cross over his grave and that prevents him from migrating among the living to inform her.

This is terribly sad. But it's not the main event that happens in the journey to Gehinnom. The main event is that while they are there, the shamash notices that there are different compartments of Gehinnom in which tortures are taking place. In two of them he sees that those who are being tortured are great scholars from all the periods, beginning from the period of the Tanna'im, the period of the Mishnah, through the Spanish age and the heads of academies, and he can't understand it. How could it be that these enormous scholars of extraordinary reputation are being tortured? And the tortures that they are undergoing are quite grotesque. In one of them, each of these scholars is bouncing around in outer space, 4000 cubits from each other, and each of them is trying to hawk their insights, their *ḥiddushim*, each of them is so important and though they are trying to speak nobody is hearing. When two of them get close to each other, and they begin to try to foist their insights on each other, the lips of the speaker begin to extend and envelop the whole body and the ears of the listener enfold the body of the listener. No communication is possible. Then they float off again.

The descriptions here are taken from the medieval ethical literature of Gehinnom. None of these are in the Talmud, but somehow in the early middle ages, the imagination of what happens in the afterlife really blossoms. We don't know exactly where it comes from, but it's very well established. Agnon took this template, and he inserted this new content of what they're being punished for. It is punishment for a kind of scholarly arrogance, the fact that they can't really overcome the need to tell somebody something in the middle of the Torah reading. This was the same problem of the young man in the synagogue who thought that his particular idea on the weekly portion was so important that it had to supersede the word of God being read from the Torah.

The shamash asks Rabbi Moshe why these people are here and Rabbi Moshe explains that even though these people were extraordinary scholars, during the service on Shabbat mornings they could not restrain themselves and they had to hock their wares to others, and for that sin they were there in Gehinnom. The shamash is incredulous and he says I know this is something we are not supposed to do, but isn't this a little extreme, to be punished in this way? This is frightening to him because the disproportion between the sin and the punishment. So they go back to this world and life goes on as usual. The fact that the rabbi had identified Rabbi Aron in the netherworld is not a halachic solution. On that basis you cannot free Zlata from her *aginut*, from her chained situation.

Coming back to the court in which the shamash is giving his testimony, we hear him say "What I did, though I understand it was a sin and I'll have to be punished for it, I was actually saving this young man and I was ready to incur this guilt myself in order to save him from something, you can't imagine how terrible it was." All of Buczacz exonerates him [the shamash]. They say, "we're sorry, we didn't know that this was such an important issue," and they reinstate him, and the whole community makes this a major responsibility to ensure there is no competition between the divine voice that is read by the Torah readers on Sabbath mornings and the voices of human beings. Buczacz makes this one of their standards.

Here we come to the end of the story. There is a 54-year gap. The events that the shamash narrates took place 54 years before the telling of the story. Buczacz has since become a mercantile center and every time they call someone up to the Torah now, they have to name all the full names of all the family members of everybody and the Torah reading has in a sense become somewhat corrupted. They commit themselves to return to the correct path, and they do this by writing down this incident in the *pinkas* of the community. The *pinkas* is a big ledger, a kind of minute book. The word *pinkas* is actually a Greek word that we have in the Mishnah, where births and deaths and taxes are written down, and if there is a fire or some anomalous event, that is written down too. But in the story we are looking at, the townspeople commit themselves to taking a fresh page of the *pinkas* and writing down the testimony of the shamash and this describes how it was written and what happened to it:

> After he made his corrections, the scribe sat down and copied everything out in a handsome script, the letters written the way they were written in Buczacz at the time when Buczacz was Buczacz, each letter distinct unto itself and each one in its place on the line, like people standing for the silent devotion, where the tall ones stick up like a lamed and the short ones are small as a yod, and all

of them are directed to the same place. Had the *pinkas* not been consumed in the flames, we could have read the entire story just as it was set down in its true and original form, with the unique blend of wisdom and faith that marked all that our ancestors wrote and did and thought and said. But now that book is no more, and Buczacz is destroyed, and many thousands of Jews have been slain, the least of them the equal of the most eminent of the Gentiles, who watched the loathsome monsters destroy the world and did nothing. From our town there were those who were buried alive in graves they dug for themselves there were those who were never buried; and there were those upon whom the murderers poured kerosene and were immolated one by one, limb-by-limb. So now, since that *pinkas* went up in the flames, and Buczacz has been destroyed, and the deeds of the former generations have been forgotten in the recent suffering, I pondered the possibility that the *Gehinnom* of our time would make us forget the that the shamash saw, and the story about it, and all we can learn from that story. So I said to myself, Let me put it all down in a book and thus create a memorial to a holy community that sanctified its life in its death as its ancestors sanctified their lives with Torah, which is our life. (67–68)

What interests me about the end of the story is two things. One is the image of the *pinkas*. We have here a description of the original *pinkas*, the large ledger. The perfection of the calligraphy of the scribe and the perfection of the phraseology is described. And then the ledger is burnt, when Buczacz is destroyed by the Nazis and the Ukranian helpers at various times around 1942–1943. And so the story we're reading, the narrator tells us, is in fact not the story that is written in the *pinkas*. That story was destroyed. The narrator has taken it upon himself to retell, to reinscribe, the *pinkas* that was lost. In other words, the kinds of stories that this narrator is telling is in fact an attempt to replace or restore the *pinkas*. What's important here in this larger project is the fact that Agnon is thinking, "How am I going to write about the early years of Buczacz, not the modern memory of Buczacz, but the early years, the 17th, 18th century? I need a model which is not about artists writing literature, but something that is more based on communal memory, such as what can be found in a *pinkas*." So the *pinkas* here is, in a sense, re-appropriated, refurbished, as a model for writing.

The second point that interests me in the passage above is, as in all Agnon's stories, a kind of wicked gesture here at the end that might sound like this: Yes, that *pinkas* was perfect, the writing was perfect. It was extraordinary. But we don't have it anymore and I've rewritten it. So let me ask you now which version you would prefer to have. Would you prefer the official version, which is extremely straightforward, no digressions, to tricks, no artistry, no literature, but a few facts? Or would you prefer to have the replacement, which is the story that I wrote, which goes into the psychology, which uses the whole kitbag of modernist literary techniques?"

Now of course we would say it's terrible that the *pinkas* is burnt, but I think any modern reader would say, "I'll take the story." So the question of the replacement of the story for the historical reality becomes one of the very self-conscious motifs of Agnon's project.

This historical Buczacz, the real city, isn't important enough to merit a name on the map. It's a small Jewish community and I think this is an extraordinarily important point. Agnon decided to write this epic sequence of stories about a city, which was maybe in the third tier of Galician cities. I often think of this in comparison to the city I came from, Worcester, Massachusetts, where there were about 10,000 Jews. There were 10,000 Jews in Buczacz as well. If I decided to devote my life's work to the Jewry of Worcester, Massachusetts, you would think that was rather strange. What is Worcester that it should deserve to be memorialized in this way? What Agnon is doing is in a sense making Buczacz into James Joyce's Dublin. He is choosing the town that he came from, which was a significant city, but not a terribly important city, and making it representative of a whole civilization. It's a choice that is driven not by patriotism and nostalgia as much as by a modernist calculation, which is that if you want to get to a larger universal truth, you have to go through the extremely parochial and specific. So the only way you can understand the classic civilization of Polish Jewry is by looking at one locality, by drilling down and going into that in extraordinary depth. So I think that's the move for Buczacz—it was Buczacz because that is where Agnon came from, it was very important to him. But it was not so much that he wanted to write a version of a memorial volume as a gesture of piety toward his hometown, but rather as a strategic choice of how this extraordinary civilization could be best rendered artistically. It was only through the particularity of that place and not trying to do it as an anthology of legends or stories from all parts of Jewish communities in the area that Agnon wanted to work.

Why did Agnon turn his attention to this in the last years of his life? He had many extraordinary projects after WWII that he was following out: great anthologies, a new cycle of stories about his years in Germany. But now it looks to us like the great organizing project for him was a cycle of about 140 stories about Buczacz. They were published from 1955 until his death in 1970. The project was left unfinished at the time that he died and he left to his daughter Emunah Yaron a series of guidelines and files and books about which stories should go into what sections and she took it upon herself to put them together according to his directives and it was published in 1973. At that time, there was not much interest in these stories.

Think of 1973 as the year of the Yom Kippur War. Of the posthumous works of Agnon, the greatest interest was in the first one, the novel *Shira*, a novel of scandal, of the goings on of the European intelligentsia at the Hebrew University. It had been a long awaited novel. And the stories in *'Ir umelo'ah*, [A City in its Fullness], a volume of about 750 pages, 144 stories, the collected stories, many of them were published during his lifetime in literary supplements, and about half of them weren't (some interesting ones were held back). But at the time they were published, and in 1973, the interest in Jewish life in Eastern Europe among the Israeli reading public was rather low.

So in the 50s and the 60s, while David Ben Gurion is building the state and all its apparatus, and ingathering the exiles, and defending the young state from a precarious security situation and establishing all that is necessary to create a state, Agnon is busy building a city in his imagination in Eastern Europe. He writes to the great critic at the time, Kurtzweil, "boneh ani 'ir" [I am building a city], in response to a query from Kurtzweil about what he was working on at the time. I think if you contrast in your mind the state building project of Ben Gurion and Agnon's city building project, the reconstruction of an imaginary city, you can understand why there is little interest in it. At that time, stories about Eastern Europe were in a sense retrograde. If you read them in Hebrew literature, they were written in order to mount a critique on the corrupt nature of the old world of exile.

Now I think it looks very different to us. What we see in this collection of stories is something unprecedented in Jewish literature. This is a magisterial modern, modernist writer deciding to go back beyond modern memory to reconstruct through the medium of the modern story the lost world of Polish Jewry. What's interesting about the collection of stories is that it ends in the early 19th century. In other words, there are books of Agnon and novels that also take place in Buczacz, such as *A Guest for the Night* and *A Simple Story* but they are much closer to the modern period. *Sippur pashut* is set in the years before WWI, and *A Guest for the Night* is in the aftermath of WWI. But here Agnon has decided to go back way before the possibility of a connection of a live memory to father, grandfather and so forth.

What's extraordinary about this is that he undertakes to bring this world back to life, but he tries to do it through the medium of modernist art. In other words, not to leave the kitbag of modernist literary techniques with his more surrealist stories, but rather to take the whole kit and caboodle and to bring that world back to life through the vehicle of modern literature. I don't know of any precedent. I think of Bashevis Singer's *Satan in Goray*, his first novel, as something that is perhaps something like that but I can't think of anything else.

It's also worth thinking about this collection as Agnon's response to the Holocaust. When I was a younger scholar I wrote a book called *Ḥurban: Responses to Catastrophe in Hebrew Literature* and I looked at Agnon, looking for stories that relate explicitly to the Holocaust. There were a few here and there, but I didn't really find the Holocaust, and I concluded in my short sightedness at the time that Agnon's was a vast literary enterprise that had been formed before the war and couldn't be recalibrated or turned around to relate to the Holocaust. I was terribly wrong. Agnon's response to the Holocaust was his dedication to a different form of Holocaust literature. We think of Holocaust literature as a literature that is about death and atrocity or about the effects on the second generation, and so forth. For Agnon, the response to the Holocaust was to go back, way back, and to try, with his tools, his kind of modernist storytelling, to revivify that world. It will be helpful to us when we think about Holocaust literature to widen the scope of that term and to not make the representation of atrocity the sole criterion of what we think of as Holocaust literature.

If you've ever taken a literature class you know that stories don't just happen, but they are told, by people, by a narrator, and every story has a narrator, whether the narrator is named and present, or implicit. Everything is told from some point of view. In the main canon of Agnon's stories, he often makes a persona of himself as a kind of narrator: a middle aged sort of religious persona, an autobiographical persona, a device that Arnold Band has called "a dramatized ego." It's a wonderful technique because it takes the egotism of the self and ironizes it, casts it in ironic terms. Agnon is always in a sense making fun of himself and using that persona as a way of viewing reality. When you go back to the 18th century you can't do that. You can't have the fictional convention of someone alive now being a witness then. So you need a narrator who belongs to that period. So what Agnon does in these stories is to invent a new kind of narrator who is a man of Buczacz, somebody of that time and place whose attitudes are aligned with the attitudes of the rabbinic elite of the time whose religious and theological beliefs are the beliefs of the serious rabbinic scholars of that time and he makes this entity (it's not a person, but a device) the narrator of those stories. So the narrator is somebody who is not in the 20th century but who belongs to the period in the stories. He is narrating events not from an ironic distance but as somebody who believes it as well, is someone who is part of that cognitive orbit. So we have a complex system here, where the narrator who is narrating to a kind of implied audience within the time of other listeners and readers who believe in the kind of things that people choose to believe in these centuries; but at the same time you have the implied author who is Agnon living in Jerusalem in Talpiot in the 50s and 60s, publishing in *Ha'aretz*, and communicating to a kind of authorial audience who are the literate readers of the literary supplements in Israel at that time. So the interplay of an implied audience of a narrator belonging to that period and a contemporary author communicating with a contemporary audience makes these narratives very interesting. And I think this is one of the great things that Agnon has done, is to invent a narrator, and that narrator takes his authority from something of the voice of the *pinkas*, of the ledger, of that kind of communal voice, and it maintains some of the crotchetiness and the digressions that we find in Agnon in general. It was a big renunciation for Agnon because he had to give up the autobiographical persona and create something that was more impersonal in which he could not, in a sense, perform his ego the way he could in the other stories.

The final point I want to move toward in getting to our last story is the question of historical truth, or historicity. What did Agnon base his stories on? Are these stories true? Can they be used as sources for East European Jewish history? It's a very fraught and difficult area. My senior colleague at JTS, Avraham Holtz, has devoted his life to tracking down the sources and realia and references in some of Agnon's major work, and in the end, it's an interesting mixture. Agnon is extremely aware of all the political changes and all the sociological differences in each period he's writing about. He is, for example, writing about the Polish period, the post partition period. But his stories tell events that are invented by the faculty of the imagination, perhaps based on kernels of local legends at the time but basically the production of an extraordinary imagination. So my question is, what is the effect of Agnon's invention? What is he doing when he takes the armature of historical events and augments it? That augmentation, that supplement of the imagination, what direction is it going in? What's its purpose? Is it to entertain, to spin a yarn? Why not, if you are going to write about history, just write about history?

The second story I want to discuss is called "Hashutafim" [The Partners]. This story is set in the middle of the 18th century and it is against the background of the fact that most cities in Galicia were privately owned by great Polish noble families. These nobles were otherwise known as magnates. A magnate could own a city and many dozens of towns around it and there were certain major families, the Potocki family, or the Rozowels, who would own hundreds of cities and hundreds of towns as well as vast tracts of forests and natural resources. One fact about the Polish/Lithuanian commonwealth is that there was no kingship, no central government. These lords were a law onto themselves. They had total control and were extremely wealthy and they owned the cities. The Jews lived in them by virtue of charters that had been granted to them. They had been originally brought to the areas of what was southeastern Poland at the time to be a managerial class and to mediate between the Ruthenian peasants and the Polish nobility. The Polish nobility wasn't interested in running shops and managing taverns. They didn't do labor, so the Jews did that for them. The scale of difference between a man like Count Potocki, who we are going to meet in a moment, and the Jews, was extraordinary.

The story is about a man who operated a tavern as his fathers did. Taverns were a very important way for Polish landowners to make use of their surplus grain. There weren't barges, there weren't trains, so if you had grain what were you going to do with it? What you were going to do with it was convert it into alcohol, and through a monopoly sell it to the peasants. It was the Jews who would do the selling because it was the Jews who remained sober, so this was a major occupational formation for the Jews. The Jews leased these taverns where the proprietary drink was the alcohol made from the grain of the Polish noble. This became an area of great debate and criticism where the Jews were accused of narcotizing the Ruthenian peasants and making the land not productive.

"Hashutafim" is about a man named Naḥum Moshe who is kicked out because he can't come up with enough of profit for the local Polish noble. He is wandering in the woods. He doesn't have a way to make a living. He comes upon a Ukranian peasant who once had been a client of his in the tavern and whom he had been good to. He is a charcoal maker and the man's children have grown up and left home so he offers to teach the Jew the art of charcoal making. The Jew learns from him, and he moves to a village that is quite a distance from Buczacz in order to make a living at this new trade. He makes charcoal, in which you cut down trees, and you put them through controlled burns. Two or three days a week he gets up in the middle of the night and he makes a very long trek to Buczacz. The reason he goes there is that he wants to pray with other Jews in the synagogue, be a part of the minyan. He gets up around midnight and takes a long trip through the trackless forest to get there. And he does this out of devotion and a burning desire to be part of the community.

One morning, very early, in the middle of the night when Naḥum Moshe is on his way, he comes across a body that is slumped at the foot of a tree. He recognizes the body and sees that it is none other than Count Potocki himself. Apparently Count Potocki had been part of a hunting part the day before, he had become separated from the hunting party when he had chased an arrow that he had shot at a deer. Isolated in this trackless forest he couldn't be found. And there he was, asleep and in danger of dying of hypothermia. So Naḥum Moshe picks him up and puts him over his shoulder, together with his bag of charcoal and his tallis and tefillin that he is bringing to go into town, and takes him another hour back to his village, puts him on the bed that is made of rocks and straw in the one room that he and his wife occupy and they bring him back to life. This is the moment that I wanted to share with you and then I'll tell you the rest of the story.

> Approximately 1800 Jews lived on Count Potocki's estates. Among them were leaseholders of farmland and taverns, grain merchants and businessmen who handled financial transactions, not to mention shopkeepers and artisans. But when it came to the customs of the Jews, he had not the least notion, and their prayers he had never heard, except for parodies of them by the banquet jesters who were a constant presence at his table. Now that fate had placed him in the home of a Jew who was preparing himself for prayer, he lay there with eyes wide open, waiting to see a Jew at prayer. But fatigue and the brandy overcame him and he fell asleep. (2c7)

Naḥum Moshe gets the wagon, and begins the journey, but of course a wagon can't get through the forest, so they have to abandon it, and the Jew has to carry Count Potocki. It takes a whole day to get back to Buczacz. All of the count's retainers are combing the area so there is nobody at the palace. Naḥum Moshe brings the count to the palace, puts him on a chair of some sort, and he leaves because he is incredibly uncomfortable being anywhere near the centralized Polish authority.

The count in the story is a man who is very grateful—very autocratic, but very grateful—and he wants to know how to reward this Jew and he has a chamberlain who advises him on the Jewish affairs of the area. Potocki says, " I want to give him some money." The chamberlain says, "He doesn't want any money." "So what does he want?" He wants to live in town so that he can go to the synagogue on a daily basis. "So let him live in town." Apparently there were no apartments available in the town, there was a great fire recently, so all the living quarters have been taken up. So the count himself comes up with an idea. He had recently built a magnificent city hall, which still exists and at the time was much greater than the city of Buczacz itself within the world of Ukraine. He said, "We built a gigantic basement in this city hall." They had built a big basement because in the 17th century there were many Tartar incursions into the area where the Tartars would come in from the east and take off nobles and ransom them. So they built this with secret tunnels for escape. Potocki said, "There have been no tartar invasions for a long time. I am going to give the basement to him for perpetuity." That's very good, but how is he going to make a living? He is going to make a living by being given the yeast concession for the town. The yeast concession is usually given to the rabbi's wife, to the rebbetzin, because the rabbis don't usually get much of a salary and the wife can be given the yeast concession as supplemental income. It turns out that the current rabbi's wife is ill. She can't do it, so the yeast concession is available.

So it's done. Naḥum Moshe has a place to live, and he has a livelihood and he and his family occupy this abandoned basement. He makes a gesture toward his co-religionists, the small merchants—the city hall is right in the center of town, right by the marketplace, and the small merchants who don't have stores but who set up stalls everyday have to lug their merchandise back to the workers' quarters which is quite a distance from the center of town. So he allows them every night to store their merchandise in the basement and to pick it up in the morning. He produces excellent yeast and the family is very happy.

This goes on for a century or so where descendants of his family enjoy this perpetual leasehold of the basement of this Polish city hall. The descendants of Count Potocki, on the other hand, are beside themselves. They are very embarrassed by this. They make offers of all sorts of money to the descendants of Naḥum Moshe, but they have this guaranteed forever. Finally it comes to an end when the Austrians take over and all these agreements are nullified. The story picks up again at the end of the 19th century when the last descendant has moved out of the basement because his wife had contracted some kind of illness from living in a basement. She's died and one of his daughters gets swept off in a bad marriage and becomes an agunah, an abandoned wife, but the other daughter becomes a ward of the narrator's mother, of the Agnon figure's mother. They help her make a very good marriage to a man named Ringelblum. Their child is Emmanuel

Ringelblum, the great social scientist who created the *Oyneg Shabbos* archive in the Warsaw Ghetto. This is where the story more or less ends, spanning about a century and a half, bringing us up to one of the distinguished descendants of Buczacz, Emmanuel Ringelblum. (Simeon Wiesenthal is also from Buczacz, as well as Freud's grandparents.) This last moment brings us to the Holocaust. The Holocaust in these stories is not foremost in the awareness of the narrator, but it's on the horizon of this awareness. He knows about it but it's not part of his world, it's more like a magical realist premise.

I want to conclude by asking the question: Where did Agnon get this? The story may have grown from the germ of the fact that there was a family living in the basement of the city hall. This is a very anomalous situation, and so he is in a sense retrofitting a story of origins for how this family could have gotten there. What's very interesting to me is the passage we read earlier—the imagining of this relationship between this humble charcoal maker and the great Count Potocki, of this very intimate body contact where the Jew saves Count Potocki, carries him, has a physical relationship with him, brings him to his house. Count Potocki sees a Jew in his natural regalia, with the black boxes and the straps and so forth, something that even though he controls the lives of thousands of Jews he knew nothing about. His only experience of these lives is through the jesters who made fun of it. He doesn't really see it because he falls asleep, but what Agnon has done is to stage a kind of intimate encounter that perhaps could not have existed in real life, but also, he staged an event in which the Jew, in a sense, saves the great Polish nobleman.

So what is Agnon's intervention in this story? I see it as an attempt to turn the tables and to create a moment in which the nobility of spirit of this humble man with this idée fixe of praying with the community prevails in this moment of opportunity that is given to him. So what is being done is the ordinary relations between the noble Poles and the managerial Jews who are much smaller in the social scale—the balance is recalibrated and even reversed. This is accomplished through the force of Agnon's imagination by creating this incident, which I'm sure he made up out of whole cloth. So the intervention is a kind of *tikkun* or repair of what the historical record actually was. Jews worked very hard for the Poles. They did their jobs. They deserved much better than they had. And Agnon's restoring of this moment in Polish Jewish history through the imagination—the imagination does not feel constrained to represent things just as they were, but rather, to use the imagination is accorded freedom to rewrite things in a way as they should have been. So it's the creation of what we might call "alternative reality" or "alternate history," which is not denial, but rather an exercise in freedom in trying to repair a tear that can be restored through the ministry of the imagination.

3 *My Life With Hebrew*[1]

Alan Mintz

In my third year as a graduate student in English at Columbia University, I came to a life-changing conclusion: as much as I enjoyed studying Victorian literature, I couldn't see myself devoting my life to it. My real passion lay instead with the study of Jewish and Hebraic culture. After finishing my Columbia doctorate in the late 1970s and sampling different sub-specialties in Jewish studies—midrash, medieval Hebrew poetry, and others—I settled on modern Hebrew literature.

By that time, my Hebrew was quite good, at least for someone who had never previously aspired to be a scholar in the field. In fact, it was a source of some pride. The Conservative movement's Hebrew school I had attended as a child in Worcester, MA had been staffed by committed Hebraists; entering college, I saw my future role in life as a rabbi or a Jewish educator, and at the summer camp where I served as a counselor during my college years, Hebrew was the semi-official language. By then, I could not only read texts in Hebrew but speak the language confidently—or so I thought. But once I decided to profess Hebrew, the rules of the game changed demonstrably. The glass that had been half-full now seemed, in my own eyes, half-empty.

I say "in my own eyes" because much of the anxiety I would experience as an American Hebrew speaker, and to some degree still experience as a long-time professor of Hebrew literature, has come from my sense of exposure to the judgment of others. (Whether that adverse judgment is a fact or largely a projection is something I'll never know.) To this day, whenever I'm among my Israeli colleagues, speaking Hebrew is always a self-conscious performance. I often think about what I want to say before I say it, pre-testing grammar and word choice. The times I have made gross errors are etched into my brain and will never be repeated; less well remembered are those gratifying times when a felicitous phrase has come to me unbidden. Even at my best, I know full well that I'll never shake my American accent, or enjoy the ease of my Israeli colleagues in skipping intuitively from ironic banter to street Hebrew and back to academic discourse within a few beats.

Writing in Hebrew is even harder. When I'm taking part in a conversation or giving a talk, there are no expectations of perfection; I can phrase and rephrase, using affect and gesticulation to enhance the message and create a bond with an interlocutor or an audience. But putting pen to paper feels like swimming with

1. *Mosaic* (April 13, 2017). Reprinted with permission from the Editors of *Mosaic Magazine*.

Building a City: Writings on Agnon's Buczacz in Memory of Alan Mintz (2022): 032–036
DOI: 10.2979/BuildingaCityWriting.o.o.04

weights, and I am thrust into a black awareness that humor, irony, nuance, and understatement are all beyond me, not to mention the deft idiom, the apt colloquialism, the *mot juste*.

When it comes to interpreting literary texts, which is what I do for a living, I'm also chastened by my awareness of how many echoes my ear will never be able to pick up. With the help of reference works I can always chase down allusions to classical sources and parse rare words, but when it comes to a bit of doggerel or a nursery rhyme or a pop song or an Israeli army acronym, let alone to slang and colloquialisms, forget about it. True, no single reader can become the "ideal reader" who catches all references and tonalities, but it's sobering to know that there will be things I'll never get.

I once had occasion to examine the voluminous hand-written journals of Mordecai Kaplan. Best-known as the founder of Reconstructionist Judaism, Kaplan had been the dean of the Teachers Institute at the Jewish Theological Seminary (JTS) for several decades in the first half of the 20th century. Although he presided over a faculty of veteran Hebraists, he himself had a background similar to mine; speaking and teaching in Hebrew were at once a challenge and a source of self-consciousness. The challenge invigorated him—about a fifth of his journals are written in Hebrew—even as it filled him with anxiety, especially at the beginning of each semester when he had to make a formal address in Hebrew to the assembled faculty and students. To tone his linguistic muscles, he spent days reading nothing but Hebrew. I think of Mordecai Kaplan, working out in the Hebrew gym, as a kindred spirit.

In my life with Hebrew, there is a term I have grown to loathe and a term I have grown to embrace. The one I loathe is "fluency." When people find out that I teach Hebrew literature, they invariably remark, "Oh, you must be fluent"—a comment that can be made only by someone who has had no serious experience learning a foreign language. Etymologically, *fluent* is related to the Latin word for river, conjuring up an effortless, spontaneous flow that has little to do with the imposing, arduous, and desultory process of mastering a language. At best, the term implies a state of arrival achieved by a fixed amount of exertion. You begin by not being fluent; you work hard at it; and then—you're fluent. I've now been working hard at it for many decades, and I'm still waiting.

Today, scholars of foreign-language acquisition shun the term "fluency" and prefer "proficiency": a word that, encouraging no mystification, defines the goal as becoming good enough to function. Instead of one proficiency, moreover, there are four: understanding speech, producing speech, comprehending a text, and writing. Each of these skills is susceptible of infinite stations of progress from the absolute beginner to the most advanced student, and in every learner the skills proceed along separate tracks at different rates. The most, and the best, we can say is that we are on the path and are moving forward.

But there's another term—"near native"—that I've come to embrace even more. I first came across it in job listings for university Hebrew instructors possessing "native or near-native" knowledge of the language. Though I've never seen the word used as anything other than an adjective, I see no reason not to make it into a noun. I'm therefore pleased to declare myself a Hebrew near-native, and one who belongs to a small but (mostly) happy band of other near-natives.

The term "near-native" is now a staple (and an ideal) in academic discussions of language acquisition. As with so many things Jewish, however, Hebrew isn't quite like other languages. Many of the American Hebraists who taught my generation never lived in Palestine, but their Hebrew was richer and more robust than that of most of their counterparts in the Yishuv (the Jewish settlement in Palestine). There, aside from the strange case of Itamar Ben-Avi, the son of the pioneering Hebraist Eliezer Ben-Yehuda (1858–1922), the members of the first generation to be actually raised in the language were born only in the early 1930s to parents who in many cases had learned their Hebrew in Europe. In short, nativeness in Hebrew is a relatively recent phenomenon.

A particular style of Orientalized Hebrew, spoken in the youth movements in the Yishuv in the 1930s and 1940s, more or less conferred upon itself the status of nativeness; subsequently, it became the form of Hebrew that gained admittance to American universities. The price of admission was the packaging of Hebrew as a modern language to be taught alongside other modern languages—in this case, the language that happened to be spoken by inhabitants of a country in the Middle East.

The effect of this packaging was to obscure Hebrew's provenance as the age-old language of Jewish culture, thus providing the ingredients of a potential culture war. Should the Hebrew taught on university campuses be only the Hebrew spoken in the present moment by literate speakers in Israel? Or was that Hebrew only the latest manifestation of a larger conception of the language that would properly encompass the achievements of both secular and religious culture over a much longer span of time?

Merely to ask such questions is to see why Hebrew has never been a comfortable fit in departments of Middle East studies. If real Hebrew speech and literature didn't develop in Palestine until the 1920s, what is one to do with the 150 or so years in which modern Hebrew was being created in Germany, Poland, Galicia, and America before arriving in the Levant? Is the poet Ḥayyim Naḥman Bialik—who wrote most of his works before settling in Tel Aviv in 1924 at the age of fifty—a Middle Eastern writer? Or the poet Shaul Tchernikhovsky, whose translations of Homer, Sophocles, and Shakespeare are still read in Israel today, and who likewise lived most of his life in Europe?

To this mix, nowadays, must also be added the isolation and demonization of Israel itself in the Western academy. So thick is the anti-Zionism in some

Middle East departments that it has become nearly impossible to teach Hebrew and Israeli culture in any but a defensive crouch.

For these reasons alone, I have felt fortunate to have taught at Brandeis University and then for a much longer time at JTS: two institutions in which no apologies for Hebrew need be made. At JTS especially I've been lucky in each semester to have had the support, and the students, to teach a literature class conducted *in* Hebrew.

Such a class, once common in the teaching not just of literature but of all subjects of Judaica in Hebrew colleges in America—and certainly so at JTS's own Teachers Institute—is now a rarity. This isn't due to some general lowering of standards but to the collapse of Hebraist ideology and the scarcity of instructors confident enough in the value of Hebrew to take the trouble of teaching their subject in it. And it does take trouble. But there is also something wonderfully bracing in the very artificiality of the situation, and for a professor of Hebrew teaching *in* Hebrew, the gains are very much worth the tradeoffs.

The prize is an unmistakable and unique intimacy with both the texts and the language in which they're written. And there are secondary gains from this sort of linguistic immersion as well. Students develop a capacity for conceptual and analytic thinking in Hebrew that is hard to acquire in any other way. New vocabulary is absorbed; the Hebrew muscles are flexed and conditioned. There is the satisfaction of succeeding at something difficult and the joy of putting one foot before the other on the path to near nativeness.

In America, alas, we Hebrew speakers must often walk that path alone. We're not watching TV or reading newspapers in Hebrew, or talking on the phone to service representatives or having fights with our spouses in Hebrew. I spent years studying the works of American Hebrew writers—there are quite a few, including some very talented ones—and this same quality of loneliness and aloneness in their work has stayed with me indelibly.

Those poor souls felt doubly abandoned. The younger generation of Hebrew readers they hoped to foster never materialized, while the Hebrew readers of the Yishuv and later of Israel evinced little interest in literary gifts from the Diaspora. For Israel Efros, Avraham Regelson, and Simon Halkin, the isolation was intolerable; each found his way to Israel around the time of the establishment of the state. More stayed on in America: Gabriel Preil, Eisig Silberschlag, Ephraim Lissitzky, Reuven Wallenrod, and others whose names are little-recognized today.

Still, no matter how quirky and perverse these figures may have been, they were not delusional. They were able to soldier on in the absence of readers because they were not dependent on them. There was something in the private relationship each had with the Hebrew language that provided the necessary nourishment. One can find a glimpse into this relationship in Regelson's magnificent ode, *Ḥakukot otiyotayikh* ('Engraved Are Thy Letters"), which he wrote at the end of World War II before his move to Israel. There the poet describes Hebrew as a sublime yet nubile beloved whom he worshipfully courts like a troubadour and to whom he pledges eternal fealty. He praises her plasticity and polymorphousness and even writes a hymn to the *binyanim*, the verb paradigms that threaten to defeat novice learners.

Regelson's ode is gorgeous and over the top, but it is right on target when it comes to identifying the gratifications experienced by the Hebraist in working the language and manipulating it. The pleasure is quasi-erotic and the fidelity quasi-religious. Despite the want of readers and despite the lack of honor, the Hebraist has no doubt that, where it counts, his or her affections are returned.

I may not be as ardent a lover or as great a believer or as erudite a possessor of Hebrew as my predecessors, but that does not prevent me from feeling something of those pleasures. And although I am definitely a Zionist, I'm grateful that the establishment of Israel and the revival of Hebrew, though deeply linked, are not one and the same thing. As the portable component of the Jewish national idea, Hebrew in the Diaspora is a source of nourishment and delight. At a time when the humanities are in trouble and enrollments for languages, including Hebrew, are down, I remain thankful that Hebrew is my daily bread. "Were not Your Torah my delight," says the psalmist (119:92), "I would have perished in my affliction."

II. Tributes

4   *Alan Mintz: A Prophet in the City*

David G. Roskies

Eldad and Medad

It was during the lengthy sojourn of the Israelites in the desert that Eldad and Medad began to prophesy in the camp, or, as the New JPS translation would have it, "to speak in ecstasy," which more accurately describes what happened to Alan and me sometime in 1980.[1] There were perhaps as many as seventy elders out there professing Jewish studies, but the existing journals in the field were either too venerable or too stodgy to serve as a platform for Jewish literary studies of a new kind. When I raised this issue with our teacher and mentor, Dan Miron, he said: "Why not start your own journal?" As it is written, "But Moses said, 'Would that all of the LORD's people were prophets, that the LORD put His spirit upon them!'" (Numbers 11: 29). And so Eldad recruited Medad that they might prophesy together in the Israelite camp.

The elective affinity between Alan and me was obvious. As children, we had both spent our summer vacations in bungalows on Cape Cod. Both of us were overachievers, who had challenged the authority of our families and communities by taking the values they advocated more seriously than they intended. While still in our teens, we had both started Jewish student magazines. *Yugntruf: Alveltekher yidisher yugnt-zhurnal* (*International Yiddish Journal for Youth*) was my creation in 1965 and *Response: A Contemporary Jewish Review*, a year later, was his. Yet for all the chutzpah of doing it alone, it was clear to the two of us that we had come late to the party. The great culture wars had already happened; the rival groups of Yiddish poets no longer sat at separate tables in Café Royale, and, a stone's throw away in Greenwich Village, the Trotskyists were no longer battling the Communists. What little remained of the recent past was insufficient to feed our hunger for serious engagement. What, then, was the historical significance of our youth rebellion? Surely it lay in the attempt of small intentional communities to reinvent a more intense and spiritually authentic Judaism. In university, both Alan and I had led a double life as we tried to combine our academic pursuits with a commitment to Havurah Judaism, and, more recently, Alan had recruited *me* to join a group of Jewish countercultural refugees on the Upper West Side in weekly prayer and study. Jointly and severally, we had undergone a gradual shift from Jewish cosmopolitanism to Jewish nationalism. Alan's shift was far more

1. This essay could not have been written without the help of the indefatigable Menachem Butler, who compiled a comprehensive bibliography of Alan Mintz's writings and made all 133 items available to me online. My thanks also go to David Stern for being the first reader.

dramatic than mine. After completing a doctorate in English at Columbia on George Eliot (which would become his first book, *George Eliot and the Novel of Vocation*), where one of his dissertation advisers was, of all people, Edward Said, he switched careers and ultimately chose to specialize in modern Hebrew literature. The decision to throw ourselves into Jewish literary studies was driven in part by the desire to foster the cultural renewal of the Jewish people. The Soviet Jewry movement was one sign that miracles were still being wrought in Israel. The State of Israel, which was to play an ever more central role in our lives, was another. Because we were both now teaching in Morningside Heights, I at JTS and he at Columbia, all I had to do was pick up the phone to arrange for us to meet. This time, Alan did not urge me to curb my enthusiasm. He allowed me to speak in ecstasy.

That their names rhymed, as if Eldad and Medad were joined at the hip, belied their differences. Their personal biographies, their very parentage, are among the many gaps in Scripture that cry out for elucidation. Alan's summer camp experience, for example, was much more positive than mine. I was not the product of a viable movement, was never elected national president of United Synagogue Youth, and the wannabe international youth movement of which I was a part did not have a leadership training fellowship. Unlike Alan, I had not separated from my parents and in some respects never would, for to do so would be to cut myself off from the source of my personal identity. I had received precisely the kind of day school education that Alan so envied: a total immersion in not one but two Jewish languages. And the Montreal Jewish community that had nurtured me was socially stratified, ideologically heterodox, linguistically diverse, and ethnically cohesive, at the farthest possible remove from the east coast urban landscape in which Alan had grown up.

Scripture reveals nothing about the content of Eldad's and Medad's prophecies. Ours, by contrast, are well documented. Despite being children of the Promised Land, our life in Jewish letters—our visionary activity, if you will—was lived within a state of exile. The first great theme that drew Alan to the study of modern Hebrew literature was the *ḥurban beit hamidrash*, the destruction of traditional faith once centered in the house of study. Young men who graduated to independent study in the *beit midrash* (in Hebrew) or *besmedresh* (in Yiddish) had already mastered the nuances of Jewish learning, otherwise they wouldn't be there, for, at least when it came to learning, traditional Ashkenaz was a meritocracy. Entering that world through the prose of Feierberg, Brenner, Berdyczewski, and the poetry of Bialik, Alan immediately experienced it as a world alien to his lived experience. "But it was also a world," he wrote,

> tinged by my romantic longing for a connection to the true matrix of Judaic knowledge. The loss of this world, the sudden collapse of its plausibility, was often presented as the tearing away of a veil of obscurantism, but what I saw

behind the ostensible liberation was a vertiginous fall, a loss of something precious and nurturing. The brutal, existential truth of their situation was luminous to me. Reading these authors, I felt something that I was to experience later on when I wrote about Holocaust writing: a vicarious connection to conditions of moral and spiritual extremity from which I had been shielded by the accident of being born in my time and my place.[2]

Alan's deliberate, apodictic style is so seductive and poetically charged that we are hardly prepared for the candor, precision, and critical self-awareness delivered by the punchline. The style says one thing, the content another. Alan admits to his vicarious attraction "to conditions of moral and spiritual extremity" in the lives of young men "banished from their father's table," the title of his second book, which in turn were comparable to experiences of "vertiginous fall" in Jewish lives cut short by the Holocaust.[3] Alive to both the agony and ecstasy of the modern Jewish experience, Alan created this synapse and used it to critical and moral advantage. He modelled a way of reading Jewish literature, its tragedies and traumas so historically removed and yet so intimately familiar.

This passage, taken from an unpublished autobiographical essay called "Stalking Agnon," which Alan circulated privately and ultimately decided to shelve, was by no means the only occasion when he admitted the reader into the personal drama of living inside the literary text. Most illuminating was his essay "In the Seas of Youth," written for the "Rereadings" issue of *Prooftexts* (21, no. 1, published in winter of 2001). The title already alluded to its double focus: a witty, self-deprecating account of the adolescent rebellion that led a young American to tackle such a richly allusive Hebrew text as Agnon's novella *In the Heart of the Seas*, and the manifold readings, both latent and manifest, that might be uncovered in Agnon's story. Nearing the end of the essay, Alan waxed lyrical:

> I have no certain way of knowing what attracted me to his stories then, but my recent return to *Bilvav yamim* has opened up what feels like a direct channel to those early promptings. As best I can tell the motive was this: the desire to experience the poetry of religion[...]. Because of the great good fortune of my having had a Hebraist education, I was able to read a novella like *Bilvav yamim* in Hebrew and feel I was peering directly into the inner romance of faith and hearing its music in its original tones.[4]

Who wouldn't want to join with Alan Mintz in a "reverie of reading" that yielded such rich and variegated fruit?

2. Alan Mintz, "Stalking Agnon" (unpublished manuscript), 15.
3. Alan Mintz, *Banished From Their Father's Table: Loss of Faith and Hebrew Autobiography* (Bloomington: Indiana University Press, 1989).
4. Mintz, "In the Seas of Youth," *Prooftexts* 21 (2001): 69.

In short, it was not a hard sell to convince an intoxicated Hebraist like Alan of the need to establish a journal of Jewish literary history. If English departments could set the bar from Beowulf to Virginia Woolf, then we could do one better. Our venture would go *mehatanakh ve'ad hapalmah* (from the Hebrew Bible to the literature of Israel's War of Independence), or further still, *'ad Natan Zach*. This was no mere lip service to three millennia of Jewish literary creativity. Both Alan and I had been inspired by our teachers, the last generation of Eastern European *maskilim*, for whom Hebrew culture was the ultimate expression of humanism. "Nothing Jewish is foreign to me" might have been their motto. With this big-tent approach, moreover, we would never feel like johnny-come-latelies to the humanities. If anything, we were johnny-come-earlies. From the outset, *Prooftexts* took on Big Jewish Topics that represented Jewish culture as continuous, cumulative, and renewable: Jewish responses to catastrophe, medieval Jewish literature, the image of women in Jewish literature, the theory and practice of translation, the role of periodicals in the formation of modern Jewish identity, reading through the lens of gender, and, most capaciously, the Jewish anthological imagination. Within each issue and especially within each thematic issue, the order of presentation was chronological, granting primacy wherever possible to the Hebrew Bible and rabbinics. For something else that Alan and I had in common was a love of midrash, which we saw as the true font of the Jewish literary imagination. My first publication was *Night Words: A Midrash on the Holocaust* (1971). Alan published both original midrash scholarship in the pages of *Prooftexts* and keenly followed developments in the field.[5] This explains why the next phone call we made was to David Stern, who had made a literary approach to midrash the focus of his academic work; why the name we finally adopted for our journal was *Prooftexts*, the *asmakhta*, or prooftext, being the main lever of rabbinic hermeneutics, the most venerable way of deriving new, and oftentimes radically new, meanings from Scripture; and why we would insist upon Judaic literacy as the *sine qua non* of Jewish literary study. (Other names that were considered for the journal included *Momentary*, suggested by Stern.) Jewish culture proceeded from the mastery of a Jewish language—the more, the better. Whoever wrote for *Prooftexts* would have to demonstrate a passion for Jewish literatures across time and space.

If Jewish literature was our eschatology, English was our prophetic idiom. Someone before us (Judah Goldin, perhaps, or Shalom Spiegel) had coined the felicitous English term "prooftext." The pluralized form was our way of signifying a concern for the text, textuality and intertextuality. Our first item of edi-

5. Alan Mintz, "The Song at the Sea and the Question of Doubling in Midrash," *Prooftexts* 1, no. 2 (1981): 185–92; Mintz, "Review of David Stern, 'Parables in Midrash: Narrative and Exegesis in Rabbinic Literature'," *Jewish Studies* 33 (1986): 75–80; and Mintz, "Review of 'Midrash and Literature', eds. Geoffrey H. Hartman and Sanford Budick," *Shofar* 4, no. 4 (1986): 46–47.

torial business, therefore, was to establish a stylesheet for the romanization of Hebrew and Yiddish, which aimed to achieve a sleek, modern look as unobtrusive as possible. We chose to de-hyphenate Hebrew (not *me-ha-Tanakh* as catalogers do, but *mehatanakh*, as Hebrew does) and to de-italicize those culturally specific terms that were indispensable for Judaic discourse. "There were many Hebrew terms that were often translated awkwardly," as Alan would later note when he explained the method adopted by his team of translators for the great Agnon project that he spearheaded (of which more anon).

> A shamash, for example, is a community employee who assists the rabbi and sees to the needs of the synagogue. Rather than translating the term as 'sexton' or 'beadle,' we kept it simply as shamash, and we further insisted that it appear on the page in roman rather than italics. We wanted to naturalize a small group of recurrent Hebrew terms for which there were no sensible English equivalents.[6]

Judaic literacy demanded a common Judaic lexicon. But English demanded a certain decorum—and universal clarity. We rejected the in-your-face hermeticism of Judeo-English, or Yeshivish.

We would not speak in tongues. To guard against gobbledygook, we held up as model the essay, "which took seriously the idea of an essay as an essai," in Alan's elegant formulation, "an attempt to say something finished within the limitations of a short piece of discursive writing. At its best, this kind of essay strove to seem like effortless but brilliant conversation and wore its learning lightly, hoping to garner the reader's assent by lapidary insights rather than by systematic demonstrations."[7] ("Lapidary," like "sanguine," was one of those words that just came tripping off Alan's tongue.) "We wanted the scholarly substance of the one and the elegant clarity of the other," he went on to explain. "In addition, these were the years of the most ferocious assaults of oracular literary theory upon plain writing. We saw ourselves as gatekeepers and mediators, opening the door just wide enough to let in the truly valuable elements of the new theoretical discourse and keep obfuscation out."

As chief gatekeeper, Alan assumed responsibility for taking on what seemed to him then to be the main competitor on the scene: the Tel Aviv School of Poetics.[8] First, he situated the Tel Aviv school within the intellectual legacy of Russian formalism, then went on to describe and evaluate its major trends, both "as a corporate phenomenon" and serially, each major figure at a time. "Even-Zohar and Toury station their constructs at so high an altitude," he wrote with great panache, "that they produce a kind of Star Wars effect, as we gaze on gigantic sys-

6. Mintz, "Stalking Agnon," 27.
7. Alan Mintz, "Editing as Intellectual Community: A Retrospective Manifesto," *Prooftexts* 24, no. 3 (2004): 273–76.
8. Alan Mintz, "On the Tel Aviv School of Poetics," *Prooftexts* 4, no. 3 (1984): 215–35.

tems 'invading,' 'infiltrating,' or otherwise interfering with each other (all these are technical terms in their lexicon)."[9] The business of this essay, however, was no less prescriptive than descriptive. "What can be left of Jewish literature," he asked rhetorically, "once history and experience have been drained to expose the fundamental structures of literature?" The problem with poetics is that it devalues the Jewish content of Jewish literature. There was a choice to be made when approaching a work of art between poetics and interpretation, and Alan urged us to choose the latter, "in which the productions of theory and poetics are used in the better understanding of specific texts, and in which theoretical insights are welcomed but unintended byproducts."[10]

Essentially, each member of the editorial board was charged with becoming the gatekeeper in his or her respective field—Edward Greenstein, Janet Hadda, James Kugel, Raymond Scheindlin, David Stern, and Hana Wirth-Nesher—and each opened the door to the new theoretical discourse with greater or lesser latitude. Greenstein took the bull by the horns in 1989 with "Deconstruction and Biblical Narrative," *Prooftexts* 9 (1989): 43–71, probably the first exercise of its kind, while Kugel and Stern launched the counterattack, Kugel in "On the Bible and Literary Criticism," *Prooftexts* 1 (1981): 217–36 and Stern in "Moses-cide: Midrash and Contemporary Literary Criticism," *Prooftexts* 4 (1984): 193–213. It was the latter that inaugurated a rubric called "Controversy." When it came to medieval Jewish literature, there was much work to be done, beginning with Stern's review essay on "New Directions in Medieval Hebrew Poetry," *Prooftexts* 1 (1981): 104–15 to Scheindlin's "A Miniature Anthology of Medieval Hebrew Love Poems," *Prooftexts* 5 (1985): 105–35, to his own studies of Ibn Gabirol and Yehuda Halevi, and culminating in the special issue on medieval Jewish literature (*Prooftexts* 23, no. 1 published in 2003).[11] The most difficult area to get a handle on was Jewish writing in non-Jewish languages, and especially the one closest to home. Wirth-Nesher managed this in several ways. She and Hadda produced two issues of *Prooftexts* (18:2–3, published in 1998) dedicated to Jewish-American autobiography, which included English and Yiddish, Ashkenazic and Sephardic within their purview, and, drawing largely from the pages of *Prooftexts*, produced a new critical canon, *What Is Jewish Literature?* (1994). But the major turn in her career came in the spring of 1990, with the publication in *Prooftexts* of "Between Mother Tongue and Native Language: Multilingualism and Multiculturalism in Henry Roth's *Call It Sleep.*" Alan's enthusiasm for this essay, carefully edited by him, was

9. Mintz, "On the Tel Aviv School," 228.
10. Mintz, "On the Tel Aviv School," 232.
11. In his review of the contribution of *Prooftexts* to the study of Hebrew poetry, Aminadav Dykman, "Twenty Years of Poetry in *Prooftexts*," *Prooftexts* 21 (2001): 121 credits Raymond Scheindlin with creating "a climate of interest" for medieval Hebrew poetry. That's not the half of it. Most of the contributions in the field were commissioned and curated by Scheindlin.

ultimately shared by Roth himself, who asked Hana's permission to place it as the afterword to the new paperback edition of the novel. Henceforth, multilingualism was to occupy the front and center both of Hana's scholarly work and of the critical discourse in the field of Jewish-American literature as a whole.

By allowing two unappointed prophets to run loose inside the camp, Moses was taking a calculated risk. What if Eldad and Medad did not rest their case until they had created a camp within the camp? "It was not only to advance the body of knowledge that *Prooftexts* was founded," Alan wrote in his valedictory address, when the two of us stepped down after twenty-five years as editors-in-chief, "but also to create an invisible intellectual community."[12] Invisible or not, community was the armature of Alan's life, from first to last.

Community

It was Alan's search for community that brought him to the study of Hebrew literature and his study of Hebrew literature that brought him the community he sought.

By accident of being born in his time and his place, Alan came of age during the great youth rebellion of the 1960s. And from the moment in 1966 that he and a number of friends he had met as counselors at Camp Ramah each put in a hundred dollars to pay for the printing of the first issue of *Response*, he never lacked a forum to express his passions and share his latest critical insights. From then on, with the English-American essay as his genre of choice, Alan appeared both as public intellectual and literary critic—sometimes in one and the same forum. Thus, the inaugural issue of *Response* featured both his critique of the youth movement in whose ranks he had so recently risen and his contemporary reading of *In the Heart of the Seas*, provocatively titled "Agnon on the Individual and the Community."[13] "I made this story about the ascent to Zion and its tribulations into an allegory about the relationship of my generation to the established Jewish community," he wrote retrospectively. "Using the Nobel Prize as a pretext, the real occasion for the article [wa]s the current crisis in American Jewish life: the disaffection of creative young people from the Jewish community."[14] If today we can say that the historical significance of that youth rebellion lay in the attempt of small intentional communities to reinvent a more intense and spiritually authentic Judaism, it is because, as early as 1971, Alan emerged as its most articulate spokesperson. *The New Jews*, a mass-market paperback anthology that

12. Mintz, "Editing," 273.
13. Alan Mintz, "Fear and Trembling: A Retrospective Critique of United Synagogue Youth," *Response Magainze: A Contemporary Jewish Review* 1, no. 1 (1967): 16–20 and Mintz, "Review: Agnon on the Individual and the Community," *Response Magainze: A Contemporary Jewish Review* 1, no. 1 (1967): 28–31.
14. Mintz, "Stalking Agnon," 5, echoing what he wrote in Mintz, "In the Seas," 59.

he coedited along with James A. Sleeper, was the first attempt to collect, explicate, and disseminate the voices of the Jewish counterculture. "I am a religious communitarian," began his programmatic essay on seeking the path to religious community. "I am interested in small fellowships of Jews who study, worship, and act together in a setting of interpersonal understanding. I am a member of the *Havurah* in New York City."[15] This was followed by a six-point indictment of the organized American Jewish community and a three-point program for inner-Jewish renewal. Yet, in closing out the volume, Alan cautioned his Jewish readers and fellow Americans that "It is important for the radical to have a deep awareness of his location in history and a sensitive knowledge of the past as composed both of moments with which he can resonate and others he must reject."[16] Allowing for the fact that hardly any female Jewish voices had yet been heard and that even progressive people still used gendered language, the call for radical conservatism and historical self-awareness was equally a call for communal responsibility. Alan's particular charge to the New Jew was to reinvent the future with a heightened awareness of the past.

By the time Alan made his second career move, from the University of Maryland to Brandeis University, his sense of crisis and urgency had shifted from prayer and politics to pedagogy. The issue was Hebrew literacy, and the root cause of the problem, he believed, had to be sought in *Tarbut 'Ivrit*, the Hebrew culture movement in America. Alan had never studied a movement before and didn't quite know how to go about it. Then again, he knew exactly what to do because he had lived it. And so his wider focus would be the function and influence of cultural elites in American Jewish life, and his narrower focus a highly successful periodical publication of one such elite grouping. In "A Sanctuary in the Wilderness: The Beginnings of the Hebrew Movement in America in the Pages of *Hatoren*," he set out to tell the largely untold story of "how a small group of immigrants formulated a radical critique of American Zionism and American Jewish life and constituted themselves into a self-appointed elite dedicated to revamping Jewish culture in America."[17] If that wasn't ownership enough, Alan had an even more compelling argument to make about the generational and ideological significance of his chosen topic:

15. Alan L. Mintz, "Along the Path to Religious Community," in *The New Jews*, ed. James A. Sleeper and Alan L. Mintz (New York: Vintage, 1971), 168.
16. Alan L. Mintz, Epilogue to *The New Jews*, ed. James A. Sleeper and Alan L. Mintz (New York: Vintage, 1971), 245.
17. Alan Mintz, "A Sanctuary in the Wilderness: The Beginnings of the Hebrew Movement in America in the Pages of Hatoren," *Prooftexts* 10 (1990): 389. This essay was reprinted in Alan Mintz, ed., *Hebrew in America: Perspective and Prospects* (Detroit, MI: Wayne State University Press, 1993), 29–67, but citations here are to the original *Prooftexts* publication. To fully appreciate the importance he attached to this essay, one should keep in mind that Alan wrote it to mark our tenth anniversary.

For the younger Hebraists, however, Hebrew served as the very existential medium through which the anguish and excitement of the nation's rebirth were taking place. Hebrew was certainly more than a national ornament and a sacred treasure for them; it was also more than a means by which the national revival was being effected or one of the planks in that program. Hebrew, in its catholic embrace, was the ground itself of the new national reality, the essence of the revolution.[18]

Hebrew culture, this essay sought to demonstrate, had once been an essential expression of Jewish revival in America proper and, as such, could serve the present generation as a usable past. More than that, he argued cogently at the annual conference of the NAPH (National Association of Professors of Hebrew) in June 1990, the cultural legacy of the *Tarbut 'Ivrit* ideology is precisely what was lacking in the teaching of Hebrew in the American university.[19] With the same fervor as he had once laid out the manifest failings of the American Jewish community, he now put forward three principles to supplement, if not to supplant, the regnant pedagogical paradigm in which Hebrew was synonymous with the State of Israel and its secular forms of self-expression.

The first principle is the conception of Hebrew as the central manifestation of the Jewish people throughout the generations and therefore Hebrew as the key to Jewish civilization[...]. The second principle [...] is that Hebrew is the language of the Jewish people in all its dispersions and not that of the state of Israel alone [...]. The third principle is the most pragmatic, and it bears on the selection of cultural materials for our more advanced courses.[20]

A Hebrew curriculum in an American university, he went on to suggest, should include the fruits of the American Hebrew culture movement.

Sanctuary in the Wilderness was to become the title of his critical introduction to American Hebrew poetry (2012). By this time, Alan had emerged as the go-to explicator and critic of contemporary Hebrew writing from Israel, thanks to such books as *The Boom in Contemporary Israeli Fiction* (1997) and *Translating Israel: Contemporary Hebrew Literature and Its Reception in America* (2001), not to speak of his elegant book reviews appearing regularly in the periodical press. By this time he had also joined the faculty at JTS, where, from my vantage point next door, I marveled at his fortitude as he ploughed through the oeuvre of another American Hebrew poet, then another, and another. "From the beginning," he wrote of this monumental project, "I had viewed these Hebrew creators in America as forgotten heroes, prophets unacknowledged in their own

18. Mintz, "Sanctuary," 392.
19. Alan Mintz, "The Erosion of the *Tarbut Ivrit* Ideology in America and the Consequences for the Teaching of Hebrew in the University," *Shofar* 9, no. 3 (1991): 50–54.
20. Mintz, "Erosion," 54.

home."[21] By the time all thirteen poets were accounted for, their ultimate failure to raise the fortunes of Hebrew in America, let alone their own, was taking its toll. Alan began to wonder whether his own efforts might not meet a similar fate and began to doubt whether his Israeli colleagues would so much as acknowledge the importance of the Hebrew literary center that once existed here, thus allotting at least a chapter to America in the still-to-be-written history of modern Hebrew literature.

Hebrew in America was the vehicle of Alan's homecoming and tracked his route to self-acceptance. For many years, the personal had become professional. Now the time had come to do the reverse, to render the professional deeply personal. Perhaps it was the dry run of writing a lengthy autobiographical piece for what was supposed to become his American biography of Agnon. But even that piece, "Stalking Agnon," was not as self-defining as the exquisitely personal essay "My Life with Hebrew," the last to appear in his lifetime and included here in this volume.[22] Here Alan revealed for the first time the anxieties he experienced as an American Hebrew speaker and to some degree still experienced as a long-time professor of Hebrew literature. It was a feeling of never measuring up to his Israeli counterparts. "I know full well that I'll never shake my American accent," he admitted openly. Writing in Hebrew was harder still, for how could he achieve "humor, irony, nuance, and understatement[...], not to mention the deft idiom, the apt colloquialism, the *mot juste*" in an acquired tongue? And most chastening of all was the awareness of how many echoes his ear would never be able to pick up when interpreting literary texts, which is what he did for a living.

It was by measuring up to the past, to the proud legacy of American Hebraists, from the founders of *Hatoren* to the JTS theologian Mordecai Kaplan, that Alan made peace with himself. ("I think of Mordecai Kaplan, working out in the Hebrew gym, as a kindred spirit.") It was by trying on the various gradations of "fluency," "proficiency," and "near-native," that he arrived at this declaration: "I'm therefore pleased to declare myself a Hebrew near native, and one who belongs to a small but (mostly) happy band of other near natives." It must have been a liberating moment for Alan, as it was for many of the younger, American-born colleagues in the field, who deeply identified with Alan's predicament.

But even that was not his greatest contribution to fostering an intellectual community. No. His singular contribution was to invent a radically new format, designed to supplant the tired—and utterly exhausting—model of the academic conference. In June 1999, I was invited to be one of eighteen participants in a colloquium held at Brandeis on "Reading Hebrew Literature." Deeply dissatisfied with the usual format of the twenty- to thirty-minute paper, which is "too

21. Mintz, "Stalking Agnon," 20.
22. Alan Mintz, "My Life with Hebrew," *Mosaic*, April 13, 2017, https://mosaicmagazine.com /observation/2017/04/my-life-with-hebrew/.

short for the adequate presentation of a coherent argument and too long for an audience to give sustained attention to an oral presentation," and with academic exchanges that "have come to resemble a kind of contest in which the scholar's performance contributes more to the enhancement or erosion of his or her reputation than to the enlarging of the body of knowledge," Alan proposed "to place the text at the center and to let a community of discourse grow up around it."[23] How exactly the time was apportioned Alan explained in the introduction to the volume that was eventually produced. Here is Alan waxing eloquent over the colloquium's common purpose: "The possibility of community arises because the illuminating of the text is the common purpose of the participants in the discourse and also because the inherent value of the text as a source of illumination is the common point of departure[...]. It is not special pleading, I think, to see in this notion of text-centeredness the hovering spirit of classical Jewish learning."[24]

So there you have it: the *beit midrash* restored through the creation of a visible, although temporary, community of readers—comprised of men and women, Israelis and Americans—who bonded around the vigorous and open-ended interpretation of Jewish texts. "The putative boundary lines between the American interpreters and the Israeli interpreters turned out to be blurred," Alan was forced to admit, which is another way of saying that one of the basic premises of the colloquium turned out to be false.[25] What the eighteen of us sitting around the table for two days had in common proved much greater than what divided us. We shared a sense of discovery, when what each of us had prepared—whether poetic or prosaic, of European or Israeli provenance—and energetically interpreted using our best interpretive methods, coalesced into a Hebrew literary canon that was larger than the sum of its parts. What's more, so long as we sat at the same table, the sources of revelation flowed every which way. *Eilu ve'eilu divrei elohim ḥayyim.*

The Great Catastrophe

Meanwhile, the Jewish bookcase was bursting at the seams. One could barely keep up with the latest novels coming out of Israel, even with the help of a study group of nonprofessional Hebrew readers that met on the Upper West Side of Manhattan. The fastest growing shelf was the one dedicated to Holocaust literature and survivor memoirs, augmented by critical studies that made competing claims about whether the Holocaust could be represented at all. This is where Alan and I were to make our most lasting contributions.

23. Alan Mintz, Introduction to *Reading Hebrew Literature: Critical Discussions of Six Modern Texts*, ed. Alan Mintz (Hanover, NH: Brandeis University Press, 2003), 7.
24. Mintz, Introduction to *Reading Hebrew Literature*, 7.
25. Mintz, introduction to *Reading Hebrew Literature*, 10.

How did we both end up writing a Big Book on the same subject? And how did our friendship survive it? In 1977, Neil Gillman, the dean of the rabbinical school at JTS, invited me to offer a synthesis course on Jewish responses to catastrophe, a topic that had been taught several years before by Neal Kozodoy and that obviously played to the strengths of the seminary faculty. The roster of guest lecturers I mobilized for this year-long course was extraordinary, including Gershon Bacon, Gerson D. Cohen, Stephen Geller, Robert Gordis, Jules Harlow, Mortimer Ostow, Raymond Scheindlin, and David Weiss-Halivni, and two of the guest lectures, by Shaye Cohen and Ivan Marcus, would eventually appear in a thematic issue of *Prooftexts* dedicated to this very subject (2, no. 1, published in January 1982). Paul Fussell's *The Great War in Modern Memory* had appeared in 1975, and I decided early on that in order to be worthy of the JTS legacy, I needed to combine Fussell with what the course had taught me, the aim being to encompass the full expanse of Jewish literary responses. Alan audited the course and came to a similar decision.

So Medad arranged to meet Eldad for lunch at the JTS cafeteria and opened the conversation by saying how much he was enjoying the course and how inexhaustibly rich was its subject. What would Eldad think about Medad carving out a discrete part of it, as pertained exclusively to Hebrew? Medad at that moment displayed his usual tact, his exquisite sensitivity, which Eldad, thin-skinned and conflict averse, completely misconstrued. Eldad replied disingenuously that the prophetic calling was best pursued severally, not jointly, so each should proceed without revealing its contents to the other. Moses, eavesdropping on their conversation, proclaimed, "Nothing spreads my Torah more effectively than creative competition. The day will yet come when my two impetuous prophets will do great things together."

And so it was. Inspired by Fussell, I was chiefly concerned with the role of Jewish literature in fashioning memory out of historical catastrophe. My first task was to understand the grammar of remembrance—both its *langue*, which I called "sacred parody," the invocation of myth and tradition through inversion and subversion, and its *parole*, the genres employed and adapted by Jewish writers. Some, like the war memoir, matched what I had found in Fussell. Most, however, were homegrown and had to be teased out of Jewish writings, both popular and highbrow, primarily in Yiddish and Hebrew.

Alan took a completely different approach. He went in an (Eric) Auerbachian *Mimesis*-like direction, moving chapter by chapter from Eikhah (Lamentations) to Appelfeld to demonstrate the unfolding of the Hebraic tradition, work by work. Both of our books were congruent with what was to become the philosophy behind *Prooftexts*, which was a conception of the unity and continuity of all Jewish literature from Tanakh to Zach.[26]

26. Here we are, sharing the same footnote and date of publication: David G. Roskies, *Against the Apocalypse: Responses to Catastrophe in Modern Jewish Culture* (Cambridge, MA: Harvard

Both of us, of course, were working in reverse chronological order. Our real point of departure was the Great Destruction, the *Ḥurban*, the Shoah. What each of us demonstrated, each in his own way, is that the literature written by Jews that witnessed and came out of the Holocaust was part of a genuine, developing Jewish tradition that could be traced back to the Bible. Because this approach was completely at odds with the dominant thinking (and teaching) in the burgeoning field of Holocaust studies, each of us had a long way to go before we could lay this awesome subject to rest.

In 1989 came *The Literature of Destruction: Jewish Responses to Catastrophe*, my 652-page, annotated companion volume, upon which the Jewish Publication Society lavished the same care it did with Scripture. It is my pride and joy. Then, working with an NEH grant over several summers, Alan began teaching Holocaust literature to college instructors, which resulted in his most densely argued work of practical criticism: "Two Models in the Study of Holocaust Literature."[27] With an academic reader in mind, Alan attached a rather off-putting multisyllabic label to each. The "exceptionalist" model, in his terse definition, "discovers in the Holocaust a dark truth that inheres in the event."[28] Just as the Holocaust was incomparable, unique, sui generis, so too its literature and language; to keep faith with its "authentic but difficult truth," one was enjoined "to eschew relativism, false consciousness, and opportunism" when they threatened to compromise that truth.[29] As much as Alan admitted to being moved by this rhetoric, he refused to be seduced by its quasitheological allure and "prophetic" appeal, especially by the notion, shared by critics and readers alike, that the prototypical site of Holocaust literature were the death camps, "because of their ultimacy."[30] The "constructivist" model, by contrast, proceeded from the Holocaust's first interpreters, the victims themselves. In this approach to Holocaust representation, one attempted to reconstruct the cultural resources, strategies, and hermeneutic frameworks that the victims availed themselves of as they grappled with their situation and the collapse of social and cultural structures, institutions, and meanings. What made this approach so morally compelling was the preservation and rescue of writings from within the Holocaust proper, primarily from the Nazi

University Press, 1984) and Alan Mintz, *Ḥurban: Responses to Catastrophe in Hebrew Literature* (New York: Columbia University Press, 1984). Since then, both our names appear together in Jewish literary studies as often as Marx and Engels in other branches of knowledge.
27. Alan Mintz, "Two Models in the Study of Holocaust Literature," *Humanity at the Limit: The Impact of the Holocaust Experience on Jews and Christians*, ed. Michael A. Signer (Bloomington: Indiana University Press, 2000), 400–428 and adapted for Mintz, *Popular Culture and the Shaping of Holocaust Memory in America* (Seattle: University of Washington Press, 2001), 36–84. Citations here are to the earlier publication.
28. Mintz, "Two Models," 402.
29. Mintz, "Two Models," 403.
30. Mintz, "Two Models," 418.

ghettos, but also from labor camps, death camps, and myriad places of hiding. As exemplars of each of these models, Alan presented Lawrence Langer's *Art from the Ashes: A Holocaust Anthology* (1995) and my *The Literature of Destruction*.

The search for the heart of darkness, Alan concluded, had led readers like Langer to deny the particularity of the Jewish victims. All was not reducible to a depersonalized and predictable symptomotology of trauma. Just so, the search for structural verities had led readers like Even-Zohar and Toury to deny the particular meanings of Jewish texts. Without regard for the victims in the fullness of their being, what was the point of studying Holocaust literature? Without regard for the fullness of time, what was the point of studying the recent, severed past?[31] Impelled to answer these questions, Alan went in search of the ultimate literary response to the Holocaust—and found his way back to Agnon.

Should anyone do a comparative study of memory maps that were appended to some of the thousand or so *yizkor* books written in commemoration of the martyred Jewish communities of central and Eastern Europe, they would be astonished to discover the one of Buczacz that Alan commissioned for his superb edition of Agnon's *A City in Its Fullness*, a collection of original translations of Agnon's "late work" (as Alan called it), which he initiated and edited.

Alan was enormously proud of this full color, two-dimensional map. Just as once upon a time he had commissioned the cover art for every volume of *Prooftexts*, each one based on another Hebrew numeral, so he delighted in this collage of architectural landmarks, topography, local lore, and Hebrew lettering. It sooner resembled a Hebrew scroll than an urban geographic. Like other memory maps of the shtetl, it wasn't drawn to scale. Who knew from maps in the shtetl? Yizkor books specifically were written by and for the survivor community, so it was important for Alan to include the point of deportation to the Bełżec death camp (unfortunately misspelled) and the two killing fields. Normally, however, Jewish memory maps were very sparing when it came to acknowledging the temporal and ecclesiastical rulers. As in shtetl fiction, so too in most maps, the shtetl was virtually *goyim-rein*. Not so Alan's rendering of Agnon's Buczacz. The castle ruins, the town hall built in rococo style in 1751, the three-storied gymnasium, the train station (the pride of every Austro-Hungarian city), as well as the Basilian monastery and massive Greek Catholic church and bell tower were so prominent that the Jewish sites—the Great Synagogue, the Old Beit Midrash, and the Jewish cemetery—were dwarfed by comparison. Yet Jewish memory traces were preserved on the map as if they were coterminous with the landmarks that have survived until this very day. Alan's map, like Agnon's Buczacz, was a palimpsest with the older layers demanding their due.

---

31. For a brilliant application of Alan's constructivist model, see Sven-Erik Rose, "Writing Hunger in a Modernist Key in the Warsaw Ghetto: Leyb Goldin's 'Chronicle of a Single Day'," *Jewish Social Studies: History, Culture, Society* n.s. 23 (2017): 29–63.

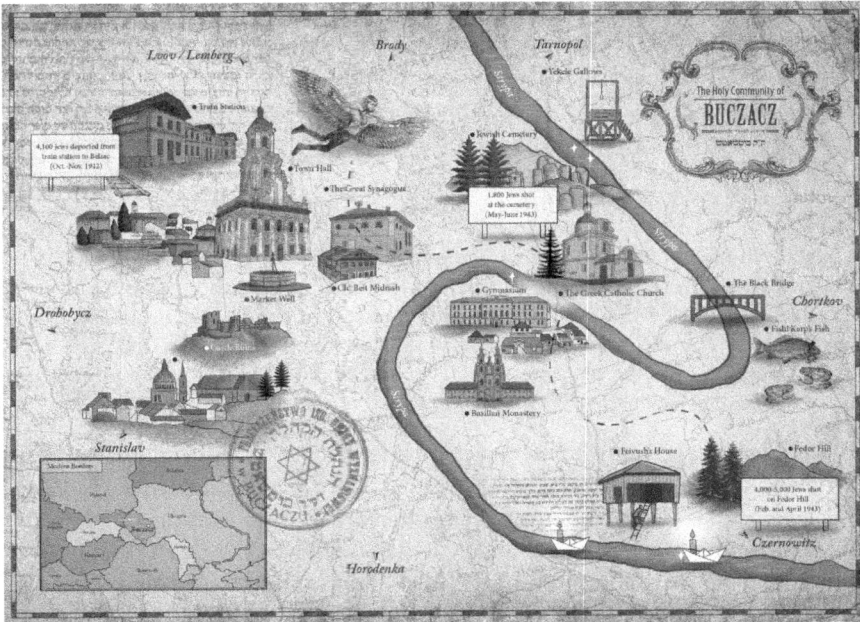

Figure 2: Buczcaz as depicted in *A City in Its Fullness*, copyright and courtesy of The Toby Press.

Some of those layers were as fantastical as they were real. Why else immortalize the figure of a Judaized Icarus hovering over the great town hall if not to commemorate the tragic fate of Theodor, *aka* Fedor, its Jewish architect, who died with his wings on in a vain attempt to escape the wrath of Count Mikołaj Potocki? And why else draw the Strypa River with paper boats floating on it carrying lit candles? Whereas Hananya's miraculous journey to the Holy Land on his kerchief in *In the Heart of the Seas* was never explained, *A Parable and Its Lesson*, which Alan published separately, told of a journey into the netherworld taken by a Buczacz rabbi and his assistant to save a young bride from abandonment.[32] Really the map should have been three-dimensional, since a number of key narratives were situated subterraneously. "The Holy Community of Buczacz" existed in time more than it did in on a topographical grid, and Jewish time had both a tragic and miraculous dimension.

It was the memorial imperative that drew Alan to this extraordinarily dense and elusive work. The love affair began with "The Sign," Agnon's most immediate and elegiac response to the destruction of his native town in the Holocaust, as

---

32. S.Y. Agnon, *A Parable and Its Lesson* (Stanford, CA: Stanford University Press, 2014), with a critical essay "Hamashal vehanimshal" by Alan on 79–158.

masterfully translated by Arthur Green in *Response Magazine* in 1973 and as later anthologized in *The Literature of Destruction*. Alan decided to present "The Sign" under a separate heading as "The Consecration Story." His profound insight about *A City in Its Fullness* was that this was the ultimate literary response to the Holocaust, a reconstruction *in toto* of the world destroyed and lost through the power of the literary imagination.

"This is the chronicle of the city of Buczacz," read Agnon's dedication page,

> which I have written in my pain and anguish so that our descendants should know that our city was full of Torah, piety, life, grace, kindness and charity from the time of its founding until the arrival of the blighted abomination and their befouled and deranged accomplices who wrought destruction upon it. May God avenge the blood of His servants and visit vengeance upon His enemies and deliver Israel from it sorrows.

Agnon's Buczacz epitomized the Covenantal Community, the *Kehillah Kedoshah*.

Agnon has had some very strong readers: Baruch Kurzweil, Amos Oz, Gershon Shaked, Dan Miron. The problem is they could be too strong, certainly too strong to be attracted to a seemingly pietistic work like *A City in Its Fullness* or to fully appreciate its restorative modernism. "Both Agnon the author and the narrator he created to tell these stories," wrote Alan in his foreword,

> held the study of Torah and the worship of God in the synagogue service to be supremely important values in Jewish society. The difference between the world depicted in *A City in Its Fullness* and East European Jewish life in the period of modernity hinges on the force and plausibility of these values.

Without for a moment forgetting the unavoidable gap between the desire of a community to live by a divine mandate and its ability to do so, Agnon insisted "on viewing that fullness through a normative grid."[33] What Alan understood, in other words, is why and precisely how Agnon had turned back the clock in order to conjure up a normative life that was as complex as it was plausible. This was precisely the theme of Alan's last monograph, *Ancestral Tales*, in which he explicated masterfully and elegantly the stories collected in *A City in its Fullness*. Alan himself considered this book the finest he had written.[34]

Buczacz became the spiritual home, the sanctuary Alan had been looking for and the greatest test of his calling. Here is how he rose to the challenge:

> Agnon took historical actualities seriously, even though he played with them incessantly, and it was crucial to know how to prise apart fiction from fact. I

33. Alan Mintz, "'I Am Building a City': On Agnon's Buczacz Tales," in *A City in Its Fullness*, by S.Y. Agnon, ed. Alan Mintz and Jeffrey Saks (New Milford, CT: Toby, 2014), xvii.
34. Alan Mintz, *Ancestral Tales: Reading the Buczacz Stories of S.Y. Agnon* (Stanford, CA: Stanford University Press, 2017).

found these challenges and the rigor they demanded to be bracing, and as I pushed through with the work of interpretation, I had the distinct sense that my vocation as a critic was finally being fulfilled. I was taking a supremely important body of Jewish writing—writing that mattered a great deal to the enterprise of Jewish self-understanding in the present moment—and, through the intervention of my efforts as a critic, making it available for readers to enjoy and appreciate.[35]

The Great Catastrophe was the *ḥurban beit hamidrash*, but not as a metaphor for the crisis of faith of a generation of highly articulate young men. It signified the destruction of thousands of temples of Torah and prayer, which had stood for centuries, and for the entire congregation of Israel—the meek and the bold, the men, the women, and the children, the beggars and philanthropists, the water carriers and tax collectors, the rabbanim, ḥazzanim, and shamashim—from the aftermath of the Khmelnitsky massacres in 1648 to the bloodbath on Fedor Hill in 1943.[36] If there was one book that deserved a place of honor in the modern Jewish bookcase, therefore, it was *A City in Its Fullness*, and if there was one interpreter, one Neal Kozodoy shamash, who would serve as its everlasting companion, it was Alan Mintz. Of Alan's Buczacz project one can truly say: *tam venishlam*.

As for the two of us, if I had it to do over again, I would have made a pact to speak only in Hebrew with Alan. Prophecies tend to last longer if they are in Hebrew.

In 1981, with Alan Mintz, DAVID G. ROSKIES cofounded *Prooftexts: A Journal of Jewish Literary History*. Both were veterans of the Havurah movement, wrote extensively on Jewish literary responses to catastrophe, belonged to the same Minyan, and since June 2001, had offices next door to each other at JTS. Roskies is the Sol & Evelyn Henkind Emeritus Professor of Yiddish Literature and Culture at JTS and has also taught for many years at the Hebrew University of Jerusalem. He was elected to the American Academy of Arts and Sciences in 2012.

---

35. Mintz, "Stalking Agnon," 26.
36. The aftermath of the destruction is the major theme of Agnon's *A Guest for the Night* (1939). This novel, however, is situated not in Buczacz but in Szybusz (which means "trifle" in Yiddish), the satiric place name that signifies the disenchanted shtetl in all of Agnon's work.

5 Remembering Alan Mintz

Encounters with Modern Jewish Culture in the Work of Alan Mintz

Anne Golomb Hoffman

In his last book, Alan Mintz described Agnon's creation of a narrative persona who is not so much "a consumer or a beneficiary of the tradition of sacred
song that goes back to the Temple" as someone who is "himself a belated link in
that chain."[1] I'd like to highlight the belatedness of our friend, Alan, as fundamental to his critical practice: the concept of belatedness brings the writer or the
critic into the long line of conversation—debate, interpretation, elaboration—
that is so central to Jewish tradition. The very distance from the sources serves to
energize the creativity of the writer or critic under the sign of belatedness. In fact,
I think this awareness occasioned Alan's goal in undertaking his last unfinished
project of an Agnon biography that would have included reflections on his *own*
Jewish journey. I didn't know Alan in the years when he made the decision to
leave Victorian literature and pursue Jewish studies, but I'm intrigued to imagine
his deliberations as he came to choose modern Hebrew literature rather than
midrash or the medieval *piyyut*. Modern Hebrew literature offered Alan a field of
engagement with existential issues that were close to his heart. It positioned him,
moreover, to highlight belatedness as a mode of critical reflection well suited to
our modernity.

From the vantage point of the twentieth-anniversary issue of *Prooftexts* in
2001, Alan looked back to his first encounter with Agnon as a college freshman
writing a paper in Hebrew on the novella *Bilvav yamim* (*In the Heart of the Seas*).
He would translate this essay into English a few years later and rework it as a
critique of American Judaism for the inaugural issue of *Response*, the journal he
helped to create in 1967. Reflecting with some bemusement on his own youthful
passion as a critic of American Jewish life, Alan nevertheless found, on returning to Agnon's novella in 2001, that his earlier encounter had been driven just as
much by "the desire to experience the poetry of religion." Whatever his youthful
frustrations with mid-century American Judaism may have been, returning to
the novella gave Alan the pleasure of an experience of reading that made him feel
again that he "was peering directly into the inner romance of faith and hearing
its music in its original tones." Looking back, he found evidence in his earlier

---

1. Alan Mintz, *Ancestral Tales: Reading the Buczacz Stories of S.Y. Agnon* (Stanford, CA: Stanford University Press, 2017), 8.

Building a City: Writings on Agnon's Buczacz in Memory of Alan Mintz (2022): 056–062
DOI: 10.2979/BuildingaCityWriting.0.0.06

reading that "I was ready to listen, and grateful to be given the chance to seize through the reverie of reading what could not be given to me in life."[2]

The word "reverie" comes up occasionally in Alan's writing and suggests something of what literary experience made available to him. The phrase conveys awareness of a reader's absorption in a text as something that is outside and yet part of the self. In this instance, for Alan, the reverie of reading opened the potential space of absorption in Hebrew literature. As he noted elsewhere, Hebrew provided "the internal resources to negotiate the distance between old and new. Substitution, retrieval, containment, synthesis, reconciliation—all the dynamics of cultural change could take place *within* Hebrew literature because in that medium alone did the new meanings and old meanings exist simultaneously."[3]

In a 1984 essay on the siddur for the anthology *Back to the Sources*, Alan took note of the "roomy space of the synagogue service," highlighting its capacity to hold the currents of Jewish life.[4] For Alan, Hebrew language and Jewish literary traditions offered spaces in which we might hear the voices of past and present mingling, arguing, and interacting in an ongoing conversation. This is abundantly evident in *Ḥurban: Responses to Catastrophe in Hebrew Literature*, a major opening move in a career devoted to the roomy spaces of Jewish textuality. Alan tells us that the motivation for the project grew out of the need to historicize the Holocaust. Yet, while his original intention may have been "to take the Holocaust literature of one interpretive community, Israeli culture and Hebrew literature, and read it against the background of its traditions," he describes the evolution of a project in which "background became foreground. The pre-Holocaust literature of catastrophe in Hebrew proved to be so rich and elaborate that it claimed equal footing with the contemporary materials."[5] In its exploration of an ongoing intertextual conversation, *Ḥurban* draws our attention not so much to the catastrophic events that have punctuated Jewish history as to the forms of "creative survival": "the exertions of the Hebrew literary imagination, as expressed in prophecy, liturgy, exegesis, and poetry."[6] Thus Alan's readings of the poetry of Ḥayyim Naḥman Bialik and Uri Zvi Greenberg, as well as the fiction of Aharon Appelfeld find their place in a history of literary responses that goes back to the book of Lamentations.

An ethics of reading informs Alan's work. Fueled by an interest in the moral imagination, Alan began his academic career with *George Eliot and The*

2. Alan Mintz, "In the Seas of Youth," *Prooftexts* 21, no. 1 (2001): 69–70.

3. Alan L. Mintz, *Translating Israel: Contemporary Hebrew Literature and Its Reception in America* (Syracuse, NY: Syracuse University Press, 2001), 230.

4. Alan Mintz, "Prayer and the Prayerbook," in *Back to the Sources: Reading the Classic Jewish Texts*, ed. Barry Holtz (New York: Summit, 1984), 403.

5. Alan Mintz, *Ḥurban: Responses to Catastrophe in Hebrew Literature* (New York: Columbia University Press, 1984), ix–x.

6. Mintz, *Ḥurban*, ix–x.

Novel of Vocation, a book that grew out of his dissertation. In his examination of Eliot's exercise of sympathy in the world of fiction, Alan refers to narrative as a "redemptive calling" that "recalls the misjudged and delivers the forgotten."[7] He gives insight into an important aspect of his own readerly commitments, as he follows the logic of an extended critical engagement with George Eliot to note that "all particulars of an imaginative universe have equal claims to sympathetic evocation." Yet, going on to consider the consequences of such a broadly inclusive view, he writes:

> To respond to each of these claims would obviously lead either to a paralysis [...] or to an endless flow of writing which, lacking any selectivity, would be formless. George Eliot seems to have been conscious of these questions when she wrote in *Middlemarch*: "If we had a keen vision and feeling of all ordinary human life, it would be like hearing the grass grow and the squirrel's heart beat, and we should die of that roar which lies on the other side of silence. As it is, the quickest of us walk about well wadded with stupidity."[8]

The passage Alan cites from chapter 20 in *Middlemarch* is well known. His critical response to Eliot's keen ethical consciousness brings the conversation into the present, as he observes:

> The either/or here is startling: either the fatal intensity of absolute sympathy or the inert silence of absolute insensibility. The only way out is a partial deafness that muffles the sound of humanity in order to make its noises sufferable, and therefore intelligible. If writing, then, is to give any articulation to human suffering, it must follow this via media by choosing some particulars for accentuation and representation and ignoring the others. Selection turns moral sympathy into narrative art.[9]

For Alan as literary scholar, I might add, selection turned moral sympathy into critical discernment. Indeed, the exercise of an ethically nuanced imaginative response is evident in the history of the choices Alan made as a literary critic. Take, for example, this account of family life in David Grossman's *Sefer hadiqduq hapenimi* (*The Book of Intimate Grammar*). Alan characterizes the novel as a portrait of the artist and describes the adolescent protagonist Aron's withdrawal from the family:

> Aron's powerlessness within the family is underscored by an extraordinary weekly ritual. Every Thursday night, while the women are doing a thorough house cleaning, the father takes a long bath and then, with his towel wrapped around his waist, he comes into the living room and lies face-down on the

---

7. Alan Mintz, *George Eliot and the Novel of Vocation* (Cambridge, MA: Harvard University Press, 1978), 160–61.
8. Mintz, *George Eliot*, 160–61.
9. Mintz, *George Eliot*, 160–61.

sofa. The women gather around him (this includes the grandmother, Moshe's mother) and scour his massive back for blackheads and whiteheads, which they fall upon with horror and rapture, squeezing with their fingernails and applying alcohol, and working in tune to the father's answering groans of submission and delight.[10]

There's something repellent and oddly enticing in Alan's account of this scene. I recall Alan telling me at the time how deep into himself he had to go in order to take in and comprehend the interactions among family members in the novel.

This is where Alan's imaginative involvement in the scene took him:

As an evocation of Stone-Age rites, the scourging and grooming of the dominant male, with its not uncomplicated exchanges of pleasure and control, presents a revealing picture of gender relations in Israeli society of thirty years ago. It is a picture in which the son does not figure. Aron takes in the scene through the doorway of the kitchen where he sits on a low stool working on his assigned chores of peeling a mound of potatoes for the Sabbath cholent. Scrawny and underdeveloped, Aron is unlikely ever to accede to the prerogatives of the father's bearlike body, nor is he even permitted to participate in the collective female tribute to it. His response to his exclusion is to daydream while performing his repetitive scullery chores, and it is in these vivid reveries, undertaken as both denial and escape, that Grossman locates the origins of Aron's aesthetic consciousness and the seeds of his identity as an artist.[11]

Let me note quickly in passing that the reference to a character's "vivid reveries" suggests, as well, something of Alan's own readerly responsiveness.

Just as importantly, Alan uses his own engagement in the novelistic depiction of family dynamics to get at some underlying issues in Israeli society. We can follow his process of inquiry as he goes on to ask "why this novel is so extravagantly preoccupied with the claims of the body." His response:

the answer lies, I believe, in Grossman's presentation of Israel as a society of immigrant survivors and in his analysis of the unseen but enormous costs of successful survival. In the conventional Zionist story the settlers of the country are not common immigrants but pioneers whose powerful spiritual longings enable them to endure privation and hostility. The truth, of course, is that the vast majority of Jews ended up in Israel because of historical circumstance rather than ideological motivation. The obstacles faced by these accidental immigrants—certainly as much after their arrival in Israel as before—were every bit as difficult as those faced by the more famous intentional immigrants, yet their struggles remained untransfigured and unmystified by a rhetoric of sacrifice and ideals.[12]

10. Mintz, *Translating*, 211.
11. Mintz, *Translating*, 211–12.
12. Mintz, *Translating*, 211–12.

Untransfigured and unmystified, to be sure, yet Alan's critical discernment highlights Grossman's "sympathetic evocation" of ordinary lives, if I may borrow Alan's phrase for Eliot's exercise of moral imagination. Indeed, Alan's critical practice gives evidence of the kind of sympathetic understanding that he so admired in Eliot.

Returning to Alan's long engagement with Agnon, I want to conclude with some thoughts about creativity and loss. In his last completed book, Alan approached Agnon's *'Ir umelo'ah* (*A City in Its Fullness*), as a volume that exists "to compensate for the loss of the *pinkas*," the minute book or registry that was for centuries the record of life cycle events in Eastern European Jewish communities. Alan explores the "epic trajectory" of Agnon's compilation of tales, while noting that, for Agnon, literary creation is a compensatory activity that can never take the place of the temple in its destruction.[13] Writing is inevitably conditioned by mourning and loss, we might say, yet mourning becomes a resource, a springboard for the creative act.

"Ma'aseh hamenorah" ("The Tale of the Menorah"), one of the ancestral tales contained in Agnon's *'Ir umelo'ah*, tells a story of changes to a physical object over time, giving us a picture of the adaptiveness of the Jewish community to a succession of rulers that includes the Polish king and the Austrian emperor. This story of a material object opens access to history. A text is also a material object, a fabric, in which we find ourselves enmeshed. A text is a weave of words that evokes presence for us, the presence of those we love and those whom we have lost. A text takes shape out of the play of absence and presence.

Alan captures this dimension of language in his discussion of "Hasiman" ("The Sign"). In this Shavuot story, the first-person narrator, living in Talpiyot, Agnon's Jerusalem home, recounts how he learned of the destruction of his town at the hands of the Nazis. "The Sign" concerns the narrator's mystical encounter with the medieval poet Ibn Gabirol, who tells him he will make a *sign* to remember the town that has been lost. As Alan puts it, Ibn Gabirol

> is modeling, in *his* own classical medium, an act of creative memorialization that he expects the narrator to imitate in *his* own—belated—creative medium. Ibn Gabirol is at once demonstrating a way out of the cul-de-sac of grief and loss and summoning the narrator to activate himself and apply his creative gifts to perpetuating the memory of his town."[14]

The narrator relates a moment of visionary encounter with Ibn Gabirol "between the doors of the Holy Ark," a moment of connection that Alan describes as "a kind of mystical telepathy."[15] I think we can take Alan's phrasing

13. Mintz, *Ancestral Tales*, 73, 18.
14. Mintz, *Ancestral Tales*, 8.
15. Mintz, *Ancestral Tales*, 4.

to acknowledge something fundamental to literary experience: the capacity of literature to dissolve existential barriers between subject and object, reader and text. "Mystical telepathy" thus links to "reverie" in Alan's critical lexicon. These phrases have particular resonance in the work of a scholar who valued the immediacy and intimacy of literary experience, yet who never lost sight of the pleasures of analytical inquiry into the dynamics of those encounters.

Alan makes the case for placing "The Sign" at the start of *'Ir umelo'ah*, rather than at the end (which had been the choice of Emuna Yaron, Agnon's daughter, when she edited the posthumous volume). In doing so, he asks us to read the story less as a memorial gesture than as an opening into the kind of storytelling that fills the volume. Rather than an epitaph, Alan writes that "The Sign" transforms lament into "an invitation to be emulated in the narrator's belated prosaic mode of creativity."[16] Belatedness here signals not only the distance between Agnon's narrator and the texts of Jewish tradition; it also points to the inevitable gap between signs and the things to which they refer.

In *Ancestral Tales*, Alan recalls the decision that he and I made to title the anthology of Agnon stories that we edited *A Book That Was Lost and Other Stories*. The title story, "Sefer she'avad" ("A Book That Was Lost," included in *'Ir umelo'ah*), offers an engaging account of the first-person narrator's efforts to track down a book that he mailed in his youth from Buczacz to Ginzei Yosef, the book collection that eventually formed the basis for the library of the newly founded Hebrew University in Jerusalem. It's a charming tale of attempted rescue on the narrator's part. He recalls how he skimped on lunch money in order to send to Jerusalem the unpublished leaves of a manuscript he discovered in the *beit midrash* of the town, a manuscript that was itself a commentary on commentaries. But the book gets lost somewhere between Eastern Europe and Palestine; it never reaches its destination. Long after making his own move to Erets Yisra'el, the narrator tells us that he continues to visit the library in Jerusalem to ask if the book has arrived. "Ḥaval 'al sefer she'avad" ("What a pity the book was lost"), he notes in closing.

A book is an object. A text is a fabric. A book that was lost: absence and presence. We wait together for a lost book to arrive. Agnon's words and Alan's, too, remind us not only of what we have lost, but also of what we have, and of what we may yet come to share. A scholarly community registers the loss and takes some measure of the life of Alan Mintz. We recall his engagement with us and his work with the texts that sustain our communal (intertextual) fabric, recognizing the opening he gives us to continue that work together into the future.

---

16. Mintz, *Ancestral Tales*, 4.

ANNE GOLOMB HOFFMAN teaches English and Comparative Literature at Fordham University and holds research appointments at the Columbia University Center for Psychoanalytic Training and Research, and the Institute for the History of Psychiatry at Weill Cornell Medical College. Her research addresses embodiment and textuality in literary and psychoanalytic writing. She collaborated with Alan Mintz on the collection, *'A Book That Was Lost' and Other Stories by S.Y. Agnon.*

6 *For Alan*

Sidra DeKoven Ezrahi

FOR DECADES—HALF A lifetime, really—you write to Alan, sharing an idea, a thought, an essay, and eagerly await his response. Always gracious, generous, even when he (oh-so-politely) takes issue with this or that claim. Then, suddenly, you are writing *about* Alan, hoping that something of his mind and spirit will be conveyed through your words. As present tense becomes past tense in your rhetoric, the presentness of his voice and his soul must somehow flow through you…

Parallel Roads and the Ones Not Taken

Alan's first book was *George Eliot and the Novel of Vocation*. But he was to find his own vocation in a different cultural space. While aware of the hubris of speaking for him, and without eliding the differences between us, I suspect that, like me, Alan would periodically return to his place of origin and savor writers like Eliot, Joyce, or James, Shakespeare or Milton … a busman's holiday for those of us who matriculated in English literature. It remained the road not taken, the road for which our graduate studies prepared us, but from which we took the detour into Hebrew and Jewish literature and culture. ("Because it was grassy, and wanted wear," as Robert Frost put it? Or because it was such a challenge for us *Amerikaner geboren* children of immigrants?)

But even as we continued to explore Hebrew literature—I in Jerusalem and Alan in Maryland, Waltham, and then in New York—we both found American spaces to which we could retreat. America itself was the site of so many different Jewish inflections, large enough to support our various curiosities and passions, its ports of entry many and its voices diverse. America and other diasporic spaces would remain central to Alan's passion. Even as he spent more time in Jerusalem, he dedicated his last decades at the Jewish Theological Seminary to inducting the next generations of American Jews, future scholars and religious and community leaders, into the intricacies and interstices of the Hebrew bookshelf. And although a kind of polemic evolved over the years between us, it was a divergence of focus rather than ideology. For Alan, the curious presence in early twentieth-century America of Hebrew writers like Gabriel Preil engaged him for a while and migrated into his fascination with contemporary novelists like Ruby Namdar and Maya Arad, who live in the United States and write in Hebrew. For me, America was, in the mid-to-late twentieth century, the theatre of the Jewish comedy as enacted by writers like Philip Roth and Grace Paley, an antidote to the heroic-epic mode in Israel that would eventually lead to the tragic hubris of post-1967 culture and politics.

Building a City: Writings on Agnon's Buczacz in Memory of Alan Mintz (2022): 063–068
DOI: 10.2979/BuildingaCityWriting.0.0.07

Diasporic Spaces

And then Europe opened up to a kind of return. For nearly half a century the inaccessible continent of the Jewish tragedy, Eastern Europe would provide new vistas for travel and scholarship in the post-Communist era. Over the past three decades, many of us have connected, physically and textually, with the places from which we had been barred; almost without noticing, our imaginations became newly engaged in the diasporic spaces of Russia, Poland, Galicia, Hungary, Romania. While North and South America continued to provide settings for cultural iterations outside of Israel, we were now able to visit and more fully envision the actual places in which the writers of the Hebrew renaissance had incubated.

And that's where Agnon comes in. In fact, I would argue that, along with access to the actual places, such as Buczacz or Lublin, certain hitherto unexamined texts in Agnon's oeuvre would themselves constitute a new diasporic space for a handful of literary scholars, among whom Alan was the most notable and consistent, along with prominent historians such as Omer Bartov. I would go so far as to say that, over the past five years or so, Agnon himself has become a new diasporic space.

Alan and I shared a romance with Agnon that went back to the early 1980s when, as cofounder and coeditor with David Roskies of *Prooftexts*, he proposed that I write about Agnon's reflections on the Holocaust in his fiction. I evinced surprise, since I was then convinced, along with so many other readers, that Agnon had avoided the subject rather assiduously. But, of course, Alan was onto something, and, as I proceeded to uncover layer upon layer of reference, some explicit but mostly implicit, I realized how deeply and persistently—but unexpectedly—Agnon had engaged that subject. It would become a major passion for me in the decades to come, as I followed these paths into presumably untrodden places where Agnon's imagination had indeed dared to tread.[1]

Meanwhile, Alan's own scholarship on Agnon began to take on its own focus that, I now believe, was of a piece with his position in and vis-à-vis the Hebrew diaspora. It was only in our last email exchange, two months before his sudden death, that the convergence of our respective work, as well as the different nuances in our passions and persuasions, began to come into focus for me. The question that had barely formulated itself in my mind, that I never got a chance to ask, was whether Alan's fascination with Agnon's Buczacz stories may be connected to his fascination with the "diasporic imagination" (my term, not his) as rendered in Hebrew.[2]

---

1. Sidra DeKoven Ezrahi, "Agnon Before and After," *Prooftexts* 2, no. 1 (1982): 78–94.
2. For two references on this subject from a vast library that has grown exponentially in the past two decades, see the seminal work by Daniel Boyarin and Jonathan Boyarin, "Diaspora: Generation and the Ground of Jewish Identity, *Critical Inquiry* 19, No. 4 (Summer, 1993),

Alan's work on diasporic writers, or on writing in diaspora, was in a way a counterpart to mine; as my own work on Agnon increasingly focused on Jerusalem, his came more and more to be trained on Buczacz. This was first iterated at a conference that Alan hosted at Cambridge University in 2015 on "Diaspora in Modern Hebrew Literature," where Namdar and Arad spoke, and where Alan and I presented our respective works-in-progress on Agnon. Alan spoke on Agnon's Buczacz stories, offering an early draft of what was to become his magisterial work on the posthumous volume, *'Ir umelo'ah* (*A City in its Fullness*). I presented a reading of another posthumously published story, "Lifnim min haḥomah," that would become the kernel of an argument I would make in an essay published two years later. My argument, briefly, is that, in many stories, Agnon's Jerusalem and his Buczacz (or its fictional surrogate, Szybusz), are mirror images—that both are diasporic in the way that the so-called shtetl was reflected in so much of Jewish literature and folklore: as a nonpolitical, supposedly homogeneous space. Crucial to this argument is the eliding of the terms *'ayarah* ("town" or "shtetl") and *'ir* ("city") in Agnon's fictions and correspondence, as well as in much of Agnon scholarship. The city as political space where conflicting interests are adjudicated and power is negotiated does not really appear in these fictions. This has major consequences for the representation of contemporary Jerusalem. My argument, in short, is that Agnon's nostalgic gaze toward his destroyed town/city reflects his "reluctance to engage the political realities and ethical challenges of contemporary Jerusalem."[3]

My essay appeared in the spring of 2017, and, of course, I immediately sent it to Alan. I quoted his introduction to *A City in its Fullness* in that essay and pointed out the problematic conflation, which can be attributed to Agnon himself, of *'ir* and *'ayarah*, or city and shtetl, in regard to Buczacz.[4] Alan's response was, as always, measured and appreciative, even as he pushed back on the differences between our positions:

> I go out of my way to say that Agnon never refers to Buzcacz as a shtetl but as a city (although not a metropolis/*krakh*). In the introduction to the book [*'Ir umelo'ah* (*A City in its Fullness*)], I do deal with stages in the image of the shtetl in order to show how anomalous it is. The section of the introduction that truly deals with the issues you raise is [...] where I talk about the dialectical relation between Buczacz and Jerusalem; that perhaps is where we differ because I don't see one as the copy of the other.[5]

693–725; and see Sidra DeKoven Ezrahi, *Booking Passage: Exile and Homecoming in the Modern Jewish Imagination*. Berkeley: University of California Press, 2000.

3. Sidra DeKoven Ezrahi, "The Shtetl and its Afterlife: Agnon in Jerusalem," *AJS Review* 41, no. 1 (2017): 146, doi:10.1017/S036400941700006X.

4. Alan Mintz, introduction to *A City in its Fullness*, by S.Y. Agnon, ed. Alan Mintz and Jeffrey Saks (New Milford, CT: Toby, 2016).

5. Private email communication, March 21–22, 2017.

The more detailed analysis of Buczacz as a "city" would appear in Alan's *Ancestral Tales: Reading the Buczacz Stories of S.Y. Agnon*, which was due to be published by Stanford in June 2017, and which Alan did not live to see. The most important note I want to sound here is that such differences between us were treated as honest disagreements in the ongoing search for better understanding—what I called in my response to him, *"maḥloqet shel ohavim"* ("disagreement between admirers")—and were never tinged with personal animus. On the contrary, the civility—*Gemütlichkeit*—that Alan always exhibited toward me was, I hope, fully reciprocated. And that was his way in the world. What made our dialogue interesting, perhaps, is that it was not clothed in ideological—and certainly not in personal—terms. The old battles between Zionists and Diasporists may not be over, but they reappear in different guises. In this arena, I find myself often on both sides of the aisle—or, more accurately, *in* the aisle—and I think Alan did, too, in a way, although we differed in our approaches to culture and to the connections between fiction and politics. But it is a source of ongoing sorrow that he did not live to help me sort out the distinctions and the convergences between us.

Alan's Most Significant Culinary Achievement: The Academy as Smorgasbord

The *Gemütlichkeit* that Alan evinced toward me, and toward all his colleagues and students, is notable because it remains all too rare in the academy. But Alan was one of those outstanding members of our generation who helped to convert the model of Herr Professor into one of access and attention. He had a genuine humility, along with a simple love of learning and sharing, and a graciousness that expressed itself in the most unexpected ways. I first experienced that humility in the early 1980s, after I had published *By Words Alone*, a typology of literary responses to the Holocaust. Just beginning what would become his pathbreaking study of Jewish responses to catastrophe, *Ḥurban*, Alan wrote me to ask if it would impinge on my own territory if he engaged in such an endeavor. I was deeply moved by what was then, and remains, such a gracious act of generosity and collegiality. Of course, not only did I not object to his wading into such waters (except to warn him of the personal toll it takes to spend your time with such ongoing misery, even through the mitigating lens of art), but I welcomed him into what was then a very small coterie of scholars. In this as in every other scholarly (and personal) endeavor, Alan himself signaled what is in the academy the equivalent of his celebrated domestic hospitality: "there's always room for one more." Of course, that principle applies only if one regards the world of scholarship as a smorgasbord and not as a zero-sum game.

It was when we had our differences, reflecting values we each held sincerely and defended vigorously, that Alan's decency and generosity showed themselves most clearly. When Alan decided to leave the university for the seminary, I challenged him publicly, saying that I believed our vocation was to teach Jewish and Hebrew studies in the American academy and not retreat into sectarian spaces. We both defended our positions vigorously, and that debate continued for years, even as the love and mutual respect remained undiminished.

But there's more: Alan has a coveted place in my own private pantheon. In his usual understated and underpublicized way, he was one of the heroes of my struggle for tenure at the Hebrew University in the early 1990s. It was his act of whistle-blowing that alerted me to the shenanigans that were going on behind my back to undermine my candidacy. His phone call to me could have cost him personally, but he exhibited the kind of quiet courage that anyone who knew him well would recognize. No posturing, no bluster, just plain human decency.

As soon as word spread—so fast, as we all know—that Alan had died, my husband Bernie Avishai and I hastily organized a *bimqom shiv'ah*, a surrogate shiva observance, in our home in Jerusalem. Thinking that a handful of people would come and share their sorrow and their memories, we were unprepared for the river of mourners that flowed into our living room, clinging to the memories and to each other, and reluctant to go out again into the heartless night.

I suspect I am not the only friend who has "seen" Alan in the streets of Jerusalem in recent months. One of the uncanny experiences of this past year has been that recurrent apparition every time a sixty-something man with an unassuming *kippah*, thinning hair, and a specific stature that is hard to describe but easy to recognize appears in front of me on 'Emeq Refaim (valley of the *ghosts*, indeed!), and I have to choke back the words, "Alan, thank God you're still here!!"

There was, for all of us, no time to say goodbye. We all wish, I suppose, to die with our boots on, but also to have the time for farewells from those we love. So we can only hope that Alan knew what each of us would have said to him. What I would have said is: "Alan, dear heart, go in peace. Your presence in my life has been a blessing. We were respectful and mutually enabling colleagues, and we were loving friends. As we moved from graduate students to young academics with one foot in the world of American and English culture and the other in Hebrew scholarship, to veterans in our respective fields, I would only have wished for one thing: more time...."

SIDRA DEKOVEN EZRAHI is Professor Emerita of General and Comparative Literature at the Hebrew University of Jerusalem. She has written on subjects ranging from representations of the Holocaust in postwar Israeli, European and American culture to the configurations of exile and homecoming in contemporary Jewish literature. Her books include *By Words Alone: The Holocaust in*

Literature (University of Chicago Press, 1980) and *Booking Passage: Exile and Homecoming in the Modern Jewish Imagination* (University of California Press, 2000). She has also published two books in Hebrew (*Ippus hamasa' hayehudit*, Resling, 2017; and *Sheloshah paytanim*, Mossad Bialik, 2020). In 2007, she became a Guggenheim Fellow for her most recent book project, *Figuring Jerusalem: Politics and Poetics in the Sacred Center* (University of Chicago Press, 2022). In November, 2019, she was awarded an honorary doctorate from Hebrew Union College-Jewish Institute of Religion.

III. Essays

Buczacz

7 "The Heavenly City": A Historiographic Paradigm in the Scholastic Cartography of S.Y. Agnon

Avidov Lipsker

Translated by Batya Stein

In memory of Alan Mintz,
a devoted scholar of Agnon

The Heavenly City of Buczacz

At the beginning of S.Y. Agnon's second posthumous book, 'Ir umelo'ah, his daughter Emuna Yaron, who edited the book, placed a dedication written by her father stating that this would be "the chronicle of the city of Buczacz." Agnon noted that he had written the book in pain and anguish "so that our descendants should know that our city was full of Torah, wisdom, love, piety, life, grace, kindness and charity."[1]

But is this indeed the case? Is 'Ir umelo'ah a nostalgic literary-historical chronicle of the city of Buczacz that is now lost? Does the content of this thick book really reflect the declaration at its opening, describing Buczacz as a utopian place full of Torah, wisdom and awe, life, grace, kindness, and charity?

This may have been Agnon's intention when he began his mythological chronicle about the foundation of his city in the section titled "Book 1: The Tale of the Town." This "foundation story," as I have already shown,[2] is a kind of literary replication of the story about the founding of the Worms community that

This research was supported by the Israel Science Foundation (grant No. 572\20).

1. S.Y. Agnon, 'Ir umelo'ah (Jerusalem/Tel Aviv: Schocken, 1986). The dedication is quoted from the English translation—A City in Its Fullness, ed. Alan Mintz and Jeffrey Saks (New Milford, CT: Toby Press, 2016), vii—which contains a selection of the stories published in the original and is cited wherever possible.
2. See Avidov Lipsker, Maḥshavot 'al Agnon, 2 vols. (Bar-Ilan: Ramat-Gan University Press, 2015–18).

appears in *Sefer ma'aseh nissim*, and is filled with hints about sin and blame.[3] Agnon's dedication was, from the start, incompatible with the opening of *'Ir umelo'ah* given his choice to follow in the footsteps of *Sefer ma'aseh nissim*, a work suffused with a sense of guilt that persisted for generations in a community that had promised to reach Zion and then stayed back in Poland for a thousand years for economic advantage.[4]

The introductory section, "The Tale of the Town," does not portray the fullness of organic Jewish life. In truth, it does not contain even *one complete story* about a community of sages, or one detailed map of the city's streets, nor any chronicled fragment presenting a metonymy of the full communal Jewish life whose destruction Agnon mourns in his dedication. Quite the reverse: the entire first part of the book is a fragmentation of a wholeness that exists no longer. Book 1 is a collection of textual shards, archeological remnants that Agnon placed *next* to one another, not as in a chronicle *after* one another but as the broken fragments of a mosaic missing most of its stones. The entire opening section of *'Ir umelo'ah* is made up of brief memory fragments, each a few pages long, lacking any unifying organizational-narrative element. They dwell next to one another only because they were collected as urban remnants in the same archeological excavation. This archeology, however, "refuses" to become a chronicle. Its findings lie on the edge of the writer's memory trenches and they glimmer in the light of the present, without any narratological-historical context. Thus, they are presented to the reader as an accumulation of fragments—"Kise shel Eliyahu" (26), "Yeter kelei hama'or shehayu beveit hakenesset haggadol" (27–29), concise memoirs tracing the profiles of local dwellers (123–128), and many many others— all mere splinters of the memory remnants from a historical reality, shards of a wholeness that was plundered in the past. Indeed, the prominent visual element in these sketches, such as "Mar'eh ha'ir" (14)—is what Agnon refers to as "the disappearing line." Buczacz is a city without contours, it "goes in and out of forests," it is a fading urban experience. It merits note in this context that "Hane'elam (The Disappeared) is also the title of a central story in the collection,[5] dealing with a youth who was conscripted into the imperial army, left the city and, when he returned, his inner world crumbled and he sunk into madness until his death.

3. Juspa Shamash, *Sefer ma'aseh nissim* (Amsterdam, 1696), 1. See also "Lamah ba'u lefanim gezerot rabot 'al yehudei vermiza umeh haya het'am," in *R. Juspa Shamash dekehilat vermiza: 'Olam yehudi bame'ah hayod zayin*, ed. Shlomo Eidelberg (Jerusalem: Magnes Press, 1991), 59. Eidelberg claims that the teleology of the story dates the beginning of Ashkenaz Jewry to the First Temple in an attempt to release it from the charge of participation in the crucifixion of Jesus, and also as a justification for their continued stay in exile after the establishment of the Second Temple. See ibid., 12. See also Shlomo Eidelberg, "Qadmut hayishuv hayehudi beGermaniyah," *Yedi'on ha'iggud hamada'i lemada'ei hayahadut* 17–18 (1981): 19–25.
4. Lipsker, *Mahshavot 'al Agnon*, 1: 65–70.
5. *A City in Its Fullness*, 369.

My claim is that, from the start, Agnon assumed the task of writing about Buczacz endorsing an approach that gave up on a full description of Jewish life. This poetic approach reverses the familiar version that readers of Jewish literature encountered, for example, in Zalman Schneur's novella *Shklover Yidn*.[6] Moreover, Agnon assigned poetic value to the decision to renounce the dimension of completeness: the greatness of the loss of his city equals the greatness of his refusal to describe its fullness! Buczacz in Agnon's writings, from the time he wrote *Vehayah he'aqov lemishor* in 1912, is always a city of collapse, of dwindling, of disappearance.

The stories in *'Ir umelo'ah* that trace the development of a cohesive narrative about life in the Buczacz community and its characters, are mainly based on plots happening outside it and reaching their climax in faraway places. Critics, who have not paid attention to the historical background of the stories in *Ir umelo'ah*, failed to note the ties and connections to these other locations. Seemingly marked by narrative coherence and by a developing storyline about a Jewish community and its characters, *'Ir umelo'ah* is a work of fiction whose roots are not at all in Buczacz and whose plot invariably culminates in settings far away from it.

The first story with a narrative of this kind is "Ha'ish halovesh badim" (The Man Dressed in Linen.)[7] Its protagonist, Gavriel the hazzan, (*dos laynen yidl*), would occasionally come to the city from far away to visit his father's grave, and the narrator wonders—what happened before his burial in Buczacz? The meaning of these sporadic visits is clarified from the life story of the protagonist's grandfather, the elder Gavriel the hazzan, who had been captivated by a copy of the book *Torat ha'olah* by R. Moshe Isserless (1530–1572), known as ReMA.[8] The plot focuses on the life of the last generation of halakhists in Kraków, the city of the ReMA, where he wrote this book. The first printing of the book[9] was magnificent by the standards of the time and, because of its splendor, the protagonist's grandfather had very much wanted it. Illustrated pages that do not appear in the original printing had been added to this copy and, because the elder Gavriel the hazzan had so much desired it, he paid a great deal for it. Yet, it was precisely the book's magnificence that led to his death, when priests caught him holding it and ascribed witchcraft powers to it. The grandfather was the victim of a cruel execution, his limbs pulled apart in the market square, and was buried in Buczacz. His grandson, "the man dressed in linen," came every year to visit his grandfather's grave without the community knowing this secret.

---

6. Zalman Schneur, *Shklover Yiden: Noveln* (Vilna: B. Kletskin, 1929).

7. *A City in Its Fullness*, 98–139.

8. Ibid.

9. Prague: Mordechai Shalom Katz, 1570. Moses Isserles, *Torat ha'olah* (Prague: Mordechai Shalom Katz, 1579)

Through this story, which only ends in Buczacz, Agnon establishes the deep connection of the Buczacz community to the communal Galician center of Kraków, the capital of the sixteenth and seventeenth-century Polish kings. This is the Kraków of ReMA's days that, together with Lublin and Lviv (Galicia), were considered "capitals" of an imagined Jewish kingdom that lacked a territory or a government. This is the kingdom of the Council of Four Lands that existed from 1520 until 1764 and, as shown below, seems to be at the center of Agnon's concerns. Agnon explicitly returned several times to descriptions of this historical era, full of wonder at this display of Jewish religious sovereignty that was renewed during the councils' biannual meetings at fairs.[10]

Agnon, as noted, related to this at length in several of his works; in his story "Meḥamat hametsiq" that was published as a booklet in 1921. In 1930, Agnon included remarks on this issue in *Hakhnasat kallah* and then again, in a similar version, in 'Ir umelo'ah:

> There they gathered, the most brilliant of the generation, the greatest Torah sages, commanders in Israel, community benefactors and leaders in Poland. And in those days, the Torah was not yet painted into a corner but was indeed the only one at the helm. The rabbis gilded themselves with the crown of Torah and the famous benefactors listened to their words. Torah and a good name wore one crown, and they would issue decrees and ordinances to strengthen Heaven's will, and all the people carefully followed them, because of humbleness and fear of sin.[11]

10. See the interesting comment of historian Shmuel Ettinger, who tied the loss of political independence in Judah after the Second Temple period to the continuous pursuit of halakhic autonomy in the Diaspora. The Council of Four Lands, he implied, is the realization of the yearning for political governance, which was translated into a supra-political halakhic autonomy. See the introduction of Shmuel Ettinger, "Va'ad arba' aratsot," to *Pinkas va'ad arba' aratsot*, ed. Israel Halperin and Israel Bartal, 2nd edn. (Jerusalem: Mosad Bialik/Hebrew University, 1990) 1:15. On the issue of Jewish autonomy at the time of the Council of Four Lands, see Gershon David Hundert, *Jews in Poland-Lithuania in the Eighteenth Century: A Genealogy of Modernity* (Berkeley, CA: University of California Press, 2004). On the participation of Kraków and its periphery in the Council of Four Lands, see Mayer Balaban, *Toledot hayehudim beKraków uveKazimierz 1304–1868* (Jerusalem: Magnes Press, 2002), 1:269–72. Meetings were initially convoked in Lublin, but other fairs were later added, mainly Yaroslav.

11. S.Y. Agnon, *Meḥamat hametsiq* (Berlin: Jüdische Verlag, 1921) 54. In the version in 'Ir umelo'ah, Agnon added that a Gentile king "sets policemen who oppress the people with sticks and leashes and coerce them to fulfill their commands ... but the holy people of Israel willingly accepted all that the leaders and guardians of the Council of the Lands enjoined them to do" (308). This description is the narrator's idealization and lacks any historical basis. Testimonies actually report on debt collectors who oppressed borrowers, to the chagrin of Polish aristocrats and landowners who did not look kindly on this "Jewish policing" that afforded Jewish institutions more effective means for collecting taxes from Jews than those available to the government through coercion, bans, and communal punishment. See Jacob Goldberg, *Haḥevrah hayehudit bemamlekhet Polin-Lita* (Jerusalem: Merkaz Zalman Shazar, 1999), 131, and historic evidence of bans, fines, imprisonment, use of the rack, consignment to

Although these councils did not meet in Kraków but rather in Lublin (the Gramenitz fair) and in Yaroslav, the sages of Kraków and of its rural periphery were significant participants in them.[12] In the perception of Agnon, who looks at the past of his urban community, Kraków, the city of R. Moshe Isserles, is "the heavenly city" in Carl Becker's "theological-political" terms.[13] This "heavenly city" is the civic-communal utopic image that the *boni viri* (טובי העיר), the townsmen-protagonists of *'Ir umelo'ah*, look up to. "The heavenly city" ranks highest in Agnon's theological-political conception, a model of community management inspired by biblical and halakhic writings entrusted to "worthy" individuals who are experts in these texts and interpret them to their community. The more they succeed in acting as a consensual leadership, the more their city will become a heavenly place, in the same sense that communities in other cities later came to perceive themselves as citizens of "Jerusalem of Lithuania" (Vilna), a "famous city" (Brest), or a "city of the mighty" (Grodno), and similar labels ascribing high sovereign value to Jewish life in a Gentile city.[14]

Agnon's attachment to the historiographic and scholastic tradition of Kraków and its sages should be credited to his early scholarly training, which began at the age of twelve in the library of the Buczacz beit midrash.

death, and more, particularly those that were decreed by the Chomsk council in 1721; Shimon Dubnov, *Pinkas hamedinah* (Berlin: Ayanot, 1925). 249–51, and also in the index of subjects under *'onashim*, 347–48. See also a contemporary testimony in the chronicle of Nathan-Neta Hanover, *Yeven metsulah* (Kraków: Fischer, 1895): "And Jews never litigated in Gentile courts, nor before any prince, nor before his majesty the king. Had a Jew gone to Gentile judges, they would have punished him with great dishonor to fulfill [what is written]: "our enemies being judges" [Deut. 32:31], 666–67. Agnon added to the *'Ir umelo'ah* version a historiosophic theological comment whereby, because of the councils' abolition in 1764, "God retaliated against the kingdom of Poland. The kingdom abolished the Council of the Lands –and He, may He be blessed, unleashed on them three ruthless countries that abolished the kingdom of Poland" (308). This comment by Agnon is copied from a memoir published when Agnon was in Leipzig, *Zikhronot R. Dov miBolihov 1723–1804*, ed. Mark Wischnitser (Berlin: Klal, 1922). The text in the memoir reads: "And after the leaders of these countries were removed from their greatness and this minor honor was taken away from the Jews ... the whole country was divided in 1772 and all honor was taken away from the people of Poland and from their king, to fulfill the verse, 'And I will lay my vengeance upon Edom' ..." (91). On R. Dov, see Meir Balaban, *Letoledot hatenu'ah haFrankit* (Tel Aviv: Dvir, 1934), 1:9–10.
12. On the election of representatives to the councils and on the place of the Kraków region, see Goldberg, *Hahevrah hayehudit*, 136–37. The fact that "the rabbi who fled" in the story "In Search of a Rabbi," is hiding in a small village in the surroundings of Kraków does appear as a retreat. His stay there did not detract from his authority since he was still in the Kraków area, which played a distinguished and decisive role in the councils' gatherings.
13. Carl L. Becker, *The Heavenly City of the Eighteen-Century Philosophers* (New Haven, CT: Yale University Press, 1932). On the theological-political interface, see, in particular, the chapter "The Laws of Nature and of Nature's God," 59.
14. On the names assigned to city representatives, which served as identification marks at the councils' gatherings in the fairs of the Council of Four Lands, see Dubnov, *Pinkas hamedinah*, 28, note 2.

The rare collections gathered in this library came mainly from acquisitions at the famous bookshop of Aharon Foist in Kraków, a commercial establishment that, indirectly, supported historical research projects that were published by the city's Yosef Fischer Press. The books were sold by Foist, who also relied on distribution to subscribers and to batei midrash in the city and outside it by means of sales catalogs. As a townsman of Agnon attested, these catalogs were also sent to the library of the Buczacz beit midrash when the young Agnon, only twelve years old, was engaged in the cataloging and organization of this library.[15]

The known chronicles of Kraków, then, had been accessible to Agnon since his youth, and it is from them that he drew his detailed knowledge about the Council of Four Lands in the generation of the *aharonim*. The detailed source for this and the closest to Agnon's times was the renowned chronicle about the city of Lviv by Hayyim Nathan Dembitzer, *Sefer kelilat yofi*, where the second part is devoted to Kraków. Another famous chronicle was *Anshei shem* by Shlomo Buber.[16] Although these two were not the first works of this kind, they must be mentioned at the start because of their immediate availability to young Agnon given that both were published by the Fischer Press and sent by Foist (owner of the Kraków bookshop) to the librarian of the Buczacz beit midrash, a subscriber to his catalogs.[17]

The important and pioneering chronicle about the city of Kraków, *'Ir hatsedeq* by Jehiel Matitiyahu Zunz, was also presumably found in this library. The Aramaic name of Kraków—*Krakha dekula bei* (the city with everything in it), citing BT Hullin 56b—features in it recurrently and prominently. Thus, in the description of a prestigious rabbi's arrival to the city, we read: "Because he had wisdom, counsel, and understanding, he was received by a city full of sages and writers, the holy community of Kraków, known as *Krakha dekula bei*."[18] This chronicle is the source of the acclaim "a city full of sages"—that is, "a city in its fullness"—as well as of the Aramaic expression taken, as noted, from BT Hullin, which evokes in its sound the name Kraka, as Jews pronounced the city's name and as its name is printed in the title pages of books. In this tradition of speech and print, the Aramaic expression as it appears in Zunz's *'Ir hatsedeq* spread widely, and only later was it found in Dembitzer's *Sefer kelilat yofi*.[19] This Ara-

15. On this issue, see in the memoirs of Naphtali Menatseah and Yisrael Cohen in *Sefer Buczacz*, ed. Yisrael Cohen (Tel Aviv: 'Am 'Oved, 1957), See also, on Aharon Foist, Hagit Cohen, *Behanuto shel mokher sefarim* (Jerusalem: Magnes Press, 2006), 55–65. For a broad description of Agnon's apprenticeship in the library, see Lipsker, *Mahshavot 'al Agnon*, 2:221–25.

16. Hayyim Nathan Dembitzer, *Kelilat yofi: Toledot harabbanim hage'onim*, vol. 2 (Kraków: Yosef Fischer Press, 1893); Shlomo Buber, *Anshei shem* (Kraków: Yosef Fischer Press, 1895).

17. S.Y. Agnon, *Me'atsmi el 'atsmi* (Jerusalem/Tel Aviv: Schocken, 1976), 7; 261.

18. Jehiel Matitiyahu Zunz, *'Ir hatsedeq* (Lemberg: Poremba, 1874), 120.

19. Babylonian Talmud, Hullin 56b: "R. Meir would expound this verse as follows: 'He has made you and established you, a city and all therein, out of it come their priests, out of it their prophets, out of it their princes, out of it their kings, as is written (Zekhariah 10:4): 'Out of

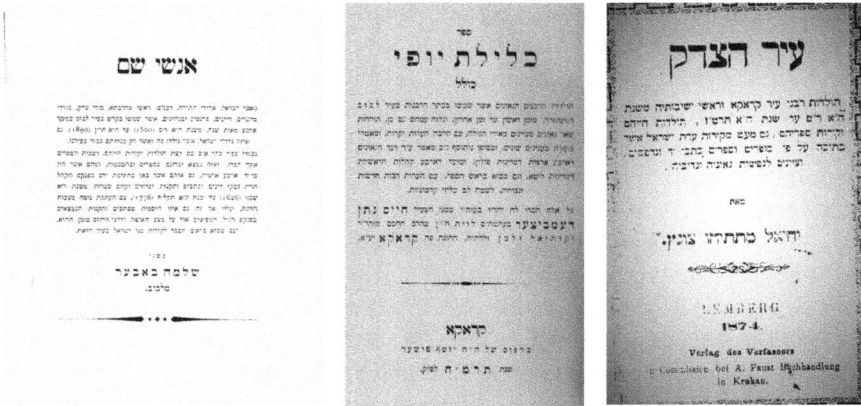

Figure 3: The chronicles of Kraków and Lemberg.

maic phrase is *ab initio* meant to denote the meaning of autonomous fullness that does not need completion from outside and resonates in particular in Rashi's comment on the Talmudic Tractate of Hullin noted above as relating to judicial autonomy, meaning that the Jewish community need not turn to foreign judges.[20]

This commentary is indeed the main concern of the story "In Search of a Rabbi, or the Governor's Whim,"[21] which condemns the way that Jews involved the Gentile governor in a legal matter and thereby brought disaster to their community. The speaker in the story is R. Moshe Avraham Abush, the rabbi of Zabno, who neither lives in the city nor is its chronicler and whose main work, *Tsiluta de'Avraham*, was about the ReMA of Kraków[22] R. Moshe Avraham Abush demanded from the

them shall come forth the corner-stone, out of them the tent peg, and so forth.'" Rashi comments: "A city and all therein, and it has been said of the community of Jews that all its rulers come from them and not from another people." On Kraków's fame as a place of Torah excellence, there is a tradition explaining the city's name by matching the numerological value of Kraków's Hebrew spelling with that of the words ending the verse in Exodus 17:6, "Behold, I will stand before you there *on the rock*" (*'al hatsur*). See Dembitzer, *Kelilat yofi*, 2:42. For a historiographic evaluation of these chronicles' relative importance and their authors' mutual relationships, see Balaban, *Toledot hayehudim beKraków*, 1:434–36.

20. See the full passage from BT Hulin in the previous note. The yearning for sovereignty is also reflected in the dry historical details about the legal conduct of Jews until the eighteenth century, both among themselves and with Gentiles. These subtleties emerge in the precise descriptions of Bernard Weinryb in the chapter he devotes to this aspect of Jewish life in Poland in general and in Kraków in particular. See Bernard D. Weinryb, *The Jews of Poland: A Social and Economic History of the Jewish Community in Poland from 1100–1800* (Philadelphia: Jewish Publication Society of America, 1972), 141–44.

21. Agnon, *A City in Its Fullness*, 253.

22. The rabbi of Zabno (1720–1802), author of *Tsiluta de'Avraham* (mentioned in *'Ir umelo'ah*, 331). Moshe Avraham Abush Margaliot, "the rabbi of Zabno," *Tsiluta de'Avraham veniqra ḥiddushei mehaReMA* (Sadilkov: Pinhas Eliezer Print, 1821). On the circumstances of his grandson's *post-*

dignitaries in the Buczacz delegation that they seek a figure such as R. Mordechai, who is hidden in their city.

In 'Ir umelo'ah, Agnon devoted to Kraków, "the other place," three stories that are the heart of the novelistic prose in this collection: "The Man Dressed in Linen," "In Search of a Rabbi, or the Governor's Whim," and "The Parable and its Lesson." The speaker in all of them is his favorite narrator, the historical figure of R. Moshe Avraham Abush, who is not a member of the Buczacz community.

The story "In Search of a Rabbi" does indeed begin in Buczacz, which had no rabbi then, but unfolds mostly outside it, when the dignitaries' delegation was sent to persuade R. Moshe Avraham Abush to leave his current home and come to serve as the city rabbi. In the story of the actual event, R. Moshe Abush explains to the delegation his refusal to do so and suggests appointing R. Mordechai, who lives in Buczacz. R. Mordechai was a disciple of "the rabbi who fled," who remains a mysterious figure throughout the story and whose name is never mentioned.[23]

Neither the reader nor the delegation listening to R. Abush knows the location of the event that led the story's protagonist, the exemplary halakhist who had been R. Mordechai's teacher, to flee the terror of Gentile law. From which city did he run away? where did he hide, and where did he teach R. Mordechai Torah? Readers are thereby branded as "suspects," with whom the narrator cannot share this important piece of information. In the details of these intimidating surroundings, which Agnon thickens in the story, he conceals the secret information in a hint that only those versed in Halakhah and Torah exegesis at the time of the Council of Four Lands might perhaps discern. The hint is given "in passing," as it were, when Agnon tells how the rabbi who fled received a volume of the Gemara that he had been studying and had intended to teach Mordechai, his disciple:

> One day a man in the village had his son circumcised. People came from the city, and one of them left behind a volume of the Gemara, but no one knew who had forgotten it. Israel Nathan took it and brought it to the rabbi. He saw the Gemara and laughed and wept. He wept for the days he had spent without a Gemara. He laughed because a Gemara had come into his possession. And which volume? The one he had been studying on the day that he fled from the duke's wrath. We, who do not wish to profit from a miracle even in a story, will reveal things as they truly happened. R. Birekh Shapira knew where his father-in-law was hiding. He brought the Gemara with him to that village and

humous publication of Tsiluta de'Avraham (a historical fact that is highly significant in the story), see Hayyim Lieberman, Ohel RaHaL (New York: Empire Press, 1980), 1:449–50. On the narrative functioning of this character as a storyteller, see Alan Mintz, Ancestral Tales: Reading the Buczacz Stories (Stanford, CA: Stanford University Press, 2006), 171–88.

23. In a long chapter that Mintz devoted to this story (ibid., 157–210), he related to this as a final interpretive datum. In the index of names (422), this figure appears under "R. Mordechai's teacher" although, as shown below, in the story his identity is only hinted at.

Figure 4: R. Berekhyah Birekh Shapira, *Zera' Birekh*, Kraków, 1646
Mentioning R. Shalom Me'elish in the introduction.

left it there, purposely choosing the volume that his father-in-law the rabbi had
been studying.[24]

The passing remark mentions by name a relative of the "the rabbi who fled"—
his son-in-law, R. Berekhyah Birekh Shapira. R. Shapira married the daughter of
R. Shalom Me'elish, a well-known community leader in Kraków.[25] This encoded
mention sheds, as it were, a glimmer of light on the genealogy of a family representing the scholarly elite of Kraków at the end of the seventeenth century, whose
details Agnon had learned from the city chronicles.[26] Seemingly, he became

---

24. *A City in Its Fullness*, 302.
25. On Me'elish and his kabbalistic leanings, see Arieh Bauminger "Toledot hayehudim
beKraka bishenot 1304–1815" in *Sefer Kraków*, ed. Arieh Bauminger, Meir Bussak, and Nathan
Michael Gelber (Jerusalem: Mosad Harav Kook, 1959), 24–25.
26. See Dembitzer, *Kelilat yofi* 20b: "And the Gaon, our illustrious teacher Berakhya Birekh Shapira, author of *Zera' Birekh*, son-in-law of our great teacher Shalom Me'elish [...] (the father of Zvi
Hirsch, who married Rivka, the daughter of Yom Tov Heller, author of *Tosefot Yom Tov*). [Shalom
Me'elish] was involved in financing the printing of books at Menachem Maisels [...]. This Shalom
Me'elish also showed kindness to the gaon who wrote the *Tosefot Yom Tov*, of blessed memory,
on his arrival to Kraków at the beginning of 1644, by generously giving money to reprint here
in Kraków, at the printing house of R. Nahum son of R. Moshe Maisels, the Mishnah treatises

aware of these kinship connections through the imprimatur of R. Yom-Tov Lipmann Heller to R. Birekh's Torah commentary *Zera' Birekh*.[27]

The protagonist of Agnon's story, then, the rabbi who fled, is R. Shalom
Me'elish, who was the father-in-law of R. Berakhiah Birekh Shapira, author of
Zera' Birekh. Agnon thus planted the story close to Kraków and presented R.
Me'elish, Kraków's important benefactor, as a victim of slanderous denuncia-
tions to the Gentile authorities. An interesting dimension is that becoming a victim of such allegations is a recurring motif in the history of several important
rabbis in central and Eastern Europe, among them two prominent figures in the
Council of Four Lands, R. Jacob Pollack and R. Yom-Tov Heller. This historical feature would later become a significant element in the popular and written
hagiography of several "leading rabbis" in the history of Eastern Europe Jewry,
and it is this historical motif of the persecution of rabbis that attracted Agnon.[28]

Alan Mintz viewed the fact that R. Abraham Abush was the main narrator
and that the story moved from the present to a remote past as the poetic foundation of the story as a whole. He, therefore, outlined a hermeneutical scheme of
"epic designs"[29] for the story "In Search of a Rabbi," which leads to a poetic conclusion: Agnon tried to set up two models of rabbinic authority, one scholarly (the
remote past at the time of the rabbi who escaped) and the other integrated into
the daily life and the spirit of Polish rule. I wish to propose here a reconstructed
historical chronology of the actual reality that Agnon had hinted at, attempting
to present it as a paradigm of autonomous Jewish life as it came alive at the time
of the Council of Four Lands, for whose cessation he blamed the Jewish community itself and whose utopian foundation he continued to long for even as he came
to reconstruct the life of his city, which had drawn away from it. The historical

---

with the *Tosefot Yom Tov* commentary." This chronicle points to the family ties, the scholarship,
the communal administration, and the close ties between these personalities in mid-seventeenth-
century Kraków. On the election of R. Yom-Tov Lipmann Heller as the rabbi of Kraków in 1643,
see Balaban, *Toledot hayehudim beKrakÓw*, 1:270. See also Yom-Tov Lipmann Heller's life story,
particularly according to his autobiography, *Megillat Evah* (Wrocław, 1837). The choice to mention the name of R. Berekhyah Birekh son of R. Yitzhak Izick Shapira conveys an interesting side
in Agnon's tendency to ascribe positive meaning to practical Sabbatean Kabbalah. R. Berekhyah
Birekh, author of *Zera' Birekh*, died in Constantinople in 1666 hoping to meet Sabbetai Zevi there.
See Balaban, *Letoledot hatenu'ah haFrankit*, 27.

27. Kraków: Menachem Naḥum Maisels, 1646.

28. The claim that R. Shalom Me'elish was persecuted adds a kind of etiological hallmark, an
identity tag that, enhances the prestige of the entire dynasty of sages in the Council of Four
Lands, branding the more distinguished ones among them as an elite. This "dynasty" opens
with the story about the escape of R. Jacob Pollack, who became entangled in a legal conflict
that forced him to flee Kraków in May 1522. See Elhanan Reiner, "R. Yaakov Pollack: Rishon
verosh lehakhmei Kraków," in *Kraka-Kazimirz-Kraków: Meḥqarim betoledot yehudei Kraków*
(Tel Aviv: Tel Aviv University, 2001), 57–60.

29. Mintz, "Epic Designs," in *Ancestral Tales*, 164–7.

model at the root of the story can only be reconstructed after identifying its vanished protagonist as a historical figure—that of Shalom Me'elish. The construct of Agnon's narrative fiction in *'Ir umelo'ah* overlaps the chronological course of historical events in seventeenth-century Kraków, and both are fully coextensive:

1641	Death of Maharam Schiff
1646	First printing of *Zera' Birekh*
1654	Death of Yom-Tov Lipmann Heller, author of *Tosefot Yom*-Tov
166?	Beginning of R. Mordechai's studies with Shalom Me'elish.
1666	Death of R. Berakhiah Birekh Shapira, son-in-law of Shalom Me'elish (the rabbi who fled)
1720	Birth of R. Moshe Abush Margaliot, "the rabbi of Zabno."
1761	The revelation of Maharam Schiff to the rabbi of Zabno
1764	Decree of Stanislav August eliminating the Council of Four Lands
1770–1800?	The delegation from Buczacz to the rabbi of Zabno
1802	Death of the rabbi of Zabno
1821	Printing first edition of *Tsiluta de'Avraham* by Moshe Abush Margaliot, the rabbi of Zabno

Agnon thus took the persecution motifs in this story from the memoirs of R. Yom-Tov Lipmann Heller as he himself had recorded them in 1643, the year he was appointed to the Kraków court. His account, *Megillat Evah*, appeared many years after his death and became his authorized biography.

By titling his last collection of stories *'Ir umelo'ah*, Agnon evoked two antithetical traditions of contextual meaning for phrases that appear to be strongly similar: *Krakha dekula bei*, and "a city and all that is in it." The former evokes the meaning of *'Ir hatsedeq*, like the title of Zunz's chronicle, epitomizing in the Aramaic expression *Krakha dekula bei* the denotation of Jewish autonomy and sovereignty. The latter, as the phrase "the city and all that is in it" in the verse of the prophecy from Amos 43:8 ("I abhor the pride of Jacob, and hate his strongholds, and I will deliver up the city and all that is in it") epitomizes the simpler meaning—the city is punished with the loss of its sovereignty.[30] The young

---

30. The title of his book does indeed hint at the devastation that will befall the "city and its fullness"—*'Ir umelo'ah*. The King James translation preserves this exact meaning: "The Lord hath sworn by himself, saith the Lord of hosts, I abhor the excellency of Jacob, and hate his palaces: therefore will I deliver up *the city with all that is therein*," rather than *A City in Its Fullness*, as rendered by Mintz and Saks, which could also suggest a positive fullness, in the spirit of Emuna Yaron's dedication.

Agnon may already have noted in his youth the title of Zunz's chronicle, *'Ir hatsedeq*, which is Kraków, *Krakha dekula bei*, and derived from it the deep substantial contrast with Buczacz—the city and all that is in it, which the prophet's rage predicts will be destroyed.

Beyond these linguistic and historical distinctions, the careful reader of these Kraków chronicles will also find that they served Agnon as a reservoir for plots in several stories of *'Ir umelo'ah*. These stories' fictional body and ideological spirit come from that same "other place" as the time of the Council of Four Lands, from that same city where everything is a "present/disappearing space" in which Agnon plants most of the stories in the collection. Kraków is the antipodal gravity center to Buczacz the *'Ir umelo'ah*. Through a set of historical allusions to the persecution of rabbis at the time of the Council of Four Lands (particularly at the time of R. Yom-Tov Heller) and to events in the Kraków seventeenth-century rabbinic literature (by R. Moshe Isserless, author of *Torat ha'olah*, and R. Berakhiah Birekh Shapira, author of *Zera' Birekh*), Agnon presents a thesis about an era he views as the "Golden Age" of Kraków, a "heavenly city." This era negates and denies the decline of rabbinic institutions in "the real place"—Buczacz, and Agnon may thereby indirectly explain the end of his beloved city as well.

This poetic strategy of casting on a narrated urban realm the shadow of a distant metropolis located in the background of the story was already evident in Agnon's previous writings from the 1930s. It can be identified, for example, in the background of *Sippur pashut* as a kind of social criticism focusing on the bourgeois provinciality of Buczacz living in the shadow of the metropolis of Vienna, where Akavia Mazal came from. This strategy was also implemented when casting the shadow of Lviv/Lemberg, the dominant center, on Brody and Rohatyn in the novel *Hakhnasat kallah*. "The other place" construct as a bi-spatial composition is obviously highly prominent in Agnon's long novels—*Temol shilshom* (Jaffa and Jerusalem) or *Shira* (Jerusalem and the kibbutz).

The Heavenly City of Leipzig

I will attempt to apply the specific claim about "the other heavenly city" beyond *'Ir umelo'ah*, to other areas of Agnon's *oeuvre*. The other city—the heavenly city—is a paradigmatic emblem. Agnon's central works from the 1930s onward reflect this writing metaphysics of the poetic space, meaning that every place has its 'other place,' its antipode location. The classic instance in this regard is the novella *Beḥanuto shel mar Lublin*, which Agnon began to write in the 1960s and wanted to conclude parallel to his efforts to finish editing *'Ir umelo'ah*.[31] At the center of this novella is his sojourn in Leipzig during the First World War, a

31. S.Y. Agnon, *Beḥanuto shel mar Lublin* (Jerusalem: Schocken, 2001). Citations are from the English translation by Glenda Abramson, *In Mr. Lublin's Store* (New Milford, CT: Toby Press, 2016).

period that became for him, as it were, an experimental literary laboratory for understanding both the ancient and the new German spirit.

The city of Leipzig features twice in Agnon's biography—once when he stayed there during the First World War, and once when he visited briefly in 1930, at the time the first complete set of four volumes of his writings was published by the local Drugulin Press. In the novella *Beḥanuto shel mar Lublin*, Agnon records the atmosphere in Leipzig in the first months of the war, when disturbances and violent demonstrations erupted after the economic hardships that followed the conscription of its young men and the food rationing measures. Civilian life was almost paralyzed and its population extremely weakened both due to the age of the inhabitants and the limited economic means at their disposal.[32] It is thus no wonder that Agnon painted Leipzig as a "nocturnal city" sunk in constant darkness whose shopkeepers, living in shops located in alleyways and inner courtyards dwell in it as if in crypts: "The shops are like crypts and the shopkeepers like bones from which the flesh has been consumed."[33]

The macabre estrangement of the dying city is spelled out in the life stories of four old shopkeepers, and particularly in that of the oldest among them, Joachim Hermann Wiezelrode, who sold odds and ends at his Böttcher Street store. This shopkeeper's fiancée was kidnapped from him in his youth and he never rebuilt his personal life. Now, during the war, he emerges as a lecherous old man courting his widowed neighbor, and, for the festive meal he is planning with her, he is raising a goose in his backyard. This goose is a metonymy for his hidden sexual passion, and itself becomes an erotic object for Wiezelrode and for his friend Götz Weigel, owner of a knife shop:

> Through love of his geese he would give them affectionate names like the ones he called the wife his mother has found for him [...]. Not only due to neighborliness but because of the geese themselves and their impertinence that amused him. He would tickle them on their necks and say "killi, killi, killi," the way he used to treat his granddaughters when they were little.[34]

In this story about the two old shopkeepers, Agnon embedded a fragment from a narrative testimony: "Rab Judah said in the name of Samuel on behalf of

---

32. Agnon reached the city seven months after the food riots that left-wing parties organized against the shortages during the week of May 14–20, 1916. Shops, already quite empty, were vandalized and destroyed. These events continued until mid-1918. There are many mentions of these shortages in the book, without any reference to the political demonstrations that accompanied them. For the historical background, see Sean Dobson, *Authority and Upheaval in Leipzig 1910–1920: The Story of a Relationship* (New York: Columbia University Press, 2001), 145–46; 150–56; 172–73.

33. *Beḥanuto shel mar Lublin*, 48.

34. Ibid., 61; 62.

R. Hanina, 'I saw a heathen who bought a goose in the market, raped it, strangled it, roasted it, and ate it.'"[35]

This testimony is cited from the Gemara as purported evidence for the fact that nothing should be bought from Gentiles, whose touch defiles everything, even the domestic fowl ritually permitted as food. This fragment is the basis for the third chapter of the novella, the first of the four shopkeepers' life stories. From the start, this is a narrative expansion of a fundamentally hostile attitude that rejects the urban life of Leipzig, the "Gentile city" that absolutely revolts him. And yet, this repugnant urban space too has a "high" version that fits into Agnon's writing metaphysic, whose construct is the space confronting "the heavenly city": just as confronting the Jewish city of Buczacz is the "heavenly city" of Kraków, the location of sages in the Council of Four Lands, so nocturnal Leipzig is confronted with its own heavenly city—Aachen, the capital of the Carolingian empire. In the second part of *Beḥanuto shel mar Lublin*, Agnon introduces a dream story about a voyage on an apocalyptic horse to the city of Aachen. In this dream, the narrator retreats to Germany's archaic sixth-century past, when Charlemagne founded the "heavenly city" as the capital of the first German Carolingian Empire. In the dream, the narrator is forced by four cavalrymen to go the emperor to help him write a thank you letter to Haroun al-Rashid for a present he had received from him—a huge elephant. *Beḥanuto shel mar Lublin* is thus built in an open and transparent symmetric pattern of two halves—the first is the story of Leipzig and the second is the story of the narrator's dream, galloping on apocalyptic horses to Aachen's historical past. The German model also relies on chronicles, of which the most important is *Vita Karoli Magni* in Einhard's Latin version. The chronicle was translated into German, adapted into a popular version, and published in several editions from 1883 onward.[36] Agnon would have had access to these editions already in his first wartime stay in

---

35. BT Avodah Zarah 22b.
36. From the end of the nineteenth century, this Latin work appeared in several German versions and Agnon could easily have read it during his stay in Germany. One translated and illustrated edition is *Das Leben Karls des Grossen, von Einhard* (übersetzt und erläutert von Hermann Althof) (Halle a. S: O. Hendel, 1893). This version served as the basis for popular adaptations of Einhard's monograph and other similar sources. See *Einhard: Das Leben Karl des Grosen*, hersg. Herman Münzel (Köln am Rhein: Hermann & Schaffstein, 1921). On the ties of Charlemagne and Haroun al-Rashid, see in this edition, 66–68. This historical document reached the height of its popularity in a series of books published in Leipzig in thousands of copies in the course of the year that Agnon returned to the Land of Israel: *Einhard: Das Leben Karls des Grossen*, Übertragen von Johannes Bühler (Leipzig: Insel Verlag, 1924).

Leipzig when he assisted in the classification and recording of books at the Otto Harrassowitz Buchhandlung.[37]

This chronicle tells how courtiers would call one another by biblical names, thereby framing the story of the new German government as a kind of imagined Christian reconstruction of King David's court. Within this symbolic act of biblical rule, which was imitated in Charlemagne's court, Agnon set a macabre fiction of his own about the desecration of a Jew's body and the use of his bones as a Christian relic. This fiction was meant to mark German evil as emerging in the imperial court of the heavenly German city. In order to link this archaic city with the concrete city of Leipzig, however, Agnon set a parallel story to that of Wiezelrode's goose. This is an imagined historical hoax about the torture of a goose whose feathers are pulled out to serve as quills when writing the letter that the narrator was called up to write in the dream.[38]

In these two parallel stories, Agnon marked the two spaces of the German rulers' cruelty—the one hiding behind a mask of Christian biblical enlightenment and the one that, in his view, reincarnated into a modern version in the city of Leipzig during the First World War.

Agnon's cartography, then, is not a synchronic cross-section in a given historical situation such as, for example, that of Charles Dickens in *A Tale of Two Cities*,[39] or like the model he chose in *Temol Shilshom* (Jerusalem and Jaffa), which is also historically synchronic. The two great works, *'Ir umelo'ah* and *Behanuto shel mar Lublin*, which Agnon labored to finish at the end of his life and never saw complete in print, set an imagined and scholastic typological cartography, where the big cities it maps represent meta-historical entities. Through the paradigm of the contrast between two cities, Agnon surveys for the last time the realized and missed possibilities of his personal biography.

Although Agnon does not follow in Dickens' footsteps, we may be able to hear him whispering at the end of his life the opening sentence of *A Tale of Two Cities*: "It was the best of times, it was the worst of times, it was the age of wisdom, it was the age of foolishness, it was the epoch of belief, it was the epoch of incredulity . . ."

---

37. On the catalogue that Agnon took part in editing, see Lipsker, *Mahshavot 'al Agnon* 2: 176–77.
38. *In Mr. Lublin's Store*, 197–98.
39. Charles Dickens, *A Tale of Two Cities* (London: Chapman and Hall, 1859). Dickens' Paris and London are synchronic historical cities. The life stories of their protagonists intersect while the cities are woven into one continuous plot.

Professor (Emeritus) AVIDOV LIPSKER is a scholar of Modern Hebrew literature. For eighteen years he was Editor-in-Chief of the journal *Biqqoret ufarshanut* (Bar-Ilan University Press). Lipsker is currently Editor-in-Chief for Bar-Ilan University Press of Thema: *Studies in Jewish Narrative*; The *Encyclopedia of the Jewish Story*; and *Uri Zvi Grinberg: Meḥqarim: uteʿudot*; and *Ofkei meḥqar*. He is the author of *Maḥshavot ʿal Agnon* Vol. I–II (Bar-Ilan Press, 2015-2018) and *Eqologiyah shel sifrut* Vol. I–II (Bar-Ilan University Press and Carmel Publish House: 2019–2021).

8 Salvage Poetics: Agnon's "Imaginary Real" in A Guest for the Night[1]

May 2013

Sheila E. Jelen

I. The World as Text

IN S.Y. AGNON's *Oreaḥ natah lalun (A Guest for the Night)* (1939), texts and textuality stand at the interstices between the real and the imagined, between the ethnographic and the literary.[2] The decline of Torah study becomes a metonymy

---

1. This essay originally appeared, in slightly altered form, under the title "Salvage Poetics: S.Y. Agnon's *A Guest for the Night*" in *The Journal of Jewish Identities* 7:1 (January 2014), 187-199.
2. Since the late 1970s ethnographers in particular, and the field of anthropology in general, have been highly cognizant of the literariness of its documentation of cultures. In their now classic anthology, *Writing Culture: The Poetics and Politics of Ethnography*, James Clifford and George E. Marcus collected essays presented in response to a conference in Santa Fe, New Mexico in April 1984. The conference was focused on "the making of ethnographic texts" and each of the essays looked "critically at one of the principal things ethnographers do—that is, write." In other words, the conference, and the writings which grew out of it, were focused on how culture is inscribed in language, even by those scientists whose aims were historically to document cultures through "participant observation," through intensive experiential and linguistic immersion in a foreign culture which resulted in a "report" on that culture—an analysis of the culture from within. Out of those in-situ experiences, those engagements between a scientist and an object of study, in its own element, and on its own terms (to the extent possible), grew texts that could no longer be understood as simply transparent. Rather every field study that was authored, every document that was written as the result of a course of ethnographic observation and study, needed to be considered first and foremost as a text.

Around the same time that anthropologists sought to understand the role of literary analysis in understanding the texts generated by their ethnographic practitioners, literary scholars were looking for anthropological tools to use in order to extrapolate culture from literature. In the late 1980s, "New Historicism," for example, drew from ethnographic terminology in order to lend credence to literary criticism's own quest to wed the practice of close readings to historical and cultural breadth. Thus, literary texts, with the help of ethnographic discourse, were deemed "artifacts" or "thick descriptions" of particular cultures. In my own formulation of "salvage poetics," particularly within the context of post-Holocaust reception of pre-holocaust arts, I draw upon this natural commingling of the disciplines of anthropology and literary analysis in order to better describe and approximate the blurring of the boundaries between aesthetic production as an ethnographically valuable enterprise and as an artistic one. *Writing Culture: The Poetics and Politics of Ethnography* Ed. James Clifford and George E. Marcus (Berkeley: University of California, 1986). Stephen Greenblatt and Catherine Gallagher, *Practicing New Historicism* (Chicago, 2000).

Building a City: Writings on Agnon's Buczacz in Memory of Alan Mintz (2022): 087–101
DOI: 10.2979/BuildingaCityWriting.0.0.09

for the very real cultural attrition experienced by the Jewish community of Galicia between the two World Wars. The argument I propose here for an intertextual "salvage poetic" takes as its starting point the idea that modern Jewish texts frequently engage in a presentation of nineteenth century East European Jewry as a world not simply devoted to texts, but constituted of texts. Traditional Jewish texts within modern literary works thus represent traditional Jewish society metonymically and are read by popular audiences as an ethnographic précis of a culture.

The classic example of a text that turns Jewish culture into a book, thus facilitating the representation of the culture as a text itself, can be found in Abraham Joshua Heschel's *The Earth is the Lord's*.[3] Heschel's essay, first delivered as an oral address in 1945 at the YIVO institute's annual conference, not only focuses on the scholarly world of traditional Judaism as if it were pervasive of all strata of the society, it also deploys a conceit of textuality, which presents the culture itself as a text. Heschel, for example, calls shtetlakh "sacred texts opened before the eyes of God, so close were their houses of worship to Mount Sinai."[4] He observes: "Yet the Jews did not feel themselves to be the People of the Book. They did not feel that they possessed the Book, just as one does not feel that one possesses life. The book, the Torah, was their essence, just as they, the Jews, were the essence of the Torah."[5]

This is partly in keeping with the notion of "ethnopoetry," as introduced in 1908 by author and ethnographer S. Ansky (Semyon Akimovitch or Solomon Rappaport). In his ethnographic expedition from 1912–1914, inspired by the contemporary Russian ethnographic movement, one of Ansky's stated goals was to collect Jewish folk art and folk artifacts in order to "salvage" them for posterity.[6] To this end, Ansky recruited artists and writers to serve as the staff for his expedition so they would not merely "salvage" artifacts of Jewish life in the Pale of Settlement, but would reinscribe these artifacts (melodies, idioms, stories, etc)

3. On the publication and reception history of this essay see Jeffrey Shandler, "Heschel and Yiddish: A Struggle with Signification" in *Journal of Jewish Thought and Philosophy* 2:2 (1993) 245–299.
4. Abraham Joshua Heschel, *The Earth is the Lord's: The Inner World of the Jew in Eastern Europe* (Woodstock: Jewish Lights, 2001), 92.
5. Ibid, 42.
6. For essays on Ansky's ethnographic expedition and its social and historical context, both within the Russian empire and within Jewish and Russian literary traditions, see selected essays from *Photographing the Jewish Nation: Pictures from S. Ansky's Ethnographic Expeditions*, Eds. Eugene M. Avrutin, Valerii Dymshits, Alexander Ivanov, Alexander Lvov, Harriet Murav, Alla Sokolova (Hanover: University Press of New England 2009). Also see, *The Worlds of S. Ansky: A Russian Jewish Intellectual at the Turn of the Century*, Eds. Gabriella Safran, Steven J. Zipperstein, Craig Stephen Cravens (Stanford: Stanford University Press, 2006).

in a uniquely modern Jewish art, or "ethnopoetry."[7] This understanding of "salvage" forged of an ethnographic consciousness but not governed by its scientific methodologies, distinguishes "salvage poetics" in a literary sense, from salvage ethnography as an anthropological science. Thus, works of salvage poetics, for purposes of the present discussion, are imaginative works that strive to balance an impulse to document with an impulse to create. They document a world in a variety of different self-conscious ways that foreground their own artistry, while inviting popular ethnographic reception.

Like Heschel in the aftermath of the Holocaust, Agnon views post-cataclysmic Jewry in light of Jewish texts. Though published on the eve of World War Two, indeed within days of the start of the war, Agnon's novel is an explicit response to the First World War.[8] What is of interest here is the way in which Agnon, focused on the depiction of the Eastern European Jewish world in the aftermath of a major war, deploys a textual thematic and an intertextual poetic designed to "salvage" the losses sustained. The particular form of "salvage" evident here posits the text as the culture itself, and therefore is not to be understood as a practical attempt to document or preserve particular texts. Rather, the sacred text is used as a conceit for a culture and as a model for future modes of representation that exist on the border of the ethnographic and the imaginative.

Here we will focus specifically on an *intertextual* salvage poetic—a poetic found in Hebrew literature just before mid-century, and which posits intertextuality as a means of institutional and cultural salvage. Our case study will be S.Y. Agnon's *Oreaḥ natah lalun* (*A Guest for the Night*) because of its explicit documentation of pre-WWI Jewish Galicia as a culture not enamored of texts, but actually constituted, sustained, and defined by them, in contrast to the physically depleted and culturally wayward Jewish Galicia the narrator visits for a year during the interwar period. For Agnon in *A Guest for the Night*, the intertextual salvage poetic is played out in a presentation of two textual institutions: one physical and one rhetorical. The physical institution is the old *beit hamidrash*, or House of Study, and the rhetorical one is the *devar torah*, or the sermon. Before we discuss the nuanced function of each of these institutions within *A Guest for the Night*, it is necessary to consider Agnon's striking treatment of the relationship between "the imaginary" and "the real" as a figure for the aspects of a salvage poetic unique to literary representations of Eastern European Jewish life in the first half of the twentieth century.

7. See S. An-sky, "Der kharakter un di eygnshaftn fun der yiddisher folks-poetisher shafung," in *Folklor un etnografye: Gezamelte shriftn* (Warsaw, 1925), 15:33–95. For a discussion of this programmatic essay, see David Roskies, *The Dybbuk and Other Writings* (New York, 1992), xxii.
8. Dan Laor, *Ḥayyei Agnon*, (Tel Aviv: Shocken, 1998), 322–323

II. The Imaginary Real

Throughout *A Guest for the Night* Agnon meditates on what he calls the "imaginary real," an apt expression of the principles underlying the salvage poetics he deploys throughout the novel:

> Since the people of my town cannot imagine that a man should describe things as they really are, they believe I am a shrewd fellow who talks much and evades the main point. At first I tried to tell them the truth, but when I found that the true truth deceived them, I left them with the imaginary real.[9]

This notion of the "imaginary real" is further developed in a conversation with Hanoch, a laborer who plays an important role in the protagonist's rejuvenation of the *beit hamidrash*, and whose death, later, will make him an important symbolic figure for the protagonist:

> This Hanoch has a weak mind, and he does not grasp anything that is higher than his cap. Nevertheless I talk to him about matters of the utmost significance and explain them to him. If he does not understand, I elucidate with a parable. But even so, he does not understand my meaning in the least, because a man needs a little imagination for that. 'Do you know what imagination is Hanoch?' I ask him. "I don't know,' says he. 'If so,' I say to Hanoch, 'sit down and I will explain it to you. Imagination is something through which everyone in this world lives: you and I and your horse and your cart. How can that be? Well, you go out to the village because you imagine that your income is assured there. The same applies to your horse and the same to your cart, for without the power of imagination the world would not go on living. Happy is the man who uses his imagination to feed his household, and woe to the man who uses it for vanities, like those who present dramas and farces.[10]

At first, we are presented with a description of "imagination" as an alternative to the "real." Indeed, Agnon was writing at the twilight of the Hebrew Revival, which valorized the capacity of the Hebrew language to represent things "as they are" ("*devarim kehavyatam*").[11] Hebrew literature had, until the Revival, been limited primarily to epic representations of the ancient world, rendered in a language comprised of biblical pastiche. During the period of the Revival, writers began to try to write about "real" things, or contemporary matters, in an unencumbered language, or a language that tried to break the fetters of allusion and liturgical diction. The idea of realism, or in some cases, even naturalism, of

---

9. S.Y. Agnon, *Oreaḥ*, 23.
10. S.Y. Agnon, *Oreaḥ*, 109. Translation in S.Y. Agnon, *A Guest for the Night*, trans. Misha Louvish (NY: Schocken, 1968), 111.
11. See Sheila Jelen, "Things as they Are: The Mimetic Imperative," *Intimations of Difference: Dvora Baron in the Modern Hebrew Renaissance* (Syracuse: Syracuse University Press, 2007) 52–102.

representing speech in its natural rhythms and society in its contemporary habitat, pervaded Hebrew letters of the Revival. Here, Agnon complicates this idea of representing "things as they are" or the "real," in combination with the imaginary.

In the first statement, Agnon's narrator introduces the idea of an "imaginary real" in order to accommodate the limitations of his neighbors' sense of propriety. Agnon's narrator cannot really tell the truth in terms that they can accept. Perhaps he has the advantage of being simultaneously both an insider and an outsider, and therefore is able to observe things and express things that someone with only one vantage point cannot. Or perhaps it is because of the copious suffering that took place during the war and in its aftermath, the senses of the town's inhabitants were dulled and their horizons limited. In any case, Agnon's protagonist-narrator must adapt the "real" to make it palatable to his peers, and he calls it an "imaginary real."

In the second statement, as Agnon attempts to define imagination for Hanoch before his untimely disappearance and death, he links imagination inextricably with the bare necessities of life. We can only survive, he argues, because we imagine the necessity to do so. Thus the real and the imaginary are linked in an assertion of the essential role of the imaginary in effecting a successful mastery of the "real." This dance of "real" and "imaginary" in Agnon's rhetoric certainly articulates an important qualification of the valorization of representing "things as they are," but also asserts a basic principle of salvage poetics: a fundamental commitment to documentary (the real) within an aesthetic frame (the imaginary) which places the documentary and the aesthetic in tension with one another.

In a continuation of his presentation of the "imaginary real" to Hanokh, Agnon's narrator asserts that there are "higher" powers of imagination (*dimyon ha'elyon*) and "simpler" powers of imagination (*dimyon pashut*). The higher powers are to be used for the work of living, as described above, but the simpler powers are to be used for the act of going to the theater:

> Happy is the man[12] who uses his imagination to feed his household and woe to the man who uses it for vanities, like those who present dramas and farces. Once I went into a theater where they were showing a kind of drama. I said to my neighbors: 'I know the end of this drama from its very beginning.' And

---

12. An allusion to Psalms 1:1. This intertextual allusion can be viewed as ironic as the passage continues on to a discussion of theater and the tension between reality and fantasy, between being an upstanding citizen and a rabble rouser. In the Psalm, "moshav letsim," "the seat of flippant people" can be understood in light of those who attend theater for entertainment instead of pursuing more scholarly or serious pursuits. Yet, the narrator says that the respectable householders are the ones who go to theater. This, you would not expect. It is, perhaps an indication of the fact that respectable householders are impoverished and need an escape into fantasy. This shift from Psalms to the unexpected validation of "petty" affairs is an important moment of irony.

what I said was fully confirmed, because all I had to do was mirror one thing with another. And this I did through the power of the simple imagination, but if I had used the higher imagination I should have been proved wrong for most plays are made with the simple imagination because the authors have not been privileged to possess the higher imagination. I see, Hanoch, that you do not know what theaters are, so I will tell you. A theater is a house to which respectable householders go. And why do they go there when they have houses of their own? Because sometimes a man tires of his own house and goes to another house. That other house, the theater, is like this: People perform there who have never seen a house in their lives, but they pretend they know everything that there is in a house; so they show the householder all that there is in their own houses, and the householders are delighted and clap their hands and say: Fine, fine. Surely they should know that it is not fine, because it is not true. But there are two groups, and each believes that what is shown in the theater is true of the other. Yet there is one man who does not believe this for that man is at home in both houses and knows what is to be found in each of them.[13]

Agnon's presentation of the theater as a foil to the domestic space, and his articulation of different levels of imagination that are deployed in each, further complicates the clear separation between the "imaginary" and the "real" which Agnon presented earlier. Here, the theater, a simulation of the real, whose purpose is to convince its audience to suspend its disbelief, is presented as a product of what he calls a more "simplistic" imaginative faculty. At the same time, the common home is presented as a product of the higher imaginative faculties, because its purpose according to the statement above, to take people out of their homes to entertain them with and to show them their own lives. The impulse to see one's life dramatized and to applaud it when one could just as well have stayed home and experienced one's own life on one's own terms, is a narcissistic foible of human nature which need not be humored, according to this statement by Agnon's narrator. The very desire for realism, for the aesthetic depiction of "things as they are," is under attack here, for what constitutes realism if not the desire to see an aesthetic adaptation of the familiar?

The scenario of a departure from home for a glimpse of one's own life in the theater strongly resembles the premise upon which *A Guest for the Night* is based. The narrator has left his home in Palestine after the destruction of his Jerusalem home in the Arab riots of 1929 in order to recollect himself, in Szibusz, his hometown. Is Szibusz being likened here to a theater? Is the narrator criticizing his own desire to view what he would imagine to be his truest self in the city of his childhood and young adulthood because, in fact, it is as if he is expecting some kind of performance that is based on the "simplistic" imaginative faculty? The Szibusz the narrator seeks out is, indeed, not the "real" Szibusz, because the Szibusz he seeks out no longer exists. The inhabit-

---

13. S.Y. Agnon, *Oreaḥ*, 109–110. S.Y. Agnon, *Guest*, 111–112.

ants of Szibusz whom he encounters during his sojourn there are performing in a play of his life that he is directing. But what he really should be doing, the narrator asserts of himself throughout the novel, is go back to his real home, his new home, the home in Palestine that he fled in order to revisit his childhood home. According to the narrator, his imaginary Szibusz conflicts with the real Szibusz in the same way that the institution of the theater reflects a problematic reflection of the real life of human beings.

This link between the imaginary and the real, between the necessities of life and the inner workings of the human spirit, as expressed through this meditation on the imagination, provides a rare glimpse into the salvage poetic underlying not only Agnon's novel *A Guest for the Night*, but his literary corpus as a whole. His attempt to represent a real world, but within the contours of his individual imagination, is more than a creed of fiction writing. It is a creed of a particular moment in the history of Hebrew literature during the Hebrew Revival. In the maelstrom of an era of tremendous social destruction and cultural change, people began to write in a modern style. For the first time Hebrew writers were writing about the world in which they lived in a usable and malleable language. Indeed they were creating that idiom as they wrote in it. That world, however, was changing dramatically through modernization, world wars, and migration. The impulse to claim the privilege of a creative language, of the individual imagination, in a world which had long limited the expression of individual creativity in the Hebrew language, in deference to rabbinic authority and notions of collective responsibility, ran up against the impulse, once again, to do a service for the collective—to represent a world teetering on the brink of oblivion. What was that world? It was a world of Torah study, of prayer, of religious communal authority.

For Agnon, it seems, the creative imagination, the faculties that are to be utilized in the development of an "imaginary" world, are secondary to the creative faculties that are to be used in an encounter with the "real." The old *beit hamidrash*, which serves as the psychic locus of the novel becomes the center of an "imaginary real" to Agnon. It is the place to which the protagonist retreats when he finds that he is essentially alone there, the place whose key is entrusted to him by people who no longer have any use for traditional Torah scholarship, the place where the protagonist becomes a kind of spiritual leader and provides physical succor to all those who have no warm place to go, and no safe place to rest. It is, as it were, a theater for the homeless protagonist to play at being home once again. But, to no avail. Like the theater, as an expression of the "simple" imagination, the *beit hamidrash* provides a digression from home, but nothing more.

III. The *Beit hamidrash*: A Home for the Text

In *A Guest for the Night*, the *beit hamidrash* is no longer a significant part of Szibusz for most of its inhabitants. Since the First World War, the interest in Torah study, the culture of prayer and scholarship has diminished and nearly disappeared. But what the protagonist manages, very nicely, to do is to re-inhabit the place, which defined the life of the town for him as a child, to reanimate it for himself, and to use it as a base for his engagement with the rest of the town. From the *beit hamidrash* in Szibusz he is able, as well, to forge a relationship with Hanoch, the emblem of loss as the story unfolds. He is able to establish a relationship with Reb Hayyim, an exemplum of humility and former splendor—an unrivaled Torah scholar and community agitator in the years before the war who is taken prisoner while doing his army service during the war years and who returns to the town a broken man. In fact, Reb Hayyim claims to no longer have any knowledge of the scholarship that made his reputation during his early years. When Hanoch, the wood gatherer for the *beit hamidrash* vanishes with his horse, Reb Hayim takes over the job of collecting wood. Each man, in his turn—the simple-minded, kindly Hanoch, and the brilliant traumatized Reb Hayim—acts as the wood gatherer and the sexton for the *beit hamidrash*, assisting the narrator in his rehabilitation of that institution, symbolically rebuilding the *beit hamidrash* with their wood and actually repopulating it by heating it and attracting impoverished townspeople to it during the wintertime.

Newly repopulated, a prayer quorum is formed in the *beit hamidrash*, and people again begin, alongside the narrator, studying the sacred texts therein contained. Reb Hayyim helps Hanoch's widow feed her children, and even teaches the children to pray, both the kaddish in their father's memory, and other prayers that Hanoch, simple as he was, was unable to teach them during his lifetime. At the end of the novel, Reb Hayyim passes away as well.

Therefore the two major figures circling the narrator/protagonist in *A Guest for the Night*, Hanoch and Reb Hayyim, who enable the protagonist to imagine the continuing viability of the *beit hamidrash,* are removed from the story as it progresses. Both Hanoch and Reb Hayyim represent the "higher" imaginative faculties, as defined earlier by the narrator. They are engaged in the struggle for survival, with even Reb Hayyim, a former luminary, sleeping in a shack and using the narrator's coat as a blanket on his deathbed. For Agnon's narrator, however, Hanoch and Reb Hayyim serve as proof of the reality of his memory of childhood and the truth of his memory of the town. Both help him to bring the *beit hamidrash* back to life, at least for the winter. But with their deaths, and with the narrator's departure from the town, it becomes apparent that the narrator's sense of the real was only imagined, that his *Szibusz* is not the *Szibusz* of the present and cannot be brought back to life, even in the imagination of its native son.

The very name "Szibusz" (a clever play on Agnon's native Buczacz), in Hebrew means a textual elision or bastardization that has been preserved and transmitted, thus becoming canonic. The narrator's memory of Szibusz is, in itself, a bastardization of the real thing, but it is all that will remain, it seems, when committed to posterity by the narrator-turned-author, in a crucial moment of homodiegetic revelation:

> Against my will I have mentioned that I am an author [sofer]. Indeed, the nomenclature of authorship [in Hebrew] comes from the notion of a "scribe" [sofer] of the words of Torah [*divrei torah*]. Yet, since they call all authors now, "sofrim" I do not hesitate to call myself an author.[14]

Here, the sacred *sofer* evolves into the modern *sofer,* just as the narrator becomes an author. In so doing, he memorializes Szibusz by textual means, through writing about it, but also through writing it in its own traditional idiom, through the words of the Torah, or in the form of a *devar torah*. His exchange of one kind of authorship for another in his confession as an author, can be understood as an engagement with the notion of modern authorship as a variation on a different kind of authorial tradition in Judaism—the composition and delivery of sermons, or *divrei torah*. His *divrei torah* therefore, throughout the novel, are a confession of authorship which demands that we consider authorship as an oral institution even in modern times, and not strictly in textual terms. Here the narrator synthesizes two senses of authorship into one—drawing upon the traditional Jewish author as *sofer* of *divrei torah* and the modern *sofer* as a literary author—thus not simply preserving, but improving upon the traditional institution of *divrei torah* through the transcription of an oral performance.

As in S. Ansky's statement about his quest to mobilize native Jewish art forms in the production of a modern Jewish art, there is an element of preservation and mobilization that must be taken into consideration in salvage poetics. How do you use your literary (or other) art to mobilize, improve upon, and preserve a culture that is in rapid decline? The imagination, the "imaginary real" as Agnon puts it in *A Guest for the Night,* is essential in the face of poverty. How is that daily struggle for survival to be applied to the broader struggle for survival expressed in a body of literary and other aesthetic work produced at the turn of the twentieth century.

In the two discrete sermons presented below, Agnon pursues the subject of "houses" or "homes." "Houses" as the theme of this *devar torah* functions tellingly within the culture of the novel and within the culture of modern Jewish salvage poetics. As discussed earlier, Agnon presents Jewish textual culture throughout the novel as the culture to which his protagonist returns from the Land of Israel in the years following the destruction wreaked on the Jewish communities of

---

14. Agnon, *Oreaḥ,* 419.

Galicia after the First World War. He does not find many familiar personages or familiar homes in his hometown. In fact, he has nowhere to spend the first night of Passover. But he finds comfort, familiarity, sustenance, and purpose in his rejuvenation of the old *beit hamidrash*. Similarly, in the very act of preaching to his fellow townsmen, he reintegrates into their consciousness an awareness of those texts that, to his mind, defined his childhood, and his memory of the town, which they continue to inhabit. In other words, he is trying to reintegrate his townsmen into the horizon of his town as he remembers it, through words of Torah and institutions thereof—through the old *beit hamidrash* and the *devar torah*. Thus, the *beit hamidrash* on the one hand, and the *devar torah* on the other hand, a physical repository of Jewish texts, and a rhetorical repository of the same, represent the home to which Agnon's protagonist is trying to return.

IV. The Sermon: At Home in the Text

The unnamed protagonist and narrator of *A Guest for the Night*, not only takes on the physical rehabilitation of the *beit hamidrash*, he also takes on the role of the spiritual guide, or the "preacher." Invited to give a sermon in the *beit hamidrash* by the men who join him there on a winter Shabbat evening, he presents the sermon lucidly, virtually anatomizing it for us as he proceeds. The first paragraph begins:

> I opened a Pentateuch, and I glossed the weekly Torah reading, beginning with the verse 'And Jacob awoke from his sleep,'[15] and he was afraid and he said, 'how terrible this place is. This must be a house of God.'[16] This is not like Abraham who said 'God will appear on a mountain,'[17] or like Isaac, of whom it is said, 'And Isaac went walking in a field.'[18] Rather, Jacob emphasizes the house. And so I sermonized about three methods for worshipping God. The first is the man who seeks out God in high places, or highfaluting ways, like on a mountain and goes through his life with lofty ideas and intentions. The second is the man who seeks out God as in a field, for the way of a field is to plant seeds in it, and to harvest them, and there is a good scent there, as it says, 'see, the scent of my children is like the scent of a field.'[19] The third, which is God's favorite, is to approach him as one would approach a house, as it is written in the case of Jacob our father, God's favorite among the forefathers. He blesses himself and praises himself saying, 'my house is a house of prayer.'[20] As it written in the *Zohar*: A mountain and a field are places of freedom, but a house is a guarded, respectable place.[21]

15. Genesis 28:16
16. Genesis 28:17
17. Genesis 22:14
18. Genesis 24:63
19. Genesis 27:27
20. Isaiah 56:7
21. Agnon, *Oreaḥ*, 128–129.

The narrator then proceeds to discuss three periods in the history of Israel as understood metaphorically through an engagement with the three concepts just introduced: Mountains, Fields, and Houses. First there was a period when the sages imagined that we don't need houses or fields. Rather, Jews should lift their eyes toward the mountains, as it says in Psalms: "I lift my eyes toward the mountains"[22] because mountains represent freedom and nothing is more beneficial than, or as desirable as, freedom. During the second period, the field is valued over the mountain, as it says, "and she went out to the field to ask after her father."[23] The third time, the time we are now living in, when we are exhausted from wandering up and down mountains and across fields, is a time of houses, where we find rest. The merit of the three forefathers can be found in the nature of the three exiles: Abraham redeemed us from Egypt, Isaac redeemed us from Babylonia, and Jacob will redeem us from our present exile. We should most aspire to emulate Jacob, "the house of Jacob, let us go and walk in the light of God."[24] And Jacob said, "and I will return in peace to my father's house," and of him it is said, "and God will be my Lord."[25]

Throughout this discourse, Agnon brings a series of prooftexts, and maintains a simple structure of triads: Three forefathers, three locales , three exiles. Each of the triads invokes other triads within it: (Abraham = Mountain = Egyptian Exile) (Isaac = Fields = Babylonian Exile) (Jacob=House=Contemporary Exile). Indeed, this triad is proposed as well by traditional commentators with the three prayer services. Abraham represents the morning prayers, Isaac represents the afternoon prayers, and Jacob represents the evening prayers. The preacher/narrator begins his sermon with a text from the Bible and ends with an allusion to the present moment, wending his way through a variety of texts from the Bible, the Prophets rabbinic literature, and even venturing into a Kabbalistic text rendered entirely in Aramaic.

The triumph of the "house" over the other two locales woven through the sermon is an allusion to the general theme, throughout the novel, of the narrator as a "guest for the night" in his own hometown. His physical house has been destroyed in Arab riots in Jerusalem, and his wife (called a man's "house" in the Talmud), and children (or "builders" of houses) have gone to Germany to be with his in-laws. For his part, the narrator has returned to his own hometown, but has no home to speak of because his own immediate family is gone, and most of the people he once knew were killed in WWI, have died of old age or grief, or have emigrated. He returns, time and again, to the notion of his own homelessness, of his having no home to return to in his chosen Palestine, and no home to inhabit

22. Psalms 121:1
23. Judges 1:14
24. Isaiah 2:5
25. Genesis 28:21

in Szibusz. He creates a home for himself in the *beit hamidrash*, not a home to merely dwell in, because he never really dwells there, but a home to study in, to teach in, to eat in when his inn-keeper's wife Mrs. Sommer is too distracted to cook for him. His notion of a home, therefore, is a place of texts, a place of textual traditions, and a place of community. By inserting this, and other fully fleshed out sermons into his novel Agnon not only furthers his thematic in a variety of different ways, but he also salvages a mode of discourse, in this case, the homiletical sermon.

Elsewhere in *A Guest for the Night*, Agnon delivers a sermon in a slightly different style, with a similar thematic. Once spring has set in, the narrator finds that his rejuvenation of the old *beit hamidrash* as a house of study and prayer has not withstood the test of the seasons. In the winter, when there was a fire blazing in the grate, it was not hard to attract a weekday daily *minyan*, a prayer quorum of ten men, and even bring in some students of the Talmud or Jewish Legal Codes. But with spring, the narrator cannot seem to get the required quorum of men for prayers, even on the Sabbath. On one particular Friday night, the narrator sits in the old *beit hamidrash* waiting for an audience to hear his gloss on the weekly Torah portion. Three men sit with him, yawning by the stove:

> I perused my book, and cocked my ears to hear if people were coming. Half an hour passed and no one arrived. I said to myself, why don't the people who are sitting here ask me to teach them? Now, even if they ask, I won't answer them. Because they were quiet I said to myself: 'if two people sit together and they share words of Torah, the holy spirit hovers between them.' Whether there are many people or few, words of Torah must be spoken. Even if only one of them wants to hear words of Torah, it is forbidden to keep them from him. While I was talking to myself, they slipped away. This man felt strange with a bellyful of Scripture verses and sayings from the sages, and no one wishing to hear them. Moreover, on other Sabbaths I did not prepare anything, but whatever God put in my mouth I would speak, and for this Sabbath I had prepared many comments...[26]

So the narrator decides to recite the *devar torah* to himself, before he leaves the empty *beit hamidrash*. It begins, like the previous *devar torah*, as a transcription of an actual rhetorical performance:

> The portion for that week was the one beginning: 'these are the regulations of the Tabernacle,'[27] and what I wanted to say was connected with the last verse of the portion: 'For the cloud of the Lord was upon the Tabernacle by day, and fire was on it by night, in the eyes of all the House of Israel, throughout their journeys.'[28] We should be precise in interpreting 'In the eyes of all the House of

26. Agnon, *Oreaḥ*, 225.
27. Exodus 38:21
28. Exodus 40:38

Israel'—do houses have eyes? And what does Rashi of blessed memory want to teach us, when he explains that the journey also includes the places where they encamped? And I went back to the verse 'And the glory of the Lord filled the Tabernacle, for the glory of the Lord was not mingled with the cloud.'[29] Then I went back to the beginning of the portion, "These are the regulations of the Tabernacle, the Tabernacle of Testimony.' Why was the Tabernacle mentioned twice? Because in this passage they were told that the Tabernacle was destined to be destroyed twice: the First Temple and the Second Temple. And we may ask: Was it for the Holy One, blessed be He, at this moment, when Israel had joy and gladness, to inform them of such an evil thing? But this is explained by the word that follows: 'Testimony.'[30] It is a testimony to all the people of the world that there is forgiveness for Israel, and these are the tidings. Since the Lord poured out his wrath on the wood and the stones, but Israel remained in existence, we learn that the Tabernacle, which in Hebrew is *mishkan*—was Israel's pledge—in Hebrew *mashkon*; and that is why it is written, 'The Tabernacle of Testimony' for it was a testimony and a pledge for Israel. And these are ancient matters.[31]

After one or two more points, based on close readings of the Tabernacle texts, the narrator begins to summarize his method and his message, instead of presenting a transcript of the sermon: "Finally I went back to the beginning and explained a number of scriptural texts about which I raised questions, and touched on a number of topical ideas which are already implied in our eternal Torah."[32]

What we see here in Agnon's approach to this sermon is twofold. First, as in the earlier sermon, he presents a biblical verse as his starting point, and, as in the earlier sermon, he focuses on the theme of a "house." Unlike the earlier sermon, what he models for us here is a gloss not on the Bible, but on Rashi, a medieval commentator and the most important and most frequently studied rabbinic voice on the Torah and the Talmud, who interprets the Biblical verse in a way that seems strange to Agnon's narrator. From Rashi's interpretation that the cloud's accompaniment of the children of Israel on all their journeys includes all the places that they encamped, he arrives at the conclusion that "encampment" is an allegory for the historical future of the children of Israel—that God's glory will accompany them on their journeys, even into future destructions and exiles. The tabernacle with which the cloud is associated in the starting verse of the sermon becomes a figure for the destroyed first and second temple.

Once this is clearly articulated, with a concluding note on the notion of the tabernacle being a tabernacle of testimony (*mishkan 'edut*), an institution that testifies to God's forgiveness of the Jewish people because God allowed

29. Exodus 40:34
30. Exodus 38:21
31. Agnon, *Oreah*, 226.
32. Ibid, 226.

the destruction of the physical temples but the Jewish people survived, Agnon shifts into a more summary mode of sermonizing. The transcription becomes an overview, and the sermon is no longer a mimetic performance in the text, but a diegetic description.

The earlier sermon, delivered to a group of interested congregants in the *beit hamidrash* on a different Shabbat evening, during the winter, is transcribed from beginning to end. We are told that that sermon was delivered upon request by those who had gathered in the *beit hamidrash* for the evening prayers, and this marks the first time the narrator takes on the role of preacher and teacher within the context of the *beit hamidrash*, of which he is now the proud possessor of the key. At this juncture, his role as keeper of the key is defined, at least for him. He is not simply a janitor, a gate-keeper, or a hanger-on. He is to foster a return of the *beit hamidrash* to its former intellectual glory, overseeing, or at least facilitating, the scholarship that can still be pursued there because the books have remained. All that is missing are the people to study the books, and the encouragement to do so.

The "key" into the beit hamidrash takes on a textual valence in the traditional rabbninic usage of the term *mafteah*. A *mafteah*, for example, is a "key" to a text—an index or a legend. The electronic portal to libraries in Israel is called, as well, a *mafteah* or a key. As both a physical artifact, a "key" and as a way into a culture through text, Agnon's "key" is the perfect sign of salvage poetics.

The second sermon, in contrast, delivered to an empty *beit hamidrash* is a cross between performance and meditation, with the first half being a performance, and the second half a meditation. Or even more poignantly, the first half exemplifies the role of the narrator as a character in the novel, and the second half reminds us that he is a narrator whose omniscience drives the novel even when he is not an actor in the story. In other words, the homodiegetic nature of the narrative, in which the narrator serves as a character as well, is emphasized because we are presented with a sermon both as it is delivered, mimetically and diegetically.

Critics have discussed the figure of the narrator in this novel, emphasizing the autobiographical nature of the "return" described herein, as Agnon did return to Buczacz in 1930, even if, as Dan Laor argues, for a much shorter time than the year described in the book.[33] Arnold Band rightly warns his readers not to assume that there is too close a correspondence between the author Agnon and the unnamed narrator of *A Guest for the Night* even if at selected moments the narrator reminds us that he is an author.[34] Agnon plays here with his readership by insisting on not naming his narrator, by having the narrator share with

33. Dan Laor, *Ḥayyei Agnon*, 316.
34. Arnold Band, *Nostalgia and Nightmare: Studies in the Fiction of S.Y. Agnon*, (Berkeley: University of California Press, 1968), 284.

himself many biographical details, and most importantly, by having his narrator, as he does in the second sermon, control both the mimetic and the diegetic levels of the story. If he is both performing the sermon and anatomizing the sermon, if he is both inside the institution being represented, and outside of it, representing it, it is harder to distinguish Agnon the author from the authorial narrator presented in his novel. Like the daughter of a rabbi returning to her hometown throughout Dvora Baron's literary corpus and serving as a homodiegetic narrator, so too does Agnon's narrator serve as a tricky alter-ego designed to maximize the auto-ethnographic premise of the work at hand.[35] Posing as the author himself, Agnon's narrator emphasizes more than just the "realism" of the novel. His seemingly autobiographical presence in the novel, and his isolation within the culture he thought he would be revisiting on familiar terms, emphasizes the gap between the actual and the expected, between that which is observable in life and that, which can be depicted in a literary text.

Agnon's *A Guest for the Night* gives us a glimpse of the kinds of changes, imposed from without, and evolving from within, experienced by Jewish communities throughout Galicia, particularly during the interwar period. Commensurate with the massive physical, communal and economic destruction wreaked on the Jews of Galicia during the First World War, the culture of Jewish scholarship, of ritual observance, and of local familial networks was in serious decline. Agnon's presentation of sermons in *A Guest for the Night,* alongside his thematization of the narrator's attempts to recuperate the old *beit hamidrash,* does not pave the way for a general articulation of the cultural changes undergone by the Jewish communities of Galicia since his departure from there about two decades earlier. Rather, Agnon creates an intertextual salvage poetic both through allusions to traditional Jewish texts and through a presentation of textual institutions. In so doing, he engages in a subtle narratological negotiation in which he has his alter-ego, the narrator of the text, pose as a kind of native informant, or a participant observer, not only lamenting the loss of textual institutions, but intervening in that loss and salvaging what he can.

SHEILA E. JELEN is the Zantker Professor of Jewish Literature, Culture, and History at the University of Kentucky, and the director of the Program in Hebrew and Jewish Studies there. She is the author, most recently, of *Salvage Poetics: Post-Holocaust American Jewish Folk Ethnographies* (2020) and co-editor of *Reconstructing the Old Country: American Jewry in the Post-Holocaust Decades* (2017). Jelen's newest book, *Israeli Salvage Poetics,* is forthcoming in 2023.

---

35. Dvora Baron, *Parshiyot* (Jerusalem: Mossad Bialik, 1968).

9 Divine Compassion at an Ironic Glance: The Experience of the Shoah in Agnon's "The Sign"

Nitza Ben-Dov, Haifa University

Translated by Wendy I. Zierler[1]

The News—Its Place and Timing

"THE SIGN," WHICH concludes *A City in Its Fullness*, is Agnon's only direct response to the Holocaust, and thus has provoked great interest among readers and scholars of Agnon. The story open as follows:

> In the year when the news reached us that all the Jews in my town had been killed, I was living in a certain section on Jerusalem, in a house I had built for myself after the disturbances of 1929 ([5]689—ט״תרפ[ה׳] in the Jewish calendar, which numerically is equal to "The Eternity of Israel"—נצח ישראל). On the night when the Arabs destroyed my home, I vowed that if God would save me from the hands of the enemy and I should live, I would build a house in this particular neighborhood, which the Arabs had tried to destroy. By the grace of God, I was saved from the hands of our despoilers and my wife and children and I remained in Jerusalem. Thus I fulfilled my vow and there built a house and made a garden.[2]

Mentioning 1929 as a year that strengthened the eternity of the people, when in reality the riots of 1929 threatened that very eternality, imbues the story with irony from its very first sentence. The strategy of interlacing a story with light irony in reference to God from the very first paragraph is characteristic of Agnon. *Sippur pashut* (A Simple Story), for example, opens with the words, "The widow Mirl lay ill for many years. The doctors consumed her savings with their cures and failed to cure her. God in heaven saw how she suffered and took her from

---

1. This article has been translated and adapted from the first chapter of Nitza Ben-Dov, *Ḥayyim ketuvim* (*Written Lives*) (Tel Aviv: Schocken, 2011), 30–51.

2. S.Y. Agnon, *Ha'eish veha'etsim* (Jerusalem: Schocken, 1962), 293. Also reprinted in S.Y. Agnon, *'Ir umelo'ah*, Emuna Yaron, ed. (Jerusalem: Schocken, 1973), 695. Translation from S.Y. Agnon, *City in Its Fullness*, Alan Mintz and Jeffrey Saks eds. (New Milford, CT: The Toby Press, 2016), 1. All future citations from these volumes will be noted in parentheses in the body of this essay.

this world."[3] God in heaven who took Mirl's life in order to lessen her suffering by the same measure could have healed her. This sentence hints oh so subtly that the doctors and medications didn't succeed in healing her, but by the same token, neither did the Omnipotent One.

Irony of the same sort can be discerned in the continuation of "The Sign." The narrator's articulation of God's love for His people when He gave them the Torah and on other occasions, is juxtaposed with the statement that human wickedness the sort of which "had not been matched seen man was placed on earth" (*'Ir umelo'ah*, p. 695 / *A City in Its Fullness*, p. 2) had annihilated God's "beloved" people. Is the omnipotent God who gave the people the Torah with great love responsible for the evil people He created? Already from the outset of the story a multi-facted, ironic opposition is established: love vs. evil, eternity vs. ephemerality, redemption vs. destruction, death vs. life, Jerusalem vs. Buczacz, the Land of Israel vs. the Diaspora, fulfilled vows vs. broken promises, the ideal vs. the real, the giving of the Torah to a Chosen People vs. a Holocaust coming down upon the heads of that same People.

In his article, "Did Agnon Write about the Holocaust?" Dan Laor notes carefully the polarity that serves as the basis of the story, based chiefly in the opposition between Jerusalem and Buczacz. In his view, "the orderly way of life of the narrator and his family, who observe the holiday Shavuot in all of its details and minutiae," and similarly, "the permanent home that the narrator built in the neighborhood and the garden he planted around it all symbolize stability and rootedness," are situated in polar opposition to the description of the city of Buczacz and its slain inhabitants.[4] No doubt this is the central contrast in the story and through it one can understand the many chapters (19–24) in the story that are dedicated to the events surrounding the founding of the neighborhood where Agnon's house was built. The long, painful settlement, riddled with obstacles and disappointments for the people of deed and vision who established a neighborhood once considered a desert and now a flourishing garden, stands in stark contrast to the sudden destruction wrought upon a bustling city like Buczacz: "Is it possible that a city full of Torah and life is suddenly uprooted from the world, and all its people—old and young; men, women and children—killed, that now the city is silent, with not a soul of Israel left in it?" (*'Ir umelo'ah*, p. 709 / *A City in Its Fullness*, p. 27). However, from the central, structural contrast that Laor observes, many other contrasts emerge, and many of them are characterized by this subtle but incisive irony. The Jewish year 5689 ט"תרפ'ה, 689 ט"תרפ (1929), the year of the riots, which corresponds in gematria with "Netsaḥ Yisra'el," is only a preface to the array of ironies that Agnon lays out in this story, a clear response to

---

3. S.Y. Agnon, *'Al kappot hamar'ul* (Jerusalem: Schocken, 1958), 55. Translation from S.Y. Agnon, *A Simple Story*, Hillel Halkin trans. (New Milford, The Toby Press, 2014), 3.
4. Dan Laor, *Hebetim ḥadashim* (*New Aspects*) (Tel Aviv: Sifriyat Po'alim, 1995), 83.

the Holocaust. (Incidentally, Agnon didn't have to mention this gematria; a mention of the year would have sufficed, had he not wished to hint at the contradiction between the promise of eternality and the stark reality of the lack thereof.) I will endeavor to prove that part and parcel of this story, as a lament for a city full of Jewish life that was annihilated in the Holocaust, is the protest it lodges against a God who did nothing to prevent this carnage. Agnon, in his way, unveils this criticism by way of ambiguous statements that feign innocence on the outside, but offer harsh criticism on the inside, that have an outer aspect and internal accusatory one all at the same time. Agnon's mask in this story is not his identity and place, rather a seemingly ingenuous tone. Therefore, this is an autobiographical story not just because it affords a glimpse into Agnon's inner world, but also because it enables a poetic inquiry into Agnon's special way of revealing the hidden precincts of the soul.

It is possible that the rumor of the obliteration of the entire Jewish population of Agnon's native city indeed reached Agnon's ears on Shavuot eve, but it is also possible for ideological, symbolic and literary reasons that it was comfortable for this shrewd writer to anchor the arrival of these terrible news in Shavuot in particular.[5] After all, according to one of the names and explanations of the holiday, the giving of the Torah at Sinai is the one time that the entire people, not just its chosen representatives "see the voices." In other words, the collective experience of covenant with God stands in stark opposition to the collective conspiracy to abrogate the covenant, with an entire people on the verge of being wiped out from under the skies of a God who chose them to receive the Torah. In addition, this holiday presents its own unique oppositions, such as those between heavens and earth and between day and night: after all, this is the holiday of the giving of the Torah from the **heavens** and the offering of first fruits from the **earth**; this is the holiday that turns night into day in the form of the Tikkun Leil Shavuot, during which one stays awake to study Torah and recite specific prayers. In the story "The Sign," where the terrible news about the annihilation of Jewish Buczacz arrives on the eve of the holiday, an additional opposition is furnished between celebration and mourning.

The second chapter of the story, which makes clear the arrival of this bad news on Shavuot eve, begins as follows:

> I made no lament for my city and did not call for tears or for mourning over the congregation of God when the enemy had wiped it out. The day when we

5. Rachel Elior uncovers a parallelism between Agnon hearing about the news of the destruction of Buczacz on Shavuot eve in World War II, while he himself resides in Jerusalem and Shavuot Eve 1533, when the news arrived about the Kabbalist messiah, Shelomo Molkho, who was burnt alive at the stake by the Catholic Inquisition, all the while his kabbalist peers celebrated a festive Tikkun Leil Shavuot, a renewal of the covenant, according to the tradition of the Zohar. See Rachel Elior, "Shai 'Agnon vehamasoret hamistit," *Kivvunim ḥadashim* 22 (2010), 232.

heard the news of the city and its dead was the day before Shavuot, so I put aside my mourning for the dead because of the joy of the season when **our Torah was given**. (*'Ir umelo'ah* p. 695 / *A City and Its Fullness*, p. 2, emphasis added)

On its declarative face, in the struggle between the dead of the city and the giving of the Torah, the Torah seems to have the upper hand. Nevertheless, the sonic similarity between "*mitah*" (death) and "*matan Torah*" (the giving of the Torah) undermines the seeming victory of giving over death. In the same way that the promise of eternity implied in the numerology of תרפ״ט failed to deliver on its promise in the wake of the 1929 riots in Jerusalem, so too the covenantal promise inherent in the giving of the Torah is broken in the face of the extermination of the people in the Shoah. The narrator's pious statements in the continuation of the passage, where he claims that God's love for His people is what endows him with the strength to divert his attention from mourning to the sacredness of the holiday, are steeped in bitter irony in the face of the mass death of tens of thousands of Jews, whose love of God offered them no protection, hence they were "killed and strangled and drowned and buried alive" (*'Ir umelo'ah*, p. 695 / *A City in its Fullness*, p. 1) and all this with great, unthinkable suffering.

Moshe Granot, in his critical appraisal of Agnon—critical in the sense that it takes a stand against the aesthetic and moral values of Agnon's work—fails to recognize the ironic aspects of "The Sign" and takes it at face value, reading literally the declaration of the narrator that the holiday of Shavuot has forced him to suppress his mourning for his city. As such, Granot angrily denounces Agnon and his values: "And so, the ostensible message from this is that the Jew continues to act according to former custom, and this total calamity has no capacity to change the ways of the world. The joy over the giving of the Torah to six hundred thousand remains undimmed even in the face of the extermination of six million!"[6] Agnon so thoroughly veiled his criticism of the Giver of the Torah that the author of *Agnon Unmasked* could not discern the mask. The difference between Granot's reading and my own (as well as that of other critics) attests to the complexity of the situation that Agnon describes in "The Sign," in particular the capacity of Agnon's rhetoric and poetics to evoke a thing and its very opposite at the very same time.

In my view, the narrator's announcement of success in diverting his attention from the terrible news that reached him in his Jerusalem home on the afternoon before the holiday of Shavuot is ironic not only because the reference to God's love in this tragic context makes it such, but also because in its entirety "The Sign" serves as a record and a monument. It is, in other words, a sign of

6. Moshe Granot, *Agnon leio masveh* (*Agnon Unmasked*) (Tel Aviv: Yaron Golan Publishing House, 1991), 17.

the city and its dead inhabitants and thus completely undermines the narrator's would-be innocent announcement. Here Shavuot serves chiefly as a window into how the holiday was observed in the narrator's native town. From now on, it seems, Shavuot there—like all other holidays and daily practices—are entirely the province of the past.

The opposition between Shavuot **here** versus Shavuot **there** is part of a system of binaries that Agnon builds throughout the story as a sign and a marker of the Jewish life that was cut off, but in so doing, he also manages to lodge a complaint against Heaven. As already mentioned, from beneath the mask of faith and adherence to the etiquette of the holiday that marks that covenant between God and Israel, there is a welling up of irony in every phase of the story.

Shavuot here, that is, in 1943 Jerusalem, which serves as a frame for the description of Shavuot in the annihilated city, is described in detail in the story: the adornment of the house and the person in preparation for the holiday, the walk to synagogue for evening prayers, the return for dinner and the unfolding conversation around the table, the nighttime departure for the Tikkun Leil Shavuot in the neighborhood synagogue, the arrival at the prayer shed that for some reason is completely devoid of people, something that allows the narrator to have an extraordinary encounter with a figure that is close to his heart, namely, himself.

Shavuot Eve and the Preparations for the Holiday

The description of the inside and the outside of the house (Chapter 3) and the declaration that "in all the days I had lived in the Land of Israel, our house had never been decorated as nicely as it was that day," (*'Ir umelo'ah*, p. 695 / *A City in its Fullness*, p. 2) distinguish Shavuot from all other holidays. That the house is exceptionally decorated specifically this year serves to sharpen the dichotomy between there and here, between Exile and the Land of Israel, between nightmare and festivity. Outer and inner, an additional binary, which plays a physical as well as a psychological role in the story, expresses itself in various ways in the text, even in terms of the house which has been dressed in holiday finery: "The sun shone down on the **outside** of the house; **inside**, on the walls, we had hung cypress, pine and laurel branches, and flowers." (*'Ir umelo'ah*, p. 695; *A City in its Fullness*, p. 2, my emphasis). The decoration of the house on the inside—a seemingly innocent, heartwarming description, meant to bring the holiday to life, moves the natural beauty of outside inside. But this description, too, carries ironic implications connected to the central theme of the story: namely the explicit diversion of attention away from mourning because of the holiness of the festival and the conflict between faith and its undoing. Thanks to the decorations, the narrator tells us,

> All of the flaws in the house had vanished, and not a crack was to be seen, either in the ceiling or in the walls. From the places where the cracks in the house used to

gape with open mouths and laugh at the builders, there came instead the pleasant smell of branches and shrubs. and especially of the flowers we had brought from our garden. (*'Ir umelo'ah*, p. 695–696 / *A City in its Fullness*, p. 2).

This description serves as a form of whitewashing; in the same way that the branches and plants and particularly the flowers cover over the cracks in an extremely temporary manner, so too this Shavuot holiday covers over the mourning for the city only very temporarily and externally. The news that arrived on the eve of the holiday will slowly seep into the narrator's consciousness. And during the Tikkun Leil Shavuot and all that occurs during it, this consciousness will reach its climax.

After describing the house and its holiday dress, the narrator moves on to describe his own holiday clothing. From this description too arises a pair of subtly ironic opposites: body versus soul. The narrator prides himself before his readers in that he holds off wearing his new summer clothes in order to wear them for the first time on the holiday itself. That's what he was raised to do by his mother. Ostensibly, this is the innocent statement of a man who guards the values of his parents in his soul and puts them into practice always and everywhere. On this Shavuot in 1943, that the narrator explains putting off wearing these new lightweight holiday clothes constitutes a special show of restraint and adherence to past custom. There had been a major heatwave before the holiday, and the narrator's old clothes were cumbersome. Even so, he did not capitulate to the dictates of his body and deferred the wearing of his new clothes until the advent of the holiday.[7]

In the broader context of the story, which concerns the narrator's seemingly great restraint in not lamenting the annihilation of his city on the holiday, the holding off of wearing new clothes seems rather natural. This kind of discipline is part and parcel of the framework of the narrator's life, wherein the holiness of the day supersedes instant gratification or expression of one's desires and emotions. However, the comment that concludes the passage ("If I haven't reached the heights of all of my forefather's deeds—in these matters I can do as well as my forefathers, for my **body** stands ready to fulfill most of those customs which depend on it," *'Ir umelo'ah*, p. 596 / *A City in its Fullness*, p. 3, emphasis added) turns it all on its head. In the same way that the branches cover over the internal defects only superficially, so too the covering provided by the clothing is merely external. The narrator's body stands at the ready to fulfill all of the bodily

7. Heavy clothes that encumber the narrator are a motif in Agnon's work. In his 1950 short novel, *'Ad henah*, the narrator finds himself in Berlin during World War I, and interestingly, his clothes there, not just in the hot Land of Israel, are out of season: "I had no summer clothes or shoes [...] Although this didn't matter as long as I stayed indoors, my clothes weighed on me as soon as I went out." S.Y. Agnon, *To This Day*, Hillel Halkin, trans. (New Milford: Toby Press, 2008 translated by Hillel Halkin), 19.

customs, but his soul is less ready. The soul, in contrast to the body, is not wearing its holiday best; disruption and lament are make their nest within it.

Indeed, when the narrator arrives in the synagogue he cannot contain his imagination, and the carnage rises before his eyes. In the future it will become clear to him and to his developed imagination, that the evil that has befallen the people of his city transcends his wildest imaginings. But that evening of the holiday, when only his imagination is available to illustrate the evil for him, he attempts to find consolation in *piyyutim* that are no longer recited in the Land of Israel, only in certain diaspora Jewish communities. Apparently, he is located in the East, but his heart is in the far West. Here, the prayers are said quickly, without the addition of the *piyyutim*. He remains unsatisfied, therefore, confused and dumfounded.

His shock increases when he arrives home and everything about the holiday is behaving according to the regular script. It is interesting that at this moment of cognitive dissonance, he doesn't lift his head to heaven in protest, rather to the contrary: "I bowed my head toward the earth, the earth of the Land of Israel upon which my house is built, and in which my garden grows with trees and flowers, and I said over it the verse 'Because of you, the soul liveth.'" (*'Ir umelo'ah*, p. 697/ *A City in its Fullness*, p. 5). The earth apparently has bested heaven. This victory has an additional ironic representation in the form of the Hallot, based for the purpose of saying the "Hamotsi" ["Who takes bread from the earth"] blessing that are baked into the shaped of the stone tablets that Moses brought down from heaven. The narrator notes that "if the bread comes down from the earth, its shape is from the heavens." (*'Ir umelo'ah*, p. 698 / *A City in its Fullness*, p. 5). In other words, the bread—the essence, the content, and the means of survival—they all come from the earth, and the heavens afford merely the pattern and the decoration.

The contrast between heaven and earth, wherein earth provides shelter, life, bread, deliverance and relief, and all Heaven provides is form, joins the other oppositions in the story: the weak, inferior side, is shown to have priority and strength, lament triumphs over celebration, evil is shown to be stronger than love, the body is listened to more than soul, the outside is brought inside in order to refresh the spirit and to cover over the defects in the house, and death exerts a greater presence than the giving (of the Torah). On this holiday of the giving of the Torah in 1943 one bows one's head toward the good mother earth to thank her, and one does not lift one's head toward a heaven that failed to prevent the Shoah. The significance of the holiday as the festival of the giving of the Torah has shrunk in relation to its meaning as a festival of first fruits of the land. "The meal which the land had given us was good, and good too is the land itself, which gives life to its inhabitants" (*'Ir umelo'ah*, p. 698 / *A City in its Fullness*, p. 6), says the narrator at the beginning of Chapter 9, which deals entirely with the wondrous garden, a real life Eden, which surrounds the narrator's house in Talpiyot and provides for all of its needs. The focus on the land makes the empty, merciless heavens superfluous.

Upon his return from synagogue, the narrator's family comes together for the holiday evening meal, and the narrator unburdens himself of the heavy load upon his heart by telling stories of Shavuot from his hometown, before the arch enemy came and killed all the Jews of his city. From these memories that the narrator shares with his wife and children, one can pull out additional oppositions: Jews / Gentiles, old / young, flowering / withering, the simple folk / the town leaders. But in contrast to these binary oppositions that arise from the description of Shavuot in the Land of Israel—mass receiving of the Torah as opposed to a massacre, land versus heaven, here versus there, outside versus inside—all of which represent irreconcilable poles, the contrasts described in the stories of the Diaspora do not retain a strict oppositional tension. A wagon filled with greens sent in honor of Shavuot by Count Potocki to decorate the Great Synagogue of the city, undoes the gap between Jews and Gentiles. The great enthusiasm on the part of the elders of the city for the artistic talent of the writer/narrator, who was a boy at the time, bespeaks a warm connection between the generations. The socio-economic gap between rich and poor is negated, though here an ironic arrow is shot; it is not for socialist humanist reasons that this gap is undone, rather "since the enemy has destroyed them altogether, I shall not distinguish between them here." ('*Ir umelo'ah*, p. 701 / *A City in its Fullness*, p. 10). Whereas a nostalgic light had bridged the oppositions and gaps at the beginning of the stories of his city that no longer is, the final statement disrupts this. As the story continues, this line becomes even thicker with irony. With a saccharine tone and self-righteous note the narrator adds: "The Holy One Blessed Be He has been gracious to Israel: even when we remember the greatness and glory of bygone days, our soul does not leave us out of sorrow and longing. Thus a man like me can talk about the past, and his soul doesn't pass out of him as he speaks." ('*Ir umelo'ah*, p. 701 / *A City in its Fullness*, p. 10) Is this the kind of graciousness that we expect from the Holy Blessed One? That he allows a total extermination and extinguishes the heart in the face of it? And this extinguishing of the heart is a true act of compassion? After all, it's clear that the heart has broken with sorrow and longings for the vibrant city that was exterminated, leaving only a story behind.

The Way to the Synagogue on Shavuot Night—Reminiscences, Meditations, and Biography of a Place

A. Childhood Memories of the Destroyed City

After the holiday dinner, during which the narrator tells stories of his city, he leaves his home to attend the Tikkun Leil Shavuot at the Synagogue (chapter 14.) "My home is near the house of prayer," the narrator will tell us later, in chapter 17 ('*Ir umelo'ah*, p. 703 / *A City in its Fullness*, p. 12), but since his intention, in typical Agnon fashion, is to meld his walk to synagogue with the thoughts and memories that arise that night owing to the information about the Shoah, the walk becomes longer and with it the comparison between there and here, the past and the present, between God and His poets, and the narrator and the others at the synagogue.

The first salient contrast is between those who read the text of the Tikkun Leil Shavuot and the narrator himself, who prefers to read the *Azharot* of Rabbi Solomon Ibn Gabirol (Rashbag). The dualism and contrast embodied in the soul and poetry of this great medieval Hebrew poetry perfectly match the framework of opposites that is laid out in "The Sign." In Ibn Gabirol's secular poetry, the poet emerges a man filled with arrogance and superiority with respect to the lowly world, whereas in his sacred poetry, he acknowledges the nothingness of human beings in relation to God. Gabirol—the haughty and proud, on the one hand, and the lowly and subservient, on the other—embodies the two-sided situation of the narrator at the Tikkun Leil Shavuot, in separating from the community in order to express his great admiration for and surrender to R. Solomon Ibn Gabirol: "I shall admit freely that I don't follow them in all of their ways. They read the Order of Study for Shavuot night and I read the book of hymns that Rabbi Solomon Ibn Gabirol, may his soul rest, composed on the six hundred and thirteen commandments." (*'Ir umelo'ah*, p. 701 / *A City in its Fullness*, p. 10)

It's worth noting that in the parallelism of arrogance and surrender shown by Ibn Gabirol and that of the narrator, there is one exception that calls for explication. While both of them raise themselves above the people around them, Gabirol surrenders to God, whereas the narrator surrenders to Ibn Gabirol. More than that: the narrator prefers Ibn Gabirol over other poets, because whereas other poets excel in praising God, Ibn Gabirol's poems "moan from the sorrow of Israel in Exile and seek out their redemption and return." (chapter 14, p. 701)

The protest against heaven is twofold: the narrator chooses a human being rather than God as an object of veneration, because his poems deal with the sufferings of Israel rather than praise of God.

Agnon drafts Solomon Ibn Gabirol in order to express veiled disappointment with God. He does this by way of a play on the word "shem," referring at once to the name שלמה (Solomon), which appears in an acrostic in the poems of the revered poet, and also serves as a name for God. Name versus name, with the second Name, that is God, failing to answer the expectations of the first one, that is Solomon Ibn Gabirol, whom the narrator identifies with and whose pains the narrator feels, in his discussion of the famous poem, "Request," which begins as follows:

At the dawn I seek Thee,
Refuge and rock sublime,—
Set my prayer before Thee in the morning,
And my prayer at eventime.
I before Thy greatness

Stand, and am afraid:—
All my secret thoughts Thine eye beholdeth.[8]

The narrator asks rhetorically: "Is it possible that such a righteous man as this, whose **name** [*shem*] was written in the prayer book, did not find God [Hashem] before him at all times and in every hour, so that he had to write "At dawn I seek Thee, Refuge and rock sublime [my rock and my strength]"? Not only did God **[Hashem]** make him see Him, but even when the poet found God [**Hashem**], fear fell upon him and he stood confused." (*'Ir umelo'ah*, p. 701 / *A City in its Fullness*, 9–10) As a way of fixing the dual meaning of the word "shem," this word will notably appear yet four more times in chapter 14 alone.

The narrator's double astonishment about the Name that fails to fulfill the expectations of the person whose name is inscribed in the siddur does not originate in Jerusalem on Shavuot eve, 1943. Rather is first arises in his hometown, when as a young boy, the narrator first alights upon Ibn Gabirol's "Request" in the siddur that his father brings back for him from the fair. Doubt begins to eat away at him back then.

From then on, Ibn Gabirol becomes the entity to which the narrator directs his prayers, his religious intentions and yearnings. Alluding to the famous verse from Song of Songs 3:1, "By night on my bed I sought him whom my soul loves; I sought him, but I found him not," traditionally interpreted as an allegorical representation of the love between Knesset Israel and the Holy One Blessed Be He, the narrator says: "As I lie down at night I see this saint rising from his bed on a stormy windblown night. The cold engulfs him and enters his bones, and a cold wind slaps at his face, ripping his cloak and struggling with its fringes." (*'Ir umelo'ah*, p. 701–702 / *A City in its Fullness*, p. 11). The young boy directs his inner world not toward God but to the man who, despite his name being inscribed in the siddur, cannot seem to find Hashem [The Name, that is, God].

Another encounter with a poem by Ibn Gabirol, "O poor captive in foreign land," (chapter 15) as sung by the old cantor in his city, prompts additional astonishment about the Master of Universe: "It was a little hard for me to understand why God didn't hurry and take her out of captivity, or why He didn't have mercy on the poor old man who stood, his head bowed, begging and praying for her." (*'Ir umelo'ah*, p. 702 / *A City in its Fullness*, p. 11) Here we have an additional contrast between a young innocent boy, who reads the poem literally and expects an

8. From Nina Davis, *Songs of Exile* (Philadelphia: Jewish Publication Society, 1901), 29. https://archive.org/details/songsofexilebyheoosalaiala/page/28/mode/2up. "At Dawn I Seek Thee" is an eleventh century piyyut by Rabbi Solomon Ibn Gabirol, one of the piyyutim of the "Reshut" for "Nishmat kol ḥai," a prayer asking for permission to recite "Nishmat kol ḥai," known in many Jewish congregations and sung to many different melodies.

immediate result, and the old cantor, who clings to the ritual and perhaps isn't even sensitive to the difficult content in the *piyyutim* he sings.

Except that the boy has grown up. As time goes on he too clings to the traditions and the rituals, and since the piyyutim of Rabbi Solomon Ibn Gabirol are so close to him, he never once misses reading them on Shavuot night, even in Erets Yisra'el where they are no longer recited. That is, the same opposition between him and the community in Erets Yisra'el that is mentioned first in Chapter 14 repeats again in Chapter 16, except that here the narrator explains the reason for the Tikkun Leil Shavuot: "in remembrance of our father who stood trembling all night in the third month after going out of Egypt to receive the Torah from God Himself. (*'Ir umelo'ah*, p. 702 / *A City in its Fullness*, p. 12) This explanation, which provides historical depth to the thousands of years of the custom of Tikkun Leil Shavuot, also indirectly explains the narrator's stubbornness in continuing to recite the Azharot of Rabbi Solomon Ibn Gabirol even in a place where it is no longer customary to recite them. From the time that he happened upon these piyyutim that captured his heart, this custom has distinguished him from others in the community.

B. The History of the Narrator's Neighborhood

All of these things about the Diaspora—about the difference between the narrator and others around him, about his childhood and the place of Rashbag in his biography—emerge as part of the narrator's musings as he walks from his house to the synagogue on Shavuot Eve, 1943. The objective closeness of the synagogue to his home does not deter his abundance of thoughts and memories. Subjectively, a mental-spiritual distance is marked out between the narrator and the neighborhood synagogue, as he himself attests: "That night the way made itself longer. Or maybe it didn't make itself longer, but I made it longer. My thoughts had tired out my soul, and my soul my feet. I stopped and stood more than I walked." (*'Ir umelo'ah*, p. 703 / *A City in its Fullness*, p. 12) This prolonged walk affords the narrator the opportunity to tell not just about his annihilated city in Eastern Europe but also to recount the history of the Jerusalemite neighborhood (Talpiot) where he now lives and where a wooden hut serves the function of a house of prayer.

But before the narrator dedicates six relatively long chapters (19–24) to the history of the neighborhood where desert land is turned into a flourishing garden, he returns in chapter 8 to the main theme of the story. Indirectly and ironically, he hints at the limits of God's power to save Israel. Like the Psalmist in his day, the narrator expresses astonishment on the night of the giving of the Torah that the heaven and the earth fulfill their destiny: "They stand and fulfill their tasks: the earth to bring forth bread, and the heavens to give light to the earth and those who dwell upon it. (*'Ir umelo'ah*, p. 703 / *A City in its Fullness*, p. 12) So in Jerusalem and so too, it seemed, in his city, which was destroyed. In light of what happened to the Jews, God didn't have to let heavens and earth function as if nothing at all had happened. But in the Diaspora, the narrator explains, as if defending the Creator of the World—but subtly criticizing Him—God behaves differently:

> In The Land of Israel, the Holy One Blessed He, judges the land Himself, whereas outside The Land he has handed this supervision over to angels. The angels' first task is to turn their eyes aside from the deeds of the gentiles who do evil to Israel, and therefore the heavens there give their light and the earth its produce—perhaps twice as much as the Land of Israel. (*'Ir umelo'ah*, p. 703 / *A City in its Fullness*, p. 13)

Is this not a sign of the powerlessness of God [*Hamakom*] in the world that is supposed to be His place [*mekomo*] entirely?

The birth of the neighborhood—the story within the story of "The Sign"—is miraculous. But it is an earthly human miracle in which God plays no part. Only at the beginning of chapter 24, the last in a series of six chapters dedicated to the sufferings associated with the establishment of the neighborhood, do we read the line. "By the grace of God upon us, we rose up and were strong." (*'Ir umelo'ah*, p. 707 / *A City in its Fullness*, p. 18) And this after the previous chapter, which culminated with a description of the riots that the Arabs unleashed against the residents of the neighborhood on Shabbat Naḥamu (the Sabbath after the fast day of the 9th of Av) 1929, that same year that symbolized Eternal Israel in gematria.

The mention of God's grace in the thoroughly secular context of resilient pioneers who stubbornly and against all odds turn a desert into a settled land is merely a hackneyed turn of phrase. The emphasis upon Shabbat "Naḥamu" (Be consoled) as the occasion for riots is no less ironic than the reference to Eternal Israel in conjunction with the riots.[9]

More ironic even than that: the presentation of the beginnings of the neighborhood as a result of one man's wonder over the beauty of the place when in reality it is a place of thorns, brambles, and rocks, but one where you can see "the Dead Sea on one side and the Temple Mount on the other" (*'Ir umelo'ah*, p. 703 / *A City in its Fullness*, p. 13). When the neighborhood is finally established after a long string of evil decrees, riots and wars, the narrator tells us that "[t]he Dead Sea would smile at us almost every day, its blue waters shining in graceful peace between the grey and blue hills of Moab. The

---

9. On the ironic connection to Shabbat Naḥamu, see the chapter on *Biḍmi yameha* (In the Prime of her Life) in Nitza Ben-Dov, *Vehi tehilatekha* (Jerusalem: Schoken, 2006, 47–48), where Agnon by choosing the eve of Shabbat Shabbat Naḥamu for the wedding of Akaviah and Tirtsa Mazal hints to unhappy marriage.

site of the Temple would look upon us. I don't know who longed for whom more; we for the Temple Mount, or the Temple Mount for us." (*'Ir umelo'ah,* p. 707 / *A City in its Fullness,* 17) In raising the possibility that the place of the neighborhood took priority over the place of the Temple, the narrator glorifies the neighborhood, but also offers ironic comment on God's dwelling place: it's not enough that from the Temple Mount God looks out on the neighborhood and makes no effort to ameliorate the sufferings of its founding; God actually seems to envy the neighborhood. The Dead Sea, with its sparkling blues looms in stark, ironic, meaningful opposition to the ruins of the Temple, which merge in the neighborhood that is situated between these two poles.

Following on this notion that the Temple envies the neighborhood, an amazingly heretical statement, to be sure, the narrator states: "We, whose minds are given over mainly to things of this world, build great and beautiful houses for ourselves, and suffice with little buildings and shacks for prayer." (*'Ir umelo'ah,* p. 707–708 / *A City in its Fullness,* p. 18) The small prayer shack as opposed to the large homes joins the priority assigned in this story to life on earth on this holiday, that is less a celebration of the giving of the Torah from heaven and more on the life and bounty of the land.

To summarize: the long digression that the narrator takes in order to tell, on the one hand, of the destruction of his Galician city, and on the other hand, of the building of his neighborhood in Jerusalem—occurs in the context of his extended walk to the prayer shack, which ought to be a relatively short walk but that takes on larger proportions in thought and spirit on this particular Shavuot night in 1943. This prolonged walk serves a literary as well as an emotional function. Emotionally, the narrator, who heard on the eve of the holiday that all of the Jews in his city were murdered, cannot return to his routine path from his house to the synagogue, as if it were just any other holiday. This departure from routine is part of his difficult reaction to the terrible news. On a literary level, this gives him the opportunity—and this too is part of his reaction to the bad news—to pit against one another the individual (that is, himself, given that the bad news pertains chiefly to him since there are few people from Buczacz in his neighborhood with whom to can share this simultaneous celebration and mourning on that holiday) and the community of those who pray at the neighborhood synagogue. Part of this are the oppositions between past and present, childhood and adulthood, destruction and building, the wooden prayer shack and the stone houses, God the merciful who seemingly offers salvation to His "chosen people" and Ibn Gabirol, the wondrous *paytan*, whose piyyutim are powerful and eternal, while he, the narrator, is a mere mortal, who exemplifies the contradictions and contrasts typical of human beings.

Alone in the House of Prayer at the Tikkun Leil Shavuot

Upon arriving at the House of Prayer the narrator finds himself all alone (Chapter 25), a continuation of his long walk, during which he is wrapped up in himself. With no one else there, he has the chance in the empty space of the prayer to contemplate the plants and flowers that adorn the neighborhood synagogue and to smell their fragrance. "Already at Ma'ariv," he explains, "I had taken note of the smell, and now every blossom and flower gave off aroma with which God had blessed." (*'Ir umelo'ah,* p. 708 / *A City in its Fullness,* p. 19) The emphasis on the blessings of God even here comes in a context that immediately renders it ironic, because the plants and flowers that give off this pleasant scent were gathered by "a young man, one who had come from a town where all the Jews had been killed." (*'Ir umelo'ah,* p.708 / *A City in its Fullness,* p. 19). And he did here what he did there "before all the Jews there had been killed." Apparently, God's blessing is limited to plants and flowers and to the scent they emit, but does not extend to the Jews who gathered these plants to decorate their houses of prayer.

More than that, in addition to the plants, flowers and roses that decorate the house of prayer there were memorial candles "without number and without end." (*'Ir umelo'ah,* p. 708 / *A City in its Fullness,* p. 20, chapter 26). Lest one forget, the lovely light these candles cast on the space of the synagogue, rendering it magical, memorializes "Six million Jews [who] have been killed by the Gentiles; because of them a third of us are dead and two-thirds of us are orphans. You won't find a man in Israel who hasn't lost ten of his people." (*'Ir umelo'ah,* p. 708–709 / *A City in its Fullness,* p. 20) Hence, this decoration is a harsh reminder of the murder and orphanhood of the Shoah.

The synagogue is adorned with flowers, but the narrator's eyes are pierced by thorns. This opposition of flowers and thorns is part of the opposition of this holiday, which the narrator ostensibly celebrates with flowers and greenery, and yet his personal feelings are all repressed mourning and a thorn in the eye. If there is a certain concealed irony in everything described above, it is hard not to sense in the description of the synagogue on the night of the Tikkun Leil Shavuot a clearly defiant tone: "The Eternal had a great thought in mind when He chose us from all peoples and gave us His Torah of life. Nevertheless, it's a bit difficult to see why He created, as opposed to us, the kinds of people who take away our lives because we keep his Torah." (*'Ir umelo'ah,* p. 709 / *A City in its Fullness,* p. 20) The paradox in the covenant between The Holy One Blessed Be He and the people of Israel is that only Israel maintains their side of the covenant, hence the expression, "a bit difficult," is difficult and ironic all at once.

Chapter 27 opens with words that connect the "grace of God" with the narrator's capacity to shift his mind from the absurd and terrible historical fate that he has been describing until this point. However, while the narrator may be able to take his mind off this difficult philosophical question—how is it that the Chosen

People can be wiped out on account of being the Chosen People?—he cannot take his mind off of the immediate and total destruction of this city that he knows as intimately as the back of his hand. His bodily reaction to this is to close his eyes. In doing so he distracts himself somehow, but this way he doesn't see the dead of his city, only those who lived in it.

In contrast to his current condition where he is standing alone in the synagogue in Jerusalem, the narrator notes that "in my town everyone came to prayer" (*'Ir umelo'ah*, p. 709 / *A City in its Fullness*, p. 21) and with his eyes closed he can see all of them. This binary distinction is fascinating: open eyes show him murder and devastation, whereas closed eyes show him life and prayer. Open eyes demonstrate that he is alone in the Jerusalem prayer shack, whereas closed eyes return him to the bustling synagogue in the city of his youth, enabling him to "put everyman in the place where he used to sit and where he studied, along with his sons, sons-in-law, and grandsons." (*'Ir umelo'ah*, p. 709 / *A City in its Fullness*, p. 20–21) Closing his eyes somehow has the power to resurrect the dead, bringing to life "the people in my city in their deaths as in their lives." (*'Ir umelo'ah*, p. 709 / *A City in its Fullness*, p. 21), as the narrator says in chapter 28. Resurrecting them by closing one's eyes constitutes a form of a distraction from their true state, which one cannot evade if one looks with open eyes at the seemingly endless number of victims who can never be brought back to life.

The narrator's personal encounters with figures who represent his lost city—the old cantor, Hayyim the sexton and Shalom the shoemaker (in other words, Life *Ḥayyim* and Peace *Shalom*, both names steeped in irony)—that hover on the thin line between dream and reality, life and death, past and present, prepare the background for the most mystical encounter of all: that between the narrator and Ibn Gabirol.

While he is still standing alone in the small Jerusalem synagogue on Shavuot eve, the doors of the ark are opened, revealing before the grieving narrator the image of a man whose head is resting between the Torah scrolls and whose voice is calling out from the ark. Similar but also different from Moses in the Tent of Meeting, who speaks with God face to face, this man with a kingly countenance, too, speaks with the narrator. But as the narrator notes, "he did not speak to me with words [*peh el peh*—mouth to mouth]. Only the thoughts that he thought were engraved before me, and these created the words." (*'Ir umelo'ah,* p. 713 / *A City in its Fullness*, p. 26) Along the way, in chapter 39, the narrator returns and recalls his naïve and simple understanding of the meaning of the *piyyut,* "At Dawn I seek Thee," and the compassion that he feels for he who seeks out God [Hashem] and when he finds Him, stands in fear, and how the *piyyut,* "O poor captive in foreign land" heaps pain upon pain. While reminiscing, he once again recalls when he heard the piyyut in the first place. It was from the old cantor in the Great Synagogue in his city, which is now desolate. These memories, and the conflict between past and present tear off the mask of necessary restraint, which nothing other than a gag order and the putting up a bodily front, which bring him to tears. Solomon Ibn Gabirol, the pains of which the narrator has mourned since he was a child, now feels the narrator's pains. In other words, the two fuse into one, and contain one another.

This fusion is not just spiritual, but also physical and emotional. Rabbi Solomon draws close to the narrator, he describes, "until I found myself standing next to him, and there was no distance between us." (*'Ir umelo'ah*, p. 715 / *A City in its Fullness*, p. 28) As they are together, cleaving to one another, the narrator can hear the name of his city coming from the lips of R. Solomon. More than that: the narrator hears Solomon looking for a sign so as not to forget the name of the city. The sign that he decides to make is very typical of him: to put the name of the city as an acrostic in a poem, as he was wont to do for his own name, Shlomo. The narrator is unable to remember the poem, but he is consoled that the name of the city sings out on high, with Hashem [God]. Indeed?

After all, we already learned that in the dichotomy laid out in "The Sign" there is a preference for earth over heaven. Therefore, the acrostic sign that Solomon, now in heaven, made for the city—is nothing other than a metaphor, a figure for the sign that the narrator himself is making for the city, here on earth. Indeed, it is here that the narrator places a monument for his city. The encounter between the narrator and Solomon Ibn Gabirol—the narrator's source of inspiration ever from the time his father brought back a siddur for him from his trip to the fair until today—is an encounter with himself. And in the same way that he himself continued to read the piyyutim of Solomon Ibn Gabirol, in the same way that he stood alone at the Tikkun Leil Shavuot in the neighborhood synagogue and wept for his city that was no longer, so too he gave his city signs that are impossible to forget. The Sign is his thoughts that turn into letters, that developed into words, and eventually became of the stories of *A City and Its Fullness*.

NITZA BEN-DOV was the 2021 Israel Prize Laureate for Hebrew and Comparative Literature. She is a Professor Emerita in the Department of Hebrew and Comparative Literature at Haifa University. She also taught at Princeton University, the University of Michigan, and the University of California, Berkeley. Ben-Dov is the author of many articles and books in Hebrew and in English, including: *Agnon's Art of Indirection* (English); *Ahavot lo me'usharot* (*Unhappy/ Unapproved Loves*, Heb.); *Vehi tehilatekha: Studies in the Works of S.Y. Agnon, A.B. Yehoshua and Amos Oz* (Heb.); *The Amos Oz Reader* (Eng.), *Hayyim ketuvim* (*Written Lives: On Israeli Literary Autobiographies*, Heb). Her latest book in Hebrew, *War Lives: On the Army, Revenge, Grief and the Consciousness of War in Israeli Fiction*, won the Itzhak Sadeh Prize for Military Literature in 2018, and will be soon published in English by Syracuse University Press. Her forthcoming book is *Where the Heart is Drawn*.

In his Generation

10   *Tales from Half-Asia: Small-Town Galicians Encounter the World*

Omer Bartov

THIS ARTICLE EXAMINES the lives and works of several individuals from Buczacz and its environs born between the mid-nineteenth century and World War I; one of them was Shmuel Yosef Czaczkes, later known as S.Y. Agnon, who was born in Buczacz in 1887. What links the people discussed below is that they all, in their different ways, were deeply rooted in the world into which they were born and, at the same time, well aware of its flaws and vulnerabilities. Most of them left their little towns in Eastern Galicia, of which Buczacz was representative, as young men and spent the rest of their lives looking at this remote part of the world from the outside. Some of them wanted to change the world they came from by changing the entire universe. Others, like Agnon, re-created their hometown as a microcosm of the world of Eastern European, especially Galician, or, as he often called it, Podolian Jewry. The drastic changes some of the characters described here had hoped to bring about ended up in catastrophe. The world that Agnon tried to depict in his writing was wiped out halfway through his creative life, and the task of representation became one of reconstruction.

Agnon's monumental attempt to "build a city"—that is, to reconstruct in writing the universe that the Nazis and their collaborators had annihilated—took up an increasing share of his energies in the wake of the Holocaust. *'Ir umelo'ah*, the tome he left unfinished at the time of his death in 1970, is the culmination of these efforts, a literary masterpiece that is at the same time a kind of biography of Buczacz and, by extension, of an entire vanished world.[1] Yet, at least until recently, this volume has not been sufficiently known and recognized, neither in Israel nor in the rest of the world. I personally came to it when I began writing a history of Buczacz. Agnon was concerned almost exclusively with Jewish Buczacz; I tried to write about it as a representative interethnic town, shared by Jews, Poles, and Ukrainians, which ended up in a frenzy of communal genocide.[2] No

---

1. S.Y. Agnon, *'Ir umelo'ah* (Jerusalem: Schocken, 1973).
2. Omer Bartov, *Anatomy of a Genocide: The Life and Death of a Town Called Buczacz* (New York: Simon and Schuster, 2018). Some of the materials in the current article appear in the book but are greatly elaborated here.

Building a City: Writings on Agnon's Buczacz in Memory of Alan Mintz (2022): 118–139
DOI: 10.2979/BuildingaCityWriting.0.0.11

Figure 5: Gravestone of Agnon's Mother, Esther Czaczkes, Jewish Cemetery in Buczacz. (Credit, Wendy Zierler).

work could provide a better, more nuanced, and deeper understanding of Jewish Buczacz than *'Ir umelo'ah*. But this was, of course, also—indeed, primarily—a work of literature. My grasp of Agnon's literary genius, however limited, was in large measure a result of my encounter with Alan Mintz and our many conversations in Jerusalem in the spring of 2015. When I spoke history, Alan responded with literature; where I saw facts, Alan saw meaning. As I was writing a history of Buczacz, Alan's coedited translation of *'Ir umelo'ah*, published under the title *A City in Its Fullness*, was about to come out, and he was hard at work on *Ancestral Tales*, his magisterial analysis of stories in that volume.[3] He was also about to launch a literary biography of Agnon that would have reflected his keen understanding of the links between history and literature in Agnon's life and work. The seminar he organized on Jewish Galicia at the Israel Institute for Advanced Studies at the Hebrew University and especially his gentle yet probing analyses of Agnon's fiction have influenced my own perception of historical writing in more ways than I can elaborate here. This article is a small tribute to that enriching and sadly all too brief intellectual and human encounter.

The great paradox of the period spanning the years between the revolutions of 1848, known as the "spring of nations," and the outbreak of World War I in 1914, is that many Europeans experienced it both as a time of unprecedented new opportunities for self-realization and collective liberation and, simultaneously, as one in which individual and collective identities came to be progressively constrained within national boundaries. History, as it subsequently unfolded during those years of great hopes and looming despair, was not predetermined, and the citizens of Buczacz, like those of many other towns in the remote Austrian province of Galicia, had more choices than ever before or after. A new world was emerging, and the restraints of the old were falling away: tradition had weakened, religious faith was waning, and authority was loosening its grip on family and society. Travel became easier, and people could go farther, change identities more easily, aspire to previously unthinkable goals, and embrace radical, exciting new worldviews.

But, at the same time, as groups and individuals began identifying themselves nationally and ideologically, they also increasingly perceived others through different eyes, distinguishing them not only by religion and ethnicity but also by whether their history gave them the right to continue living where they were. By the same token, those who adopted nationalist discourse restricted their own horizons by determining who they were, where they belonged, and what they could and should hope and struggle for. In this brave new world, vast collectives were being transformed into communities of fate, whose history and future were

3. S.Y. Agnon, *A City in Its Fullness*, trans. Arthur Green et al., ed. Alan Mintz and Jeffrey Saks (New Milford, CT: Toby, 2016) and Alan Mintz, *Ancestral Tales: Reading the Buczacz Stories of S.Y. Agnon* (Stanford, CA: Stanford University Press, 2017).

determined by national affiliation; it was a fate from which others were excluded by definition, yet one from whose repercussions there was no escape.

In the wake of the 1848 revolution, the Habsburg Empire abolished serfdom in Galicia. Over the next few decades, a new nation emerged from the Ruthenian (later known as Ukrainian) peasants in the larger, more populous eastern part of the province. It was a long process: most of the former serfs remained wretchedly poor, illiterate, and the target of ruthless exploitation by the landowners. Instilling "national consciousness" into the rural masses and crafting them into a nation that would eventually claim Eastern Galicia for itself was the singular accomplishment of an increasingly radical national movement.[4]

The Jews of Galicia were also transformed into a modern nation in the second part of the nineteenth century. Jewish activists initially focused on civil rather than national emancipation. Emperor Franz Josef's "constitution" of 1867 had guaranteed equal rights to all citizens and thereby emancipated the Jews.[5] This fundamentally changed relations between Jews and non-Jews. Efforts by the Ukrainian national movement to educate peasants coincided with the return of Jews to the countryside after restrictions on occupation and residence were lifted. As rural Ukrainians were being nationalized, the growing presence and economic role of Jews in the villages created a popular sense of material exploitation and cultural decimation. Jews were presented as fleecing the ignorant peasants, tricking them into alcohol and tobacco addiction, and lending them money at cutthroat rates. Some accused the Jews of retarding the development of a healthy Ukrainian nation, and anti-Jewish comments in the new Ukrainian press soon surpassed attacks on Polish landlords.[6]

Ironically, then, the realization of the Enlightenment's lofty aspiration of liberating the individual from collective feudal constraints culminated in the unleashing of forces that undermined the very core of humanism. As nationalism became the carrier of ideologies that often generated mass violence, one of its central obsessions entailed unmasking assimilated Jews, perceived as a major obstacle to the creation of ethnically homogeneous nation states.

4. John-Paul Himka, *Religion and Nationality in Western Ukraine: The Greek Catholic Church and the Ruthenian National Movement in Galicia, 1867–1900* (Montreal: McGill-Queen's University Press, 1999); Paul Robert Magocsi, *The Roots of Ukrainian Nationalism: Galicia as Ukraine's Piedmont* (Toronto: University of Toronto Press, 2002); and Kai Struve, *Bauern und Nation in Galizien. Über Zugehörigkeit und soziale Emanzipation im 19. Jahrhundert* (Göttingen: Vandenhoeck & Ruprecht, 2005).
5. J. Shanes, *Diaspora Nationalism and Jewish Identity in Habsburg Galicia* (New York: Cambridge University Press, 2012), 31–37. In 1900, Buczacz numbered 3,078 Roman Catholics, 1,918 Greek Catholics, and 6,730 Jews. *Galizien*, vol. 12 of *Gemeindelexikon der im Reichsrate vertretenen Königsreiche und Länder* (Vienna: K. K. Statistische Zentralkommission, 1907), 100.
6. John-Paul Himka, *Galician Villages and the Ukrainian National Movement in the Nineteenth Century* (London: Macmillan, 1988), 158–75 and Struve, *Bauern*, 384–433.

The Ukrainian author Ivan Franko was among the most influential advocates of national independence in the latter years of the nineteenth century in Galicia. Born in 1856 in a small village near the town of Drohobycz, Franko was deeply engaged with the links between social and national oppression and, in his works of fiction, relentlessly defended the rights of the peasants for dignity, identity, and material well-being. Simultaneously, he produced a series of stark literary representations of Jews as parasites sucking the blood of the Ukrainian nation in the service of Polish landowner exploitation and oppression. Still widely read in Ukraine, Franko's fiction has been influential in creating an image of "the Jew" as young Ukraine's explicit "other" within the setting of a social-realist depiction of Galician rural and small-town life at the turn of the nineteenth century.[7]

It was for that reason that Franko responded enthusiastically to the publication in 1896 of Theodor Herzl's *Der Judenstaat* (*The Jewish State*): his preferred solution to the "Jewish question" was the Jews' departure from Ruthenian lands, and he believed that Jews choosing to remain in a future Ukrainian state should be categorized as "aliens" with restricted political and civic rights.[8] Franko's Jewish contemporary, the social-realist author Karl Emil Franzos, had a rather different view of this matter. Born in 1848, Franzos spent his childhood in the town of Czortków, some twenty miles east of Buczacz. As the son of a physician, he had an atypical upbringing and sense of identity. Decades later, he still recalled his father's admonition: "Your nationality is not Polish, nor Ruthenian, nor Jewish— you are German," but, "as for your faith, you are a Jew." In providing him with that hybrid identity, hardly sustainable in a mid-nineteenth-century shtetl, his father's goal was "that I should not see Galicia but rather the West as my homeland," concluded Franzos.[9]

As a child in a largely Hasidic town, Franzos attended school in the Dominican monastery, had little contact with other Jews, and never went to synagogue. At age ten, following his father's death, Franzos was sent to secondary school in the city of Czernowitz, a site of increasing Jewish assimilation into German cul-

7. Yaroslav Hrytsak, "A Strange Case of Antisemitism: Ivan Franko and the Jewish Issue," in *Shatterzone of Empires: Coexistence and Violence in the German, Habsburg, Russian, and Ottoman Borderlands*, ed. Omer Bartov and Eric D. Weitz (Bloomington: Indiana University Press, 2013), 232–35 and Ivan Franko, *Boa Constrictor and Other Stories*, trans. F. Solansko (Moscow: Foreign Languages Publishing House, 1957?).

8. Theodor Herzl, *Der Judenstaat. Versuch einer modernen Lösung der Judenfrage, 1860–1904* (Leipzig: M. Breitenstein, 1896); Hrytsak, "Strange Case," 233–37; Ivan Franko, *Zur Judenfrage—Do iudeiskoho pytannia. Statti* (Kiev: Mizhrehionalna akademiia upravlinnia personalom, 2002); and Myroslav Shkandrij, *Jews in Ukrainian Literature: Representation and Identity* (New Haven, CT: Yale University Press, 2009), 69–80.

9. Karl Emil Franzos, *Der Pojaz. Eine Geschichte aus dem Osten* (Frankfurt am Main: Athenäum, 1988), 5–6, trans. Enrique Lerdau as *The Clown of Barnow* (New Orleans, LA: University Press of the South, 2004).

ture. And while "it was entirely out of the question that I would ever even think of changing my faith," he stressed. "I thought just as little that Judaism would play a decisive role in my life."[10]

Shortly thereafter, Franzos was denied a government scholarship to study Classics at Vienna University. His Jewish identity, he now wrote, had demanded "a terrible sacrifice from me: that I give up the profession I chose." While he went on to study law, he decided to learn more about Jews and, as a consequence, ended up as an author whose novels were largely dedicated to explaining the fate of Galician Jewry to German readers. To be sure, stressed Franzos, he "did not become pious," yet his "feeling of belonging to the impoverished caftan-wearing Jews" of the province "became incomparably greater than before." It was this sense of belonging, yet also of peering from afar, that became the core of his entire oeuvre.[11]

Franzos had no qualms about railing against the tyrannical hold of Jewish religious leaders in Galician towns over the lives of young men and women, their dismissal of love as a poor substitute for a well-arranged marriage, and their vehement opposition to any intimate relations with gentiles.[12] But, unlike Franko, he did not call for Jewish national consciousness and reassertion; instead, he sought a trans-European culture of openness and mutual understanding, and the fulfillment of individual aspirations divorced from ethnic identification. The tragic content of his writing is derived from the impossibility of realizing these goals in Galicia.[13]

Franzos's greatest literary achievement is his novel *Der Pojaz* (*The Clown*), an inverted *bildungsroman* about a Jewish youth's failed quest for self-emancipation.[14] The main protagonist is Sender, the son of a famous wandering jokester, who inherits his father's extraordinary acting talent. While the father represents the quintessential "wandering Jew," the son pines to play Shylock, the archetypical Jew of the Christian imagination. Paradoxically, in order to be allowed to act the Jew on the European theatrical stage, Sender must first become European by shedding his Jewish attributes, a transformation he fails to accomplish.

For Franzos, Shylock was the ultimate embodiment of irreconcilable yet complementary perceptions of the world.[15] When Sender proposes to play Shylock in a wandering theater troupe, the director exclaims enthusiastically that

10. Franzos, *Der Pojaz*, 6–7. See also Salo W. Baron, "The Impact of the Revolution of 1848 on Jewish Emancipation," *Jewish Social Studies* 11, no. 3 (1949): 195–248.

11. Franzos, *Der Pojaz*, 8.

12. Barnet Phillips, "Preface to the American Edition," in *The Jews of Barnow: Stories by Karl Emil Franzos*, trans. M. W. Macdowall (New York: D. Appleton, 1883), v–vi.

13. See, e.g., his novella, *Leib Weihnachtskuchen and his Child*, trans. Michael Mitchell (Riverside, CA: Ariadne, 2005 [1896]).

14. Jeanette R. Malkin, introduction to *Jews and the Making of Modern German Theatre*, ed. Jeanette. R. Malkin and Freddie Rokem (Iowa City: University of Iowa Press, 2010), 10.

15. See his early story "The Shylock of Barnow" (1873), in *The Jews of Barnow: Stories by Karl Emil Franzos*, trans. M. W. Macdowall (New York: D. Appleton, 1883), 19–71.

The Merchant of Venice "is a play for Galicia. It is interesting for Jews and Christians and both can be pleased or angry about it to their hearts' content. Shylock is always a sellout." If Christian audiences see a money-grubbing, parasitical, self-hating and vengeful Jew, the Jews see in Shylock a personification of their predicament, eternally dependent on the tender mercies of the gentiles no matter how much wealth he acquires. As the dying Sender watches his idol, the great actor Dawison, perform Shylock's soliloquy in Lemberg, "If you prick us, do we not bleed? If you tickle us, do we not laugh?" he observes: "This was no longer an actor, but rather a poor, unfortunate man who had long kept his and his brethren's misery bottled up within himself, who had long suffered without complaint, and who had suddenly found words for his terrible pain."[16]

This appears to have been Franzos's own state of mind when he wrote the novel. Completed in 1893, *Der Pojaz* was published only in 1905, after its author's death.[17] By all accounts, Franzos delayed publication in response to the rise of anti-Semitism in central Europe. As a prominent proponent of Jewish integration into the mainstream of European culture, Franzos was shaken by the growing tide against emancipated Jews in the culture and nation he had adopted. Ironically, despite the novel's commercial success when it was published, German critics greeted it as "too Jewish," and Zionist detractors saw it as "too German."[18]

Both Franko and Franzos felt that, by accurately yet both critically and empathetically describing the ills of the present, they would motivate society to progressive action. For Franko, the purpose of the historical novel was "to lay bare the human heart, its fervent aspirations and consuming passions, its struggles, triumphs and defeats [...] portrayed against the backdrop of a historical

16. Franzos, *Der Pojaz*, 312, 354. Dawison is based on the celebrated Warsaw-born actor Bogumil Dawison (or Davidsohn), who went insane and died at age fifty-four in 1872; see Herma Rosenthal and Edgar Mels, "Dawison (Davidsohn), Bogumil," *Jewish Encyclopedia* (1906): http://www.jewishencyclopedia.com/articles/5005-dawison-davidsohn-bogumil.
17. Jost Hermand, afterword to *Der Pojaz. Eine Geschichte aus dem Osten* by Karl Emil Franzos (Frankfurt am Main: Athenäum, 1988), 360.
18. Hermand, afterword, 371–73. See also Peter Pulzer, *The Rise of Political Anti-Semitism in Germany & Austria*, rev. ed. (Cambridge, MA: Harvard University Press, 1988). In Agnon's novel *Shira*, his protagonist, Manfred Herbst, who was born and raised in Germany and served as a lecturer at the Hebrew University, returns to reading German literature during World War II. It was only then, writes Agnon, that he "saw and recognized that even Germany's best bards were not free of that malice, so much so that they lyricized it and made it into a virtue, so that all manner of cruelty to the Jews became acceptable [...] It should be mentioned here that many books ringing out with malice and cruelty came to Herbst as presents given to him by Jews for his Bar Mitzvah. The Jewish spirit had become enslaved to such an extent to Germany that they did not perceive the hatred of Jews lyricized by these books. But what the Jews did not feel the Germans did feel [...]"; see S.Y. Agnon, *Shira*, 3rd ed. (Tel Aviv: Schocken, 1999), 296 and translation by Zeva Shapiro (New York: Schocken, 1989), 295.

event."[19] Franzos, who called himself "the historian of the Podolian Ghetto" and referred to the Galician world he had come from as "half-Asia," insisted that, despite his "great desire to give these stories an artistic form," he would never do this "at the cost of truth [...] I am confident," he wrote, "that I have described this strange and outlandish mode of existence precisely as it appears to me."[20] But these two writers saw the same world through utterly different eyes: their very insistence on factual accuracy betrayed the gaping fissures between the perceptions of reality by their respective ethnic groups, which eventually widened to unbridgeable chasms, irretrievably shattering that entire universe.

Unlike Franzos, most Jews of his generation had to chart their own course into the world directly from a traditional Jewish upbringing. Some, such as David (Zvi) Heinrich Müller, who was born in Buczacz in 1846 and was Agnon's maternal cousin, made subsequent use of the skills they had acquired as children and youths. They also always retained a whiff of foreignness about them and, much as they were admired by the communities they left behind, were suspected both by the Orthodox and by the emerging Zionists of having abandoned the fold: too Jewish for the Germans, too German for the Jews.

For a man of his generation, Müller was a rare exception. By the time of his death in 1912, he had become a renowned scholar, a university professor, and the holder of a heredity noble title, all without abandoning his Jewish faith as was conventionally required for such official recognition. A child prodigy, Müller was banished from his father-in-law's home because of his interest in the Haskalah and set out on an educational journey throughout Europe, ending up at the age of thirty-one as an assistant professor of Semitic philology at Vienna University, where he remained for the rest of his life.[21]

---

19. Sonia Morris, introduction to *Winds of Change: Selected Prose by Ivan Franko*, trans. Roma Franko, ed. S. Morris (Winnipeg: Language Lanterns, 2006), 8–9.

20. Karl Emil Franzos, preface to *The Jews of Barnow: Stories by Karl Emil Franzos*, trans. M. W. Macdowall (New York: D. Appleton, 1883), ix–xx. See also Franzos, *Aus Halb-Asien. Culturbilder aus Galizien, der Bukowina, Südrussland und Rumänien*, 2nd ed. (Leipzig: Duncker & Humblot, 1878). In a letter to Karl Jaspers describing the trial of Adolf Eichmann in Jerusalem in 1961, Hannah Arendt wrote: "On top, the judges, the best of German Jewry. Below them the persecuting attorneys, Galicians, but still Europeans. Everything is organized by a police force that gives me the creeps, speaks only Hebrew and looks Arabic. Some downright brutal types among them. They would follow any order. And outside the doors, the oriental mob, as if one were in Istanbul or some other *half-Asiatic country*. In addition, and very visible in Jerusalem, the peies [sidelocked] and caftan Jews, who make life impossible for all the reasonable people here." Quoted in Amnon Raz-Krakotzkin, "Jewish Peoplehood, 'Jewish Politics,' and Political Responsibility: Arendt on Zionism and Partitions," *College Literature*, 38, no. 1 (2011): 72 (emphasis mine).

21. Getzel Kressel, "Professor David Zvi (Heinrich) Müller," in *Sefer Buczacz*, ed. Yisrael Cohen (Tel Aviv: 'Am 'Oved, 1956), 109–11; "David Heinrich Mueller," *Ost und West. Illustri-

To be sure, not everyone admired Müller. The Palestine-based Zionist newspaper *Hatsevi*, for instance, accused him of having betrayed the cause of Hebrew and "worshipping only German literature."[22] Conversely, the Berlin-based liberal Jewish monthly *Ost und West* described Müller as "a sharp-witted grammarian, text critic, decipherer of ancient inscriptions and texts, editor and cultural historian."[23] Müller's most important contribution was his assertion that the Hebrew Bible had a major impact on later sacred and secular European writing, which flew in the face of the contemporary wisdom, according to which the Bible was largely derivative of earlier Assyrian and Babylonian texts. In 1903, he published an annotated German and Hebrew translation of Hammurabi's code, discovered two years earlier in Persia, where he showed the vast differences between Mesopotamian and biblical concepts of law and morality.[24]

Learned in Jewish and secular scholarship, equally comfortable in the company of rabbis and professors, committed to traditional erudition and to the Haskalah, and publishing in both German and Hebrew, Müller had all the makings of the ideal modern Jew. Contrary to the reproaches of his Orthodox and Zionist detractors, he spearheaded the establishment of the Jewish Theological Institute in Vienna, where he began teaching in 1893. As *Ost und West* noted, Müller also encountered much "resentment and envy" from "Protestant German colleagues eager to deny a Jew the right to have a word on Biblical questions," especially at a time when "antisemitism raged at its fiercest in Austria." While the journal insisted that Müller had prevailed over his opponents, *Hatsevi* claimed that Christian scholars had eventually adopted Müller's views only at the price of denying his original contribution and even accusing him of plagiarism. Indeed, the old professor was said to have been so "consumed by rage" that "his health was destroyed." As "this Jew descends to the Netherworld in discontent,"

erte Monatsschrift für das gesamte Judentum 13, no. 2 (1913): 162; "Dr. Zvi Heinrich Müller *z"l*," *Ha-Zvi*, January 9, 1913, 2.

22. "Dr. Zvi Heinrich Müller *z"l*," *Ha-Zvi*, 2.

23. "David Heinrich Mueller," *Ost und West*, 163.

24. Kressel, "Professor David Zvi (Heinrich) Müller," 111; David Heinrich Müller, *Die Propheten in ihrer ursprünglichen Form. Die Grundgesetze der ursemitischen Poesie erschlossen und nachgewiesen in Bibel, Keilinschriften und Koran und in ihren Wirkungen erkannt in den Chören der griechischen Tragödie* (Vienna: Hölder, 1896); and Müller, *Die Gesetze Hammurabis und ihr Verhältnis zur mosaischen Gesetzgebung sowie zu den XII Tafeln. Text in Umschrift, deutsche und hebräische Übersetzung, Erläuterung und vergleichende Analyse* (Vienna: Hölder, 1903). Agnon refers to this last book in Agnon, *Shira*, 77 (75 in the Shapiro translation). *Shira* is filled with insights on the lives, views, and fates of German Jewish scholars who ended up in Mandatory Palestine.

concluded *Hatsevi* in its 1913 obituary, "his entire intellectual work will be ignored by the sages of Semitic languages."[25]

Müller's hometown also viewed him with a mix of admiration and resentment. In 1893, Müller was sent word by his mother "that an evil rumor has come to the city of Buczacz and that informers have denounced and slandered me and that she would rather die because of this affair." Deeply distressed, Müller responded that he was "the strong pillar upon which the house of Judah rests," and that "the whole congregation of Vienna honors me and the Name of God is sanctified through me." But there is little doubt that, for some of those who stayed behind, his very accomplishment on the European stage cast doubt on his commitment to Jewish faith and tradition.[26]

For others, not least Agnon, Müller was "a great and famous sage of whom all Galicia was proud." In 1908, the twenty-one-year-old Agnon was instructed by his mother to visit their relative in Vienna on his way to Palestine. Perhaps the mother hoped that the venerable scholar would dissuade her son from this adventure. Indeed, as Agnon recalled in his autobiographical novel *Ḥemdat*, Müller impressed on him that "settling Erets Yisra'el is a great deed, but its climate is harsh, and its inhabitants suffer, and you will not be able to withstand the suffering of the land. Better that you settle down in Vienna and prepare yourself for the university and I will support you." Agnon did not heed this advice. But four years later he abandoned Jaffa and moved to Germany, where he stayed for well over a decade.[27]

Although Agnon's later writings betray the influence of Freud, who was also teaching at Vienna University, he is unlikely to have heard of him at the time or to have known that he, too, was linked to his hometown.[28] In fact, Freud's paternal

25. "David Heinrich Mueller," *Ost und West*, 164–66 and "Dr. Zvi Heinrich Müller *z"l*," *Ha-Zvi*, 2. Müller has recently been rediscovered; see Gertraud Sturm, *David Heinrich Müller und die südarabische Expedition der Kaiserlichen Akademie der Wissenschaften 1898/99* (Vienna: Verlag der Österreichischen Akademie der Wissenschaften, 2015).
26. Letter by Müller, April 12, 1893, reprinted in Yisrael Cohen, ed., *Sefer Buczacz* (Tel Aviv: 'Am 'Oved, 1956), 118.
27. Dan Laor, "Pgisha be-Vinna, May 1908," *Ha'arets*, August 8, 2008, http://www.haaretz.co.il/literature/1.1341697; S.Y. Agnon, "Ḥemdat" (1947), in *Me'atsmi el 'atsmi* (Tel Aviv: Schocken, 2000), 18.
28. For Freud's impact on Agnon's writing see, e.g., Arnold J. Band, *Nostalgia and Nightmare: A Study In the Fiction of S.Y. Agnon* (Berkeley: University of California Press, 1968); Avraham Band, "Agnon megaleh penei Freud," *Moznayim* 11 (1989): 17–21; Malka Shaked, "Ha'im haya Hirshel meshuggah? Likrat re'iyah pluralistit shel ha'alilah be*sippur Pashut*," *Hasifrut* 32 (1982): 132–47; David Aberbach, *At the Handles of the Lock: Themes in the Fiction of S. J. Agnon* (New York: Oxford University Press, 1984); Yael S. Feldman, "The Latent and the Manifest: Freudianism in a Guest for the Night," *Prooftexts* 7, no. 1 (1987): 29–39; Avner Falk, "Agnon vehapsykho'analizah," *Itton 77* 156 (1993): 28–39; Shmuel Faust, "'Kaḥalom ya'uf:' Pesher hasippur 'Tallit Aḥeret' me'et Shai Agnon," *Ha'arets: Sefarim* (October 5, 2005),

grandfather and great-grandfather were born in Buczacz and there is evidence to suggest that both were rabbis, while his father was born in the nearby town of Tysmenitz (Tyśmienica, Tysmenytsya) moving later to Freiberg (Příbor) in Moravia, where Sigmund was born to his second (or possibly third) wife Amalia. The family settled in Vienna four years later, where Freud was raised, having had no direct contact with Buczacz.[29]

But a century later, in 1958, Freud's sixty-nine-year-old son Martin recalled his grandmother Amalia, who "came from East Galicia" and was of "Jewish stock." These "Galician Jews," he commented, "were a peculiar race, not only different from any other races inhabiting Europe, but absolutely different from Jews who had lived in the West for some generations." On the one hand, they "had little grace and no manners; and their women were certainly not what we would call 'ladies.' They were highly emotional and easily carried away by their feelings." On the other hand, "they, alone of all minorities, stood up against the Nazis" and "fought the German army on the ruins of Warsaw." Martin firmly believed that, "whenever you hear of Jews showing violence or belligerence, instead of that meekness and what seems poor-spirited acceptance of a hard fate sometimes associated with Jewish people, you may safely suspect the presence of men and women of Amalia's race."[30]

Martin Freud had served as an officer in the Austro-Hungarian army in World War I and in the British army in World War II. As tall and broad-shouldered as his

https://www.haaretz.co.il/literature/1.1048977; and Yael Halevy-Wise, "Reading Agnon's *In the Prime of Her Life* in Light of Freud's *Dora*," *Jewish Quarterly Review* 98, no. 1 (2008): 29–40.

29. Max Grunwald, "Pegishot 'im Sigmund Freud," in *Sefer Buczacz*, ed. Yisrael Cohen (Tel Aviv: 'Am 'Oved, 1956), 119–22; Ernest Jones, *The Formative Years and the Great Discoveries, 1856–1900* (New York: Basic, 1953), 1–3, 12–13, vol. 1 of *The Life and Works of Sigmund Freud*, 3 vols. (New York: Basic, 1953–57). Freud's father, Jacob, referred to his own father and grandfather as "haRav Shlomo son of ha-Rav Ephraim," although they may not have practiced as rabbis. See Benjamin Goodnick, "Jacob Freud's Dedication to His Son: A Reevaluation," *Jewish Quarterly Review* 82, nos. 3–4 (1992): 329–60, which analyzes both father and son's relationship to Judaism (and 347 for this specific quote) and Goodnick, "A Well-Deserved Sabbath Rest: Three Freud Patriarchs," *Journal of the American Academy of Psychoanalysis* 21 (1993): 107–15 (esp. 107). See also, e.g., Marianne Krüll, *Freud and His Father*, trans. Arnold J. Pomerans (New York: Norton, 1986); William J. McGrath, "How Jewish Was Freud?" *New York Review of Books* (December 5, 1991): https://www.nybooks.com/articles/1991/12/05/how-jewish-was-freud/; Alain de Mijolla, "Freud, Jakob Kolloman (Or Kelemen Or Kallamon) (1815–1896)," *International Dictionary of Psychoanalysis* (2005): https://www.encyclopedia.com/psychology/dictionaries-thesauruses-pictures-and-press-releases/freud-jakob-kolloman-or-kelemen-or-kallamon-1815-1896; and Robert Kaplan, "Soaring on the Wings of the Wind: Freud, Jews, and Judaism," *Australian Psychiatry* 17, no. 4 (2009): 318–25.

30. Martin Freud, *Sigmund Freud: Man and Father* (New York: Vanguard, 1958), 11. See also Helen P. Fry, *Freud's War* (Stroud: History, 2009) and Judith Bernays Heller, "Freud's Mother and Father: A Memoir," *Commentary* (May 1, 1956), https://www.commentarymagazine.com/articles/freuds-mother-and-father-a-memoir/.

paternal grandfather, he appreciated physical resistance to one's enemies and took pride in what he believed to be the laudable qualities of his heritage, about which he otherwise knew close to nothing. One can imagine that Martin acquired some of his views of Jews from his father. The rabbi and ethnographer Max Grunwald, who encountered Sigmund Freud a few times, has left us some telling observations on the topic.[31] At their first meeting, following a lecture he delivered in Vienna in 1898, Freud remarked that he was "pleasantly surprised" to see Grunwald in "an elegant tailcoat," because "he had imagined a Jewish rabbi in the image of John the Baptist, wearing a shaggy coat, with unkempt hair and tormented features." Several years later Grunwald attended a lecture by Freud on Hammurabi's code, where Freud rejected his colleague Müller's views and insisted that the Hebrew Bible and thus Judaism as a whole were derived from ancient Mesopotamian mythology. Raising the issue again at their third and last encounter, Freud asserted "resolutely that the Jews had given nothing to culture" in recent times as well.[32]

One cannot but be struck by the irony of Freud's statement considering his own incalculable impact on modern culture. Freud's discernible influence on Agnon is only one, albeit significant, instance, both in terms of Hebrew literature in general and, more to the point of this article, by way of linking these two singularly creative offspring of late nineteenth-century Eastern European Jewry to each other. Freud, as we know, also shared with Müller a fascination with ancient Jewish mythology. These two Jewish men made the most of the opportunities that had opened up to members of their generation, however differently they related to their own heritage, yet their personal fates were the function of changing times and circumstances: Müller, ten years older, died just before World War I as a respected Austrian scholar. Freud fled Vienna as a hunted Jew shortly after the *Anschluss* with Germany in 1938 and lived just long enough to witness the outbreak of World War II. His four sisters were murdered in the camps. One of his last books was *Moses and Monotheism*.[33]

Most of those who left their Galician hometowns never came back, but some did. They brought with them a trace of the new world and the possibilities of a different life, as well as books, newspaper subscriptions, ideas, and opinions. But they also found themselves irretrievably back in the drudgery of provincial life. Their children, growing up among those books and magazines, ideas and disillusionments, at times decided to act where the fathers had not: to transform not

31. Grunwald, "Pegishot," 119–22; Isidore Singer, "Max Grunwald," *The Jewish Encyclopedia* (1906), http://www.jewishencyclopedia.com/articles/6911-grunwald-max.
32. Grunwald, "Pegishot," 119–22.
33. Sigmund Freud, *Moses and Monotheism*, trans. Katherine Jones (London: Hogarth, 1939) and David Cohen, *The Escape of Sigmund Freud* (London: JR Books, 2009), 178, 205–7. See also Yosef Haim Yerushalmi, *Freud's Moses. Judaism Terminable and Interminable* (New Haven, CT: Yale University Press, 1991) and Michael L. Miller, "Sigmund Freud: Reluctant Galitsianer" (paper presented at the Israel Institute for Advanced Studies, Jerusalem, May 13, 2015).

just their hometowns but the entire world. They were often adventurous, reckless, and tragic figures: their high hopes were irreparably dashed, their firm beliefs betrayed, the world of their youth wiped out, and the one that replaced it turned out to be infinitely crueler and more cynical. Many died young; some of the survivors adapted to the new reality and served its masters, while others ended their days sheltered in the margins of irrelevance. They tended to be bitter and, toward the end, were occasionally given to rather unrevolutionary nostalgia. The youngest among them belonged to my grandparents' generation.

This generational trajectory is well illustrated by the case of the Nacht family. The father, Fabius, was born in Buczacz in 1848 and raised in an affluent, German-speaking home already touched by the Haskalah. After matriculating from the Polish-language state gymnasium in Stanisławów, Fabius went on to study medicine at the University of Vienna. (He had originally aspired to acquire a degree in mathematics but abandoned that quest when he found out that Jews were not allowed to teach it in schools.) In 1879, he came back to Buczacz and opened a private medical practice. Fabius was soon recognized as one of the most respected members of the Jewish community on account of his university degree, his position as a doctor, and his "higher" German culture.[34]

But as his son Max recalled almost a century later, in response to the limitations imposed on him by "the reactionary, church-ridden Vienna regime," Fabius Nacht had also become a socialist in the early 1870s. Indeed, it was from his father, wrote Max, that "I got my first radical indoctrination."[35] Yet unlike Franzos, his exact contemporary, who was forced to study law but never practiced it, Fabius dedicated himself to his role as the most prominent medical authority in Buczacz. In 1891, a modern hospital was established in Buczacz under the direction of Fabius Nacht, a position he held for thirty-four years until his retirement at the age of seventy-seven in 1925. He was fortunate to pass away just before the outbreak of World War II. In 1942, the German occupiers, together with Ukrainian and Jewish policemen, deported the approximately 100 patients to the Bełżec extermination camp, while shooting those too sick to move in their beds. Nowadays all that is left of the hospital is an empty lot.[36]

An obituary published in the Polish Socialist Party's weekly in 1938 acclaimed Dr. Nacht as "a socialist out of conviction, a freethinker without hateful intolerance ... a rationalist filled with deep feelings, [and] an internationalist who

34. Werner Portmann, *Die wilden Schafe. Max und Siegfried Nacht. Zwei radikale, jüdische Existenzen* (Münster: Unrast, 2008), 12–15.

35. Max Nomad, *Dreamers, Dynamiters, and Demagogues* (New York: Waldon, 1964).

36. Ḥaya Roll, "Beit haḥolim uveit hamaḥseh lizqenim," in Sefer Buczacz, ed. Yisrael Cohen (Tel Aviv: 'Am 'Oved, 1956), 181–82 and Portmann, *Die wilden Schafe*, 15–17. Bundesarchiv Berlin 162/5182: "Aufklärung von NS-Verbrechen im Kreis Czortków/Distrikt Galizien, 1941–1944, Sammelverfahren gg. Brettschneider u.a.," deposition by Yehuda Bauer, January 10, 1968, 6212–14.

sympathized with all liberation movements." Even toward the end of his life, the doctor's "desk was overflowing with piles of socialist newspapers and magazines of all shades and languages."[37] It was in this home that Fabius Nacht's sons were raised as members of the first activist socialist generation in Buczacz.

In *'Ir umelo'ah*, Agnon depicts those early days of social mobilization: "An explosive new word is making the rounds in Buczacz and it is socialism." Suddenly, those who used "to work for you as servants" assert that "every person is his own master and does not belong to anyone else"; they "used to work from daybreak till midnight," but now they "stop working after eight hours." As Agnon observed, in this struggle for social justice, not a few Jewish "sons of the wealthy who appeared to want for nothing [...] joined the socialists, and no father could be certain that his son would not carry out some action that would land him in prison or that he would not marry the daughter of a worker." All those who thought that "Zionism is the worst of all upheavals in the world" now "discovered that there are even greater upheavals," since Buczacz had become "a city of socialists."[38]

One center of political ferment was Fabius Nacht's home, described in his obituary as "the meeting point for socialist youths of all nationalities."[39] The local leader was Anselm Mosler, whom Max Nacht recalled as "the only citizen of our town ever to accomplish" the "intellectual feat" of earning two doctorates from Vienna University, in law and philosophy. Having spent eighteen months in a Russian prison for smuggling illegal literature, Mosler returned to Buczacz and organized a socialist association that, despite its Ukrainian name, was, according to Max, "exclusively Jewish, for the Gentile workers, Roman Catholic Poles and Uniate Catholic Ukrainians were under the influence of their respective clergymen and would not join such a society." In any case, as he pointed out, the majority of the population in Buczacz "consisted of Yiddish-speaking Jews," while the remaining Polish and Ukrainian inhabitants "hated and despised each other even more than they did the Jews."[40]

Born in Buczacz in 1881, Max Nacht became a Marxist by the ripe age of fourteen and was an early member of Mosler's group. He and his older brother Siegfried attended public school, where they learned Polish and Ukrainian. Siegfried soon joined the social democratic movement and was expelled from two secondary schools in a row for conspiratorial activities before finally matriculating in the larger city of Stanisławów in 1895.[41]

37. *Tydzień Robotnika* (Warsaw, Lemberg Edition) no. 6, February 6, 1938, cited in Portmann, *Die wilden Schafe*, 18–19.
38. Agnon, *'Ir umelo'ah*, 644–46. See references to socialism in pre-1914 Buczacz in S.Y. Agnon, *Sippur Pashut* (1935), in *'Al kappot haman'ul* (Tel Aviv: Schocken, 1998), 58, 71.
39. *Tydzień Robotnika*, in Portmann, *Die wilden Schafe*, 23.
40. Nomad, *Dreamers*, 7.
41. Portmann, *Die wilden Schafe*, 11–12, 23–27, 30; "Autobiographical Sketch," in *Max Nomad Papers 1902–1967*, Tamiment Library, New York; Zvi Heller, "Mezikhronotai," and Naftali

By then, Max, too, had become radicalized; turning to anarchism, he broke with his former idol Mosler, whom he accused of wanting to go "beyond cultivating his own garden, with its few scores of Jewish tailors, carpenters, locksmiths, salesmen, butchers, and shoemakers," so as "to play a more important role," especially "in the Polish section of the Austrian Socialist party." Yet Mosler's "first bid for leadership," recalled Max, "met with such bitter abuse that he resigned from that party and joined the newly organized Jewish Social-Democratic Party," formed after it had been denied recognition both by the Austrian socialists and by the Polish section. To Max, writing about these events six decades later, this demonstrated the effects of Polish and Austrian socialists' anti-Semitism, leading to Mosler's "utterly ridiculous... sudden conversion to Yiddish separatism," considering that he was a former "assimilationist who was unable to speak Yiddish."[42]

In fact, Mosler had not entirely given up on trying to revolutionize the local population. In 1905, he began publishing a bilingual Polish-Ukrainian monthly newsletter directed at the "peasants of the Buczacz district and other districts of Podolia" with the goal of enlightening the largely illiterate farm laborers about their rights and helping them resist abuse and exploitation.[43] Yet, as many of the peasants' letters to this short-lived newsletter show, their sense of injustice and resentment often translated into rage against the Jews. Disillusioned and impoverished, Mosler finally put an end to his career as an agitator and receded from the scene. Living in Vienna during World War I, he finally succumbed to the tuberculosis he had contracted in the Russian prison as a young revolutionary.

But Mosler did make one last ghostly appearance in Agnon's great novel, *Oreaḥ natah lalun* (*A Guest for the Night*), over two decades after his death, under the evocative fictional name Knabenhut. Based on Agnon's last visit to his hometown in 1930, the novel depicts his protagonist's encounter with Aharon Schützling, a character bearing a striking resemblance to Max Nacht. Both the narrator and Schützling had left Buczacz many years earlier and are keenly aware of how profoundly both the city and their own outlooks have changed since their departure. "Although we differed in our opinions," observers the narrator, "for I was a Zionist and he an anarchist, we were glad to talk to each other."[44]

Menatseach, "Miyemei ne'urai," in *Sefer Buczacz*, ed. Yisrael Cohen (Tel Aviv: 'Am 'Oved, 1956), 158 and 173, respectively.

42. Nomad, *Dreamers*, 8–9.

43. *Służba dworska: Gazeta dla robotników rolnych powiatu buczackiego i innych powiatów podolskich* 1 (June 1905): 1–3, *Biblioteka Sejmowa*, P. 50730. See also Heller, "Mezikhronotai," 150.

44. S.Y. Agnon, *Oreaḥ natah lalun*, rev. ed. (Tel Aviv: Schocken, 1998), 228–29. The novel was translated by Misha Louvish as *A Guest for the Night* (Madison: University of Wisconsin Press, 1968). See also references to Knabenhut in Agnon, *Sippur pashut*, 58, 71, 200–201.

As they contemplate their respective disillusionments, they remember Knabenhut, who is "dead and gone." Schützling is beset with nostalgia: "Days like those will never return. Strikes during the day and wild parties at night." But then he recalls a chance meeting with Knabenhut in wartime Vienna. The latter, he says, had "fumed at me for becoming an anarchist, and some said that he had denounced me to the authorities, and I had to flee to America." This time, the disheveled Knabenhut lectured him "about the war and the destruction that is in store for us and the entire world." He was gravely ill, and his last words were just a whisper: "The generation that is about to come will be worse than all the generations that preceded us," he prophesized. "The world is becoming ever uglier, uglier than either I or you had ever sought to make it."[45]

This prophecy expressed Agnon's own foreboding at the time of the novel's publication in 1939. His narrator recalled how Knabenhut had empowered the "wretched boys" of Buczacz, "who were treated like cattle, tyrannized day and night by their masters." But the anarchists blamed him for refusing to accept that "the world can only be repaired through eradication," whereas he viewed them, in Agnon's words, as "rabid zealots, ready to sacrifice themselves and the whole world as well."[46] To be sure, while the fictional anarchist Schützling somehow wound his way to wartime Vienna, the real Max and Siegfried Nacht were already in the United States by the time the war broke out, having also given up on their efforts to change the world after years of revolutionary activities across Europe.

In the years between his departure from Buczacz and immigration to the United States, Siegfried was transformed into an itinerant revolutionary. Having acquired a degree in electrical engineering in Vienna, he could not find an appropriate position because of his Jewish background and socialist politics. At the same time, as a member of the Austrian Social Democratic Party, he came out against Zionism and, in 1897, officially left the Vienna Jewish community. But shortly thereafter he also grew disenchanted with what he perceived as the nationalism, anti-Semitism, and parliamentarism of the Social Democrats, embraced anarchism, and moved to Berlin, from which he traveled, mostly on foot, from one revolutionary cell to another. In April 1903 he crossed into Gibraltar and was promptly arrested on suspicion of plotting to assassinate King Edward VII during his planned visit to the British territory. The pistol he regularly carried did not help matters.

Siegfried's arrest made waves throughout Europe. Polish émigrés in Paris and Ruthenian socialists in Vienna protested. In London, a committee was formed under the leadership of Russian anarchist Peter Kropotkin and the philosopher Herbert Spencer (who died just a few months later). Siegfried's younger brother

45. Agnon, *Oreaḥ*, 234–35.
46. Agnon, *Oreaḥ*, 235–41. See also Yehuda Mosner, "Maine yugent yoren in Buchach," in *Pinkes Galitsye*, ed. Nekhemya Tsuke (Buenos Aires: Galitsyaner Farband, 1945), 476.

Max described the response to the arrest in Buczacz, noting sarcastically that Siegfried was transformed overnight from "the disgrace of the town," into "a national hero, the fame and pride of the place." Moreover, Siegfried was called "an engineer" and "an author" in Polish newspapers and was said to have come under the protection of "a former minister, a real countess," and "an actual prince." With such credentials, commented Max, the town of Buczacz came to view Siegfried as nothing less than an "eighth wonder of the world." In Agnon's *Oreaḥ natah lalun*, Siegfried appears as Sigmund Winter, "the son of a doctor and one of Knabenhut's disciples," who "was distinguished among his friends by his black hair and beautiful eyes that he would make at young women." The narrator recalls Winter's victorious visit to his hometown following his release for lack of evidence a few weeks after his arrest in Gibraltar. He was "holding his head high like a prince, a black cape over his shoulders with its hem flowing down below his knees, a black hat on his head slightly tilted to one side, his moustache rolled upward and his beard descending in the shape of a half Star of David." Indeed, the young revolutionary "was walking as if" the whole city "belonged to him," surrounded as he was by "beautiful maidens from the best families" with "all the officials making way for him." It all sounded a little like Mordecai the Jew's triumphant march through the city of Shushan following his victory over Haman the Agagite.[47]

This was Siegfried's finest hour. In 1912 he immigrated to the United States and was joined there by his brother the following year. Max had begun studying law at Vienna in 1900, but he soon teamed up with fellow student Mykhailo Lozynsky, a Ukrainian poet, journalist, and political agitator, to produce a single issue of a projected anarchist periodical, which led to their arrest and indictment for high treason by the Austrian authorities. Max, who somehow escaped to Switzerland, ruminated years later that, had it not been for this event, "I most likely would have remained in Austria to die for my Emperor during World War I, or, in case of survival, to be gassed by Eichmann during World War II." By then, he rationalized his adoption of anarchism as "compensation for the personal sense of inadequacy and insecurity of the impractical son of a radical Jewish physician." Conversely, he saw his Ukrainian comrade's anarchism as the "expression of a nationalist intellectual's protest against the Austro-Polish landed nobility," who "were oppressing four million Ukrainian peasants" in Galicia. Yet, in the wake of World War I, Max noted, Lozynsky "capitulated to Moscow, taking a job with one of the Ukrainian scientific institutions in Kiev." Nevertheless, during the Great Purges of the late 1930s he

---

47. Portmann, *Die wilden Schafe*, 55–58, citing Maxt Nacht, "Anarchistenjagd," *Neues Leben* 23 (June 6, 1903) and 24 (June 13, 1903) and Agnon, *Oreaḥ*, 236–38, where the narrator also praises Knabenhut for having "learned to speak Yiddish, so that he could speak with his comrades [in the Buczacz socialist cell] in their language. Which was not the case with most of our [Zionist] leaders, who were too lazy even to learn the Hebrew alphabet."

"was shot along with all the other well-known Ukrainian intellectuals who had ever shown any Ukrainian nationalist inclination."[48]

In the United States, the brothers changed their names to Stephen Naft and Max Nomad and lived most of the rest of their lives in New York City.[49] Max achieved certain notoriety in the American left. The eminent critic Edmund Wilson wrote an introduction to Nomad's 1961 book, *Aspects of Revolt*, where he described him as a "connoisseur of radicals" not least because he was, in his own words, "a Socialist in my high-school days, an Anarchist as a college student, a Syndicalist *sui generis* during the years of my romantic and not-so-romantic vagabondage, and finally a Soviet sympathizer some forty years ago when Lenin and Trotsky were still glorious legends, between 1917 and 1920."[50]

To lifelong professional revolutionaries, Mosler and the Nacht brothers would have appeared as mere dilettantes who ended up betraying their ideals. Adolf Langer, born in Buczacz in 1892, just eleven years Max Nacht's junior and five years younger than Agnon, had the temperament and perseverance of the numerous apparatchiks who have populated so much of the twentieth century. After his death, his communist colleagues noted vaguely that he was raised "in an atmosphere of patriotism and democratic ideals." In fact he was the son of Joachim Langer, director of the Baron Hirsch School, where classes were held in Polish but German, Ruthenian, and some Hebrew were also taught; Joachim's wife, described by one of her former students as "a beautiful blond," taught there as well, while he offered additional extracurricular classes on Jewish religion at the Buczacz state gymnasium, which his son Adolf also attended.[51] In the small universe of Jewish Buczacz most people knew each other: Markus (Mordechai) Kanfer, a teacher at the Baron Hirsch School and an essayist for Hebrew-language magazines, also taught Agnon German and some Polish; Markus's son Mojżesz (Moshe) attended gymnasium with Siegfried Nacht and later became an important intellectual figure in interwar Kraków. He and his wife were murdered in the Holocaust but their daughter, Irène (Irma) Kanfer, became a well-known postwar French poet. Markus Kanfer's daughter Sabina (Sara) became romantically involved with Max Nacht and apparently had a son by him in Paris before he left for the United States. I met Alain Kanfer, a retired physician and Sabina's

48. Portmann, *Die wilden Schafe*, 30–34 and Nomad, *Dreamers*, 11–14. See also John Kolasky, ed., *Prophets and Proletarians: Documents on the History of the Rise and Decline of Ukrainian Communism in Canada* (Edmonton: Canadian Institute of Ukrainian Studies Press, 1990), 212–13.
49. Portmann, *Die wilden Schafe*, 117–18.
50. Edmund Wilson, introduction to *Aspects of Revolt: A Study in Revolutionary Theories and Techniques* by Max Nomad (New York: Noonday, 1961), vii. Siegfried's pamphlet "The Social General Strike," published under the name Arnold Roller in 1905, is still available; see Robert Graham's Anarchism Weblog, September 10, 2010, https://robertgraham.wordpress.com/2010/09/10/siegfried-nacht-the-social-general-strike-1905/.
51. Menatseach, "Miyemei ne'urai." 168–69; "Droga życiowa Ostapa Dłuskiego," n.d., Akta Ostapa Dłuskiego, *Archiwum Akt Nowych* (AAN), 450/I-1, 1; *Sprawozdanie dyrekcyi C. K. Gimnazyum w Buczaczu za rok szkolny 1901* (Lwów, 1901), 36–39.

(and likely Max's) grandson, in 2001 in Paris; raised as a Roman Catholic, he was trying to recover his roots in Jewish Buczacz.[52]

By the time Adolf enrolled as a philosophy student in Vienna University in 1914, he had become a member of the Austrian Social Democratic Party but, two years later, shifted his loyalties to its "revolutionary left wing grouped around Lenin."[53] A founding member of the Austrian Communist Party in 1918, Langer led the establishment of the Communist Party of Eastern Galicia the following year. In 1921, he chaired its national conference in Lwów, where the mostly Ukrainian Galician communists clashed with the Polish representatives over the demand to retain their autonomy in newly independent Poland. Ironically, the twenty-nine-year-old Jewish communist Adolf Langer, now known by the more Polish-sounding name Ostap Dłuski, was charged with resolving this largely ethnonational crisis within the new Polish Communist Party.[54]

Not unlike Mosler, and despite being a loyal communist, Dłuski had much sympathy for the Ukrainians. He spoke frankly about Poland's "brutal suppression of the Ukrainian nation" in 1919, and stressed that even the Polish communists "came to us not with a vehement, all-inclusive protest against the horrors that were committed, but rather with the slogan 'Polish Soviet Republic,' which to us was incomprehensible, alien, and aroused suspicion." In fact, while three quarters of the Galician communists were Ukrainian, and Jews were prominent among the leadership, the majority of the Ukrainian population of Eastern Galicia, mostly made up of peasants, was strongly anti-Polish. As Dłuski noted at the time, the "simple Ukrainian" responded to assertions by Polish communists that "this was one state" by saying: "You are nationalists, you are exactly like the other bourgeois parties."

The 1921 conference came to an abrupt end when the Polish authorities arrested all the delegates. At the trial, Dłuski unflinchingly professed his belief

52. Dan Laor, *Ḥayyei Agnon* (Tel Aviv: Schocken, 1998), 22; Heller, "Mezikhronotai," 155–58; David Pohorille, "Pirqei havai," in *Sefer Buczacz*, ed. Yisrael Cohen (Tel Aviv: 'Am 'Oved, 1956), 199–200; letter to author from Alain Kanfer, Paris, March 22, 2010, and enclosed documents, including Sara Kanfer's certificate of residence in Buczacz dated 1912, and a certificate by a police prefect in Paris dated May 1915, stating that she was born in Buczacz to Markus and Civje Herman Kanfer and arrived in Paris in August 1912; email to author from Alain Kanfer, June 14, 2010; Portmann, *Die wilden Schafe*, 85 and n. 522, 111 and n. 673, 117–18; Eugenia Prokop-Janiec, "Mojżesz Kanfer a teatr jidysz," in *Teatr żydowski w Krakowie*, ed. Jan Michalik and Eugenia Prokop-Janiec (Kraków: Uniwersytet Jagielloński, Międzywydziałowy Zakład Historii i Kultury Żydów w Polsce, 1995), 125–50; and Sean Martin, *Jewish Life in Cracow, 1918–1939* (London: Vallentine Mitchell, 2004), 66, 111–19, 218–33. Irène Kanfer also translated from Yiddish and Polish the volume *Le Luth brisé. Première anthologie en français de poèmes du ghetto et des camps* (Paris: Presses du temps présent, 1965).
53. Droga życiowa, 1. See also "Dłuski Ostap—Langer Adolf (1892–1964)," *Słownik Biograficzny Działaczy Polskiego Ruchu Robotniczego*, ed. Feliks Tych, 2nd ed., 2 vols. (Warsaw: Książka i Wiedza, 1985, 1987), 2:585–86.
54. "Dłuski," *Słownik* and Droga życiowa, 1–2. See also Roman Solchanyk, "The Foundation of the Communist Movement in Eastern Galicia, 1919–1921," *Slavic Review* 30, no. 4 (1971): 774–94.

that "only communism could eliminate the oppression, poverty, and misery of humanity," and that the Soviet Union marked "a new beginning in the progress of humankind."[55] Throughout his life, at least publicly, Dłuski never wavered from this position and, following his release from prison in 1923, made a career in the Polish Communist Party, becoming a member of the Central Committee and later head of its National Secretariat. In 1936, he moved to France in order to liaise with the French Communist Party.[56] When the Polish government dissolved the Communist Party in 1938, Dłuski remained in France, resuming underground activities following the German invasion of the Soviet Union in 1941. With the French police hot on his heels, in 1942, he went into hiding in a shack owned by Dr. Edgar Longuet, Karl Marx's grandson and mayor of Alfortville near Paris, where he spent several months composing a lengthy German-language indictment of Nazism. In his only known written reference to the ongoing Nazi genocide, Dłuski condemned Hitler's "bloodhounds," who "drag millions of unarmed Jews in all occupied lands out of their houses, bring them to Poland, and heinously slaughter them there in slaughterhouses built especially for this purpose, among them hundreds of thousands of Jewish children."[57]

By 1943, Dłuski was back in action, organizing a Ukrainian underground in France, editing the Ukrainian-language magazine *Fatherland*, and justifying Stalin's takeover and reordering of Eastern Europe in a series of French-language articles. The Soviet Union, he asserted without a trace of irony, "had made the principle of liberty and independence of peoples into the basis of its *raison d'état* and of its foreign policy," because "a nation that oppresses another people cannot be free."[58] In a victory speech he delivered in liberated Paris in 1945, Dłuski blamed the recent crushing of the Polish uprising and the destruction of Warsaw by the Wehrmacht as the Red Army stood by on "the egotistical politics" of those who "wanted to drive a wedge into the Allies' front," to which "the heroic people

55. Stefan Królikowski and A. Hołówka, eds., *Proces komunistów we Lwowie (sprawa świętojurska) sprawozdanie stenograficzne* (Warsaw: Książka i Wiedza, 1958), 114–28; Franciszka Świetlikowa, *Komunistyczna Partia Robotnicza Polski 1918–1923* (Warsaw: Książka i Wiedza, 1968), 279–306; Solchanyk, "Foundation," 788–91; "Relacje tow. Dłuskiego," AAN, 450/I-3, 1–5 (c. 1960); and Droga życiowa, 2.
56. "Relacje tow. Dłuskiego," 8–12 and "Dłuski," *Słownik*. See also, e.g., O. Dłuski, "Pan Beck oszukuje społeczeństwo polskie," *Correspondance Internationale*, published in Paris, AAN, 450/IV-4 (1937). For Dłuski's interwar Polish police file, see AAN, 450/I-2.
57. Oswald Ostenrode (Ostap Dłuski), "Die Rostowlüge und ihre Folgen. Ein Kapitel aus der Broschüre 'Deutschland ein Schauermarchen oder der Weg zur Freiheit,' mit einem Aufruf an den Leser. Beitrag zur Entlarvung des Hitlerismus," manuscript, January 7, 1943, AAN, 450/VI-1, 4–5.
58. Ostap Dłuski, "Il n'y a qu'un seul chemin qui mène à la l'indépendance" and "Aux immigrants slaves en France," AAN, 450/II-69, 20–23, 72–76, respectively (undated, likely late 1943 and early 1944).

of Warsaw fell victim."[59] He made no reference to the Warsaw Ghetto uprising of 1943 or to the extermination camps overrun by Soviets.

Dłuski's firm Stalinism seems to have been shaken only once. On July 4, 1946, the bloodiest postwar pogrom in Europe took place in the Polish town of Kielce; over forty Jewish survivors of the Holocaust were butchered. Altogether between 500 and 1,500 Jews were murdered in Poland in the immediate aftermath of the war.[60] Back in Warsaw as member of the Central Committee, on July 29, Dłuski proposed to his colleagues "that an institution be established which would facilitate departure of the Jews from Poland, so that they could join their families." He went so far as to take note of the Jewish community's disappointment with the lack of democracy in Poland and the fact that Władysław Gomułka—at the time deputy prime minister and de facto ruler of Poland—had not made a single reference to the situation of the Jews in a five-hour speech to the Communist Party.[61] In 1968 Gomułka, by then leader of the renamed Polish United Workers' Party, expelled the remaining Jews from the country.[62]

Dłuski's brief preoccupation with anti-Semitism in Poland may have been mostly motivated by the communists' attempt to accuse their enemies at home and abroad of inciting anti-Jewish sentiments, but it is at least possible that he was also personally shaken by the violence that followed the destruction of the world into which he was born.[63] Subsequently, Dłuski became engaged mainly in propagandistic humanitarian activities.[64] When given the opportunity to speak publicly about Nazi crimes, as on the occasion of Goethe's 200th anniversary in 1949, Dłuski refrained from any mention of Holocaust.[65] Conversely, after Sta-

59. "La Pologne nouvelle et la France en face de l'impérialisme germanique," attributed to "M. André Dluski, Représentant du Comité Polonais de Libération Nationale en France, Centre d'Étude de Politique Étrangère," February 28, 1945, AAN 450/II-71, 9–10. In a questionnaire for admittance into the Central Committee of the Polish Workers' Party dated July 17, 1945, he identified himself as "Andrzej Dłuski (Adolf Langer)," being "of Jewish origins, Polish," and "leader of the Ukrainian resistance movement in France." AAN 450/I-1.
60. Jan T. Gross, *Fear: Anti-Semitism in Poland after Auschwitz. An Essay in Historical Interpretation* (New York: Random House, 2006), 35 and David Engel, "Patterns of Anti-Jewish Violence in Poland, 1944–1946," *Yad Vashem Studies* 26 (1998): 43–85.
61. Gross, *Fear*, 125 and Joanna Beata Michlic, *Poland's Threatening Other: The Image of the Jew from 1880 to the Present* (Lincoln: University of Nebraska Press, 2006), 211.
62. Dariusz Stola, "Fighting against the Shadows: The Anti-Zionist Campaign of 1968," in *Antisemitism and Its Opponents in Modern Poland*, ed. Robert Blobaum (Ithaca, NY: Cornell University Press, 2005), 284–300.
63. "Dłuski," *Słownik*; *Droga życiowa*, 4; and Bożena Szaynok, "The Role of Antisemitism in Postwar Polish-Jewish Relations," in *Antisemitism and Its Opponents in Modern Poland*, ed. Robert Blobaum (Ithaca, NY: Cornell University Press, 2005), 274–75.
64. See, e.g., Dłuski's article for the organ of the World Peace Council in 1955: "Pour une vaste tribune de discussion," AAN, 450/IV-24.
65. Ostap Dłuski, "Aussprache während der 'Goethefeier in Warschau,'" AAN, 450/III-103, 6–7.

lin's death in 1953, which put an end to the anti-Jewish campaign he had just unleashed, Dłuski depicted his memory as "eternally alive, warm and sincere," and described the Bolshevik Party as representing "the highest achievements of advanced human thought."[66] No wonder that, following his death in 1964 at the age of seventy-two, he was described as "a model communist."[67] He certainly had impeccable timing; four years later he would likely have been unmasked as the crypto-Jew Adolf Langer and expelled from Poland as a fifth column Zionist.

Still, for all the ideological baggage Dłuski piled up between himself and Buczacz, he always remained within the Polish sphere on whose periphery he was raised. Others, who had wandered much farther, remained attached to the world they had striven to leave behind. Max Nacht acknowledged toward the end of his life that his worldview had initially been forged in Buczacz. Müller, whose move across the Carpathians to a Vienna professorship was a giant step for members of his generation, drew greatly on his early years in Buczacz and was pained by rumors about his lack of loyalty to its community. Agnon spent a lifetime writing about Galicia; had he lived longer, he might have continued compiling ever more stories about Buczacz because, in the aftermath of destruction, "building a city," as he depicted the writing of *'Ir umelo'ah*, "in its fullness," could not but be a never-ending labor of love:

> For if my city has been wiped out of the world, its name exists in the poem that the poet has written as a sign of my city. And if I do not remember the words of the poem because of its greatness, the poem resonates in the heavens above among the poems of the holy poets beloved of God.[68]

In different ways, they were all trailblazers: coming from the margin they struggled to make themselves known to the world and in the process became part of its remaking.

OMER BARTOV is the John P. Birkelund Distinguished Professor of European History at Brown University. He is the author of *Anatomy of a Genocide: The Life and Death of a Town Called Buczacz*, along with several other well-respected scholarly works on the Holocaust and genocide, including *Hitler's Army, Germany's War and the Holocaust: Disputed Histories* and *Erased: Vanishing Traces of Jewish Galicia in Present-Day Ukraine*. His new book, *Tales from the Borderlands: Making and Unmaking the Past*, will be published in 2021.

66. Dłuski on Stalin, AAN, 450/IV-21, 1, 9. See also Joshua Rubenstein and Vladimir P. Naumov, eds., *Stalin's Secret Pogrom: The Postwar Inquisition of the Jewish Anti-Fascist Committee*, trans. Laura Esther Wolfson (New Haven, CT: Yale University Press, 2001).
67. "Dłuski," *Słownik*; *Droga życiowa*, 5. See Dłuski's death certificate, AAN, 450/V-1.
68. Agnon, *'Ir umelo'ah*, 716.

11 *Beaking the Idyll: Rereading Flaubert's Madame Bovary and Agnon's* Sippur pashut *through Devorah Baron's "Fradl"*

Wendy Zierler

Tucked away among the hundreds of volumes in S.Y. Agnon's personal library in Beit Agnon is a copy of Devorah Baron's 1933 book, *Ketanot*, inscribed with the following dedication:

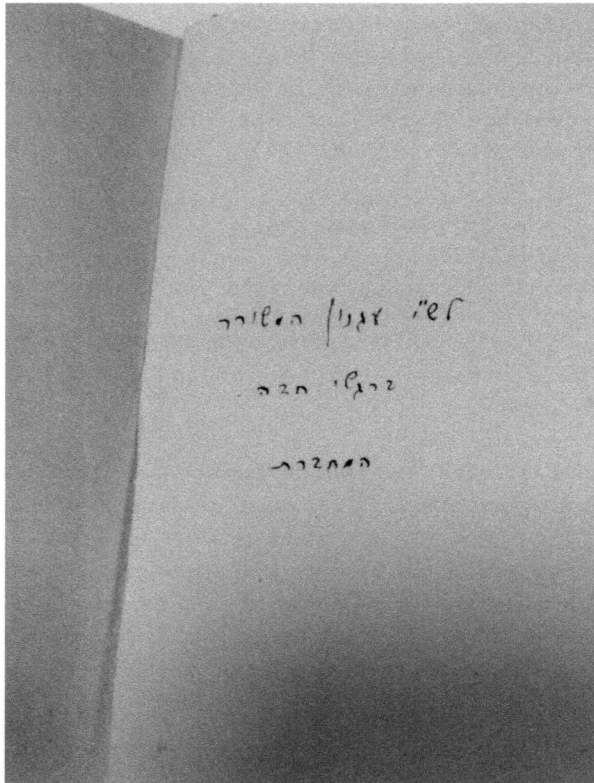

Figure 6: Courtesy of Agnon House.
To Shai Agnon, the Poet
With Fond Feeling
The Author

Building a City: Writings on Agnon's Buczacz in Memory of Alan Mintz (2022): 140–166
DOI: 10.2979/BuildingaCityWriting.0.0.12

At first blush, the inscription seems unexceptional, significant only as a marker of an ongoing, connection between Agnon (1888–1970) and Baron (1887–1956) that dates back to 1910 when they both lived in Neve Tsedek and Baron served on the editorial staff of *Hapo'el Hatsa'ir*, where both writers published early works of fiction.[1] Baron's reference to Agnon as "Hameshorer" (the poet) rather than as "Hasofer" (the writer) might seem odd given Agnon's major reputation as a prose artist.[2] Then again, Agnon filled his 1931 novel *Hakhnasat kallah* with verse, ending with a rhymed coda that includes both terms used in the inscription: "Tamu divrei hamehabber / vehameshorer beshir yedabber" ("The words of the author have been completed / the poet will speak in verse").[3] Agnon fancied himself a Levite, a descendant of the biblical *meshorerim*, and employed the term *meshorer* as a high form of literary praise.[4] We see this in a 1916 letter to his patron Zalman Schocken about Gustave Flaubert, where he praises the French realist master's unstinting dedication to his craft, describing him as "hameshorer shehayah mei-

I began working on a joint study of Agnon and Baron in 2013. Alan Mintz was one of the first people to respond to my preliminary efforts to establish the contours of this new project. His February 5, 2014 email to me in response to an early draft of this paper was helpful in prodding me to consider "some consideration of the role that genre plays here," given that "*Sippur pashut* is a novel, although not in the epic, sprawling tradition of *Hakhnasat kallah* and the others," while "Fradl is something else, a long short story [...] This must be a factor," Alan insisted, "in the compositional options each writer takes advantage of and is limited by." Alan also urged me to consider the interpretive benefit of comparing these three texts. Five years later, this article attempts to address Alan's queries. I only wish he would have been able to read and comment on whether they had been properly answered. I also wish I could be consulting with him in the editing of *Prooftexts, the journal* that he helped found. Thanks go out to the Hadassah Brandeis Institute for their financial support of this project; to Nitza Ben-Dov, Yael Halevi-Wise, David Aberbach, and Robert Alter for sources and insight; to Yoram Bitton, Tina Weiss, and Marilyn Krider of the HUC-JIR Libraries for research assistance; to Allison Schachter and Sheila Jelen for helpful feedback; and to Jeffrey Saks, who not only commented carefully on an early draft but also hosted me at Beit Agnon, and located a copy of Baron's translation of *Madame Bovary* as well as the copy of Baron's *Ketanot*, inscribed by Baron, featured above.
1. For evidence of the early correspondence between Agnon and Baron's husband Yosef Aharonovitz that also refers to Baron, see S.Y. Agnon, *Missod ḥakhamim: mikhtavim 1909–1970* (Jerusalem: Schocken, 2002), 18–20, letters 8 and 9.
2. Young Agnon also wrote a good deal poetry. For more on his earliest writings, see Yitzhak Bakun, *Agnon hatsa'ir* (Tel Aviv: Dekel, 1989).
3. S.Y. Agnon, *Hakhnaset kallah*, vol. 1 of *Kol sippurav shel Shmuel Yosef Agnon* (Jerusalem: Schocken, 1952), תע (translation mine).
4. See, e.g., Ezra 2:41; 10:24; Nehemiah 7:44; 10:29; 11:22, 12:28, 12:29, 12:42. In his story "Ḥush hareiaḥ" ("The Sense of Smell"), Agnon writes of how, as a Levite, he would be standing together with his brothers, the *meshorerim*, singing the daily Levite song if the temple in Jerusalem were still standing; see S.Y. Agnon, *Eilu ve'eilu*, Volume 2 of *Kol sippurav shel S.Y. Agnon*, (Jerusalem: Schocken, 1959), רי"ז. See also Shmuel Agnon, "Banquet Speech," The Nobel Prize, December 10, 1966, https://www.nobelprize.org/nobel_prizes/literature/laureates/1966/agnon-speech.html.

meit 'atsmo be'oholah shel hashirah" ("a poet who mortified himself in the Tent of Poetry").[5] By the time she inscribed this book for Agnon, Baron had already published her classic translation of Flaubert's *Madame Bovary*[6]; without doubt, she shared Agnon's regard for Flaubert's economical style and psychological characterizations, as well as his detailed depiction of small-town life. Given their common admiration of Flaubert, Baron's inscription to Agnon as "Hameshorer" (the poet) might be understood simply as way of praising the major literary achievements of a respected colleague.

Closer inspection, however, reveals another potential meaning for the inscription, given that, from early on, critics often characterized Baron's fiction as a form of poetry in prose. In one of the earliest published articles about her fiction, Dov Kimḥi, avers that, in essence, Baron doesn't write stories at all; "these [works] are really tiny idylls."[7] The title of a 1934 article in *Hado'ar* about her fiction boasts the title, "meshoreret ha'ayarah Devorah Baron" ("Shtetl poet Devorah Baron")[8] Yaakov Fichman describes her fiction as "hashirah hamutsaqah hazo't" ("this solid poetry"), while Asher Barash would later dub Baron, in his introduction to *Parshiyot*, her 1951 volume of collected stories, "hameshoreret

---

5. In this using this expression, Agnon substituted the word *shirah* for *torah*, thereby revising a statement from BT Berakhot 63b: Reish Lakish said: Whence do we learn that the words of the Torah are firmly held by one who kills himself for it? Because it says, 'This is the Torah, when a man shall die in the tent'" (Soncino translation from https://halakhah.com/berakoth/berakoth_63.html). For more on Agnon's admiration of Flaubert as a model "for the painstaking devotion to the writer's craft," see Robert Alter, "The Great Genius of Jewish Literature," *New York Review of Books* (April 6, 2017), http://www.nybooks.com/articles/2017/04/06/sy-agnon-great-genius-jewish-literature/. For the letter, see *Sh. Y. Agnon–Sh. Z. Schocken: Ḥilufei iggerot* (Jerusalem: Schocken, 1991), 36–37. In a letter from Agnon to Dov Sadan, in which Agnon denies being influenced by Kafka, he admits to reading Homer, Cervantes, Balzac, Gogol, Tolstoy, Flaubert, and Hamsun; see S.Y. Agnon, *Me'atsmi el 'atsmi* (Tel Aviv: Schocken, 1976), 245.
6. Gustave Flaubert, *Madam Bovary: roman*, trans. Devorah Baron (Tel Aviv: Sifriyat Hapo'alim, 1966). "Misfrei ha'onah," *Lamerḥav* (January 17, 1958), 8, a roundup of the season's literary offerings, includes a hundred-year anniversary reprinting of *Madame Bovary* in Baron's translation (it had already been reprinted several times since its original 1932 publication), which it describes as a "targum mofet," a classic translation that maintains the clarity and precision of Flaubert's style. See also Y. Livkhi, "Haroman ladorot," *Ma'ariv* (January 17, 1958), 15.
7. See Dov Kimḥi's essay, "Devorah Baron: Lidemutah hasifrutit," in Ada Pagis, ed., *Devorah Baron: Mivḥar ma'amarim 'al yetsiratah* (Tel Aviv: 'Am 'Oved, 1974), 23. A later review by Kimḥi of Baron's book, *Ketanot*, refers to the stories as *shirah hazo't shelah* ("this poetry of hers"); see Dov Kimḥi, "Me'aron hasefarim," *Do'ar hayyom* (11 August 1933), 6. F. Laḥover's essay, "Devorah Baron," in Pagis, *Devorah Baron*, 26 makes a similar observation, referring to "the almost idyllic quiet" of Baron's descriptions. Likewise, Y. Lichtenbaum's essay, "Devorah Baron," in Pagis, *Devorah Baron*, 31 writes of the reader passing from "the tiny, from the extremely quiet idyll, to the lofty and the sublime [...] of poetry sprouting as if organically from ugly matter."
8. Y. Ovsei, "Meshoreret ha'ayarah Devorah Baron," *Hado'ar* 13, no. 16 (Adar 8, 1934): 315–16.

biprosah," or the "poetess of prose."[9] On the one hand, this talk of the poetic quality of her fiction reads as admiring praise of her concise, resonant style. On the other hand, the habit of calling her a poet in prose becomes a way of lumping her together with the other prominent female Hebrew literary figures of her day, all of whom were poets: Rachel Bluwstein, Esther Raab, Yokheved Bat Miriam, Elisheva Bikhovsky, and Anda Pinkefeld Amir. This, together with the frequent attention to the idyllic, retrospective, shtetl-centered subject matter, drawn as if unfiltered from Baron's own memories of her shtetl youth, serves to downplay the element of currency, invention, and narrative ambition in Baron's work.[10] Add to this Baron's relatively slim literary output, which Agnon himself lamented in a letter to Baron, even as he praised the stories in her book, *Ketanot*: "May you be blessed for the good hours that I spent next to your stories. Were I to come and write you all that I liked and took pleasure in from this book, I would have to copy over every page and verse. You have so much in you and yet you write so little. A pity."[11] In this context, being a *meshoreret*, a short-form artist, amounts to being something decidedly less than a novelist—a creator, very literally, of idyllic *ketanot*, small works too brief and few in number to earn serious literary regard.

In dubbing Agnon "hameshorer" and calling herself "hamehabberet" might Baron have been trying shrug off the sense of limited or stereotypically feminine accomplishment associated with being labeled an idyllic, small-form poet in prose? Was Baron attempting for a moment to shed the poet moniker and foist it on her better known male contemporary, who, like she, often wrote about the town of his youth, yet, in marked contrast to the difficulty she had in securing a publisher for her first book (which finally appeared in 1927, twenty-five years after she published her first story), was never charged with being a mere memoirist or writer of simple shtetl idylls?[12]

To be clear: Baron wrote short stories and novellas; she practiced brevity and restraint and never undertook to write an epic novel about Erets Yisra'el like Agnon's *Temol shilshom*. Her book *Ketanot* was indeed quite small, not just in

9. Yaakov Fichman, "Yetsirat Devorah Baron," in Pagis, *Devorah Baron*, 59 and Asher Barash, "Hameshoreret biprosah," in *Parshiyot* by Devorah Baron (Jerusalem: Mossad Bialik, 1968), 5–6, respectively. Barash's introduction also appeared in *Hapo'el hatsa'ir*, Shevat 16, 5711/January 23, 1951 and was reprinted in Pagis, *Devorah Baron*, 46–47.
10. For a discussion of the mythic/idyllic aspects of Baron's fiction, see see Dan Miron, "The Endless Cycle: The Poetic World of Dvora Baron," in *Hebrew, Gender, and Modernity: Critical Responses to Dvora Baron's Fiction*, ed. Sheila E. Jelen and Shachar Pinsker (College Park: University of Maryland Press, 2007), 17–32.
11. Letter dated Tuesday, Parashat Vayera Eilav, תרצ"ד [October 31, 1933], from the Genazim Archives. Published in *Yedi'ot genazim* 99, no. 8 (year 14, 1981), 16.
12. Note that, while Baron labels Agnon "hameshorer," she labels herself "hamehabberet," a title that might be seen as invoking, in feminine form, the masculine authority of R. Yosef Caro, author of the *Shulhan 'arukh*, known in halakhic discourse as "the Mehabber."

terms of the number of pages, but also in terms of the physical size of the volume, measuring roughly 4 x 6 inches. Even smaller in size was her 1946 book, *Halab-ban,* where she first published "Fradl," the story I will be analyzing late in this article in relation to Flaubert's *Madame Bovary* and Agnon's *Sippur pashut* (1935).

All this does not mean, however, that Baron did not have grand literary aspirations. Indeed, a careful reading of her fiction indicates the extent to which her taut, compact, emotionally restrained short stories and novellas manage to engage and reconfigure the narrative perspective, plot, and motifs of canonical (male) writings. As one of the only early female prose writers in a company of men who often dramatized the silencing of women, Baron found a way to register her desire to gain entry into the Hebrew literary "male-stream" even as she departed significantly and conspicuously from it, often highlighting alternative female communities. The provincial short story genre, with its seemingly modest proportions and the shtetl subject matter, with its concern for patterns and mores from the past, suggests for some readers a modest and conservative orientation on Baron's part. Yet the presence in many of her stories of a controlling, first-person female narrator, who lives apart from the world being described and engages in multilayered intertextuality and independent ars-poetic reflection, points to Baron's effort to craft an image of the woman writer as author of narratively sophisticated, modernist prose.

The extent to which Baron's undersized reputation as poet in prose endures to this day is noteworthy, even in some feminist re-readings and reevaluations of her work. In *Spoiling the Stories,* a recently published study of Israeli women's novels, scholar and novelist Tamar Merin reinforces the impression of Baron as an admired but marginal poetic prose writer who insisted on "the short, lyric impressionistic, mode" and "never developed into a novelist, nor did she become fully integrated into the evolving Hebrew canon."[13] Throughout the introduction to her study, Merin defines the importance of a writer on the basis of having written novels rather than shorter stories. Each of the writers she includes in her book, she writes, "successfully passed the most crucial test of a Hebrew author by writing novels."[14] Merin's study attempts to look beyond the hierarchical relationship between the female text and the canonical male text by identifying what she refers to as "intersexual dialogue" in the works of Israeli women novelists, "a literary technique which allowed the first Israeli prose fiction authors [read: novelists] to join with the Hebrew canon while still challenging its gender boundaries, unmanning it, imagining it anew."[15]

13. Tamar Merin, *Spoiling the Stories* (Evanston, IL: Northwestern University Press, 2016), 20 and 5, respectively.
14. Merin, *Spoiling,* 24.
15. Merin, *Spoiling,* 24.

Yet her insistence upon privileging the novel over other forms of prose even as her study includes analyses of works of short fiction by Israeli novelists essentially upholds the very hierarchy it seeks to undo. By beginning her book with a 1947 short story by Yehudit Hendel that engages in intersexual dialogue with two short stories by Agnon rather than with a comparable work by Baron, Merin bypasses the ways in which Baron's fiction anticipated many of the intersexual engagements she seeks out in the writings of the next generation of women novelists. Merin's study focuses on literary daughters and canonical fathers, but Agnon and Baron were contemporaries—literary siblings, as it were—who edited, read, and responded to each other's work. Not just that: several scholars have identified occasions when they seemed to have borrowed from and revised one another's work: Nurit Govrin has suggested that Baron's early story "Hasavta Hanye" (1909) might have served as a template for Agnon's beloved novella "Tehilla" (1950).[16] Marc Bernstein has argued that Baron's story "'Agunah" (1920) responds directly, from a feminist perspective, to Agnon's signature story, "'Agunot."[17] And my own work on Baron's "Mishpaḥah" (Family) shows how Baron's novel revises aspects of Agnon's "'Aggadat hasofer" (The Tale of the Scribe).[18]

This article adds to the account of the literary dialogue between Agnon and Baron by focusing on one hitherto unexplored nexus between their work, namely, their shared admiration for and common intertextual engagements with Flaubert's *Madame Bovary*, as seen in Agnon's realist novel, *Sippur pashut* (1935) and Baron's 1946 novella, "Fradl."[19] Critics like Robert Alter, Dan Miron, Nitza Ben-Dov, and David Aberbach have already identified allusions to certain key symbolic passages from *Madame Bovary* in Agnon's realist novel, showing how Agnon remade Flaubert's story of female adultery into a story of a man who learns to renounce the romantic allure of such escapades and return in peace to family life.[20] Baron's two-volume Hebrew translation of *Madame Bovary* was

16. Nurit Govrin, *Hamaḥatsit harishonah* (Jerusalem: Mossad Bialik, 1988), 174. For more on this, see Wendy Zierler, "From Harve to Tehilla," in *Agnon's Stories of the Land of Israel*, ed. Jeffrey Saks (New York: Wipf and Stock, forthcoming).
17. Marc Bernstein, "On the Story 'Agunah'," in *Hebrew, Gender, and Modernity: Critical Responses to Dvora Baron's Fiction*, ed. Sheila Jelen and Shachar Pinsker (College Park: University of Maryland Press, 2007), 117–44. See also Sheila Jelen, *Intimations of Difference: Dvora Baron in the Modern Hebrew Renaissance* (Syracuse: Syracuse University Press, 2007), 79–97.
18. Wendy Zierler, *And Rachel Stole the Idols: The Emergence of Modern Hebrew Women's Writing* (Detroit, MI: Wayne State University Press, 2004), 192–201.
19. In her postmodern psychobiography of Baron, Amia Lieblich seems to draw a direct connection between Baron's translation of *Madame Bovary* and the subject matter of "Fradl" by treating them right next to one another; see Amia Lieblich, *Conversations with Dvora*, trans. Naomi Seidman (Berkeley: University of California Press, 1996), 259–64.
20. See Robert Alter, "Blind Beggars and Incestuous Passions," *New York Times*, December 22, 1985, https://www.nytimes.com/1985/12/22/books/blind-beggars-and-incestuous-passions.html; Nitza Ben-Dov, *Agnon's Art of Indirection* (Leiden: Brill, 1993), 98–106; Dan Miron, *Haro-*

published between 1931 and 1932, and, while Agnon had already read Flaubert in German during his long sojourn in Germany, he owned a copy of Baron's translation and might very well have consulted it in the writing of *Sippur pashut*. A close reading of Baron's later story "Fradl" also discloses the intertextual traces of both *Madame Bovary* and Agnon's novel, references that can be read as overturning elements of both masterworks in specifically feminist and non-idyllic ways.

As Naomi Seidman notes, translation theorists often employ a marriage metaphor to describe the relationship between the original text and its translation, with the original being seen as the husband and the translation, the wife and the accuracy of the translation being assessed in terms of fidelity or faithfulness to the original.[21] It is significant in this context that Baron, a founding feminist modern Hebrew woman writer known for her negative literary representations and caustic statements about the institution of marriage, undertook to translate a novel, the deep center of which, as Charles Baudelaire first observed in 1857, "resides in the adulterous woman; she alone possesses the attributes of worthy hero."[22] Baron publicly insisted on the fidelity—namely, accuracy—of her translation of Flaubert's novel; in a somewhat carping early review of the first volume of the translation, S. Tsemah took Baron to task for specific "negligent" changes to Flaubert's original, minute modifications that Baron herself defended in a subsequent letter to the editor.[23] According to Allison Schachter, Baron takes such pains to refute the minutiae of Tsemah's critique because they threaten to undermine her authority as a (woman) translator; Schachter points out, however, that Tsemah overlooks the far more significant ways in which Baron transforms, and in that sense is explictly "unfaithful" to, Flaubert's novel.[24] As Arza Tir-Appelroit's 2004 doctoral dissertation demonstrates, Baron's Zionist-socialist commitments, as well as her critical attitudes about the conventional role of women in society, can be detected in numerous swerves away from the meaning

feh hamedummeh (Tel Aviv: Hakibbutz Hameuchad, 1995), 207; and David Aberbach, "Beggars of Love: Flaubert and Agnon," *Journal of Modern Jewish Studies* 2, no. 7 (2008): 157–74.

21. Naomi Seidman, *Faithful Renderings* (Chicago, IL: University of Chicago Press, 2006), 37–38.

22. Charles Baudelaire, *"Madame Bovary* by Gustave Flaubert," first published in *L'artiste* (October 18, 1857) and reprinted in translation by Paul de Man in *Madame Bovary*, ed. Paul de Man (New York: Norton, 1965), 340. Regarding Baron's view of marriage, her daughter, Tsipporah Aharonovitz recalls her mother reading in the paper about a play entitled "I Murdered my Wife" and saying in response that "All husbands could say that." Also, when an acquaintance was getting married, and someone in Baron's house recommended they send a note of congratulations, Baron suggested that they send a message of consolation instead. See Devorah Baron, *Agav orha* (Tel Aviv: Sifriyat Hapo'alim, 1960), 108–9.

23. See Sh. Tsemah, "Madam Bovary be'ivrit," *Moznayim* 30 (Tevet 14, 1931), 12–14 and Devorah Baron "He'arot," *Moznayim* 31 (Tevet 21, 1932), 14–15.

24. Allison Schachter, "Dvora Baron's Aesthetic Labor," in *Women Writing Jewish Modernity 1919–1939* (Evanston: Northwestern University Press, 2021), 55–79.

of the original French text.[25] And, while in Baron's translation the basic contours of the plot and Emma's tragic fate clearly remain the same, according to Schachter, Baron's translation subtly but substantively rewrites Emma as a woman aware of her limitations but nevertheless intent on pursuing "her desire for personal and aesthetic redemption to the death."[26] I would add to this Baron's decision in various places in the translation to endow Emma's otherwise ludicrous musings and observations with an almost revelatory, biblical quality, as I will demonstrate below.

Madame Bovary as (Anti-)Feminist Text?

What does it mean for a pioneering feminist Hebrew woman writer, a student of both sacred and secular literature and a serious writer in her own right, to translate and respond in her own fiction to *Madame Bovary*, a novel that depicts the dire consequences of religion, reading, and aesthetics on a middle class woman's life and confirms many misogynist stereotypes even as it explodes others? What does it mean for this woman writer to revise the plots of two prior realist masterworks, one in French and the other in Hebrew, each of which hinge on the killing off and/or silencing of a female reader-protagonist?

The question of what Flaubert's *Madame Bovary* offers the woman/feminist reader or writer is complicated, to be sure. Male and female critics alike, beginning with Baudelaire, have called attention to the ways in which Emma Bovary flouts contemporary norms of femininity and motherhood and assumes masculine behaviors and postures, thereby undoing rigid gender stereotypes.[27] According to Baudelaire, Emma is endowed with a scandalous variety of masculine qualities that defy contemporary gender expectations, including a manly capacity to enjoy life, great imaginative faculties, "forcefulness and quickness of decision," and "an unlimited urge to seduce and dominate."[28] Baudelaire also points to the centrality of hysteria in *Madame Bovary* and refers to Emma as a

25. Arza Tir-Appelroit, "Hatargum betselem uvidmut" (PhD Dissertation, Tel Aviv University, 2004).

26. Schachter, "Aesthetic Labor."

27. For a feminist novel that grapples with the figure of Emma Bovary as a potential feminist icon, see Dorothy Byant, *Ella Price's Journal* (New York: Feminist Press, 1997 [1972]). See also Gayle Greene, *Changing the Story: Feminist Fiction and the Tradition* (Bloomington: Indiana University Press, 1991) and Suzanne Leonard, "I Really Must Be an Emma Bovary: Female Literacy and Adultery in Feminist Fiction," *Genders 1998–2013*, May 1, 2010, https://www.colorado.edu/gendersarchive1998-2013/2010/05/01/i-really-must-be-emma-bovary-female-literacy-and-adultery-feminist-fiction (accessed 1/1/2018).

28. Baudelaire, "*Madame Bovary*," 336–43. For more recent articles on this subject, see Dorothy Kelly, "Flaubert's Androgynous Representations," in *Fictional Genders* (Lincoln: University of Nebraska Press, 1989); Tony Williams, "Gender Stereotypes in Madame Bovary," *Forum for Modern Language Studies* 28, no. 2 (1992): 130–39; and Roger Huss, "Flaubert and Realism: Paternity, Authority, and Sexual Difference," in *Spectacles of Realism: Body, Gender, Genre*, ed.

model of the "hysterical poet," an image that more recent critics have associated with Flaubert himself.[29]

According to this reading, Emma not only challenges gender norms but also becomes a serious figure of literary aspiration in her own right. As feminist critic Naomi Schor highlights, "Emma seeks a lover not only to become a novelistic character, but especially to become an author. When, in the early stage of her marriage, Emma settles in to wait for 'something to happen,' she outfits herself in advance with a writer's tools."[30] Later, during her affair with Léon, she becomes an avid writer of love letters, as if emulating the epistolary romance novels that initially inspired her adolescent longings even before marriage.

In the end, of course, Emma patently fails—in love, in life, and in literature. As Ashley Hope Pérez observes, "Emma's only narrative strategy, it seems, is pastiche," rendering her writing at best derivative and at worst "a Frankenstein monster of romance made grotesque by his many contradictory attributes."[31] Thus, in writing her letters to Léon, Emma summons up a

> phantom fashioned out of her most ardent memories, of her favorite books, her strongest desires, and at last he became so real, so tangible, that her heart beat wildly in awe and admiration, though unable to see him distinctly, for like a god, he was hidden beneath the abundance of his attributes. He dwelt in the azure land where silken ladders swung from balconies in the moonlight beneath a flower-scented breeze." She felt him near her; he was coming and would ravish her entire being in a kiss.[32]

So it is that Emma's life of writing culminates quite literally with self-destruction. Even her last piece of writing—a suicide note—proves fragmentary and unrealized. The gendered nature of this literary failure is glaringly evident in the way in which Flaubert juxtaposes the failed writing efforts of Emma, whose name approximates the French word *femme* ("woman") with the literary successes of the writer/apothecary, Homais, whose name approximates *homme* (man).[33]

Margaret Cohen and Christopher Prendergast, Cultural Politics 10 (Minneapolis: University of Minnesota Press, 1995), 179–95.

29. Baudelaire, *Madame Bovary*, 341. For the association of this image with Flaubert himself, see Elisabeth Bronfen, "Gustave Flaubert's *Madame Bovary* and the Discourse of Hysteria," *Nineteenth Century Prose* 25, no. 1 (1998), 65–101. For more on Flaubert and hysteria, see Janet Beizer, *Ventriloquized Bodies: Narratives of Hysteria in Nineteenth-Century France* (Ithaca, NY: Cornell University Press, 1994), particularly chapters 4, 5, and 6.

30. Naomi Schor, *Breaking the Chain* (New York: Columbia University Press, 1985), 15–16. For this passage see Gustave Flaubert, *Madame Bovary*, trans. Paul DeMan (New York: Norton, 1965), 43 and Flaubert, *Madam Bovary* (trans. Baron), 54.

31. Ashley Hope Pérez, "Against 'Écriture Féminine': Flaubert's Narrative Aggression in *Madame Bovary*," *French Forum* 38, no. 3 (2013), 37.

32. Flaubert, *Madame Bovary* (trans. DeMan), 211.

33. Schor, *Breaking*, 12.

Michael Danahy points to "Emma's utter deprivation [at the end of the novel] of a tongue of her own," a condition that in my view, Baron clearly registered and endeavored to counter both in her fiction and in her translation.[34]

One can discern this countereffort quite clearly in Baron's Hebrew rendering of the passage quoted above, which subtly transforms Emma's misguided letter-writing into a sacred literary endeavor. Whereas Flaubert dismissively describes the Léon of Emma's letters as a phantom, Baron translation renders him a *demut*, an artistic image, evocative of God's creation of Adam in Genesis 5:1 as "bidmut Elohim"—in the image of God. As opposed to Flaubert's French, which has Emma fashion Léon out of "ses lectures les plus belles, de ses convoitises les plus fortes" ("her most beautiful reading and her strongest passions or lust"),[35] Baron's Hebrew translation describes Léon's image as "'utsvah meme'avyyehah vetupehah beruah tovei hasefarim" ("fashioned out of her longings and cultivated in the spirit of the best books").[36] Here "ruah" and "tovei hasefarim" considerably elevate Emma's sources and efforts, and "utsvah meme'avyyehah" evokes and plays on the famous opening of Y. L. Gordon's "The Tip of the Yud," in which the poet laments the sorrows ('otsbekh) of the Hebrew woman and her quashed hopes (ma'avayyayikh).[37] Baron renders the "contrée bleuâtre" ("azure lands") where her imagined Léon resides as "be'olam shekulo tekhelet," an expression that calls to mind the expression *tallit shekulah tekhelet* ("a completely blue prayer shawl"), a figure for absolute purity without blemish. And, while in the French original, Emma envisions Léon carrying her off and ravishing her entire being with a kiss—"il allait venir et l'enlèverait tout entière dans un baiser"—in Baron's translation, Emma imagines that "hinneh yavo veyeqaddesh otah binshiqah" ("Behold he will come and sanctify her with a kiss"). Admittedly, Baron's revisions of Flaubert's novel are subtle and semantic and easy to overlook. The literary revisions of Flaubert and Agnon that she undertakes in her own fiction, I would argue, are even more fundamental and sweeping, involving a reconfiguration of prior plots from female to male infidelity, and from emphasis on female indiscretion to the transformative capacity of women's empathy, community, and storytelling.

34. Michael Danahy, *The Feminization of the Novel* (Gainesville: University of Florida Press, 1991), 147. In the story "Madame Bovary bineveh tsedek," the poet and prose writer Nurit Zarhi has Madame Bovary rise up out of the Mediterranean Sea and visit Devorah Baron, who chides Flaubert's heroine for many of her bad choices and assumptions about men; see Nurit Zarhi, *Oman hamasekhot* (Tel Aviv: Zemorah Bitan, 1993), 59–67.
35. Gustave Flaubert, *Madame Bovary*, Édition du groupe "Ebooks libres et gratuits" (1857, French), https://www.ebooksgratuits.com/pdf/flaubert_madame_bovary.pdf, 330.
36. Flaubert, *Madam Bovary* (trans. Baron), 245–46.
37. See Y. L. Gordon, "Qotso she yod," פרייקט בן-יהודה, https://benyehuda.org/yalag/yalag_086 .html.

Agnon Meets Flaubert

In order to flesh out this argument relating to Baron's revision of Flaubert and Agnon in her fiction, I need first to establish certain important connections (as well as certain crucial distinctions) between Flaubert's novel and Agnon's *Sippur pashut*. Agnon's novel, like Flaubert's, takes place in a provincial town, tells the story of an unhappy marriage that results in an emotional breakdown, and features a woman, Blume Nacht, whose first name half rhymes with Emma, and who is frequently seen in the novel reading by candlelight.[38] Like Emma and Léon, Blume and Hirshl share and talk about books as they begin to fall in love; eventually, however, Hirshl acquiesces to the wishes of his mother, Tsirl, and marries the more wealthy Mina Ziemlich, while Blume goes from serving (Cinderella-like) as an unpaid domestic servant in the Hurvitz household and romancing with her cousin, Hirshl, to working as a paid domestic servant in the household of Akavia and Tirtza (Mintz) Mazal. The Mazal house, located on the outskirts of the community, is a noteworthy place of employ insofar as Tirtza Mazal, the protagonist of Agnon's 1925 novella, *Bidemi yamehah*, is the one major female protagonist created by Agnon who writes herself—in biblical Hebrew, no less! Because of Tirtza's authorship, one might expect Blume to develop some manner of agency and voice. The lack of information about Blume's life after Hirshl thus looms at the novel's end as thick absence.

Instead of giving voice to Blume, Agnon's *Sippur pashut* foregrounds the inner life of Hirshl and his nervous breakdown, a form of hysteria unleashed in the wake of his marriage to Mina, even as he continues to love Blume, his would-be spiritual "twin."[39] If, as Baudelaire argues, Flaubert's achievement in *Madame Bovary* consists in his representation of Emma's tortured, "ambiguous temperament," Agnon's achievement centers on his complex psychological depictions of Hirshl's madness and consequent therapy.[40] Dr. Langsam, Hirshl's therapist in Lemberg, lends Hirshl his dead wife's romance novels—like Emma Bovary, Langsam's wife commits both adultery and suicide—yet urges him to shun their tawdry plots, dealing as they did with nothing but "'iskei semalot veqishutei nashim," matters of dresses and women's decorative accessories.[41] Everything about Dr. Langsam's treatment of Hirshl—Miron and other critics

---

38. S.Y. Agnon, *Sippur pashut*, in *'Al kappot haman'ul*, vol. 3 of *Kol sippurav shel Shmuel Yosef Agnon* (Jerusalem: Schocken, 1958), עג׳ ,עב׳ עא׳. For English translation, see S.Y. Agnon, *A Simple Story*, trans. Hillel Halkin (New Milford, CT: Toby, 2014), 21, 22, 24.
39. Agnon, *Sippur pashut*, עו׳; Agnon, *Simple Story*, 28 translates the sentence "Zo Blume haytah bivhinat te'umato," as "In age she was almost his twin," which I think misses the psychological or spiritual point of the description.
40. Direct quote from Baudelaire, *"Madame Bovary,"* 341.
41. Agnon, *Sippur pashut*, רלד׳, my translation. On shunning tawdry plots, see Miron, *Harofe*, 218.

connect Dr. Langsam's story therapy to Agnon himself—seems to hinge on dislodging him from Bovaryian impulses and ambitions and restoring him to proper small-town family values.[42]

And so, if Flaubert's novel highlights an aspiring female literary hysteric only to squelch her romantic fantasies and kill her off, Agnon transmutes hysteria into a plot that elevates a bourgeois male (anti-)hero and mutes his female, spiritual twin. In this sense, the silencing of Blume in *Sippur pashut* outstrips that of Flaubert's Emma—a fact symbolized in the oxymoronic double meaning of Blume Nacht's name as "night flower," destined to open up and elaborate through maturation, and as completely sealed or blocked off in the darkness.[43] The silencing of Blume is underscored by the respective narrative structure of each novel. *Madame Bovary* initially focuses on Charles Bovary's point of view but shifts early on to Emma; likewise, the narrative focus of *Sippur pashut* begins with Blume but quickly moves to Hirshl. But, whereas *Madame Bovary* returns to Charles's point of view after Emma's suicide, *Sippur pashut* never revives Blume's storyline, offering only a few tantalizing glimpses (from Hirschl's perspective) of her life at the home of the Mazals. At the very end of the novel, Agnon's narrator concedes that, while the story of Hirshl and Mina has reached its conclusion, that of Blume has not yet been told, although it merits of a book of its own. "God in heaven knows when that will be," says Agnon's narrator, when this book will ever be written."[44] According to Miron, this concluding "remark testifies openly to the narrator's discomfort with this ending."[45] Baron's "Fradl," I would like to argue, responds, as it were, to this uneasiness, decidedly countering and unsealing the twin literary fates of Emma Bovary and Blume Nacht.

Tritextual Engagements: Flaubert, Agnon, Baron

A number of additional intertextual connections between the novels of Flaubert and Agnon, and, by extension, to Baron's story "Fradl," serve to ground this

42. Miron, *Harofe*, 222–30. See also Yair Koren Maimon, *Yaḥasei metappelim-metuppalim biytsirotav shel Agnon* (Tel Aviv: Resling, 2015), 161–96.
43. According to Harold Fisch, *S.Y. Agnon* (New York: Frederick Ungar, 1975), 93, Blume's name, which is Yiddish for "flower," marks her specifically as the *hortus inclusus*, the closed garden of Song of Songs 4:12. That is why is she mysterious and unattainable. In Hebrew, her name also suggests "closed off" or "sealed." This interpretation essentially blames Blume's character for the failure of their love, rather than focusing on the way in which Hirshl and the narrative within which he predominates seals her off from opportunities or voice. Along similar lines, Amos Oz, *The Silence of Heaven*, trans. Barbara Harshav (Princeton, NJ: Princeton University Press, 2000), 45–60 (translation of *Shetiqat hashamayim* [Tel Aviv: Keter, 1993]). charges Blume with frigidity and emotional aridity, making her ultimately an unfit partner for Hirshl. For a counterargument that opposes the notion of Blume's frigidity and unattainability, see Nitza Ben-Dov, "Ha'im Blume frigidit?" *'Alei siaḥ* 34 (1994): 43–50.
44. Agnon, *Sippur pashut*, רעב; Agnon, *Simple Story*, 239.
45. Dan Miron, "Domesticating a Foreign Genre," *Prooftexts* 7 (1987): 9.

reading. To begin, *Madame Bovary* and *Sippur pashut* share a whole list of common motifs and themes, including cakes and sweets, coins, orphanhood, physical and mental illness, the role of literature and reading in abetting romance and promoting freedom; women's education (Emma and Mina), and the adoption of aristocratic names, as well as the recurrent use of bird imagery to symbolize a (thwarted) quest for freedom and romantic passion.[46]

Yet the most prominent critically acknowledged borrowing from *Madame Bovary* in Agnon's *Sippur pashut* is that of the blind singing beggar who follows the Hirondelle, the coach that Emma rides to her trysts with Léon and that appears in the novel on three separate occasions.[47] The beggar is first mentioned after Emma and Léon begin their affair, serving as lurid externalization of what Emma's dreams as a younger girl have now become.

> There was a wretched creature on the hillside, who would wander about with his stick right in the midst of the carriages. A mass of rags covered his shoul-

46. On women's education: Mina Ziemlich is a wealthy farmer's daughter-turned-*maskilah*, who knows how to play piano, just like Flaubert's Emma Rouault; this parallel does not bode well for Hirshl insofar as Emma's study of piano becomes the pretext for her visits to Rouen to pursue her affair with Léon. At the very end of *Sippur pashut*, though, when Hirshl and Mina are out strolling in the snow, Hirshl recalls gratefully that Mina had not asked him for an instrument even though she had once learned how to play piano, an intertextual nod to the fact that Mina might have turned out just like Emma. See Agnon, *Sippur pashut*, רסח; Agnon, *Simple Story*, 235.

On the adoption of aristocratic names, the name Berthe/Bertha appears in both texts and follows a similar pattern. Emma Bovary chooses the name Berthe for her daughter because she heard this name in the house of the Marquise, lending the name an aristocratic association. Likewise, Mina's mother changes her name from the Yiddish Brayndel to the more German Bertha, as a mark of her rise in social station given her husband's wealth. But, whereas Flaubert's Berthe is orphaned and reduced to poverty and servitude (like Agnon's Blume Nacht!), Bertha Ziemlich remains a God-fearing Jew and enjoys a comfortable rural life, affording her the opportunity to help care for her grandson. The sad fate of Flaubert's orphaned, destitute Berthe constitutes a major critique of French bourgeois culture, whereas Agnon's Bertha seems to support and undergird the middle-class status quo.

47. Hirondelle, which means "swallow," strengthens the association between bird imagery and Emma's quest to be free of her marriage in order to indulge in other passions. Later, when her affair begins to peter out and her debts reach a crushing height, she muses on how "she would have liked to take wing like a bird, and fly off far away to become young again in the realms of immaculate purity" (Flaubert, *Madame Bovary* [trans. DeMan], 212). Agnon's novel includes too many references to birds to cite individually, but two are worth mentioning: Early on in Agnon's *Sippur* pashut, Blume is described as "as quick on her feet as a bird in flight." (Agnon, *Simple Story*, 28; Agnon, *Sippur pashut*, עד) Later, after his marriage to Mina, lovesick Hirshl develops insomnia and muses how drinking coffee makes you feel light like a bird (Agnon, *Simple Story*, 169; Agnon, *Sippur pashut*, רח). When he has his nervous breakdown Hirshl begins to crow like a rooster, less a bird of flight than one of domestic breeding or farming—the purview of his in-laws, the Ziemlichs—a mark of how will never truly flee his family's expectations.

ders, and an old staved-in beaver hat, shaped like a basin, hid his face; but when he took it off he revealed two gaping bloody orbits in the place of eyelids. The flesh hung in red strips and from them flowed a liquid which congealed into green scales reaching down to his nose with its black nostrils, which kept sniffing convulsively. To speak to you he threw back his head with an idiotic laugh;—then his blueish eyeballs, rolling around and around, would rub against the open wound near the temples. He sang a little song as he followed the carriages:
　　Often the warmth of a summer day
Makes a young girl dream her heart away.[48]

In Baron's Hebrew translation of this passage, Emma's encounter with the blind beggar takes on a luridly revelatory quality, as his hat is likened to a *gigit* ("tub" or "cask"),[49] a Hebrew word choice evocative of the famous midrash about the coercive and fearsome nature of the revelation of Sinai.[50] The second time the beggar appears and sings, he is seen rolling his eyes, sticking out his tongue, and howling like a famished dog, provoking outright disgust in Emma. To counter this disgust, Emma tosses the beggar a five-franc coin, the only money she has left, a gesture she considers beautiful, but that clearly presages her financial and physical ruin.[51] Fittingly, the third time the blind beggar appears coincides with Emma's suicide, during which he sings a longer, smuttier version of his original song. Emma erupts into bitter wild laughter in the middle of the song; by its conclusion, she experiences a final spasm and is thrown back onto the mattress, at which point, in Flaubert's words, *Elle n'existait plus*—she "had ceased to exist,"[52] a moment that Baron more reverently renders as "yats'ah nishmatah" ("her soul departed"),[53] in effect refusing to write Emma out of existence in her death.

The figure of the blind singing beggar also appears three times in Agnon's *Sippur pashut* but in a much more positive guise. When Hirshl has his mental breakdown, he is sent for treatment to the hospital of Dr. Langsam who treats Hirshl by telling him stories of the shtetl of his own youth, including references to blind beggar-musicians "who sat on empty sacks in the marketplace of his town and coaxed from their instruments such boundlessly sweet music that it could put one into a trance."[54] In marked contrast to Flaubert's grotesque, blind *vagabond*, the singing beggars in Agnon's novel are nostalgic, folkloric figures

48. Flaubert, *Madame Bovary* (trans. DeMan), 193.
49. Flaubert, *Madam Bovary* (trans. Baron), 227.
50. See BT Shabbat 88a, Soncino translation, http://halakhah.com/pdf/moed/Shabbath.pdf.
51. Flaubert, *Madame Bovary* (trans. DeMan), 219; Flaubert, *Madam Bovary* (trans. Baron), 254.
52. Flaubert, *Madame Bovary* (1857, French), 372; Flaubert, *Madame Bovary* (trans. DeMan), 238.
53. Flaubert, *Madam Bovary* (trans. Baron), 274.
54. Agnon, *Sippur pashut*, רל"ג; Agnon, *Simple Story*, 196–97.

who sing pleasing songs that provoke a sense of warm sadness, maternally wrapping and swaddling the heart—thus standing in for the cradle songs that Hirshl never heard from his emotionally stinting mother.

The image of the singing blind beggar appears a second time mid-way through Hirshl's treatment, as part of Hirshl's renewed struggle with insomnia and nightmares, including one in which a blind beggar sings songs that have no beginning and no end, followed by a cloaked woman who cuts him a piece of cake and a man who throws coins in his eyes.[55] According to Ben-Dov, this dream, with its references to the singing beggar, the cake, and the coins, recalls the cakes that Blume served the Hurvitzes the morning after her arrival, as well as the domed cake, topped with sugar coins that is presented at the home of the Ziemlichs after Hirshl and Mina's engagement; as such, it is a compressed representation of the conflict between Tsirl and Blume, which Hirshl wishes somehow to resolve.[56] The conclusion of this dream reflects Hirshl's guilt that, in abandoning his love for Blume, he has emotionally beggared himself to his family and their pursuit of money. Hirshl's telling cure at the hands of Dr. Langsam ultimately leads him away from such self-incriminating thoughts and back to his wife and newborn child. Indeed, by the end of the novel, when the blind singing beggar appears for the third time, Hirshl has returned to Mina; together they are strolling in the country in the snow, where they come upon a blind musician sitting and playing sad music that "seemed to have no beginning and no end" and to whom Hirshl throws a valuable coin.[57] In Flaubert's novel, the image of Emma, throwing her last coin to the blind beggar who follows the coach, appears just as Emma's world is falling apart, while, in *Sippur pashut*, Hirsh's tossing of a coin coincides with the restoration of stability to Hirshl's life and marriage. Critics of Agnon's fiction differ as to whether this moment in the novel is meant to be seen as truly restorative or lamentable, with some straddling both positions.[58] All of that discussion, of course, pertains to an evaluation of Hirshl's life with Mina; none of it directly

55. Agnon, *Sippur pashut*, רל'ו; Agnon, *Simple Story*, 199–200. The image of the blind beggar who sings songs that have no beginning and no end also appears in Agnon's unfinished posthumously published novel, *Shira*; see S.Y. Agnon, *Shira* (Jerusalem: Schocken, 1971), 8.

56. Ben-Dov, *Agnon's Art*, 73–106.

57. Agnon, *Sippur pashut*, רסח; Agnon, *Simple Story*, 234–35). Gershon Shaked interprets the scene where Hirshl throws the coin at the blind beggar who plays that song that has no beginning and no end as an external representation of Hirshl's resolve to "close his account" with fate and with a world that has no boundaries and to embrace his relationship with Mina. See Gershon Shaked, *Omanut hasippur shel Agnon* (Tel Aviv: Sifriyat Hapoʻalim, 1973), 220.

58. See, e.g., Malka Shaked, "Haʾim Hirshl hayah meshugaʻ," *Hasifrut* 32 (1982): 81–113, who sees the novel as accommodating both interpretations. Others have suggested other hybrid readings, where the narrator of the novel stands at an ironic remove from novel's seeming resolution. See, e.g., Gershon Shaked, *S.Y. Agnon: A Revolutionary Traditionalist* (New York: New York University Press, 1989), 131–32 and Alter, "Great Genius."

addresses the status and future of Blume, which is where, I would argue, Baron steps in to break the idyll.

Baron's Revisionary Narration

I began this article with a discussion of the reception history of Baron's fiction and the tendency on the part of critics to view her stories as poetic idylls: small, static, lyrical evocations of places and times gone by. In *The Dialogic Imagination*, Mikhail Bakhtin critically targets what he sees as the idyllic, petit bourgeois, provincial setting of Flaubert's *Madame Bovary*:

> In Flaubert's *Madame Bovary* the provincial town serves as a locus of action [...] Such towns are the locus for cyclical, everyday time. Here there are no events, only "doing" that constantly repeat themselves. Time here has no advancing historical movement; it moves rather in narrow circles: the circle of the day, of the week, of the month, of a person's entire life. A day is just a day, a year is just a year—a life is just a life. Day in, day out the same round of activities is repeated, the same topics of conversation, the same words and so forth. In this type of time people eat, drink, sleep, have wives, mistresses (casual affairs), involve themselves in petty intrigues, sit in their shops, play cards, gossip. This is commonplace, philistine cyclical everyday time... Time here is without event and therefore seems to stand still. Here there are no "meetings," no "partings." It is a viscous and sticky time that drags itself slowly through space. And therefore it cannot serve as the primary time of the novel.[59]

It would seem to be an interpretative simplification to view either *Madame Bovary* or Agnon's Flaubertian *Sippur pashut* as mere idyllic, inhabiting an eventless world where time stops; both master novels actually include "meetings," "partings," and historical disruptions to the way things have always been. The famous obscenity trial following the publication of Flaubert's novel indicates just how threatening the novel's representation of gender norms and sexuality was to nineteenth century France.[60] Likewise, Agnon's novel offers considerable evidence of the changes afoot in Galicia in the early twentieth century and the chaos of modernity.

That said, both *Madame Bovary* and *Sippur pashut* reinstate the prior patriarchal social order in some manner and, in that sense, evince a conservative, idyllic aspect, one which, I would argue, Baron's "Fradl" subtly disrupts. In my reading, Baron's story subverts both novels , compensating, as it were, both for the killing of Emma, and for narrative silence surrounding Blume Nacht in

---

59. Mikhail Bakhtin, *The Dialogic Imagination*, trans. Caryl Emerson and Michael Holquist, ed. Michael Holquist, University of Texas Slavic Series 1 (Austin: University of Texas Press, 1981), 247–248.
60. For more on the trial that followed the publication of Flaubert's *Madame Bovary*, see Dominick LaCapra, *Madame Bovary on Trial* (Ithaca, NY: Cornell University Press, 1984).

Sippur pashut by offering an entire story about orphaned Fradl, one that supplies her with a happy ending befitting a character whose Yiddish name means "happiness" or "joy."[61]

It might seem strange to argue for the subversive or disruptive quality of a story that offers a happy ending in marriage, especially because, with few exceptions, Baron avoids writing in a happily-ever-after vein.[62] In fact, in the *sefer "zuta"*—the tiny book in which "Fradl" was initially published in 1946—it appears alongside "Halabban," a tragic narrative about a brick maker who slaves his entire life, loses his wife and two sons to death, and, by the end of the story, loses his only daughter, too. And it is this tragic tale that caps the book and furnishes its title.[63] In his introduction to *Halabban*, A. Kariv refers to the unstinting honesty of Baron's prose, noting Baron's practice as a writer of looking directly "upon the lot of each person without an averting of the eyes, never embroidering her vision with sweet delusion."[64] Even in "Fradl," I would argue, the happy end comes only at great cost and as a result of a fundamental break with the past—both anti-idyllic narrative features. Beyond that, the restitutive ending of the story itself can be read as subtly ironic, given its Lithuanian shtetl setting and the publication date of 1946.

On the most basic level, the eponymously title "Fradl" engages with the idea of happiness, pointing back to the centrality and ultimate failure of the search for happiness in Flaubert's *Madame Bovary*. Note that Emma's narrative strand begins with her quest, after her marriage, to understand the meaning of "bliss, passion, and ecstasy."[65] Surrounding Emma in Yonville are figures whose names literally mean "happiness"—Felicité ("joy") and Lheureux ("the happy one")—underscoring Emma's quest and ultimate failure to achieve the bliss she so desires. Reading errantly leads Emma to admire heroines who are famous, beautiful and unhappy ("nashim mefursamot o **keshot** hayom"/"**rabbat haḥen**",

---

61. The name of Baron's eponymous protagonist also gestures back to a minor character with the same name in Agnon's "'Agunot." In that story, Fradl is the poor daughter of a servant woman and the beloved Yehezkel, the talmudic luminary who abandons her in Poland in order to become a Rosh Yeshiva in Jerusalem and to marry Dina, the daughter of wealthy Ahiezer. After marrying Dina, Yehezkel sadly learns that Fradl has been married off to someone else. Aside from this, Agnon provides no other information about Fradl's fate. Baron "Fradl" might be seen as compensating for this omission as well.

62. Gershon Shaked, *Modern Hebrew Fiction* (Bloomington: Indiana University Press, 2000), 60 notes that "Baron's plots often record the trajectory of a protagonist's life from an 'idyllic' point of departure to an 'anti-idyllic' ending. Being orphaned is the pivotal event in the lives of many of her female characters." Stories such as "Fradl" and "Mishpaḥah" reverse this tragic course but upend the idyll in other ways.

63. Devorah Baron, *Halabban* (Tel Aviv: Zuta/Dvir, 1946).

64. A. Kariv, introduction to Baron, *Halabban*, 3.

65. Flaubert, *Madame Bovary* (trans. DeMan), 24.

according to Baron's rendering[65]), figures whom she tragically mistakes as models for her own life. Fittingly, Baron's story of a young woman with a happy name but an unhappy marriage begins with a description that repeats verbatim elements of Baron's translation of Emma's misguided reading: "**Rabbat ḥen** aval 'atsuvat ruaḥ haytah be'ir moladetah shel Ḥannah ha'ishah Fradl, asher goralah heimer lah ve'asher ne'evqah 'imah **kashot** bemeshekh hashanim."—"Beautiful but unhappy was the woman Fradl in Hannah's shtetl, whom fate had dealt with harshly and she struggled long and hard against it."[67] What Emma romanticizes, Fradl unromantically and unwittingly suffers, beginning with the match made for her by her guardians with the erstwhile *maskil* Avraham Noah, a biblical name that connotes regressive (from Abraham backward to Noah) rather than progressive development. As in *Sippur pashut,* where *maskilim* are seen as petty, cigarette smoking, chess playing, and materialistic, Avraham Noah is a selfish, taciturn, inattentive husband, a kind of gamester and playboy who eventually leaves home altogether, seeking employment out of town and rendering Fradl an undeclared *'agunah.*[68]

Like Hirshl, Fradl is unhappy despite apparent familial and financial advantages. She, too, comes from *benot tovim,* a good (read: wealthy) family.[69] But, like Blume, she is orphaned, forced to spend her youth living with other relatives. In this sense Baron's Fradl is a hybrid figure, combining aspects of Agnon's Hirshl, Blume, and Mina. Upon marrying, Fradl returns to her family's large house in the center of town, which is outfitted (presumably by her relatives) with furnishings from the city, while she herself is dressed "kenusakh benei hakerakhim," in city fashion. All of these trappings, though, serve only to reinforce Fradl's sense of loneliness, enveloping her in "demamat qipa'on."[70] a frozen silence that Baron herself invokes in personal correspondence as a figure for loneliness in the absence of family and that also recalls the motif of orphanhood and silence

---

66. Flaubert, *Madam Bovary* (trans. Baron), 36 (emphasis added).
67. Devorah Baron, "Fradl," *Parshiyot* (Jerusalem: Mossad Bialik, 1968), 97 (emphasis mine). Translation from Dvora Baron, *The First Day and Other Stories,* trans. Naomi Seidman and Chana Kronfeld (Berkeley: University of California Press, 2001), 26.
68. "Fradl," like other stories in Baron's corpus, resists the use of the category of 'agunah as allegory, as it appears in stories such as Agnon's "'Agunot," insisting instead on attending to actual women's suffering and possible remedies. For more on Baron's deallegorization of the 'agunah, see Bernstein, "On the Story 'Agunah,'" 117–44.
69. The epithet of "benei tovim" appears several times in Agnon's novel, including one passage that considers Blume's decision not to marry anyone else after Hirshl marries Mina: "Kelum metsapah hi shetitnasse levaḥur ben tovim? […] Lifnei yamim lifnei shanim natnah 'eineihah bevaḥur ben tovim Hirshl Hurvitz shemo," (*Sippur pashut,* קצ). "Did she really believe some wealthy young man would still come along and marry her? . . . Once, long ago, she had given her heart to a [wealthy] young man named Hirshl Hurvitz (Agnon, *Simple Story,* 157).
70. Baron, "Fradl," 97.

in Agnon's *Bidemi yamehah.*[71] This silence persists even in the presence of her husband, who is seen early on in the story reading a book or a newspaper, "davar shehasheqet yafeh lo," an activity befitting silence.[72] As for Fradl herself, she sits alone on a bench outside. The narrator describes in free indirect discourse how the female neighbors observe Fradl's lack of newlywed joy, a condition that the town *rebbetzin* (mistakenly) attributes to Fradl's "emptiness"—that is, her current lack of a child.

At this point in the story, a typographic break marks a shift to backstory and draws attention to the perspective of the narrator. In the same way that Flaubert shifts back in time after Emma's wedding to Charles in order to provide the backstory of her convent education, Baron's narrator announces: "umin hanimna' hu shelo lehazkir"[73]—it would be remiss not to mention the widow Sarah Leah and her son Ḥayyim Raphael, both of whom were close companions to Fradl when she was a small child. The narrator notes how Sarah Leah, who did not herself have a daughter, would delight in giving sugar cakes to the orphan Fradl. In Agnon's *Sippur pashut*, Blume Nacht presents sugar cakes to the Hurvitzes the first breakfast after her arrival. Hirshl delights in Blume's cakes and whispers in his mother's ear: "You must admit, Mother, that these cakes are delicious," an intimation of his attraction to Blume that Tsirl will eventually set out to block.[74] Later in the novel, at a dinner party, Mina's mother, Bertha Ziemlich serves a pudding, topped with sugary coins, suggesting the sweetness of money.[75] In the context of *Sippur pashut*, sugar cakes come to represent Hirshl's ultimate acquiescence to the lure of money over love. Likewise, Flaubert scholar Barbara

71. In a letter to her hospitalized daughter Tsipporah, dated January 23, 1947, Baron describes the sad emptiness of her house without her there: "shoreret po kemo beveit Fradl, demamat kipa'on" ("frozen silence prevails within, as in the house of Fradl"), suggesting the significance of this fictional description to Baron's own state of mind. See Baron, *Agav Orḥa*, 149–50. Cf. Baron's Hebrew rendition of the description of Emma Bovary in the convent as situated, "betokh demamat ḥeder hamitot, leqol sha'on raḥoq shel eizo 'agalah" (Flaubert, *Madam bovary*, 37), "within the silence of the dormitory against the distant clamor of some carriage or another" Flaubert, *Madame Bovary* (trans. DeMan), 27. In both narratives the static silence of the narrative is destined, for better or worse, to be broken. For a discussion analogous themes in Agnon's *Bidemi yamehah*, see Naomi Sokoloff, "Narrative Ventriloquism and Muted Feminine Voice," *Prooftexts* 9 (1989): 115–37 and Ruth Ginsburg, "'Bidemi yameha metah tirtsah' o: 'yafah at ra'ayati ketirtsah nava kiyrushalayim ayumah kanigdalot'," *Dappim lemeḥqar besifrut* 8 (1991–92): 285–300.
72. Baron, "Fradl," 98. Jelen, *Intimations*, 90–91 notes a similar silence in Baron's "'Agunah."
73. Baron, "Fradl," 98.
74. Agnon, *Sippur pashut*, 'הנ; Agnon, *Simple Story*, 6. For a detailed analysis of the cake/pudding motif in Agnon's novel, see Ben-Dov, *Agnon's Art*, 73–88.
75. Agnon, *Sippur pashut*, 'פכק; Agnon, *Simple Story*, 84.

Vinken notes the excess use of sugar in the Bovary household, as if to compensate for a lack of authentic spiritual nourishment.[76]

In opposition to use of the cake motif by Agnon and Flaubert, Sarah Leah's cakes in "Fradl" represent a simple offering of love and kindness from a widow to an orphan, a gift that accords her the merit not just of the two matriarchs for whom she is named but of all four.[77] Sarah Leah's surrogate maternal gestures are free of guile and charge; they do not originate, as in the case of Tsirl, with a desire to squelch freedom. Insofar as Sarah Leah seeks out a relationship with Fradl, the daughter she never had, Baron's story also affirms the value of daughters and not just sons.

Not so in the case of Flaubert's novel. In *Madame Bovary*, Emma's sense of feminine limitation, inferiority, and self-hatred finds specific expression in her fervent desire to have a black-haired, brave-hearted son. To her great chagrin, she has a daughter instead, whom she goes on to neglect in egregious ways as she pursues extramarital affairs. Baron's Fradl *does* give birth to a son, and, for a brief time, happiness replaces gloom in her home and marriage. But when Fradl's baby suddenly dies of illness, her husband Avraham Noah begins to escape whenever he can, going down to the garbage dump to play chess with his buddy Zanvil Elkes and seeking other undisclosed (Bovaryian) pleasures outside the house.[78]

In Flaubert's novel, as previously mentioned, it is the blind beggar who appears three times and sings a song about a young girl who dreams her heart (and her petticoats) away, who embodies and broadcasts the ugly truth about Emma's financial indiscretions and infidelities and augurs her ruin. Instead of a blind (male) beggar, the socially marginal "seer" in Baron's "Fradl" is a woman, *Gitl hamevulbelet* ("Mixed-Up Gitl"), whose Yiddish name implies both goodness and Fradl's need for a *get* (a divorce) to free herself from her unloving and, by implication, unfaithful husband.[79] Like the blind singing beggars in the novels of Flaubert and Agnon, Mixed-Up Gitl appears in "Fradl" on three crucial occasions in order to bear witness to Fradl's suffering, beginning with the following scene:

> Mixed-up Gitl, Fradl's neighbor on the kitchen side, once saw him [Avraham Noah] steal into the house through the back entrance, and then from the

76. Barbara Vinken, "Loving, Reading, Eating: The Passion of Madame Bovary," *MLN* 122, no. 4, French Issue (September 2007) 771.

77. Baron, "Fradl," 101.

78. Implied in the story is that Avraham Noah is interested in other forms of female company, as he pays more attention to his beautiful, city-dwelling sister when she comes to visit than he does to his wife; see "Fradl," in Baron, *Parshiyot*, 103–4.

79. Ben-Ami Feingold in "Devorah Baron kesoferet feministit," *Sadan* 4 (5760/1999–2000), 329–30, notes that the motif of the *get* in Baron's fiction functions alternatively as a symbol of oppression (as in "Keritut") or of liberation (as in "Fradl").

inside came the sound of worlds and a moaning cry, and the next day she told the women about it at the community bench, where the relations between the couple was now a frequent subject, and little Hannah, who was playing there listened to the story.[80]

Her nickname notwithstanding, Gitl is neither mixed-up nor blind when it comes to her observations about things going on around her. On the contrary, she witnesses with wide-eyed clarity the abuse suffered by unhappy Fradl as a result of her husband's behavior and reports it to the town *rebbetzin* and others in the community, thereby fulfilling an important communal function. Gitl's reports also find their way into the mind and later the stories of the young Hannah, who emerges later, in her adult guise, as the narrator of the story."[81]

Adult narrator Hannah reports that she managed to learn about the sufferings and ultimately the joys of Fradl because her shtetl community made no effort to shield children from harsh reality:

In that place, in those days, they did not believe in shielding the eyes of a child by throwing an elegant blue prayer shawl [*tallit shel tekhelet*] over life's nakedness, and so, along with the song of sun-dazzled birds and the scent of dew-drunk plants, she also absorbed impressions of daily life, bits of local color, of heartache and heart joy, which in the course of time—when they had been refined and illuminated by the light of her intellect, and experience had bound them into life stories—became for her, in the solitary nights of her wandering, a source of pleasure and comfort.[82]

Baron's use of the phrase *tallit shel tekhlelet* recalls the famous midrash on the biblical rebellion of Koraḥ, based on the episode's proximity to the commandment of wearing *tsitsit*.[83] According to this midrash, Koraḥ questions Moses's interpretive authority by posing a halakhic question in the form of a *reductio ad absurdum*: if one were to have a tallit that were completely blue (*kulah tekhelet*), would that tallit not be exempt from the mitzvah of *tsitsit*? The phrase *tallit shekulah tekhelet* thus indicates a notion of complete purity, as well as an attitude of smug certainty and arrogance.[84] Recall Baron's use of a version of this sancti-

80. Baron, "Fradl," 102; Baron, *First Day*, 33.
81. For a discussion of the role of Mixed-Up Gitl (or Crazy Gitl) as well as the layers of narrative mediation in the story, see Jelen, *Intimations*, 57–59.
82. Baron, "Fradl," 102; Baron, *First Day*, 33.
83. See Numbers Rabbah 18:3.
84. Agnon alludes to this same midrashic tradition in the preamble to his story "'Agunot," when he describes God enfolding the feminized people of Israel in a "tallit shekulo ḥen," a mark of God's protection of the people that nevertheless proves ephemeral, as all it takes is for one thread in this same tallit to unravel leaving the people entirely exposed and abandoned. See S.Y. Agnon, "Agunot," *Eilu ve'eilu*, Volume 2 of *Kol sippurav shel S.Y. Agnon*, (Jerusalem: Schocken, 1959), תה׳-תטז.

fying phrase in her translation of Emma's outsized image of Léon, in which he inhabited an *'olam shekulo tekhelet*, an azure land.[85] Here in "Fradl," this phrase similarly refers to a romanticized, idyllic depiction of reality, a mode of storytelling that stands in the way of depicting *yesurei lev vehedvat lev*, authentic pains and joys of the heart.[86]

Fradl herself clings for a time to an unrealistic, idyllic hope that she can save her marriage. Baron's narrator likens her to a terminally ill person who nevertheless pursues every sort of therapy,[87] a connection between love and medicine that calls to mind Emma's lovelorn hysteria and Charles's ineptitude as a doctor, as well as Hirshl's dubious cure in *Sippur pashut*. The real cure for Fradl (and perhaps for Hirshl) would be to let the marriage die; nevertheless, she employs various desperate means to win over her husband's affections that recall Emma's frenetic and ultimately financially ruinous purchases from Lheureux: wearing bright colored dresses that only accentuate her pallor and eating rich dairy foods to fatten herself up.[88] All of this renders her an object of curiosity and derision among many in her town, like a misguided character in a tawdry novel of the sort devoured by Emma Bovary or Dr. Langsam's wife. To Baron's narrator, Fradl's behavior recalls the *senu'ah* of the Bible, Jacob's hated wife Leah "who degrades and humiliates herself by chasing after a little bit of husbandly affection."[89] In Agnon's *Sippur pashut*, Hirshl, who hates his wife Mina, invokes the same biblical story about Leah giving away the mandrakes in exchange for a night with her husband in order to question why God made one of the wives hated, and why Jacob ever married Leah in the first place. Had he never married her, she never would have been hated.[90]

Of course, God has little to do with any of this. It is Tsirl who engineers Hirshl's marriage to Mina and Hirshl who acquiesces. Fradl's relatives similarly arrange her marriage to Avraham Noah, preferring him to the (poorer) neighbor, Hayyim Raphael, although, in Fradl's case, there is no discussion of her feelings about the marriage. Is it possible that, when she gets married, she is simply too young and naïve to know how she feels? In her naïveté, does she (like Hirshl) blindly and pliantly acquiesce to her relatives, agreeing to marry Avraham Noah (instead of Hayyim Raphael) for purported financial reasons?[91] How do the

85. Flaubert, *Madam bovary*, 246.
86. Baron, "Fradl," 103.
87. Baron, "Fradl," 104; Baron, *First Day*, 36.
88. In her dissertation on Baron's translation, Tir-Appelroit, *Hatargum*, 191 argues that Baron does not look down on the efforts of either Emma Bovary or Fradl to arouse greater love in their mates.
89. Baron, "Fradl," 104; Baron, *First Day*, 36. See Genesis 30:16, where Leah goes out to meet Jacob to claim the one night with him that she had purchased by giving Rachel the mandrakes.
90. Agnon, *Sippur pashut*, ר; Agnon, *Simple Story*, 160.
91. Raheli 'Ofer, "Meha'atah shel bat harav: Feminism ve'ortodoxiyah bisheloshah sippurim shel Devorah Baron," in *Ishah veyahadutah*, ed. Tova Cohen (Jerusalem: Reuven Mass/Kolech,

various intertextual resonances from *Madame Bovary* and *Sippur pashut* help us interpret her story and its implications?

As previously noted about *Madame Bovary*, critics disagree about feminist implications of Emma Bovary's behavior. Some maintain that Flaubert gives voice, through Emma, to the fundamental inequities of middle-class women's lives and to the quest for self-expression beyond the roles of wife, mother, and nun. Others emphasize her inability to see through the clichés of romance fiction and her easy seduction, unremitting narcissism, and financial irresponsibility render her a veritable misogynist stereotype. A similar interpretive ambiguity and debate surrounds the meaning and implications of the ending of Agnon's *Sippur pashut*. Does Hirshl actually ever cure himself of his love for Blume and embrace the life and marriage staged for him by his mother? Is the end of the novel a comedy of strengthened marriage or a tragedy of unconsummated love that leaves both Hirshl and Blume in a condition of unending emotional abandonment or *'aginut*?[92]

This much is clear: if Agnon vacillates in his novel between a condemnation of traditionalism and the bourgeois middle class and a countervailing condemnation of modernity, he does so all at the narrative expense of Blume Nacht. Similarly, if Flaubert's novel introduces the feminist complaint but replaces it with a female adulterous stereotype, if he teases the reader with the idea of the woman writer/reader but delivers a mere writer of love letters, Baron counters with a story about a woman who is mistreated by the man she ought never have married, and about a community of women who witness her torments, including young Hannah, whom we know from other stories where she is featured, eventually becomes a student/reader/writer in her own right.[93] Hannah is introduced in the very first line of the story together with Fradl herself, a twin narrative presence that challenges Fradl's silence and suggests an alternative to her way of life.

In the ars-poetic *tallit shel tekhelet* interlude in the story discussed above, Hannah's childhood impressions and storehouse and memories fuse with those

---

2013), 268, 271 suggests that Fradl plays a major role in her own unhappiness. When Ḥayyim Raphael attempts to court her, she holds herself aloof from him. And later, when married to Avraham Noah, she humiliates herself in all sorts of ways in order to capture his affections.

92. On one side of the debate are Baruch Kurzweil, "Ba'ayat hadorot besippurei Agnon," in *Masot 'al sippurei Shai Agnon* (Jerusalem: Schocken, 1963), 38–49 and Ben-Dov, *Agnon's Art*, who read Agnon's novel waging a battle between the collectivism of traditional Jewish life and the individualism and dynamism of modernity. On the other side are readers such as Hillel Halkin in his afterword to Agnon, *Simple Story*, 240–54, who see Agnon's novel as repudiating modern life, which Agnon viewed as "synonymous with chaos." For a summary of this debate see Maimon, *Yaḥasei metappelim*, 161–96.

93. See "Fradl," "Beit Kayitz," "Halabban," "Metsulah," "Matmid," and "Ameriqah," in Devorah Baron, *Parshiyot* (Jerusalem: Mossad Bialik, 1968), 97–113, 207–12, 216–24, 278–90, and 426–44.

of the narrator, presumably an older Hannah who has already left home and begun to read and write realist literary fiction based on lived experience.

The distinction drawn here between imagined and lived experience is crucial. In *Sippur pashut*, when Hirshl Hurvitz has his nervous breakdown and begins crowing, he begs not to be slaughtered, for he is a man rather than a rooster.[94] Hirshl's fear of being slaughtered is either a paranoid delusion or a conscious strategy to appear insane so as to escape military service and, for a time, his marriage. Mixed-Up Gitl's reports of Fradl's suffering employ a similar vocabulary of slaughter: "Come and look how he has butchered her now," she tells the Talmud students in the community house the second time she appears in the story,[95] once again calling urgent attention to the emotional abuse of Fradl by her husband. Gitl's use of the vocabulary of slaughter suggests, however, that Fradl's misery can be escaped only by attentive, realistic witness and real-life action, rather than fantasy or escapism.

Fradl's misery mounts significantly when Avraham Noah escapes from her and takes a job away from town. Upon his departure, Fradl is consigned like many other women of her time whose husbands have gone away to seek their fortunes elsewhere, to live "*ḥayyei niyyar*" ("a life of paper/letters")—a tragic echo of Emma's romanticized epistolary exchanges. As Fradl's sense of abandonment intensifies, Hannah's writerly life of paper, exemplified through her narration of Fradl's story, begins to emerge as an alternative to the dead-end writing of both Emma and Fradl.

All this becomes clear when, suddenly, after months of being away and without previous warning, Avraham Noah returns to town for a visit. Because of his prolonged absence, Fradl has not been adhering to the laws of family purity, so her relatives submit a question to the rabbi regarding the permissibility of Fradl proceeding immediately to the ritual bathhouse for immersion. At this point in the story, Baron's narrator briefly digresses from the storyline to offer an ethnographic description of Jewish women's observance of the laws of mikvah, with their attendant humiliations and hardships:

> About this commandment, and how the daughters of Israel in the shtetls fulfilled it, it's worth writing a special section.
>
> They, these shy women, who concealed themselves within their kitchens, would make their way, when the time came, through the alleyways to the bathhouse before the eyes of the curious, each of whom knew them by name.
>
> The kerchief was too small to obscure their flushed, shamed faces, and the ground beneath was stiff and unforgiving, and so slippery that it was easy to trip.

---

94. Hirshl's obsession with not being a rooster also calls to mind R. Nahman of Bratslav's famous parable of the Hindik; see ברסלב - ספרי רבי נחמן מברסלב / ספרי ברסלב :ז http://breslev.eip .co.il/?key=5517.

95. Baron, "Fradl," 107; Baron, *First Day*, 39.

And behind them, had they not left a house in disorder, a goat waiting to be milked, hungry children crying for their supper, and an unperturbed husband who paid them no mind? He was a moody man, who did not pamper his household or speak softly to them, and against him, the heart swelled with rage. And indeed, it not the desire for a little lovemaking that propelled these women, but rather, the holy duty, a matriarchal inheritance, the commandment of life itself.[96]

Fradl had previously been described as demeaning herself like the hated biblical wife, Leah, "by chasing after a little husbandly affection." In casting Fradl's trip to the *miqveh* against the backdrop of this description of Jewish matriarchal fortitude and devotion to ritual, the narrator explicitly dissociates Fradl and her female community from a demeaning pursuit of "a little love." At the same time, the presence of an authorial voice that subtly judges and laments the suffering of these women points to the need for another way, one made more urgent when, in a cruel twist of fate, Fradl emerges from the ritual bath only to discover that her husband's coach—an ironic nod, perhaps, in the direction of the Hirondelle from *Madame Bovary*—has already left town.

In her third appearance in the story, Mixed-Up Gitl observes Fradl's reaction to this climactic act of betrayal, saying, "You see, I told you he was a murderer; now he's really spilled her blood."[97] Gitl's exclamation points to the potential for a tragic Bovaryian ending to the story. In happy contrast to Emma Bovary, however, who dies at her own hand against the background of the beggar's last song, Gitl's outcry presages an emotional and intellectual breakthrough: Fradl finally musters "me'at hasekhel asher natan Elohim belibbah" ("the little common sense God had put in her heart)[98]—and seeks a divorce from Avraham Noah. The above reference to God instilling a bit of wisdom in her heart recalls the moment at the end of *Sippur pashut* when Hirshl resigns himself to his life with Mina because "our father in Heaven inserts love for his son, Meshulam, into his heart."[99] Divine intercession in Agnon's novel results in Hirshl remaining bound to a woman he previously did not love, whereas, in Baron's story, it allows a woman to read the truth of her own life and seek a better course.

Recall the moment before Emma Bovary's final breakdown and ultimate demise when, on a whim, she tosses the blind beggar the five-franc coin, as well as Hirshl's

96. Baron, "Fradl," 110; Baron, *First Day*, 42–43. Tir-Appelroit, *Hatargum* 176–77 refers to this scene in "Fradl" in her analysis of feminist issues pertaining to Baron's translation of Baron's *Madame Bovary*, specifically the demand that women conform to the image of the virgin/Madonna. In a letter to Yosef Rappaport dated May 9, 1955, Devorah Baron makes clear that she will not agree to re-publish "Fradl" without this *miqveh* observance scene, indicating how important this section was to her conception of the story; see Baron, *Agav orḥa*, 196.
97. Baron, "Fradl," 111; Baron, *First Day*, 44.
98. Baron, "Fradl," 112; adapted from Baron, *First Day*, 45.
99. Agnon, *Sippur pashut*, רמו (my translation).

recapitulation of this gesture at the end of *Sippur pashut*. "Fradl" boasts a similar moment: After recovering from her breakdown, Fradl gives away to poor girls the dresses that she had previously bought merely to please her husband, a deed that aids the poor and also signals a purging of her prior, deluded ways. If that isn't enough, Fradl also burns the love letters she once received from Avraham Noah, a move that both counters Emma Bovary's saving of all her letters from Rodolphe and recalls Leah's burning of Mazal's letters in Agnon's *Bidemi yamehah*.

After these symbolic acts of dissociation from her former life—distinct literary swerves, as it were, from the plots of *Madame Bovary* and *Sippur pashut*—the story finally supplies its happy ending. Fradl marries her neighbor, Hayyim Raphael, leading to a taking down of the *gader* ("fence") between the two properties; this recalls the moment in Baron's translation of *Madame Bovary* where Emma is seen longing for a son because, unlike women, only men can burst through every *gader*,[100] a translation choice that departs somewhat from Flaubert's *traverser les obstacles*.[101] The taking down of the fence signals a blurring of class, family, and gender (*migdar*), enabling Fradl to assume control of her own decision making and personal life. Her new mother-in-law, Sarah Leah, who had always longed for a daughter and had fed her sweets when she was a young girl, now indulges Fradl even more thoroughly. Sweet treats are associated here not with an acceptance of bourgeois norms (as in *Sippur pashut*) or with romantic indulgence (as in *Madame Bovary*), but with a socially conscious attitude of caring for the orphan, something conspicuously lacking in the novels of both Agnon and Flaubert, where two orphans (Bertha and Blume) languish in servitude.

At the very end of the story, Fradl gives birth to another son. Like his father Hayyim Raphael, who is described earlier in the story as frequently risking his life to save people during town fires, this son, Yeruham David, will grow up and become known among his townspeople for teaching his fellow Jews the principles of self-defense against anti-Semitic aggressors. Compare this to Hirshl's evasion of military duty in *Sippur pashut* and Emma's complaints about Charles's lack of physical, manly aptitudes such that "he could neither swim, nor fence, nor shoot."[102] To be sure, Baron's ending hardly overturns gender norms or expectations insofar as Fradl's redemption seems to hinge on her having a heroic masculine husband and son (rather than a daughter). As Sheila Jelen explains, "Fradl" is "a story about the possibility of happy endings for a Jewish woman in a nineteenth-century shtetl within the confines of proscribed tradition" and the conventional marriage plot.[103]

---

100. Flaubert, *Madam Bovary* (trans. Baron), 79.
101. Flaubert, *Madame Bovary* (1857 French), 98.
102. Flaubert, *Madame Bovary* (trans. DeMan), 29).
103. Jelen, *Intimations*, xv.

That said, one cannot ignore the role of Baron's female narrator and her *ḥayyei niyyar* ("life of letters") in the shaping of this seemingly conventional plot. This narrator, who enters into the story's world and comments upon it at various crucial junctures, repeatedly reminds us that the events in this story do not unfold naturally or inevitably. Rather, they are shaped by a narrative hand that remains both bound to and set apart from this world of the past. The narrator's metapoetic reflections and ethnographic descriptions of Jewish women's ritual observances set Fradl's story against a broader communal story of continuities and discontinuities, of insiders and outsiders to that world. Describing events from several years before, but published in 1946 in the tragic aftermath of the Shoah, "Fradl" grants its female narrator the voice and prerogative to conjure up a wistful and restitutive dream of stability and self-preservation at the very moment when the shtetl idyll has been irretrievably lost. Having grown up among honest folk, Baron's narrator knows better than to cover that world and its history in a narrative *tallit shel tekhelet*. Nevertheless, she rejects the long-standing deterministic script that imagines only tragedy or ridiculousness for its yearning, aspiring female protagonists. In a stubborn assertion of agency, and faith, the narrator offers a story about a suffering woman, who—in marrying Ḥayyim Raphael, whose name means both "life" and "cured by God," and in having a son named Yeruḥam David ("David will be pitied")—manages at long last to find hope, happiness, and security. After 1946, readers know that no Ḥayyim Raphael will be able to stave off the afflictions to come; no amount of pity will suffice to save Yeruḥam David and his community. Only in *ḥayyei niyyar*—a life on paper within the stubborn, inventive life of Baron's story—will they endure.

WENDY ZIERLER is Sigmund Falk Professor of Modern Jewish Literature and Feminist Studies at HUC-JIR in New York. She is the author of *Movies and Midrash: Popular Film and Jewish Religious Conversation* (SUNY Press, Finalist for the National Jewish Book Award in Modern Jewish Thought and Experience, 2017), *And Rachel Stole the Idols: The Emergence of Hebrew Women's Writing* (Wayne State UP, 2004) and co-editor with Carole Balin, of *To Tread on New Ground: Selected Writings of Hava Shapiro* (2014). In 2017 she became co-editor of Prooftexts: A Journal of Jewish Literary History. Together with Josh Garroway she is editor of *These Truths We Hold: Judaism in an Age of Truthiness* (HUC Press, 2022).

12   Last Translations: Gershom Scholem's Renditions of S.Y. Agnon's Polish Tales

Maya Barzilai

> In Agnon's rendering of its origins ... Buczacz is a way station on the path to the Land of Israel, the result of an arrested journey.
>
> —Alan Mintz, "'I am Building a City': On Agnon's Buczacz Tales"

S.Y. AGNON'S TRAVELS AS a young man took him, in 1908, from Buczacz, Galicia to Jaffa, Palestine and from there, in 1912, to Germany. Agnon's stay in Berlin was intended as a "way station" on route back to the Land of Israel, but the outbreak of World War I arrested his journey and he ultimately remained in Germany until 1924. The notion of a "way station" that becomes a home is crucial to understanding Agnon's writing and its dissemination during his extended sojourn in Germany. Agnon continued to write and publish in Hebrew during this period, working on stories and novellas such as *Giv'at haḥol* (*The Hill of Sand*). He also actively promoted the translation of his stories into German, intended for publication in reputable journals such as the *Jüdische Rundschau* and *Der Jude*. Agnon collaborated, furthermore, with German Jewish editors and translators to produce volumes of tales concerning Polish Jews, thus enhancing his creative output in the German language.[1]

While this formative period in Agnon's career might pale in comparison to his post-World War II voluminous activities, and, specifically, to his "epic" project of *'Ir umelo'ah* (*A City in its Fullness*), the two periods of Agnon's writing resonate with one another through a shared preoccupation with the Jewish past in Poland. The stories that ultimately constituted the volume *Polin* (*Poland*), published first in the journal *Hatekufah* in 1919 and, in an expanded volume, in Tel Aviv in 1924, were composed, in part, during Agnon's stay in Germany, and these were also the stories that Gershom Scholem selected to translate. Unlike the spatial focus of the later Buczacz stories, the tales of the *Polin* volume have a broader geographical range across Poland. At the same time, the far slimmer 1924 book

---

1. See, for example, Shmuel Yosef Agnon and Ahron Eliasberg, eds., *Das Buch von den polnischen Juden* (Berlin: Jüdischer Verlag, 1916); Hugo Herrmann and Shmuel Yosef Agnon, eds., *Chad gadja: Das Pessachbuch* (Berlin: Jüdischer Verlag, 1914).

167

Building a City: Writings on Agnon's Buczacz in Memory of Alan Mintz (2022): 167–180
DOI: 10.2979/BuildingaCityWriting.o.o.13

contains, like *'Ir umelo'ah*, an opening legend, concerning how the Jews came to live in Poland, as well as stories that depict the spiritual life of the poor and violent relations between Jews and non-Jews. *Polin* and *'Ir umelo'ah* thus provide book ends, of a sort, for Agnon's writing career: while both combine a mythical and historical Polish Jewish past, the former was written under the sign of Agnon's years in wartime and interwar Germany, while the latter was heavily shaped by the events of the Holocaust.

In *Ancestral Tales* Alan Mintz discusses Agnon's approach to memorialization, contending that the Hebrew author conjured "the lost world of Polish Jewry, viewed not in its fallen, belated aspect but in the vigor of its golden age." Agnon's indirect response to the events of the Holocaust was to "reanimate … what was most valuable in the civilization that had been destroyed."[2] These claims can help to distinguish between the *Polin* tales and the *'Ir umelo'ah* project: most significantly, many of the earlier stories depict a society in decline, on the verge of its complete disintegration, rather than a world in the "vigor of its golden age." An examination of Scholem's translations into German shores up one explanation for this difference: while the earlier stories depict Jews in Poland, they also implicitly reflect upon the current situation of Jews in Germany, as witnessed by Agnon. Working on his translations of Hebrew lamentations around the same time period, Scholem selected precisely those stories that concern cultural decline and end on a note of ironic resolution. Rather than suggest that these translations into German take part in the cult of the Eastern European Jew in Germany during that period, I argue instead that they expressed a specifically German Jewish sense of loss in relationship to the Jewish past and its scriptural traditions.[3] They did not serve the agenda of the German Jewish revival but rather suggested the decline of this culture and offered the long history of Hebrew textual traditions as an antidote to a more nationalistically-driven route toward Hebrew modernization.

The Task of the Translator, Scholem

Scholem and Agnon met during the World War years at the home of another translator of Agnon's, Max Strauss, the brother of Ludwig Strauss.[4] At Agnon's urging, Scholem assisted Strauss with his translation of the novella *Vehayah he'aqov lemishor* (*And the Crooked Shall Be Made Straight*), advising him about rabbinical Hebrew terms.[5] In letters from this time period, Agnon urges

2. Alan L. Mintz, *Ancestral Tales : Reading the Buczacz Stories of S.Y. Agnon* (Stanford: Stanford University Press, 2017), 13.
3. See Steven E. Aschheim, *Brothers and Strangers: The East European Jew in German and German Jewish Consciousness, 1800-1923* (Madison: The University of Wisconson Press, 1982).
4. Gershom Scholem, *From Berlin to Jerusalem: Memories of My Youth*, trans. Harry Zohn (New York: Schocken Books, 1988), 91.
5. Ibid., 92.

Scholem to translate more of his writings and compliments him on the existing translations, asking also that he oversee Max Strauss's subsequent rendition of "Hanidaḥ" ("The Outcast"), ultimately published in 1920 as "Der Verstossene."[6] Agnon also offered to deliver to Scholem unpublished manuscripts, copied by his wife, Esther Marx, but he did not manage to lure Scholem away from his translation project of the kabbalistic work *Sefer habahir* (Book of Brightness).[7] Scholem undertook in total four short translations, the first one appearing in 1920 and three subsequent stories appearing in 1924, after Scholem himself relocated to Palestine in 1923.

A letter from Scholem to his first wife, Else (Escha) Borchhardt, dating July 2, 1923, recounts his visit with Agnon one Shabbat at the author's home in Bad Homburg, during which Scholem read to him Scholem's translation of "Ma'aseh Azriel Moshe shomer hasefarim" ("The Tale of Azriel Moshe, the Book Keeper"). Agnon, he reported, was very enthusiastic and enjoyed the reading, despite his recent bad spirits.[8] The correspondence between the two men also reveals that Scholem had previously sent Agnon drafts of one of his translations, to which Agnon responded: "My friend, I was happy with the translation, which I believe turned out well. I wrote my comments on the margins. Accept the good and ignore the bad. You know that I am not a speaker of Ashkenaz [German] and my knowledge of this language is weak."[9] Despite his protestations to the contrary, Agnon's German did allow him to review the translations of his work and assist Strauss and Scholem in the translation and editing process.

Several decades after the publications of his translations from Agnon's stories, Scholem would assess his friend's contribution to Hebrew literature in a London lecture, claiming that the writer was "heir to the totality of Jewish tradition" while also being able to give artistic form to "the historical forces that made for the disintegration of Jewish tradition." Agnon's early stories, according to Scholem, "succeeded in expressing an infinite wealth of content in infinitesimal space." More importantly, they are, in his words, "suffused by a spirit

---

6. "כידוע לך תרגם [שטרויס] את הנדח אלא שתרגומו צריך שכלול. בבקשה ממך לכשתבוא לברלין גלגל עמו בתרגום או כתוב לו שישלח לך את התרגום ואת המקור למינכן והיה לו לעזר מרחוק. ואף אתה אמור לו שיפרסמו במהרה" ("As you know, [Strauss] translated Hanidaḥ but his translation requires improvement. When you come to Berlin please discuss the translation with him or write to him so that he sends you the original and the translation to Munich and be of help to him from afar. And tell him also to publish it quickly.") S.Y. Agnon to Gershom Scholem, undated letter, in Gershom Scholem Archive, ARC.4 1599 01 0016.1, The National Library of Israel.
7. "התרגמת את במצולות? ואת בית הכנסת הישן? היש א'. לבבך ישר לתרגם איזה דבר משלי? מה?" ("Have you translated 'Bametsulot'? And 'Beit hakenesset hayashan'? Would you honestly like to translate something that I wrote? Which one?"). S.Y. Agnon to Gershom Scholem, August 1920, in ibid.
8. Stefan Litt, Hasafranim: blog hasifriyah haleumit, 11.30.2017, https://blog.nli.org.il/gershom_escha/.
9. S.Y. Agnon to Gershom Scholem, undated, in Gershom Scholem Archive.

of immense sadness and at the same time hold out a great promise of consolation." This intertwinement of sadness and consolation became, for Scholem, "a profoundly Jewish feature of Agnon's creativity."[10] In the German version of the same essay, Scholem used the term "Trauer," denoting sadness and mourning, to describe Agnon's writing.[11] Scholem's appreciation for Agnon thus ties in with his own preoccupation with mourning, which he described, in his 1917 essay, "Über Klage und Klagelied" ("On Lament and Lamentations") as a paradoxical condition or "mental being," rather than as a psychological state of loss. Mourning, moreover, entails a linguistic destruction. In Scholem's words: "Thus mourning partakes in language, but only in the most tragic way, since in its course toward language mourning is directed against itself—and against language."[12] Scholem wrote this essay as an afterward to his translation of Eikhah (Lamentations), but it appeared in print only posthumously.[13] Itta Shedletzki has described his process of using translation and commentary to better understand Hebrew lamentations as a "labor of mourning" ("Trauerarbeit") for the lost Jewish tradition as a result of his secularized upbringing. Using terms reminiscent of Scholem's own assessment of Agnon, Shedletzki explains that mourning, for Scholem, had a positive outcome: "Only after a break with Jewish tradition and a distancing from it, one might, through a serious attempt at approaching it, freely celebrate a sense of renewal."[14] Galili Shachar likewise maintains that Scholem found in the form of the lamentation, "the potential for the renewal of language and thought from the points of silence and extinction."[15]

The process of translating Agnon's stories can be understood within the framework of the "labor of mourning," especially in view of the particular stories Scholem selected for translation. "Ma'aseh Azriel Moshe shomer hasefarim," first published in the Berlin art and literature journal *Rimon* in 1923, tells of a simple man, a porter who, after realizing the extent of his ignorance in Jewish scripture, falls into a deep sorrow. Azriel Moshe finds partial relief through his study of the names of all the Jewish books and their authors in the Beit Midrash. He then

10. Gershom Scholem, "S.Y. Agnon—The Last Hebrew Classic?," in *On Jews and Judaism in Crisis: Selected Essays* ed. Werner J. Dannhauser (New York: Schocken Books, 1976), 95, 104.
11. "S. J. Agnon - der letzte hebräische Klassiker?," in *Judaica 2* (Frankfurt am Main: Suhrkamp Verlag, 1995), 104.
12. "On Lament and Lamentation," in *Lament in Jewish Thought: Philosophical, Theological, and Literary Perspectives*, ed. Ilit Ferber and Paula Schwebel (Berlin: De Gruyter 2014), 315-316.
13. Galili Shachar and Ilit Ferber, eds., *Haqinot: Shirah, hagut, vetugah be'olamo shel Gershom Scholem* (Jerusalem: Carmel, 2016), 88.
14. Itta Shedletzki, "Auf der Suche nach dem verlorenen Judentum. Zur „historischen Gestalt" Gershom Scholems," *Münchner Beiträge zur Jüdischen Geschichte und Kultur 2* (2007), 36.
15. Galili Shachar, "Lekonen ulehokhiaḥ: 'al darko hamukdemet shel Gershom Scholem bayahadut," in *Haqinot: Shirah, hagut, vetugah be'olamo shel Gershom Scholem*, ed. Galili Shachar and Ilit Ferber (Jerusalem: Carmel, 2016), 32.

becomes the keeper of the books and is murdered in a pogrom after attempting to guard them from destruction. For Scholem, "Ma'aseh Azriel Moshe" exemplified the "intermingling of consolation and sadness" in Agnon's work.[16] He translated Azriel's sadness at his ignorance about the Jewish sources through the term "Kummer," meaning sorrow or pain: "...sein Kummer so groß war..." ("his sorrow was so vast").[17] Azriel Moshe experiences this sadness when he recalls how Jews sit on the ground on the Ninth of Av and mourn the destruction of the Temple. He then recognizes that he does not know in which Jewish source this destruction was recorded.[18] The translated term, "Kummer," provides a lexical juncture between Yiddish and German, and Agnon would later name the protagonist of *Temol shilshom* (*Only Yesterday*) Yitzhak Kummer. Scholem's choice of this word allows a Jewish-inflected melancholia to permeate his German. When rendering Eikhah into German, Scholem used the word Kummer to translate the Hebrew "*makh'ov*" meaning grief and pain.[19] Scholem's word choice linked his scriptural and literary translations, since the same German term translated both Azriel Moshe's sorrow, *tsa'aro*, and the grief of Jewish collective lament.

After writing all the names he has learned in the Beit Midrash on the walls of his home, Azriel Moshe feels joy intermingled with sadness for while he has learned the names of wise Jews and their writings, he cannot read the contents of these books. He cries and his tears erase the very names that he wrote in chalk in order to memorize them: "umerov hadema'ot hayah haketav holekh venimhah" ("And the abundance of tears was erasing the writing").[20] In Scholem's German, this same phrase reads: "Und der Menge der Tränen halber verlöschte die Schrift immer mehr" ("And because of the quantity of tears the writing was wiped out more and more").[21] The German verb *verlöschen* refers, ordinarily, to the extinguishing of a source of light, but here the tears perform the destruction, erasing that which has been obtained through study. Azriel Moshe's tears in the story function in a manner akin to the language of lamentations, in Scholem's iteration: they destructively erase, in a performative gesture, the very names that they mourn, resulting in a potentially endless cycle of mourning. However, Azriel Moshe subsequently decides to rewrite: he purchases paper and records the names with pencil on it, providing a somewhat definite framework for retaining and transmitting his knowledge.[22] This shift in medium, from chalk on the walls

16. Gershom Scholem, "S.Y. Agnon," 104.
17. S.Y. Agnon, "Zwei Erzählungen: Die Geschichte von Asriel Moshe, dem Bücherwart; Die große Synagoge," *Der Jude*, 1924, 232.
18. "Ma'aseh Azriel Moshe shomer hasefarim," *Rimon*, 1923, 35.
19. Galili Shachar and Ilit Ferber, eds., *Haqinot: Shirah, hagut, vetugah be'olamo shel Gershom Scholem*, 53.
20. S.Y. Agnon, "Ma'aseh Azriel Moshe," 36.
21. "Zwei Erzählungen," 233.
22. "Ma'aseh Azriel Moshe," 36.

to paper and pencil, might be compared to the mournful work of translation that has the potential of resulting in a sense of restoration.

Scholem's choice of the term "Schrift" in his translation of the above-quoted passage is overdetermined since it denotes not only writing but also the holy text, Die Schrift. The translation thereby foregrounds an implicit aspect of the original story: Azriel Moshe's tears do not merely erase chalk names on walls, but extinguish the holy books themselves, thereby alluding to the holy names of God. Elḥanan Shilo has discussed the Kabbalistic origins of this passage in tales from the Zohar about the angle Azriel who reinscribes the names of God that were erased by false oaths and thereby protects the world from the waters of the deep, of *tehom*.[23] If Scholem undertook a "labor of mourning" through his work on Hebrew lamentations, his translations of Agnon's stories addressed German Jews who had experienced a distancing from tradition and a desire to take up the study of Jewish texts, enabling a sense of restoration. Specifically, he had his brother-in-law, Moshe Marx, in mind since, as Scholem recounted, Marx collected Hebrew books and took excellent care of them, even though he could barely understand their contents.[24] Scholem's German version thus spells out for readers the resonances of Agnon's Hebrew, rendering writing as scripture and turning the erasure of the names into their utter extinguishment.

From yet another perspective, Scholem himself, as a translator between Hebrew and German, might be compared to Moshe Azriel who, after erasing his own writing on the walls, decides to transcribe the (holy) names again. In his diaries, Scholem described the translation of the Bible as an act of redemption since through this process the "structure of God's language" can be rediscovered. He viewed the translation of Eikhah and the Bible more generally as a "parting gift" (*Geschenk beim Abschied*) of the Zionist Jew to the German language, or else "the gift that enables parting." In other words, German Jews cannot be delivered into Hebrew until they pay off their "debt of gratitude" (*Dankesschuld*) to German society and culture through the task of scriptural translation.[25] When approaching works of literature, such as Agnon's stories, rather than "God's language," the hefty notion of a debt of gratitude is only partially applicable. However, in view of Scholem's departure from Germany in 1923, his translations of Agnon became literal gifts, which he left behind for a German readership.

23. Elchanan Shilo, *Haqabbalah biytsirat S.Y. Agnon* (Ramat-Gan: Universitat Bar-Ilan, 2011), 187-188.
24. "This memorable man [Moses Marx] was a partner in a textile firm on Spittelmarket, but his heart belonged to Hebrew typography and bibliography, though he was hardly capable of understanding the contents of the books which he so lovingly tended and had so wonderfully bound by Berlin's most outstanding craftsmen." Gershom Scholem, *From Berlin to Jerusalem: Memories of My Youth*, 143.
25. *Tagebücher nebst Aufsätzen und Entwürfen bis 1923*, vol. 2 (Frankfurt am Main: Jüdischer Verlag im Suhrkamp Verlag, 2000), 346.

The reverence with which Scholem upheld Agnon might also explain his decision to translate his stories into German, even when most of his other translations were not of a literary nature. When reading out loud another tale by Agnon, "Aggadat hasofer" ("The Tale of the Torah Scribe") to Walter Benjamin in the summer of 1918, Scholem describes how Benjamin thought that this story is comparable to the Bible, so that if the ending were better executed then "the purpose of the Bible" would no longer be evident.[26] Scholem too considered Agnon's Hebrew writing a continuation of Hebrew scriptural and literary tradition, claiming that Agnon "worked for [the renaissance of Hebrew] in the quarries of tradition." Agnon did not treat the Bible as a mere "national saga," devoid of religious or mystical significance, but rather recognized the "continuity of tradition and its language in their true context." In this respect, Agnon, for Scholem, was the last of a near-extinct species of Hebrew writers, the master of an obsolete medium, or, from a different perspective, "the occupant of the most advanced outpost of the Hebrew language in its old sense."[27] The question arises, how could a translation into any language, including German, capture Agnon's sensibility as a Hebrew writer who was able to bridge the Jewish past of this language with the present and future of its users? When seeking to mediate Agnon for a German readership, Scholem could not preserve the full extent of the Hebrew writer's allusions and the range of his Hebrew that drew from past textual traditions. Rather, his German texts evoked, more than anything, a sense of loss and mourning, perhaps as a first steps towards recovery of the past. They provided a glimpse of the Hebrew original without suggesting that the German translation could supplant knowledge of Hebrew and its legacy.

The Voices of Past Hebrew

In the same issue of the 1924 *Der Jude*, Scholem also published his translation of Agnon's "Beit hakenesset haggadol" ("The Great Synagogue"). This story shares with "Ma'aseh Azriel Moshe shomer hasefarim" the sense that a body of knowledge and tradition has been lost and cannot be fully restored, despite the protagonists' attempts. "The Great Synagogue" first appeared in the Hebrew journal *Hatekufah* in 1919 and Agnon then collected it, with some modifications, in the *Polin* volume of 1924. It describes a group of Jewish children who, when digging in the ground in order to construct their own new Temple, uncover the shingles of a roof. At first, when only the roof is in sight, the Polish town folk believe it is an old palace in which a local lord suffocated to death his wife's lover. After the entire structure has been uncovered, they believe it is a church, and only

26. Gershom Scholem, *Lamentations of Youth: The Diaries of Gershom Scholem, 1913–1919*, trans. Anthony David (Cambridge, Mass.: The Belknap Press of Harvard University Press, 2007), 250.
27. "S.Y. Agnon," 95–96.

when they hear voices coming from within and fear that these are unburied souls, do they call the Jews to try and open the locked building. When the doors swing open, the local Jews find a splendid synagogue within, filled with trappings of the original Temple as depicted in the Bible. However, the last line reads: "Everything was in its place. Only the eternal light was about to go out."[28]

Scholem's choice to translate this tale of unearthing a synagogue from a past era of greatness was overdetermined, when we consider his view of Agnon as a writer who worked for the modernization of Hebrew in "the quarries of tradition." The epigraph, a verse from Psalm 31, alludes to this point: מָה רַב־טוּבְךָ, אֲשֶׁר־צָפַנְתָּ לִּירֵאֶיךָ: "How great Your goodness that You hid for those who fear you."[29] Those who seek God might find a hidden goodness, the Psalmist promises, but Agnon's story is far bleaker. Ironically, the synagogue appears to be the very Temple that the children were planning to build so that their utopic project transforms into a site of decline and death, hinted at through the discussion of the local lord who turns into a vengeful murderer. Rather than uncover a preserved space and tradition that possesses an "eternal life"—in Scholem's description of the Hebrew language—Agnon's ending reveals, in Robert Alter's words, that "the wondrous renewal of the past ... comes too late in the history of faith and culture—the return can no longer take place."[30] In the historical Jerusalem Temple, the Western candle was the one that always remained ablaze and was used to light the other candles. Considering that Agnon used the term *ner hattamid*, his story points to the decline of Western Jewish culture. Scholem translated the final verb, *shqi'ato* (its setting or extinguishing) with the nominalized verb, *Erlöschen*, which denotes both extinguishment and death, thereby intensifying the original Hebrew. The German translation can be viewed as a lamenting one, mourning the loss of Jewish traditions and the Hebrew language itself, suggesting that the past can perhaps be dug up but not fully resurrected.

Scholem's German includes, in a gesture of preservation, specific Hebrew terms—such as *Tischa b'ab*, the day of mourning for the destroyed Temple, *Gemara*, and *Shamir* (legendary worm used to cut the Temple's alter stones). This incorporation of Hebrew terms notwithstanding, the German version provides, as a whole, an accessible narrative that forgoes the intricate web of allusions evoked in Agnon's Hebrew, precluding the very process of probing into the past

---

28. S.Y. Agnon, "The Great Synagogue," *The Reform Jewish Quarterly* (2016), 129. "Beit hakenesset haggadol," *Hatequfah*, 1919, 30. והכל על מקומו בשלום, רק נר־התמיד היה סמוך לשקיעתו"
29. Alter Psalm 31.
30. Robert Alter, *Necessary Angels: Tradition and Modernity in Kafka, Benjamin, and Scholem* (Cambridge, Mass: Harvard University Press, 1991), 17.

that the story describes.[31] The opening of the story posed a particular challenge for Scholem (and later translators) since it draws on Talmudic idiom, also alluding thereby to the relevant rabbinic commentary. Here are the story's opening sentences:

תינוקות של בית רבן משתעשעים היו יום של קיץ אחד אחר הצהרים בחצר בית רבן על

ההר הגדול: במחבואים ובזקנה ודוב; בארבעים שודדים ובגימ"ל אחין; במלחמת דוד

וגלית ובכהן משוח-מלחמה,–עד שנתיגעו משעשועים אלו ונתנו לבם לבנות את בית-

המקדש. אמרו: הרי אתמול תשעה באב היה, יום שהחריבו את הבית, הבה נתחיל בבנינו.[32]

Die Kinder aus der Schule spielten nachmittags an einem Sommertage im Hof der Schule auf dem großen Berg: Versteck, die Alte unter der Bär, Vierzieg Räuber, Drei Brüder, Davids Kampf mit Goliath, und den Priester, der die Krieger auswählt, bis sie dieser Spiele müde wurden und darauf sannen, das Heiligtum zu bauen. Sie sagten: gestern war ja Tischa ba'ab, der Tag, an dem die Feinde das Haus zerstörten, nun wollen wir anfangen es wieder zu bauen.[33]

School children [*tinoqot shel beit rabban*] were playing on the hill: Games such as Forty Thieves and Three Brothers, the Battle of David and Goliath, and the Priest Anointed for Battle. When they had tired of these pastimes they said, "Yesterday was Tishah B'Av, the day that the enemies destroyed the Temple. Let's begin to rebuild it.[34]

The Hebrew idiom, *tinoqot shel beit rabban*, is a Talmudic term originating in BT 119b that refers to children studying in a traditional Jewish school or *ḥeder*. In the context of this story concerning the children's shift from typical games to the more serious project of rebuilding the Temple, the idiom activates a passage in the Babylonian Talmudic warning against the neglect of Jewish children's studies, even for the sake of rebuilding the Temple.

> R. Hamnuna said: Jerusalem was destroyed only because they neglected [the education of] school children; for it is sad, pour it out [sc. God's wrath] because of the children in the street: why pour it out? Because the child is in the street.

---

31. In 1917, Scholem published in the Zionist *Jüdische Rundschau* a scathing critique of Alexander Eliasberg's translation, from the Yiddish, of three story collections by writers such as Y. L. Peretz, Sholem Aleichem, and Sholem Asch. He accused Eliasberg of succumbing to modern norms and bourgeoisie expectations, producing texts that ignore or replace Jewish terms and create a sentimental atmosphere unbefitting the originals. Gershom Scholem, *Tagebücher nebst Aufsätzen und Entwürfen bis 1923*, vol. 1, ed. Kalfried Gründer, Herbert Kopp-Oberstebrink, and Friedrich Niewöhner (Frankfurt am Main: Jüdischer Verlag im Suhrkamp Verlag, 2000), 495–497.
32. S.Y. Agnon, "Beit hakenesset haggadol," 28.
33. "Zwei Erzählungen," 235.
34. "The Great Synagogue," 126.

Resh Lakish also said in the name of R. Judah the Prince: School children may not be made to neglect [their studies] even for the building of the Temple.[35]

Playing secular games like "Forty Thieves and Three Brothers," the children in Agnon's story participate in the neglect of studies denounced by R. Hamnuna and Resh Lakish. Their games progress, furthermore, from the more innocuous "hide and seek" to enactments of biblical battle scenes such as "David and Goliath." Not only do these children neglect their sacred studies but they then turn to the "game" of rebuilding the Temple. They work sacrilegiously in direct opposition to the rabbinic notion that the neglect of study caused the destruction of Jerusalem and that children should not be permitted to stop studying even for the sake of rebuilding the Temple. When their teacher, the Rabbi, comes out to the sound of their calls as they happen upon the roof tiles, he does not scold them, moreover, but appears interested in using the tiles to repair the roof of his own home.

This passage concerning the children's work outside of the *heder* environment can also be interpreted from within a Zionist framework: as they leave behind the religious world, the children embark upon warring games that bring them to take matters into their own hands and attempt to rebuild the Temple. By setting his tale on the day after the Ninth of Av, a day that Agnon adopted as his birthday, Agnon implicitly shows how the destruction of the Temple might be subsumed within a Zionist agenda, alluding to the rebuilding of a Jewish nation through imagery of children as construction works: "One brought a pocket full of clay, and another a mouth full of water. This one a stone and that one a broken brick... they decided to cut the stone with their teeth."[36] Using their clothes, mouths, and teeth rather than any construction tools, these young students embody Zionist labor, using and sacrificing their own bodies as they toil and become subsumed in the earth that they dig up.

The loss of the Talmudic allusion to the *tinoqot shel bet rabban* in German translation—"Kinder aus der Schule spielten nachmittags...im Hoff der Schule"— thus enacts the logic of the story itself. It abolishes the world of Jewish *heder* and religious studies and secularizes the story, downplaying the sacrilegious dimension of the children's play. Additionally, just as the townspeople misidentify the structure and believe it to be a church, so readers of this translation might first misinterpret who these children are, mistaking them for Christians, only to encounter terms like *Tischa b'ab* that force a renewed perception of the truth. The dissonance between the German-language opening and the game of rebuilding the Temple, "das Heiligtum," performs the distance that a secularized German Jew would need to overcome in order to return to Zion as a religious,

35. The Babylonian Talmud, (I. Epstein), 818–819, https://archive.org/details/TheBabylonian TalmudcompleteSoncinoEnglishTranslation.
36. S.Y. Agnon, "The Great Synagogue," 126.

not merely political, site. Scholem's translation constitutes, in this manner, a portal in its own right: it is a door that will not easily unlock and that hides its inner Hebrew contents; it also can, potentially, lead the reader into the house, *habayit* in Hebrew, which means both home and Temple. Just as the children uncover the old synagogue when trying to rebuild the Temple, so the readers too, once entering the story, come across terms and ideas that, like the shingles of the rediscovered roof, must be deciphered, ultimately revealing their innermost Jewish significance.

If Scholem uses the more neutral words "Kinder" (children) and "Schule" (school) in the opening of the story, as the tale progresses he includes explanations within the translation for terms that do not require such elaboration in the Hebrew. For instance, where Agnon writes "*harei matsinu bateshuvot*" ("we have found in the responsa"), Scholem translates "Wir finden ja in den Bescheiden der Rabbinen" ("we find in the legal decisions of the rabbis"). When a voice is finally heard from within the locked abode, Agnon writes and translates that the Jews hear the voice, "and behold: the voice is the voice of Jacob." Scholem diverges here from Agnon and writes: "und sieh, wie die Stimme von Juden war ihr Klang" ("and behold, its sound was like the voice of Jews").[37] As in the example of *tinoqot shel beit raban*, here too the German version avoids an allusion to another Jewish text, in this case the theft of the birthright in Genesis 25, when Isaac identifies Jacob's voice while incorrectly mistaking the hands for Esau's. In Agnon's tale, the allusion concludes a debate concerning the identity of the building itself. Initially perceived as a palace, further digging reveals the structure to be a house of worship, but it remains unclear whether it is a church or a synagogue. Only when the door does not open and the Polish townfolks supposedly hear the voices of an unburied soul from within do they call upon the Jews to approach, fearing spirit possession. In other words, the synagogue itself appears masked, as though it were a church with "stained glass windows," reminiscent of the manner in which Jacob covered himself with lamb skin in order to appear akin to Esau while his voice betrayed his true identity. Considering that Agnon witnessed the flourishing of Reform German Jewry in Germany, including the construction of a massive and richly-decorated synagogue in 1912 in West Berlin, the allusion to the "voice of Jacob" could be understood as a stab at the Christian façade of the modern German synagogue. Agnon further underscores the importance of this allusion with the description: "And when they put their hands on the gate, the gate opened before them." It is not enough to hear the voice of Jacob, that is the voice of the Israelite brother, the Jews must also, like Jacob, use their hands to recover the space of this structure as their own.

37. "Beit hakenesset haggadol," 29; "Zwei Erzählungen," 237.

The verse that the voice from within the synagogue sings includes the name Jacob: "How goodly are thy tents, O Jacob, thy dwelling places, O Israel."[38] Since Jews traditionally utter this phrase from Numbers 24:5 prior to prayer, upon entering the space of a synagogue, Agnon uses it at this point in the narrative just prior to the magical opening of the old synagogue's doors. However, in conjunction with the previous mention of Jacob and his mistaken blessing, this allusion to Numbers also might remind readers that Bal'am sought to curse the people of Israel, rather than bless them. Israel's fate depends on such reversals, from curse to blessing, and the dug-up synagogue represents this potential transformation from poverty to wealth, from destitution to redemption. Still, the decline of the eternal flame at the end of the story indicates an unclear resolution and brings this fairytale like narrative to an ominous conclusion. While Scholem transposed the verse from Numbers into German—"Wie schön sind deine Zelte, Jakob"—he translated the first mention of Jacob as "Juden" (Jews), revealing that he did not rely on his audience to understand the biblical allusion or to consider Jacob as representative of the people of Israel. He also rendered the singular Jacob as a plural "Juden," linguistically cementing the connection between the Polish Jews whom the Christian villagers call to "do their work" and enter the structure and the voice emanating from within.

In an unpublished 1926 essay entitled "Bemerkungen über Hebräisch und Hebräischlernen" ("Notes on Hebrew and the Study of Hebrew), Scholem distinguished between Hebrew as the literary language of the book and the Hebrew spoken in Palestine. He argued for the life force of the former in contrast to the ghostly, almost demonic power of the latter. Despite the ongoing processes of secularization, Hebrew had retained, for Scholem, the glint or reflection ("Abglanz") and "the constant resonance of that revelation" to which it owes its eternal life. Even more so, this language possesses, through its tradition, "a weighty treasure chamber of nuances" ("Ballast Schatzkammern von Nuancen") and, most importantly, "it promises us the silent realms, without which we cannot conduct a spiritual, that is a linguistic life."[39] Scholem perceived Agnon, alongside the poet Ḥayyim Naḥman Bialik, as one of the few modern Hebrew writers capable of drawing from these "treasure chambers of nuances" and writing in the spiritual mode of the language. For Scholem, "Agnon's writing is distinguished by a singular stillness, by an absence of pathos and exaltation." It is also, as he recognized, informed by "the extraordinary sobriety of rabbinic prose," in addition to Agnon's saturation in kabbalistic literature and the early writings of Hasidism.[40]

In view of Scholem's own positioning of Agnon at the "crossroads" of Hebrew language tradition and modernity, translation into any language,

38. "The Great Synagogue," 128.
39. Gershom Scholem Archive, ARC. 4* 1599 07 277.1.25, The National Library of Israel.
40. Gershom Scholem, "S.Y. Agnon," 106-107.

German included, could not possibly convey this bridging function. As we have seen, while contending with the dying out of the Jewish past and the inability to fully resurrect it, "Beit hakenesset haggadol," nonetheless performs the ongoing presence of the past in the Hebrew language through its intricate web of biblical and Talmudic allusions. Incapable of replicating these resonances in German, Scholem could still imitate the "sobriety" of Agnon's prose, or else its stillness and "absence of pathos." Furthermore, his German story points to the duality of (secularized) Hebrew as a potentially demonic voice emanating from within an unidentified locked chamber versus (literary) Hebrew as a decipherable voice emerging from within an identified synagogue. His decision to take up this particular story, alongside "Ma'aseh Azriel Moshe shomer hasefarim," suggests, moreover, that both tales addressed Scholem's concern with the demise of German Jewish culture. The German translations were intended to lead readers to the Hebrew source, rather than leaving them satisfied with its German replication. Like the Christian townspeople, who are denied entrance to the unearthed house of worship, so readers of the German text are led to understand that they remain themselves outside the structure of Hebrew spiritual life that contains treasures for those who seek. Thus, for instance, the final sentence of the Hebrew story includes terms that allude to the Temple's brass ritual objects (*kiyyor neḥoshet* and *neḥoshet kelal*) and to the symbolism of the dove. While the interior opulence can be expressed in German, the provenance of the Hebrew terms in scriptural descriptions of the Temple remains buried in translation.

For Scholem, the figure of Azriel Moshe and the image of the Great Synagogue encapsulated some of these tensions concerning the study of Hebrew in modern times and the preservation of written Hebrew as a quarry of tradition. Both stories represent, through imagery of erasure, misidentification, and extinguishment the arduous process of coming to terms with and striving to obtain a hidden and buried past. Agnon's stories do not suggest that these losses can be recuperated but posit, instead, a structure of mourning that ends on a tragic-ironic note. The act of translating these stories from Hebrew into German constituted, I maintain, a loss of a second order, distancing the reader further from the original and from "the heavy ballast of historical tones and overtones accumulated through 3,000 years of sacred literature," as Scholem put it.[41] In this respect, the translations performed, even more decisively than the original texts, the rupture between past and present, tradition and modernity. They offered German Jewish readers a form of literary lamentation, a path for mourning the erasure of holy Hebrew names, also through the very process of translation away from Hebrew. And, at the same time, they extend into the German language something of the Hebrew "Abglanz," the reflection of revelation: they depict a glint of that light in

---

41. Ibid., 95.

the process of its extinguishment. Scholem's German translations radicalize, in this manner, the Hebrew lament, marking a site of linguistic annihilation and suggesting that the rich silence of this language might only be accessed through the dialectic of study and mourning.

In writing this essay, I too mourn the tremendous loss of Alan Mintz z"l, a wise and caring mentor. Not unlike Scholem, Mintz too engaged in the translation and interpretation of Agnon's writing, focusing on works about the Jewish Polish past. In the "introduction" to *Ancestral Tales*, Mintz openly tells us that he was "wrong" in his past assessment of Agnon's engagement with the Holocaust. While previously underestimating the significance of World War II in this author's oeuvre, he came to realize that he could not see the Holocaust because it did not appear in the forms he was used to—"ghettos, camps, victims, perpetrators, survivors, traumatic memory, and so on." "The Great Synagogue" can provide a useful analogy for Mintz's claim: how does one go about identifying what one encounters? The entire population in the story (*kol ha'ir kulah*), and not merely the Christian Poles, see in the unearthed building what their eyes are trained to perceive: a palace or a church. The idea of a Temple-like "great synagogue" has been lost, to some extent, and cannot be imagined until very late in the story. Mintz understood Agnon's project as an attempt to "restore, if only through the medium of the storyteller's art, the world of Jews and Judaism that had been brought to its final extermination."[42] In order to appreciate this project of restoration one must, as Mintz instructed us, retrain one's scholarly vision, allowing the previously unimaginable to appear and become recognized for what it truly is. And for this late-life lesson, an intellectual parable if you like, I am eternally grateful to Alan Mintz.

MAYA BARZILAI is Associate Professor of Hebrew literature and Jewish culture at the University of Michigan. Her first book, *Golem: Modern Wars and Their Monsters* (NYU Press 2016) received the AJS Jordan Schnitzer Book Prize. Her second book, *Golem, How He Came into the World*, appeared with Camden House in 2020. She currently researches twentieth-century German-Hebrew translation practices and cultural exchanges.

42. Alan L. Mintz, *Ancestral Tales*, 14.

Early and Late

13 From "A City of the Dead" to A City in Its Fullness: Evolving Depictions of Buczacz in the Long Agnonian Arc

Jeffrey Saks

> Dr. Langsam returned for one of his stimulating talks. These chats must have stimulated the doctor, too, for the more he said, the more he had to say. In fact, though he had spent only the first twenty years of his life in his native town, a thousand years seemed not long enough to tell about them. Sometimes he repeated old stories to Hirshl and sometimes he related new ones. Though he had studied in famous universities, lived in great metropolises, and frequented celebrated theaters and opera houses, all these places might as well never have existed: nothing had remained in his memory, it seemed, but the little town he grew up in.
>
> —S.Y. Agnon, *A Simple Story*

COSMOLOGY, THE STUDY of the origin and evolution of the physical universe, posits that every observable thing in creation can be traced back to events that took place in the earliest moments immediately following the Big Bang. The seed for all material objects originated with the formation of the first light elements—

Forming a connection with Alan Mintz *z"l* was surely one of the most pleasant and beneficial surprises of joining the community of Agnon scholars. His warm friendship and wise counsel informed the fifteen volumes in the Toby Press S.Y. Agnon Library, and the *chavrusashaft* we shared in coediting *A City in Its Fullness* was a source of particular joy and learning for me. Alan's legacy remains his deep belief in the power of Hebrew literature, and Agnon's writing in particular, to inform and invigorate Jewish life and learning. This essay was first presented at a session of the Galicia Group at the Israel Institute for Advanced Studies, convened by Alan at Hebrew University in June 2016. The ideas behind what I write here came about through my work with Alan and James S. Diamond *z"l* on *A City in Its Fullness* and were sharpened through Jim's penetrating insights and gentle encouragement only two weeks before his own tragic death. May the memories of Alan and Jim, and the memory of their teachings, remain blessed. For their friendship and advice in preparing this essay I am grateful to Omri Ben Yehudah, Yitzhak Blau, Gila Fine, Steven Fine, Rhonna W. Rogol, Wendy Zierler, and especially Rafi Weiser *z"l*.
The epigraph is from S.Y. Agnon, *A Simple Story* (New Milford, CT: Toby, 2014), 196.

Figure 7: The Jewish cemetery in Buczacz. Credit: Wendy Zierler.

hydrogen and helium—out of primordial energy during the first three minutes of creation, a theory popularized by the Nobel physicist Steven Weinberg.[1]

Rarely can the roots of literary or artistic creations be analyzed with the same type of scientific precision. However, careful examination of the often overlooked early works of S.Y. Agnon offers crucial insight into the original raw material from which he crafted a literary universe over his long career. Agnon's adolescent writing in Yiddish and Hebrew prior to his departure for *Erets Yisra'el* in 1908, aged twenty, are the protons and neutrons he would rearrange in stories, novellas, and novels from the moment his career is conventionally considered to have begun, with his arrival in Jaffa, up to and including material he was working on shortly before his death in 1970. As a young teenage author whose ambition was outstripped only by his talent, Agnon already saw himself as the chronicler of his native Buczacz. Understanding the writings of young S. Y. Czaczkes (his name prior to adopting his pseudonym) is essential for understanding the mature author.[2]

Agnon seems to have been self-conscious of the weaknesses in his early works, those published while still living in Galicia and even some early material composed after his aliyah. With time, he came to moderate the excesses of his immature, romantic narrative voice in favor of a style marked by "a singular stillness, by an absence of pathos and exaltation [...] free from even a trace of expressionistic hysteria," as described by Gershom Scholem, who noted the "profound influence" of the "extraordinary sobriety of rabbinic prose" on Agnon's writing.[3] He certainly came to recognize that his strength was as a prosaist, not as a poet, and assessments of his adolescent verse (and its shortcomings) bear out the wisdom of this artistic choice. Indeed, A. M. Habermann's bibliography of the early writings of Czaczkes, almost none of which were later included in the various editions of collected works, is a reader's guide of material Agnon chose to leave behind.[4]

1. Steven Weinberg, *The First Three Minutes: A Modern View of the Origin of the Universe* (New York: Basic, 1977).
2. The most trenchant treatments of Agnon's early writings are Yitzhak Bakon, *Agnon hatsa'ir* (Beersheba: Ben Gurion University, 1989); Arnold Band, *Nostalgia and Nightmare: A Study in the Fiction of S.Y. Agnon* (Berkeley: University of California Press, 1968), 29–53, which is an expanded English version of Band, "Agnon lifnei heyoto Agnon," *Molad* 175–76 (1963): 54–63; Dov Sadan, *'Al Shai Agnon*, 1st ed. (Tel Aviv: Hakibbutz Hameuchad, 1959), 125–54; and Shlomo Zucker, "Sippurei Czaczkes vetiqqunei Agnon" in *Shai Agnon: Meḥqarim ute'udot*, ed. G. Shaked and R. Weiser (Jerusalem: Mossad Bialik, 1978), 11–29. In 1958, Sadan had already speculated whether it would have been possible to predict Agnon's later greatness from his earliest work. For his felicitous metaphor of distinguishing kittens from lion cubs see Sadan, *'Al Shai Agnon*, rev. ed. (Tel Aviv: Hakibbutz Hameuchad, 1978), 57.
3. Gershom Scholem, "S.Y. Agnon—The Last Hebrew Classic?" in *On Jews and Judaism in Crisis* (New York: Schocken, 1976), 106–7.
4. A. M. Habermann, "Shmuel Yosef Czaczkes: Ḥomer bibliografi," *Gilyonot* 7, nos. 4–5 (1938), 471–72. While Agnon did recycle certain themes or plotlines from the adolescent works (e.g.,

In fact, in what seems to be a clear autobiographical projection, the Guest in *A Guest for the Night*—returning to his hometown as a now middle-aged, accomplished author—is embarrassed when Yeruham Hofshi declaims the Guest's early poetry. The doggerel's cheesy rhymes such as *Shamayim* and *Yerushalayim* or *Qodesh* and *Ḥodesh* cause him to beg for the younger man's silence:

> [Yeruham] placed his two hands on his heart, and repeated melodiously:
>> Devotion faithful unto death
>> I've sworn to thee by God above,
>> For all I have in Exile here
>> I'll give, Jerusalem, for thy love.
> …"If you are not silent I will leave you and go," I said to Yeruham. He paid no heed but recited:
>> And though the tomb may close me in
>> With all the dead beneath the ground,
>> In deepest pit thou art my strength,
>> O fortress city, world-renowned.
> "I know you don't like this poem," said Yeruham. "Your taste has improved and you are sick of rhyming "God above" and "Jerusalem's love.""[5]

Agnon's dismissal of his adolescent writing aside, there is value in turning our attention to a remarkable and largely overlooked item in the catalog of early works. This is the short piece, " 'Ir hametim" ("A City of the Dead"), which appeared in the Lvov Hebrew newspaper, *Ha'et*, on March 14, 1907, and was signed with the pseudonym *Eḥad min Ha'ir* ("One of the City" or "A Man of the City," which I presume was a salute to Aḥad Ha'am, as well as a claim of rootedness in the locale he was coming to document).[6] The work is hard to categorize. It is a string

---

the 1907 "Hapanas" is an early iteration of the themes found in "Meḥolat hamavet"), only three very short stories were reworked and salvaged in any recognizable way in the later collected works: "Or Torah" (1906), "Hapinkah hashevurah" (1906, retitled "Yatom ve'almanah"), and "Ger tsedeq" (written prior to Agnon's departure from Buczacz, publication was delayed until 1910 in the first issue of the Zloczow newspaper, *Hatsa'ir*). All of these stories today appear in *Elu ve'elu*. Habermann's bibliography was later slightly expanded by Band, *Nostalgia*, 525–26 as Appendix I (Hebrew works, 1903–8) and Appendix II (Yiddish works, 1903–7).

5. S.Y. Agnon, *A Guest for the Night* (New Milford, CT: Toby, 2014), 97–98. This early poem of the Guest had in fact been published by Czaczkes in the Kraków newspaper *Hamitspeh* (July 15, 1904)! The treatment of Agnon's early poetry in Sadan, *'Al Shai Agnon* (1959 and 1978) remains the most insightful.

6. S.Y. Agnon, " 'Ir hametim," *Ha'et* 19 (March 14, 1907), 2–5. Y. L. Peretz published a Hebrew story by the same title in the Warsaw newspaper *Hatsefirah* 164 (August 5, 1892) and 165 (August 7, 1892), then published an expanded Yiddish version as "Di Toyte Shtot" in 1895. The Yiddish version was collected in his *Shriften* 4 (Warsaw, 1901), 138–48 and translated by Hillel Halkin as "The Dead Town" in *The I. L. Peretz Reader*, ed. Ruth R. Wisse (New Haven, CT: Yale University Press, 2002), 162–71. It is possible that young Czaczkes had read the story in either Hebrew or Yiddish by 1907. While our story does not appear to be in dialogue with that by

of vignettes about the history of Buczacz, around 1,450 words long, presented as reportage of the type he had been publishing in Galician newspapers for about three years.

Had young Czaczkes entered the family fur trade or the rabbinate (as his father and grandfather might have hoped), or if, God forbid, the ship carrying him to Jaffa's shores had never reached its port, we would little note nor long remember "'Ir hametim." The importance of this story, perhaps more than any other publication prior to the colossal success achieved early on with "'Agunot," first published in Ha'omer in October 1908, is in the cataloging of a variety of themes and plots in miniature, which Agnon would rework over the next sixty years, culminating with his monumental *'Ir umelo'ah* (whose major stories have now been published in English as *A City in Its Fullness*). The sheer artistry of "'Agunot" (even in its first edition; it was substantially revised in 1921, then again when included in the collected works), is remarkably advanced relative to his pre-aliyah works published only a number of months earlier. One wonders what—aside from the proverbial "air of Erets Yisra'el"—caused such an accelerated maturation in the artist as a young man.

In February 1907, young Czaczkes answered the call of Gershom Bader to move to Lvov and serve as assistant editor at his newly launched *Ha'et*, which styled itself as a thrice-weekly "political and literary newspaper."[7] Yitzhak Bakon observed that this short period in Agnon's career marks the earliest emergence of what would later evolve into his distinctive "narrative voice."[8] Part of the assistant's job must have been to provide much of the copy himself. As was common in small newspapers of the day, one writer would publish under a variety of pen names in order to give the impression that a small paper with an even smaller staff was serviced by a team of journalists. (*Ehad min Ha'ir* was only one such pseudonym used by Czaczkes at that time.) However, *Ha'et* was not long for the world, and, after only six weeks, the newspaper went out of business. After his abbreviated stint in the big city, a center of Hebrew and Yiddish publishing and journalism, where he came into contact with literary circles unimaginable back home, it must have been a bitter disappointment to return to Buczacz, unpaid for his efforts, for Passover 1907. It is not surprising that he could not be kept down in the town after he'd seen grand Lvov, or, in Arnold Band's terms, "perhaps the contrast between the big city and the provincial town made him more aware of

Peretz, nor are there explicit thematic resonances aside from the title and a general description of a town in decay, future comparison of the two tales may provide further insight.

7. Gershom Bader (1868–1953) was a Hebrew and Yiddish author, editor, and journalist. For more on Bader and on this particular chapter in Agnon's life see the depiction in S.Y. Agnon, *Me'atsmi el 'atsmi* (Jerusalem: Schocken, 2000), 29 and Dan Laor, *Hayyei Agnon* (Jerusalem: Schocken, 1998), 34–39.

8. Bakon, *Agnon*, 78.

the failings of the latter."[9] Presumably this contributed to his decision to set out once again within a year—this time bound for Erets Yisra'el.

"'Ir hametim" was overlooked because the newspaper *Ha'et* has remained largely unavailable to researchers. Having ceased publication after only a few weeks (only twenty issues were ever released), it disappeared from view. To the best of my knowledge, the National Library of Israel possesses the only microfilm copy, and it is incomplete and of exceedingly poor quality. Band was the first scholar to discuss the piece, fifty-seven years after its publication, and he reported that Agnon himself had brought it to his attention, telling him that it had aroused some controversy in Buczacz when published in 1907.[10] Band cites the opening of "'Ir hametim," quoting only the first two paragraphs (about 18% of the whole), with a brief discussion of its themes. Almost all subsequent writers who deal with the text do so secondhand through Band's presentation of it.[11] However, at least one print copy of the entire run of *Ha'et* remains in existence: all twenty issues in a bound volume, property of Agnon himself. Upon his death, this volume was gifted, along with his manuscripts, to the National Library of Israel, where it resides as part of the Agnon Archives. However, it is uncatalogued and unavailable to general researchers due to its extremely brittle state, so it remains under the radar. Through the generosity of the archive's legendary director emeritus, Rafi Weiser, I have come into possession of the complete text of "'Ir hametim."[12]

Upon full examination, we quickly assess the article's significance. In it, Agnon surveys a number of themes that would occupy him for years to come, some of which were part of the town's indigenous folklore, others actual history, and presumably much drawn from his own imagination. As I hope to demonstrate in the coming pages, and as should be clear from a reading of "'Ir hametim" (appended in an annotated English translation below), these aspects of the story are recast in a more mature voice throughout Agnon's later writings, culminating in *'Ir umelo'ah*.

Among the later works that inherit elements first presented in "'Ir hametim" are the Gothic story "Toitentants" in Yiddish, probably written around the same time as "'Ir hametim" and published in subsequent Hebrew iterations as "Meholat hamavet" ("The Dance of Death") and "Aggadat hasofer" ("The Tale of the Scribe"); an array of short stories such as "Earth of Israel" ("'Afar Erets Yisra'el"), "In the Depths" ("Bimtsulot"), "Canopy of Love" (Huppat dodim);

---

9. Band, *Nostalgia*, 38.

10. Band, "Agnon," 61 n. 19.

11. Some writers even err in their bibliographical citation of "'Ir hametim": adding the subtitle "Toledot ha'ir Buczacz" ("A History of the Town Buczacz") reveals their knowledge of its existence only through the bibliographies by Habermann and Band, which carried these words as a descriptor of the content, not as part of the title.

12. An annotated English translation is appended to this article; the Hebrew text, with my introduction, appeared in *Ha'arets: Tarbut vesifrut* (July 20, 2018), 4.

two novellas, *And the Crooked Snall Be Made Straight* and *The Outcast; A Simple Story* (*Sippur pashut*, especially chapter 15) and *A Guest for the Night* (*Oreah natah lalun*), in which the themes of physical and spiritual decay are brought to novel-length perfection; and, of course, more stories in *'Ir umelo'ah* than can be listed here. (The specific elements reprised in each work are enumerated below and in the annotations to "'Ir hametim.") In a different but perfectly applicable context, Gershon Shaked stated that this early work "serves as the seed for later works and contains within it developments which would only reveal themselves later in Agnon's writing—in the manner of 'a bit that contains the abundant' or a type of foundation story. Later stories become variations [of these themes] or transformations and inversions."[13]

"'Ir hametim" begins with a description of the earliest Jewish graves in the town, and the omnipresence of death is presented as a macabre point of pride— Jews are literally dying to get into Buczacz. The obsession with graves as a sign of Buczacz's death urge, leading to a type of eternal memorialization in the object of the grave and basis for the connection of the residents to their town, is recycled in conversations of the Guest and his friend Schutzling, depicted powerfully in *A Guest for the Night*:

> "It is the tragedy of my life that I do not live in Szibucz," [said Schutzling. The Guest replied:] "Do you love Szibucz so much?" said I. "When a man sees that there is no place in the world that he loves, he deceives himself into thinking he loves his town. And you, do you love Szibucz?" "I? I haven't thought about it yet." My friend took my hand, and said, "If so, let me tell you that all your love for the Land of Israel comes to you from Szibucz; because you love your town you love the Land of Israel." "How do you know that I love Szibucz?" "Is it proof you want? If you did not love Szibucz, would you be dealing with it all your life? Would you be digging up gravestones to discover its secrets?"[14]

The morbid atmosphere is further marked by the halakhic question regarding ritual defilement of *kohanim* who walk the streets where death is underfoot at each turn.[15] These sentiments reappear in the persons of Yona Toyber in *A Simple Story* and Akavia Mazal of *In the Prime of Her Life* (*Bidmi yamehah*), both of whom fancy themselves historians of the town who know the bedrock of that history is in the graveyard. "'Ir hametim" reports:

13. Gershon Shaked, "Qabtsan mul sha'ar na'ul," *Biqqoret ufarshanut* 35–36 (2002): 75. Shaked's remark concerned Agnon's first novella, *And the Crooked Shall Be Made Straight*, published just five years after "'Ir hametim."
14. Agnon, *Guest*, 339. Szybusz, an anagramic pseudonym for the town Buczacz, was used often by Agnon in his pre-Holocaust writings to depict the town as a place of confusion, muddle, and breakdown (all meanings of the Hebrew root *shin-bet-shin*).
15. *Kohanim*, male members of the priestly class, are under biblical injunction against the ritual impurity brought about by close exposure to human remains (Leviticus 21:1).

To this day there is a street called by everyone "Shul-gas" [Synagogue Street], even though there is no sign of Judaism or Jews there. In fact, when a Jew wishes to remove himself from the community, he rents a house on that street. Yet it is reported that once a grand synagogue stood there... [O]ne of the [church] walls is at a slant, and is the remnant of the synagogue upon which their church is built. The wall stoops in great sorrow in mourning for the desecration of its holiness.

This desecrated synagogue makes cameo appearances in any number of stories; the old Jewish neighborhood now abandoned by members of the faith becomes the refuge for Jews wishing to live on the periphery, such as Yeruham and Rachel Hofshi (in *A Guest for the Night*) and Akavia and Tirtza Mazal ("In the Prime of Her Life") who are later joined by their housemaid, Blume Nacht (*A Simple Story*).

The banishment of a Hasidic master by the town's anti-Hasidic leadership (among whom was counted Agnon's maternal grandfather), is repurposed as the opening of "The Outcast," setting that novella's plot in motion. The late novel *In Mr. Lublin's Store* contains the surrealistic intrusion of old Mr. Jacob Stern, in a scene that could have been perfectly placed in Agnon's *Sefer Hama'asim* cycle of stories. Stern and the narrator sit in the empty Leipzig store in the final days of World War I reminiscing about their common Galician town. Recollecting the cemetery and an episode of the surprising discovery of two old graves, in a manner identical to "'Ir hametim." sends them on an imaginative journey back to the unnamed "our town" (which readers immediately recognize as Buczacz)—one in which they are transported from Germany to Galicia and from present to nostalgic, idealized, and mythologized past. Once again, now at the opposite end of his career, Agnon depicts gravestones and morbidity as touchstones for memory, but his tone had shifted dramatically over the ensuing decades.

In *'Ir umelo'ah* that church on Shul-gas takes on a mystical air as the walls of the "once grand synagogue" weep.[16] The legend of the jealous and vain count who erects Buczacz's monumental town hall and then murders the master builder "so that he would never be able to construct such a building anywhere else" is spun into one of *'Ir umelo'ah*'s most well-known tales: a Judaized Icarus myth of the builder Theodor (known as Fedor), which also generates the origin myth of the nearby Fedor Hill, later the site of the mass extermination of thousands of Jews at the hands of the Nazis, the resting place of at least 13,670 martyrs in fourteen mass graves. In doing so, the kernel of the story from "'Ir hametim" takes on mythical depth as it foreshadows the final destruction and casts an eerily prescient light on Agnon's depiction of a town riddled with unmarked graves.[17]

16. "Letorah ulitefillah," in S.Y. Agnon, *'Ir umelo'ah* (Jerusalem: Schocken, 1999), 14–15.
17. "The Great Town Hall," in S.Y. Agnon, *A City in Its Fullness* (New Milford, CT: Toby, 2016), 192–99. On the executions and mass graves on Fedor Hill, see Omer Bartov, *Anatomy of a*

It must, however, be noted that, aside from the shift in tone between "'Ir hametim" and these later works that bear resonance with that 1907 text (and these are but a sample of the intratextual links within his writing), there is an even more striking difference. "'Ir hametim" is marked by an almost complete absence of the intertextual matrix for which Agnon was famous, his Hebrew prose being a richly woven tapestry of allusions to and wordplays with rabbinic literature. This intertextuality, which later becomes almost the very subject of his writing, was not yet in place in the earliest publications.[18]

The most significant *intra*textual connection between "'Ir hametim" and Agnon's later writing is situated at the very end of the piece. The main part of the concluding vignette reads:

> One of the founders of Hasidism in town was a learned Torah scholar, the father of the man Yekele, who was eventually executed by hanging at the command of the head of the community. This Yekele, son of the first hasid in town, was executed 82 years ago having been charged on suspicion of theft and found guilty. At the moment they brought him up to the gallows the hangman, who was an apostate Jew from Czernowitz, said to him: "Make confession in the name of the God of Israel." He confessed many misdeeds, but denied any responsibility regarding this theft. A moment before they slipped the noose around his neck he declared that he had not committed this sin. In fact, this man was killed because of the wrath of the communal leader, who had a gripe against him and feared him. A few days after he was hanged, a court order arrived absolving him of all punishment—but it was too late as the deed was done. On the day they took Yekele to the gallows all the townsmen left the city, wandered the fields and forest in tears, stretched out their hands towards heaven, and cried out: "Our hands have not shed this blood!"[19]

This passage is a précis of what would become two parallel stories, "Yekele I" and "Yekele II," published posthumously in 'Ir umelo'ah.[20] Agnon's daughter and literary executor, Emuna Yaron, discovered the manuscripts for these stories among her father's files for the work in progress. Unable to determine which was meant to be the final version, she made the unconventional decision to publish

---

Genocide: The Life and Death of a Town Called Buczacz (New York: Simon and Schuster, 2018), 179–82, 277–80.

18. Another distinguishing feature of the style of "'Ir hametim" is an excess of commas and an unfortunate number of typographical errors (presumably at the hands of the editor and typesetters, respectively). These were two things Agnon was insistent, almost obsessive, about avoiding, often imploring his editors and publishers to take special care in this regard. His life-long distaste of editorial meddling can be seen in his response to the addition of a concluding sentence to "'Ir hametim" by Bader; see n. 65.

19. See annotations on the passage in the translation of "'Ir hametim."

20. In Hebrew in Agnon, 'Ir umelo'ah, 516–33; in English in Agnon, *City*, 427–52. On the Yekele stories see Alan Mintz, *Ancestral Tales: Reading the Buczacz Stories of S.Y. Agnon* (Stanford, CA: Stanford University Press, 2017), 279–90.

them both, assigning them subtitles "Nusaḥ eḥad" ("One Version") and "Nusaḥ aḥer" ("Another Version"). Alan Mintz, James S. Diamond, and I decided to style the translated titles with roman numerals. This is a decision I now regret, because the use of numbering inadvertently telegraphs a sense of sequence, that version I was the draft, later revised as version II. In light of comparison to the much earlier source material in "'Ir hametim," I now believe that the opposite is true, as I will demonstrate momentarily. I should state that Yaron's decision at the time was perfectly reasonable; neither manuscript is a first draft, as is clear from the minimal amount of correction and revision on each, both were rewritten by Agnon in his own hand in preparation for later typing, and they appear to have been transcribed around the same time, on identical paper stock. Both are titled "Yekele," with no subtitle or indication of which was intended for publication.[21]

As the twinned stories grow from the seed in "'Ir hametim," the issue around which their common plot revolves becomes the challenge to Jewish legal authority once Galicia comes under Austrian rule with the first Partition of Poland in 1772. Aside from ritual matters still adjudicated by a local *beit din*, rabbinic authority, or the power of the Jewish communal leadership headed by a *parnas*, authority had been largely ceded to and usurped by the civil authorities. This results in the question: How do you solve a problem like Yekele? How can the Jewish community rein in an insolent youth or a juvenile delinquent, especially an orphan without parents to have guided him in his growing up? The most significant transformation that the story undergoes from 1907 to its expanded versions published in 1973 is the identification of the anonymous "head of the community" (*rosh haqahal, parnas*) as none other than Reb Yisrael Shlomo—a character from Agnon's *The Bridal Canopy*, described by Dan Miron as that novel's "most vivid and interesting character, and one of the best portrayals of a pathological narcissist in all of Hebrew literature." Yosef Dan said, "It would be hard to find a more negative character in *The Bridal Canopy* than Yisrael Shlomo."[22] This legendary *parnas* of Buczacz is the hero of three long stories in *The Bridal Canopy* (book I, chapters 11–13), told as stories within the story, as he is now long dead but related to the assembled listeners by his namesake, another Yisrael Shlomo (just one more example of the doppelgänging for which that novel is famous). The most important of these stories, "Meḥamat hametsiq" ("From the Wrath of the Oppressor"), has been called the best precursor to Agnon's later stories

21. A facsimile of the opening page of "Yekele II" from the Agnon archives (AC4025) at the National Library of Israel can be seen in Agnon, *City*, 437.
22. Dan Miron, *Histaklut baravnekher* (Tel Aviv: Hakibbutz Hameuchad, 1996), 82 and Yosef Dan, "Shivḥei Hamari"sh," in *Hanokhri vehamandarin* (Ramat Gan: Masada, 1975), 181. Both of these works present extensive treatments of Yisrael Shlomo (as he appears in *The Bridal Canopy*).

collected in *'Ir umelo'ah*.[23] If so, then it draws attention to the first appearance of its main character in "'Ir hametim" and further strengthens the importance of that early work as being connected to the late *magnum opus*. The novella is a kind of Agnonized Pygmalion story, in which Yisrael Shlomo, in a cruel practical joke, attempts to pass off a poor, young ignoramus as a learned scholar and marriage prospect for the daughter of his rival. In the end, Yisrael Shlomo is hoisted on his own petard when the unlettered fellow has improved himself from the time spent as an "imposter" in the *beit midrash*, and, by the time the wedding arrives, he has, in fact, been transformed into an authentic, fêted *talmid hakham*!

"Mehamat hametsiq" opens with a portrait of the *parnas* as a high-handed, thin-skinned communal leader who subjects his opponents (if they are sufficiently lower class that he can get away with it) to humiliation via public punishment. In this case, a young man has been placed outdoors in the pillory on a freezing cold winter day. Such punishment was deemed appropriate for the "crime" of public insolence (chutzpah) toward the wealthy head of the town. This characteristic is instantly recognizable to us from its earliest kernel in "'Ir hametim" and in its later reappearance in the "Yekele" stories.[24]

In the "Yekele" stories, the confrontation between the *parnas* and the delinquent remains the focus. Yekele is suspected, presumably falsely, of a robbery and attempted murder, leading to his execution, which conveniently ameliorates Yisrael Shlomo's egotistical annoyance at the young whippersnapper's presence. Among the essential differences between the two versions of the story is that Yekele is the center of his own story in version I; Yisrael Shlomo is the focus of version II. In both, however, we encounter, in Mintz's synopsis, "the story, in short, of a lopsided duel between a powerful oligarch and a boy who refuses to

23. Avidov Lipsker, *Mahshavot 'a' Agnon*, 2 vols. (Ramat Gan: Bar Ilan University Press, 2016), 1:101. For "Mehamat hametsiq," see S.Y. Agnon, *Hakhnasat kallah* (Tel Aviv: Schocken, 1998), 99–118 and Agnon, *The Bridal Canopy* (New Milford, CT: Toby, 2015), 155–83. "Mehamat hametsiq" was originally published in the Warsaw periodical *Ha'ogen* 2 (1917) and then as a freestanding novella by Jüdischer Verlag (Berlin, 1921), before it was subsequently incorporated as part of the novel *Hakhnasat kallah* (1931). On this novella, its publishing history, and the character of Shlomo Yisrael, see Lipsker, *Mahshavot*, 1:99–126.
24. I agree with Dan, "Shivhei Hamari"sh," 183, who acknowledges the chronological difficulties with fitting Yisrael Shlomo into these different stories: "Mehamat hametsiq" places him as a well-established, adult *parnas* at the final session of the Council of Four Lands in 1764; this segment of "'Ir hametim" and presumably the Yekele stories are set in 1825. Nevertheless, in order to resolve the anachronism, Dan suggests that Agnon is painting him as a universal type (linked through the name), the kind of reviled communal leader who could have been found in each generation. See also Lipsker, *Mahshavot*, 107. In all cases, "Yekele II" offers a resolution by explaining: "There was in our town a *parnas* who had no equal, neither among those who preceded him in that position nor among the provincial leaders [....] His name was R. Yisrael Shlomo, named after the pride of the family, the first Yisrael Shlomo, of blessed memory, who we have often mentioned" (Agnon, *City*, 438).

acknowledge his authority. Cowed and enfeebled, the community fails to play a mediating role in the confrontation."[25]

The salient plot differences between the two versions of the story are as follows: In version I, Yisrael Shlomo passively enables Yekele's execution through silence; in version II, Yisrael Shlomo plays a more active role, moving "quickly to bring the matter to the attention of the regional judges, and he was not satisfied until they condemned Yekele to the gallows." In version I, the whole town, as well as we the readers, are aware that Yekele was present at a communal celebration of the Burial Society during the crimes of which he is accused, giving him a solid alibi against claims that he was the perpetrator; in version II, his whereabouts on the night in question are unclear.

Version II contains a lengthy roster of the many charitable institutions in the town, over twenty organizations that care for the sick, clothe the orphans, feed the needy, and the like. It comprises approximately one-third of the story and, in honesty, taxes the reader's patience. Agnon's purpose in describing these charities was to highlight the gap between Buczacz's ideals and their execution in practice, shining the spotlight on the spilling of innocent blood because of the egos and arrogance of the wealthy and the inability or unwillingness of the townsmen to push back against such wickedness.[26] This section is completely absent from version I.

In version II, the hangman imported from out of town to carry out the execution is an apostate Jew, an element missing from version I of the story.

In version I, the townsmen go to the outskirts to proclaim, "Our hands have not shed this blood!" while Yekele's body is being lowered from the gallows, at which point "a runner arrived from the court in Stanislav. In his hand was a letter from the court officials to the emperor's deputies. The letter said that Yekele, the son of Moshe, was not to be given the death penalty." In version II the tardy stay of execution arrives "a few days later" (from an unspecified court).

A half-century after "'Ir hametim" was published, it seems clear that Agnon had that copy of Ha'et in front of him as he sat down to compose what would become the two versions of "Yekele." In light of these textual differences, it becomes clear that what we titled "Yekele II" is in fact Agnon's first iteration, his initial version of an expanded Yekele tale on the skeleton outlined in the concluding section of "'Ir hametim." He spun the 1907 version of the story, only a few short paragraphs, into "Yekele II" (totaling 3,754 words in Hebrew). A perusal of "'Ir hametim" shows a high level of correspondence between that early text and details in "Yekele II," including, among others: Yisrael Shlomo's more activist position in the story, the identification of the hangman as an apostate, and the

25. Mintz, *Ancestral Tales*, 289.
26. For further analysis of this section of the story see Yosef Dan, "Panim aherot leBuczacz'" in *Hanokhri vehamandarin* (Ramat Gan: Masada, 1975), 193–97.

arrival of the court messenger a few days after Yekele's death (instead of having the horses gallop up as he's being lowered from the noose). In the rewriting of the story as (what we called) "Yekele I," we witness a tightening of the text (it weighs in at only 2,662 words). Agnon excised the lengthy listing of the charitable associations, aware no doubt of how it slowed the story's pace. The drama is heightened by the arrival of the messenger just a moment too late to spare Yekele's neck (instead of "a few days later"). These are the types of revisions for which Agnon was famous, polishing his prose toward greater artistry. Perhaps most significantly, "Yekele I" elevates the rascal's role as the victim, unsympathetic a character as he may be. Only in this version do we the readers know he is indubitably innocent of the crime for which he swings.[27] This resonates perfectly with the themes of the section of *A City in Its Fullness* in which the story is situated. Compare Yekele (in version I) to Dan in the neighboring story, "Disappeared" ("Hane'elam"). They are both expositions on the theme of how the communal authorities misuse the limited autonomy and power granted to them under their non-Jewish hosts to police members, and neutralize young men (through the noose or military conscription) who have become inconvenient. To accomplish this the "Yekele" story had to evolve with the boy at the center. (Yisrael Shlomo, who has his own star turn in *The Bridal Canopy*, appears here in a supporting role, either as a character or mere typology.) Interestingly, "Disappeared" contains a different variety of a second version, in which the tale is recounted through the point of view of the Polish noblewoman, the story's villain, in an account appended to the main narrative.

I am further convinced that "Yekele I" was Agnon's intended telling of the tale for public consumption when we consider one other story, wholly overlooked in any analysis of "Yekele." In the portion of *A City in Its Fullness* that contains our story, "Disappeared," and others, we find a brief interstitial section entitled "Shivḥah shel 'ireinu" ("Our City's Praise").[28] It is part of a cycle of short stories in book III called "The Upheavals of Time" that portray the city in decline. In passing, the narrator summarizes the plot of "Yekele," telling us that it is "a story he has written in detail, in his possession in manuscript." In other words, "Shivḥah shel 'irenu" postdates "Yekele," but its plot summary aligns completely with our "Yekele I." The narrator concludes the rehearsal of the story with:

---

27. Admittedly, version II *implies* Yekele's innocence and concludes with an ironic postscript encouraging restraint in storytelling from showing deeds in a negative light, but only version I provides the reader with the solid alibi that not only establishes the fact but also indicts the fellow townsmen, who should have spoken out in his defense but were intimidated by Yisrael Shlomo.

28. "Shivḥah shel 'ireinu" in Agnon, *'Ir*, 511–12. Like the Yekele stories, this was not published in Agnon's lifetime. Unfortunately, a translation of the story was not included in Agnon, *City*.

I will add here, *after they lowered Yekele from the hanging tree* [i.e., on the same day, unlike version II] a speedy messenger came from the high court in *Stanislav* [a detail only present in version I] with papers to the local judge in Buczacz informing him that the ministers of the high court examined the case of Yekele and found him innocent of the crime.

This latter recounting of the "Yekele I" plot confirms the final trajectory of the story begun in "'Ir hametim."

Taken as a whole, the presence of these many foreshadowings of later works in the adolescent "'Ir hametim" testifies to how long Agnon carried these stories in his mind throughout his life. It also undermines the common notion that only late in his career, with the compositions that would become *A City in Its Fullness*, did he make the conscious decision to undertake his chronicling. The awareness that his home town was on the verge of collapse, spiritually as well as physically, and the impulse to document Buczacz in literature was obviously deeply rooted in his childhood experience. In fact, from his first years as a writer he had already set this as one of his areas of focus, although his narrative voice would mature and, indeed, sharply transition over the ensuing decades. In 1956, when his published output had slackened, he answered Baruch Kurzweil's inquiry as to where he was focusing his energy with: "I am building a city—Buczacz!"[29] Mintz carefully observed that this statement was the

> proprietary stamp of a veteran writer who writes using an established repertoire of modernist techniques. Reimagining Buczacz through the filter of this imagination that abandons nothing from the toolkit of modernism must of necessity mean creating something new, a new city. The bricks and mortar may be taken from the historical record, but the building will be a new creation. No other writer in modern Jewish culture has attempted a project of similar scope or ambition."[30]

This last point has become clearer especially in this past decade as *'Ir umelo'ah* has begun to receive the level of critical attention it deserves, in no small measure thanks to the scholarly work of Mintz. *'Ir umelo'ah* was Agnon's epic literary memorial to Buczacz. Published in 1973, the book was largely overlooked, partially due to the bad timing of appearing on the eve of the Yom Kippur War, but more so due to the lack of appetite of that generation's Hebrew readers for old world stories.[31] Nevertheless, Yaron asserted that, "To my mind *'Ir umelo'ah* is the best and most important of the volumes I published from my father's estate...

29. *Kurzweil-Agnon-U.Ts.G.: Ḥilufei iggerot*, ed. L. Dabi-Guri (Ramat Gan: Bar Ilan University Press, 1987), 56.
30. Mintz, *Ancestral Tales*, 2.
31. For a survey of the reception history of the book, see Mintz, *Ancestral Tales*, 20–28.

One should read the book as my father intended: As a monument to Polish Jewry which was destroyed in the Holocaust."[32]

However, the arc of writing from "'Ir hametim" to '*Ir umelo'ah* is long, and it bends toward nostalgia, creativity, and memorialization. Agnon's early writings are marked by a harsh critical eye, spotlighting hypocrisy and deception, especially relating to financial matters and social injustice. Consider the short story "Ger tsedeq," written around the same time as "'Ir hametim," in which a crafty Jew disguises himself as a Russian prince converted to Judaism to defraud the entire community.[33] Only as Agnon matures is his focus on physical poverty (which admittedly remains ever present in his writing) overtaken by a portrayal of the spiritual poverty of Buczacz, as a synecdoche of Jewry writ large.

The cynical feel of "'Ir hametim" is palpable. Compare it to another relatively early work, "Old and Young Together," which was first published in 1920 but set in Buczacz in 1907 (the very year "'Ir hametim" is written).[34] This story, Agnon's first substantial literary treatment of his Galician youth, presents a satirized depiction of an array of personalities, institutions, and issues of the day. Among the objects of his humor (which fluctuates from gentle mocking to acerbic biting) are the pompous windbags who pass as Zionist leaders and the cowardice behind their words; the internecine fighting about the purposes of Zionism (whether to ameliorate Jewish suffering in Europe or to build a new Jewish settlement in Palestine); literary figures with inflated egos; the Yiddish versus Hebrew language wars; arrogance, ignorance, and hypocrisy of rabbis, Hasidim, and *maskilim* alike; and the perennial penchant for Jews to act as their own worst enemies despite the external threats of anti-Semitism. Yet the reader still senses the love for the world coming under critique at the tip of the author's pen. In addition, perhaps for the first time, his critique is not pitched exclusively toward the town. The narrator, Hemdat (universally understood to be Agnon's autobiographical projection of himself into his fictional universe), is himself the target of the novella's scorn. His self-depiction introduces a well-intentioned youth, hungry for fame yet seemingly incapable of any effective action. An ancillary cause for self-flagellation is his depiction of the generational divide represented by the conflict between himself and both his father and grandfather, who disapprove of his lax religious commitments and his Zionist affiliations. Hemdat's desire to gain glory as a writer, like that of his author-creator, prevents the fulfillment of his family's aspirations for him as a Torah scholar and rabbi. *A Simple Story*,

---

32. Emuna Yaron, *Peraqim mehayyai* (Tel Aviv: Schocken, 2005), 221–22.
33. On "Ger Tsedeq" see n. 4.
34. In Hebrew as "Bine'arenu uvizkenenu" in the volume '*Al kappot haman'ul* (Jerusalem: Schocken, 1998), 215–74, available in English in *The Orange Peel and Other Satires* (New Milford, CT: Toby, 2015), 1–120. See also my foreword to that volume, "The Metaphysics of Agnon's Political Satire," vii–xvii.

similarly set in Buczacz/Szybusz during the first decade of the twentieth century, serves as an additional example of the more muted criticism diluted with nostalgia, conveying the warmth he feels for the town. Dr. Langsam's longing for the *alte heim*, cited in the epigraph above, could have been written by Agnon about himself. (In fact, I presume it was.)

A penchant for self-mockery (especially by a middle-aged writer of his adolescent self), does not imply that Agnon lost or abandoned his critical perspective on his hometown as he aged. This was an authorial voice not available to a teenager unable to feel nostalgia for a town he had not yet left! Agnon departed Buczacz at age twenty, and, aside from two very brief visits, he essentially never returned—yet his literary imagination is never far from the hometown, as if to say, "you can take the boy out of Buczacz, but you can't take the Buczacz out of the boy." Similar observations can and have been made about other great novelists: Mark Twain, James Joyce, William Faulkner, and Philip Roth all come to mind. Aharon Appelfeld's appreciation for what he learned as a young author from Agnon expresses this quite precisely:

> Most of my generation [of fellow authors] invested a huge amount of effort into suppressing and eradicating their past. I have absolutely no complaints against them; I understand them completely. But I, for some reason, didn't know how to assimilate into the Israeli reality. Instead, I retreated into myself. For this, Agnon served as an excellent role model. It was from him that I learned how you can carry the town of your birth with you anywhere and live a full life in it. Your birthplace is not a matter of fixed geography. And you can extend its borders outward or raise them to the skies. Agnon populated his birthplace with everything the Jewish people had created in the past two hundred years. Like any great writer, he wrote not literal reminiscences of his town, not what it actually was, but what it could have been. And he taught me that a person's past—even a difficult one—is not to be regarded as a defect or a disgrace, but as a legitimate source to be mined.[35]

All this suggests that Agnon had to "leave his country and his homeland and his city and ascended to Erets Yisra'el to build it from its destruction and to be rebuilt by it," so that he could turn his attention back to that city of Buczacz to rebuild it in literature. Dov Sadan observed that "the difference between what the author knew about his town while he was a young man residing there and what he came to understand over the course of the rest of his life was akin to the difference between a puddle and a raging river."[36] We might amend this statement to read: It is akin to the difference between "A City of the Dead" and *A City in Its Fullness*.

35. Aharon Appelfeld, *The Story of a Life* (New York: Schocken, 2014), 153.
36. Dov Sadan, *Ḥadashim gam yeshanim*, 3 vols. (Tel Aviv: 'Am 'Oved, 1987), 1:43.

This is not to say that Agnon ever abandoned his critique, nor that he was unable to retain his cynicism as he aged. Indeed, *'Ir umelo'ah* is awash in such social criticism, bordering on outright indictment of the communal leadership and the corrosive effects of vanity and power on Jewish life. Among the objects of particular concern are the oppression of the poor and the gap between the town's expressed ideals as a religious community versus its sometime shoddy application in practice—or the widening chasm between ideal Buczacz and real Szybusz. The book bears a dedication to a city that "was full of Torah, wisdom, love, piety, life, grace, kindness and charity"; its content often tells a different tale (alternatively with acid or good humor). The essential difference between early and later career is how Agnon learned to temper the youthful critique. He did this out of artistic impulse: writers who cannot evolve past the persona and voice crafted by their teenage narrators tend not to be recognized by the Nobel committee. But it was also a desire not to be a shill for the old world, nor attempt to deconstruct it. The proclivity of an author to venerate or alternatively satirize a world he depicts does not, in and of itself, indicate his stance vis-à-vis that world. In the case of Agnon, it was neither one nor the other but a desire to simultaneously skewer and sacrilize and, in so doing, ask what that world of the past has to say to the present and future.

Agnon expressed pride in his ability to walk this careful line, especially as it distinguished him (in his own mind at least) from earlier giants of Jewish literature, figures he often saw as role models against whom to compete:

> Consider what I did with the pauper Reb Yudel Hasid in my novel *The Bridal Canopy*. I created him as a person of substance, with charm after his own fashion, despite the events that befell him. What would our other writers have done with a character like this? Mendele would have made him ridiculous, in order to twist and poke; Sholem Aleichem would have made him the object of simple mockery. I sweetened the bitterness of Reb Yudel's poverty, removing the ridicule, making the pauper a more perfect character.[37]

Agnon's particular mode of balancing the critical and the self-critical with the nostalgic was, in his own eyes, part of what set him apart from other authors. He saw himself as an inextricable part of both the good and the bad that was Buczacz's reality and legacy. Many have wondered at what it was that made him so successful and well received in Jaffa and Jerusalem of the Second Aliyah, as well as in the early state, despite his focus on the old world of Eastern Europe. Perhaps it was precisely these intertwined threads of the self-consciously self-critical and the respectful distance that made him acceptable to his early readers.[38]

---

37. Cited in A. M. Habermann, *Massekhet sofrim vesifrut* (Jerusalem: Reuven Mas, 1977), 129.
38. My thanks to Sheila Jelen for suggesting this observation to me. For more on the reception history of early Agnon, see Yehudit Halevi-Zwick, *Reshitah shel biqqoret Agnon* (Haifa: Haifa University Press, 1984).

Agnon's long career can be traced as an arc from youthful, almost cynical focus on death and decay to a more mature and creative form of writing. With tragic irony, this later voice was surely informed by the knowledge of Buczacz's final destruction but was already formed prior to the Holocaust. The unripe narrator of "City of the Dead" had to give way to enable the formation of the canon of Agnon's work, leading to the culminating project that took shape in 'Ir umelo'ah. Because Alan Mintz viscerally understood the power of Jewish literature and culture as a reviving force in Jewish life, he recognized the creative achievement of A City in Its Fullness. This enabled him to read and analyze Agnon's entire literary output through the lens of his late masterpiece and present it to us as an "imaginative chronicle.... [A]n alternative to forms of memorialization that brought destruction and loss to the forefront. For Agnon the path was not lamentation, martyrology, theodicy, or conventional forms of consolation but the re-creation in words of what was lost in fact."[39]

Appendix

"A City of the Dead"
Translated and annotated by Jeffrey Saks

Buczacz, in Galicia, is a city of the dead in every way. Not merely because wherever one excavates he finds human remains and dead corpses, or because a halakhic inquiry has already been posed to the leading authorities if it is permitted for *kohanim*, men of priestly lineage, to reside in Buczacz and to walk her streets.[40] Rather, it is a city of the dead due to the absence of life within it. If you wish to know how fond Buczaczers are of death, listen to the legend that circulates in town about the first grave in the Jewish cemetery: An important person was

---

39. Alan L. Mintz, "Between Holocaust and Homeland" in *Translating Israel* (Syracuse, NY: Syracuse University Press, 2001), 109.

Annotations to "A City of the Dead"
Appeared in Hebrew as Eḥad min Ha'ir (pseudonym), "'Ir hametim" in the Lvov newspaper *Ha'et* 19 (March 14, 1907), 2–5 and republished with an introduction in *Ha'arets: Tarbut vesifrut* (July 20, 2018), 4.
40. See n. 15. The halakhic question to which Agnon alludes was discussed by R. Avraham Teomim, rabbi of Buczacz from 1853 until his death in 1868. See his responsa *Ḥesed le'Avraham, Yoreh De'ah* 107–10. Three years earlier, Agnon wrote in the Kraków newspaper *Hamitspeh* (June 10, 1904), 4: "Last week they excavated in our town and found three human remains buried in lime. It is said these were victims of the Black Plague."

passing through Buczacz and saw men digging. When asked what they were doing, they answered that they were digging graves for the local Jews. The man envied the good fortune of those Jews, who would merit eternal rest in those graves, and he longed to dwell in this place as well. He died at that very moment and was buried in that graveyard, with a large monument erected over his plot. They engraved his name as "Wayfarer Ḥayyim," that is, "a passerby whose name was Hayim, who passed this way unto the light of Eternal Life." His tombstone is the oldest in the graveyard of the holy community Buczacz.[41]

The Jews of Buczacz yearn so much for death that they hark back to a legend about a wayfarer who wanted to die. Furthermore, as soon as any Jews settled there, they immediately dug themselves graves. Who knows how many years the wayfarer was the only one interred there and how much money the community spent to pay a cemetery watchman so that he would not lie alone in the grave. Who knows whether those Jews had died of natural causes or whether the local count had thrown them into the river, as he did many times. Once, when a wagonload of Jews traveled to town, he gave orders to hurl them into the Strypa River.[42] Consequently, we don't know when the first congregation was established in Buczacz. There are, to be sure, several ancient tombstones sunk into the ground, but it is impossible to read them and to grasp their content, not because reading graves with raised lettering causes forgetfulness, but because the inscriptions are worn away and illegible.[43]

Yet one tombstone remains legible, in particular its date: Year 91 AM [=1331 CE], although it is unclear if the final letter of the preceding word belongs to the numeral itself, making it 491 AM [=1731 CE] instead.[44] Local scholars insist that

41. The legend of "Wayfarer Ḥayyim" reappears in Agnon's early story "Haḥuppah hasheḥorah" (1913); substantially revised and retitled "Ḥuppat dodim" in *ʿAl kappot*, 336–50. Band, *Nostalgia*, 83 suggests that this piece of local folk legend may have shared a "common ancestor" with the Yiddish *Der Yored* (1855) by Isaac Meir Dick, which in turn may have served as source material for Agnon's later *And the Crooked Shall Be Made Straight*.

42. On the legend of Count Potocki's slaughter of the Jews as they crossed the river, see, e.g., "In the Depths," in S.Y. Agnon, *Forevermore and Other Stories*, ed. Jeffrey Saks (New Milford, CT: Toby, 2016), 171–77, and Agnon, *Simple Story*, 143–44.

43. A variety of things that cause forgetfulness, are listed in BT Horayot 13b, including "one who reads the writing that is on the stone of a grave." R. Isaac Luria limits this to a case where the letters of the inscription are raised (not sunken or engraved into the stone); Arizal, *Shaʿar Hamitsvah*, Vaʾetḥanan 13.

44. The lack of clarity is due to the fact that the year is represented in *gematria*, which assigns numerical value to letters, instead of Arabic numerals. The question is whether the final letter *tav* (whose value is 400) in the word "Shenat..." ("In the year...") is part of the numeral. It is either folklore or fantasy to imagine that there was a Jewish grave in Buczacz in 1331, as by all historical accounts the Jewish community dates from around 1500. In the short news report he filed in *Hamitspeh* (see n. 40) Agnon claimed, "In the cemetery I found an ancient gravestone, sunk into the ground, from the year 91 A.M. [1331 C.E.] (?)."

the correct date is 91 AM, demonstrating the importance of the city as among the most ancient. However, according to the historical facts available to us, and according to the local traditions, we cannot deduce anything about the founding of the Jewish community from this cemetery, since it has been demonstrated that this was not the town's original graveyard.

Apparently, the Jewish community was originally situated in a different neighborhood. To this day there is a street called by everyone "Shul-gas" [Synagogue Street], even though there is no sign of Judaism or Jews there. In fact, when a Jew wishes to remove himself from the community, he rents a house on that street. Yet it is reported that a grand synagogue once stood there, and the local chroniclers decided that the location where their church now stands was previously occupied by the Jews' Great Synagogue. And this on account of the fact that one of the walls is at a slant and is the remnant of the synagogue upon which their church is built. The wall stoops in great sorrow in mourning for the desecration of its holiness.

The Great Synagogue we possess today is distant from that "Shul-gas."[45] It is built in the same style as their church, and it is even said that the same builder built both. This builder also constructed the Town Hall, with its marble masonry and magnificent statues. These statues were quite well known throughout the surrounding villages, and when a villager would visit Buczacz and return home, no sooner would he be greeted by his friends than they would ask: And how are the Town Hall statues faring?

And just like all legends that circulate in other towns, it was told in our town that after the builder did all this, when he completed his labors and finished his work, the Count brought him up to the top of the tower and cast him down to the earth, so that he would never be able to construct such a building anywhere else.[46]

One way or another, it seems that the Jewish street in Buczacz was originally in a different location, in the place called "Shul-gas." This can be determined by a variety of factors, including, as is known, that when a town is first established they would build it near the water, and not far from the castle.

Buczacz was apparently not among the more prominent Jewish communities in the area and was not well known among them, for in the writings of the great rabbinic sages we find it referred to as: "Buczacz, nearby to Yazlovets"—and

---

45. The Great Synagogue of Buczacz was constructed in 1728 and demolished in 1950; see "The Great Synagogue," and a variety of stories which follow it, from Book I of Agnon, *City*, starting on 38–39.

46. Buczacz's town hall, completed in 1751 and still standing today, was commissioned by the Polish nobleman Mikołaj Bazyli Potocki and designed by the renowned rococo architect Bernard Meretyn. The story of the murdered builder took on greater depth (and a Jewish back-story) as Agnon expanded it as "The Great Town Hall" in Agnon, *City*, 192–99; see also "The Partners" in Agnon, *City*, 201–23 (in Hebrew as "Beit hamoʾatsot haggadol" and "Hashutafim").

Yazlovets is a very small town.[47] In the responsa of another distinguished rabbi: "Buczacz, nearby to Barysz"—and Barysz is so small, that for years it has not even ranked as a village.[48]

Buczacz has been known as a city for 800 years. In the thick woods is the ruin of a monastery, which housed monks 600 years ago and was destroyed in the war of the Tatars against the Poles. While the monks were hiding there, a certain gypsy betrayed them, and the Tatars slaughtered them to the last man. Even now one can see red grass growing by the entrance to the monastery—stained red with the monks' spilled blood.[49]

To this day the remains of the monastery still stand: tall, ruined walls. A spring bubbles forth from that spot, its waters trickling through the forest.

On "Shul-gas" is the castle of the Polish lord, but it was destroyed by the lord himself, forced by the Tatars so that the Poles would have no secure hiding place when they refused to pay the tribute tax imposed on them by the Tatars. Many times he had refused to pay the required tax. This was the Tatars' strategy: teams would enter Buczacz, uproot trees from the forest, and dam the waters and lay a bridge. When they ascended the hill to the castle where the lord resided, boiling millet was cast down upon the heads of the Tatars, forcing them to flee.

Once when the Tatars overcame the Poles a conditional peace treaty was signed, forcing the Poles to destroy their own fortress so they would have no place of support or base for rebellion. This treaty is known in the annals of Poland as the "Shameful Peace."[50] To this day the ruined castle stands outside of the city limits, surrounded by a fence, and the treaty is housed there in an iron chest. An elderly cook reported that his father, who had died at age ninety, had remembered that at the edge of the mountain where the ruined castle stands were two tombstones with Hebrew inscriptions, but the waters overran them and washed them away.

A notable figure in the kingdom—that is, a Jewish turncoat in the old lord's castle—told me that he had heard with his own ears that which was read from the old town chronicles: "And now it is permitted for Jews to settle here," and the first area listed was the one next to the castle.

---

47. Yazlovets (or Jazłowiec in Polish) is a village about 16 km south of Buczacz.

48. Barysz is a village about 14 km southwest of Buczacz.

49. The trope of grass stained in perpetuity with martyrs' blood appears in a variety of places in Agnon's writing; see, e.g., Agnon, *Simple Story*, 144.

50. Treaty of Buczacz (signed October 18, 1672). "Shameful Peace Treaty" works as a Hebrew wordplay that would have delighted Agnon: the word *buz* ("shame," "disgrace") resonates with Buczacz. Agnon errs here: The treaty ended the first phase of the Polish-Ottoman War (not a war with the Tatars). The Tatars and Cossacks had previously aligned with the Ottoman Empire against the Polish-Lithuanian Commonwealth during the Polish-Cossack-Tatar War of 1666–71.

No written chronicle of the Jewish community survives, and we know nothing for certain, only hearsay. For example, we do not know which rabbi served the holy community Buczacz with honor prior to Rabbi Tsvi Hirschele, author of *Neta sha'ashuim*,[51] the father-in-law of the Tsaddik.[52] However, the elders relate that they themselves had seen the seal of a rabbi in the old chronicle about testimony regarding set places in the Great Synagogue, and it was signed "Avram, that is Avraham."

We know nothing more about this rabbi, for he is not buried in the Jewish cemetery here, and in the villages none remember his name. Perhaps something was written of him in the communal chronicle, but that chronicle was destroyed in the great fire over thirty years ago.[53] Or perhaps that generation's community elders were guilty of destroying it, not wanting to leave evidence of their vile and ugly deeds, some of which we have heard reported by word of mouth.

However, in the introduction to the book *Zikhron devarim*[54] the author mentions a certain Rabbi Eliyahu, who had also served as rabbi in Zlotchov,[55] yet he tells us nothing about when he lived, nor if he served first in Buczacz and afterwards in Zlotchov, or vice versa.

Buczacz was, however, a city full of Torah scholars, as is recorded in the introduction to *Sefer haberit* by Rabbi Eliyahu Pinḥas.[56] He spent a period of time in Buczacz and praised the city, its scholars and students of Torah.

The author of *Penei Yehoshu'a*[57] also lived for a while on Moldy Lane, on account of which everyone called it Gold Street.[58] On that same street lived Rabbi

---

51. R. Tsvi Hirsch ben Yaakov Kra (1740–1814), rabbi of Buczacz from 1794 until his death. He appears in Agnon, *City* in various stories, including but not limited to "Feivush Gazlan," "In Search of a Rabbi," "In a Single Moment," and "The Frogs."

52. The Tsaddik of Buczacz was R. Avraham David ben Asher Wahrman (1771–1840), author of the halakhic works *Da'at qedoshim* and *Eshel Avraham*, served as rabbi of the town from the passing of his father-in-law in 1814 until his own death. He appears in Agnon, *City* in, among other stories, "The Hazzanim," "Feivush Gazlan," and "The Earliest Hasidim." A list of the known rabbis of Buczacz (from the seventeenth century until the Holocaust) can be found in the appendix to Agnon, *City*, 606–8.

53. Buczacz suffered an extensive fire on the Sabbath before Tishah B'Av in 1865; its long-lasting effects are described in "In a Single Moment" in Agnon, *City*, 455–97.

54. By R. Aleksander Sender Safrin (1770–1818), founder of the Komarno Hasidic dynasty.

55. In Polish, Złoczów, a town 110 km northwest of Buczacz.

56. R. Eliyahu Pinhas Hurwitz (1765–1821), rabbi and mystic, student of R. Hayim of Volozhin, lived for a few years in Buczacz where he began composing his *Sefer haberit*, a wide-ranging work of halakhah and ethics (published anonymously in 1797).

57. *Penei Yehoshu'a* is the halakhic work by R. Yaakov Yehoshua Falk (1680–1756), later rabbi of Lvov, Berlin, and Frankfurt am Main. He lived in Buczacz between 1720 and 1730, while his father-in-law, R. Aryeh Leibush Auerbach, served as the town's rabbi.

58. In Hebrew the name of the street is given as "Me'uppash," meaning "rotten" or "moldy," perhaps a now forgotten nickname from an unpleasant odor due to proximity to the bend in the river. In the short story "Or hatorah," Agnon, *'Ir umelo'ah*, 201 adds to this description of

Meshulam of Pressburg,[59] author of *Igra Ramah*, who served as rabbi in Pressburg prior to Rabbi Moshe Sofer, the great genius, who eulogized him and published the eulogy in his book *Ḥatam Sofer*.

In Buczacz they told of the arrival of Rabbi Meshulam to our town. His father was a simple Jew from a nearby village, who brought his son to our town so he might study Torah. He toiled away at his study until his reputation as a scholar became well known. It is also said that the father of Rabbi Meshulam is buried in the Buczacz cemetery, but we do not know the location of the grave.

A community of Hasidim was founded in Buczacz before the arrival of the Tsaddik Rabbi Avraham David, of sainted and blessed memory, the renowned author of many talmudic works. He instructed that during the recitation of the Incense Offering Passage one ingredient, whose pronunciation was unclear, be read "*hakosht* or perhaps *hakost*"—not wishing to decree a bad end on transgressors, for just as "one who omits even one of its ingredients is guilty of a capital offense" so, too, one who should mispronounce one of the ingredients.[60] That is why he decreed that we recite: "*hakosht* or perhaps *hakost.*"

Ten Hasidim separated themselves from the Jewish prayer-house and built themselves a sanctuary of their own, making a Hasidic minyan, and imported a certain rebbe, but their opponents in town banished him with derision. The

R. Falk's residence: "His home was in the upper part of town, on the road leading out to Podheitz. Today the place is called after the *kloiz* of the Chortkov Hasidim. In the past it was called Gold Street, on account of the light of Torah that would shine forth like fine gold from that great rabbi's window. One night, a band of thieves exiting the tavern saw the light and said, 'An alchemist is spinning gold! Let's go and fill our sacks with his gold.' Before they could even break into his front door they dropped dead in a pile of corpses." That street leading northwest out of town toward Podheitz (Pidhaytsi) is today called, in Ukrainian, Pidgayetska Street. The street is also mentioned as the residence of famous rabbis in the opening chapter of "The Outcast" ("Hanidaḥ"). Elsewhere Agnon mentions that the street was named after R. David Halevi Segal, author of *Turei zahav* (*Rows of Gold*); see S.Y. Agnon, "Mitsnefet hashabbat" in *Takhrikh shel sippurim* (Jerusalem: Schocken, 2001), 96. For more on this rabbi's connection to the town, see "The Rabbi Turei Zahav and the Two Porters of Buczacz" in Agnon, *City*, 175–80.

59. R. Moshe Meshulam Igra (b. Buczacz, 1752–1801), talmudist and halakhist, served as rabbi in Buczacz until 1794 when he decamped to the Hungarian city of Pressburg (today, Bratislava, the capital of Slovakia). Agnon describes him in "Igra Ramah" in Agnon, *'Ir*, 204–6, and he appears in the stories "Disappeared" and "In a Single Moment" in Agnon, *City*.

60. The ingredients of the temple incense mixture (known as "Pittum haqetoret") are outlined in BT Keritot 6a, the recitation of which makes up part of the liturgy (the recitation of the offering taking the place of the actual temple service). Lack of clarity about the pronunciation of one particular ingredient leads to a case of doubt, which caused R. Avraham David Teomim (see n. 40) to suggest reading both possibilities, a sh or s consonant depending on the undifferentiated letter *shin/sin*. This is recorded in Avraham David Teomim, *Birkat Avraham* (Kolomyia, 1888), 3b. This ingredient *kosht/kost* has been identified by some as *costus speciosus* (crape ginger).

khsidim-shtibl, that is, the Hasidic house of prayer, is to this day called the *leyt-sim-shulekhl*—"The Clowns' Shul."

One of the founders of Hasidism in town was a learned Torah scholar, the father of the man Yekele, who was eventually executed by hanging at the command of the head of the community.[61]

This Yekele, son of the first hasid in town, was executed 82 years ago,[62] having been charged on suspicion of theft and found guilty. At the moment they brought him up to the gallows, the hangman, who was an apostate Jew from Czernowitz, said to him: "Make confession in the name of the God of Israel."[63] He confessed many misdeeds but denied any responsibility regarding this theft. A moment before they slipped the noose around his neck, he declared that he had not committed this sin.

In fact, this man was killed because of the wrath of the communal leader, who had a gripe against him and feared him. A few days after he was hanged, a court order arrived absolving him of all punishment—but it was too late, as the deed was done.

On the day they took Yekele to the gallows all the townsmen left the city, wandered the fields and forest in tears, stretched out their hands towards heaven, and cried out: "Our hands have not shed this blood!"[64] [In order to cleanse themselves of responsibility, they contemplated performing the ritual of the "broken-necked calf," but they feared provoking the fury of the head of the community.][65]

61. The story of Yekele was expanded in two versions which appeared posthumously; see Agnon, *City*, 427–52.
62. Namely, in 1825. To the best of my knowledge, this story has no corroborating historical evidence.
63. Cf. Joshua 7:19 and BT Sanhedrin 43b.
64. Deuteronomy 21:7, a line from the ritual of the *'eglah 'arufah* ("broken-necked calf") which allows a town to make expiation for an unsolved murder or unexplained death, as outlined in Deuteronomy 21:1–9. The reference here is ironic: this ritual is performed in the case when the identity of the guilty party is unknown, yet the townsmen know precisely who is responsible for Yekele's death: Yisrael Shlomo!
65. The final sentence ("In order to cleanse...") was not authored by Agnon. In Agnon's personal copy of *Ha'et*, housed in the archives of the National Library of Israel, he marked the sentence in pencil with square brackets and wrote in the margin: "This was added by the editor"! The editorial amendment implies that the townsmen would have performed the actual *'eglah 'arufah* ceremony, absolving them of blame in Yekele's death (instead of merely evoking the theme through the associated verse), were they not cowering before Yisrael Shlomo. I am certain Agnon resented Bader taking this liberty with his story, for artistic concerns, as well as for its lack of authenticity. Agnon would have known that the *'eglah 'arufah* ritual had been abrogated already in the mishnaic era (see m. Sotah 9:9), and in all cases was never in effect outside of Erets Yisra'el (Sifre, Shoftim 62 and Maimonides, *Hilkhot Rotseah* 10:1).

RABBI JEFFREY SAKS is the founding director of ATID—The Academy for Torah Initiatives and Directions in Jewish Education, in Jerusalem, and its WebYeshiva.org program. He is the Editor of the journal *Tradition*, Series Editor of The S.Y. Agnon Library at The Toby Press, and Director of Research at the Agnon House in Jerusalem. A three-time graduate of Yeshiva University (BA, MA, Ordination), Saks has published in a variety of scholarly journals on Jewish thought, education, and literature, and authored *Spiritualizing Halakhic Education* (Mandel Foundation). His edited volumes include *Wisdom From All My Teachers: Challenges and Initiatives in Contemporary Torah Education* (Urim); *To Mourn a Child: Jewish Responses to Neonatal and Childhood Death* (OU Press); and *Agnon's Stories of the Land of Israel* (Wipf and Stock).

Figure 8: The Strypa River. (Credit, Wendy Zierler).

14   *A Simple Story: Szybusz and the Crisis of Parenting*

Michal Arbell

Arranged Marriages and Moral Values: "In a Single Moment" and *A Simple Story*

In the final chapter of his last book, *Ancestral Tales*, Alan Mintz offers a brilliant interpretation of Agnon's story "Besha'ah aḥat" ("In a Single Moment"). With great sensitivity to the smallest detail and nuance, Mintz interprets the loving relationship and dynamics between Avraham David and Sarah Rachel and their only son, Menaḥem, and portrays the family drama in the context of the historical decline of the old moral order of the Torah in Buczacz in the second half of the nineteenth century. Menaḥem is the only surviving child of Sarah and Avraham David, a gifted *talmid hakhamim*. Although he has reached the ripe age of fifteen, Menaḥem is not married yet. According to the custom, his parents should have betrothed him two years earlier, when he became a bar mitzvah. Mintz suggests that the parents failed to execute their duty to their son because they unconsciously resisted the thought of parting from him, their only child, but then he adds another, stronger, interpretation: The source of the problem lies not in the emotional dynamics of a specific family, but in the historical time of the Austrian rule of the city, when "Buczacz has become complacent, and the force of God's word [...] has been blunted and obscured beneath a mesh of protocols based on social status."[1] The world of the Torah is declining; there are fewer accomplished young scholars, and Menaḥem's value in the matchmaking market, which still offers *talmidei ḥakhamim* to the rich fathers of young daughters, is soaring. Dazzled by the high prospects of their promising son, Avraham David and Sarah cannot make up their minds about the right match.

Menaḥem's marriage predicament is resolved in a single moment. While walking together through the city, father and son encounter a dramatic scene. A young bride is abandoned under the *ḥuppah*, just before the wedding ceremony is about to begin, by her prospective groom. The girl comes from a known Buczacz family. She is the daughter of a highly respected (although poor) scholar and the

I am grateful to Michael Gluzman, Sheila Elana Jelen, Jeffrey Saks, and Wendy Zierler for their very helpful remarks.
1. Alan Mintz, *Ancestral Tales: Reading the Buczacz Stories of S.Y. Agnon* (Palo Alto, CA: Stanford University Press, 2017), 338.

Building a City: Writings on Agnon's Buczacz in Memory of Alan Mintz (2022): 206–228
DOI: 10.2979/BuildingaCityWriting.0.0.15

granddaughter of a famously righteous woman who dedicated her life to assist the marriage of penniless young girls. The groom, on the other hand, is a newcomer, an older widower who bought some property in the city. The fire that devastated Buczacz in 1865 enabled strangers like him to purchase real estate at very low prices. The bride's father has promised the groom a dowry of a certain amount, but he does not manage to get together the money by the time of the wedding. The groom refuses to accept his future father-in-law's word to make good on the promise as soon as he comes to funds and abandons the wedding place. The shocked, abandoned young bride faints and lies on the ground of the synagogue courtyard. In the spur of the moment, Avraham David asks his son to marry the girl, and Menaḥem accepts. A huge outburst of joy unites the city: Avraham David and Menaḥem ignore the latter's prospects of affluence in order to do the right thing. Mintz observes that Avraham David's decision "is fueled by another unacknowledged source: a desire to overcome his own unimportance." Nevertheless, Avraham David is also driven by a strong moral impulse: "Rescuing the girl is tantamount to rescuing Buczacz from the threats that have beset it."[2] For one glorious moment, this generous and compassionate act restores the moral order in the city. Mintz stresses: "It is a moment of redemption, not Redemption itself."[3] Unlike in older times, when Buczacz "was united in reverence for its magisterial spiritual leader and obeisant to his will," after the partitions of Poland, "that capacity for inner reform seems exhausted," and a lasting redemption is no longer a viable option for the community.[4]

A similar constellation of a mother, a father, and their single son caught in the drama of an arranged marriage lies in the center of Agnon's highly praised and probably most popular novel, *Sippur pashut* (*A Simple Story*). Agnon published the novel in 1935, twenty years before "In a Single Moment," but the story is set almost forty years later than "In a Single Moment," at the beginning of the twentieth century.[5] By that time, applying Mintz's observation about the portrayal of Buczacz in *A City in its Fullness*, the city (called Szybusz in the novel), certainly had "become wholly unmoored from its connection to Torah" and had reached a state of "moral debasement."[6] In "In a Single Moment," the father—

2. Mintz, *Ancestral Tales*, 385.

3. Mintz, *Ancestral Tales*, 391.

4. Mintz, *Ancestral Tales*, 338.

5. S.Y. Agnon, *Sippur pashut*, vol. 5 of *Kol sippurav shel Shmuel Yosef Agnon* (Jerusalem: Schocken, 1935). "Besha'ah aḥat," *Ha'aretz*, September 16 and 25, 1955. Gustav Krojanker, *The Works of S. J. Agnon*, trans. Jacob Gottschalk (Jerusalem: Mossad Bialik, 1991), 53 claims that the time of the story is 1905. According to Dan Miron, *Harofe hamedummeh* (Tel Aviv: Hakibbutz Hameuchad, 1995), 182, the story concludes in 1903, before the Russo-Japanese War.

6. Mintz, *Ancestral Tales*, 337, 339. In *A Simple Story*, the narrator keeps referring to the abandonment of the study of the Torah and of the old moral order. On the debasement of the traditional values and the historical transition to modern times in the novel, see Dov Sadan,

with the later approval of the mother—asks his son to value kindness, compassion, and moral duty over money and marry the poor abandoned girl; it is the right thing to do. In marked contrast, in *A Simple Story*, Tsirl, the mother of the young protagonist, Hirshl, with the pleased approval of his father, Boruch Meir, manipulates her son to betray the bond of love between him and Blume, his poor orphaned relative, in order to marry a rich man's daughter. In Tsirl's eyes, this is the right thing to do. It is not merely that money outranks moral values; for Tsirl, and, as it seems, for her social milieu as a whole, *there are no values except money*. Because Tsirl is a very clever woman (as the narrator keeps telling us) who exercises great power over her son, and because Hirshl, like his father, typically follows his mother's lead, he is manipulated to abandon Blume, whom he loves deeply and who had put her trust in him. He becomes the man, like the erstwhile groom in "In a Single Moment," who cruelly abandons his betrothed because her father does not have enough money.

Agnon's interest in the emotional and ethical aspects of matchmaking spans five decades of writing. In the first story he published after immigrating to Erets Yisra'el, "Agunot" (1908), from which he took his own name, Agnon, he describes the catastrophic consequences of an arranged marriage that ends in divorce. The mismatch goes beyond personal suffering to symbolize a national and even cosmic eternal state of *'aginut*, of loss and separation, longing and alienation. In his novella, *Bidmi yamehah* (*In the Prime of her Life*, 1923), he deals with the confused ethics of arranged marriages, when the good intention of a father to protect his daughter from her heart disease condemns her to a sorrowful life of heartbreak. In those stories, as well as in *A Simple Story* (1935) and the later story "Tehilla" (1950), Agnon rewrites—albeit in a much more sophisticated way—the popular theme of the wrongs of arranged marriages in earlier modern Hebrew literature. The literature of the Jewish Enlightenment harshly criticized the practice of the *shidukh*. In his autobiography, *Ḥaṭ'ot ne'urim* (*The Sins of Youth*, 1878), Moshe Leib Lilienblum powerfully portrays the devastating effects of his arranged marriage at a young age, which prevented him from having a love life as well as achieving higher education. Similar descriptions also appear in earlier Jewish autobiographies like *Avi'ezer* by Mordechai Aharon Ginzburg (1863). Negative representations of arranged marriages or the attempts to arrange them also appear in the first portrayals of contemporary society in modern Hebrew fiction, in Y. L. Gordon's long short story "Aḥarit simḥah tugah" ("Rejoicing Ends in Grief," 1868) and the debut novel *Avot uvanim* (*Fathers and Sons*, 1868) by S. Y. Abramovitsh (Mendele Mocher Seforim).[7] These works, like many others that

'Al Sh. Y. Agnon (Tel Aviv: Hakibbutz Hameuchad, 1979), 32–35; Krojanker, *Works*, 141–48; and Baruch Kurzweil, *Masot 'al sippurei S.Y. Agnon* (Tel Aviv: Schocken, 1975), 38–49, 353–58.
7. The first Hebrew novel, *Ahavat Tsiyyon* (*The Love of Zion*, 1853) by Avraham Mapu, is set in Erets Yisra'el in the time of King Hezekiah and revolves around a convoluted scheme of an

follow them, including Abramowitch's masterpiece Yiddish novel *Fishke der krumer* (*Fishke the Lame*, 1869), describe the traditional *shidukh* as a backwards and obsolete practice that oppresses the erotic life of the Jews and goes against both nature and reason.[8] The personal and social wrongs created by arranged marriages also stand at the center of relatively later modern Hebrew works like Abramowitch's novel *Be'emeq habakhah* (*In the Valley of Tears*, 1909) or M. Y. Berdyczewski's "Klonimos veNaomi" ("Klonimos and Naomi," 1909).[9]

Agnon's literary portrayals of arranged marriages are much more complex and multifaceted than those of the Hebrew Haskalah. It is important to note that the traditional *shidukh*, as well as the Jewish Enlightenment's agenda to eradicate it, are not a part of Agnon's social world. Still, the abovementioned works by Agnon do all point out the heartbreak, suffering, and even disasters caused by arranged marriages. Regarding the ethics of *shidukh*, two works stand out: "In a Single Moment" and *A Simple Story*. Agnon's "In a Single Moment" portrays, in an unprecedented way, the abrupt decision of a father to marry his son to a girl whom they both do not know, as an altogether positive act. The story suggests that, because of the goodness invested in the father's decision, the couple had a very happy and fruitful marriage. "In a Single Moment" is far from being a sentimental or even forgiving portrayal of Buczacz, but, in a way, this late story implies that, if a man like Avraham David is, in a single moment, totally true to the old moral values, even the much vilified traditional practice of *shidukh* can become a source of momentary redemption. The ethical dynamics in *A Simple Story* are almost the opposite. When the old values are totally abandoned, the use of the traditional *shidukh* has no justification; its wrongs cannot be mitigated on the basis of religious beliefs (as in "Tehilla") or by fatherly guilt and apprehension (as in *In the Prime of Her Life*). The arranged marriage in *A Simple Story* is totally devoid of any moral value.

arranged marriage. At the end of the novel, the crimes of the antagonists are revealed and the true identity of the young protagonist, Amnon, is restored. It comes out that he and Tamar, who fell in love although they supposedly belonged to very different social strata, are not defying their fathers' old pact that their not-yet-born children would marry, but actually fulfilling it. Mapu thus ingeniously succeeds in promoting the value of romantic love without undermining the authority of the father over his daughter's marriage.

8. Abramovitch published the Hebrew version of the novel, *Sefer haqabtsanim* (*The Book of the Paupers*), in 1909. Naomi Seidman, *The Marriage Plot: Or, How Jews Fell in Love with Love, and with Literature* (Palo Alto, CA: Stanford University Press, 2016) offers a comprehensive discussion on the relationship between love, matchmaking, and the emergence of Modern Jewish literature.

9. There are several similarities between Berdyczewski's story and *A Simple Story*: the two children grow together as adolescents, Naomi falls in love with Klonimos, and loses her mind when his father arranges his marriage to another girl.

In this respect, "In a Single Moment" and *A Simple Story* stand as mirror images of each other: parallel and opposite, reflecting and negating one another. (Agnon has a penchant for the mirror trope in his works, both as a motif and a narrative structure). As such, in the following discussion, I would like to use Mintz's observation about the connection between parenthood, arranged marriage, and moral values in a time of historical transition in "In a Single Moment" in order to illuminate similar themes in *A Simple Story*. I will try to point out the inevitable connection between the abolishment of moral order and the failure of parenthood not only on the level of the family, but also in the town as a whole. Furthermore, I would like to suggest that the much-discussed therapy of Hirshl by Dr. Langsam serves to reestablish parenthood through reenacting the process of rearing a child as well as by evoking the historical memory of moral order.

Moral Values and Melancholia

When Blume Nacht, the penniless orphaned girl, alone, enters the house of her rich relatives, the Hurvitz family in Szybusz (the literary name of Buczacz in the novel), the son of the family, Hirshl, is very nice and welcoming, but his mother is as cold as a stone. Tsirl treats Blume as a liability and makes it very clear how unwelcome she is. Lucky for Blume, Tsirl soon realizes that the intelligent and hard-working girl has the making of a very good servant. Not only is Blume a perfect housekeeper and an accomplished cook, but, since she is family, there is no need to pay her a wage: "'After all,' said Tsirl to her husband, 'she is one of us, isn't she? He who rewards us will reward her too.'"[10]

The narrator, who keeps shifting from irony to empathy, ostensibly defends Tsirl's exploitation of the girl. It only *seems* "that Blume was being taken advantage of." He is confident that "when Blume's time came to marry,"[11] Tsirl "would surely compensate her for each year of work."[12] This, of course, will never materialize. Not only will Tsirl not pay Blume a dime, but, when the girl's time comes to marry, she will also ruthlessly shatter all her hopes. Tsirl is quick to notice that Hirshl and Blume, who grow up together and share the same intellectual interest in books, have fallen in love with each other. Surprisingly, she takes no action and says nothing: "The same good sense that make her think, Why, the boy would have to be mad to fall in love with a penniless orphan, made her keep silent too. Let him have his flirtation with Blume, she thought. Once he grows up, he'll marry someone suitable." Tsirl's attitude toward Blume is utterly instrumental: "she felt grateful to Blume for keeping Hirshl away from other girls, for even

---

10. S.Y. Agnon, *A Simple Story*, rev. ed., trans. by Hillel Halkin, ed. Jeffrey Saks, (New Milford, CT: Toby, 2014), 7. All the further references to the English translation of the novel are from this edition.
11. Agnon, *Simple Story*, 7.
12. Agnon, *Simple Story*, 8.

in Szybusz, she knew, youthful morals were not what they once were."[13] It does not matter to Tsirl *at all* that the girl will fall more and more in love with her son as time passes, and that eventually her heart will be broken.

Tsirl never shows even a morsel of empathy toward Blume. Undoubtedly, she dislikes Blume, but the lack of empathy is not just personal; it characterizes Tsirl in general. For example, unlike Boruch Meir, she refuses to give a dime to the town's beggars and condescendingly tells them off, ignoring the Jewish ethical obligation of *tsedakah*.[14] Nevertheless, Tsirl is not totally devoid of empathy. She feels sorry for her future daughter in law, Mina, with regard to her most minor discomforts as well as for her real suffering when she is pregnant and Hirshl loses his mind. The difference in her attitude toward the two young women stems from the fact that Mina is "one of us"—namely, a relative—while Blume, who is left unpaid because she supposedly is "one of us," is not truly "one of us." This is why, for example, when the Hurvitzes go to visit friends, they never take Blume with them; she is not *really* one of the family. For Tsirl, the broad distinction between "one of us" and "all the others" corresponds with the distinction between the rich and the poor. Her knack as a shopkeeper is her ability to tell the financial status of her customers even when they try to disguise it, and she treats them, as well as everybody else, in keeping with their relative wealth or poverty.

At the same time, although Mina is rich and Tsirl likes her very much, and Blume is poor and Tsirl dislikes her very much, her fundamental attitude toward both of them is similar. Except for her nearest kin, her husband and son, with whom—in her own mind—she forms one entity, Tsirl regards everybody else as "others," as mere objects of exploitation. She does not abide by Immanuel Kant's categorical imperative, never to treat the other "merely as a means to an end, but always at the same time as an end."[15] For her, neither Mina nor Blume is by any sense an "end"; both are just means for an end that only she contrives. The only difference between them is that Mina is a cherished object, an asset, while Blume is unwanted, and a threat at that.

Tsirl's animosity toward Blume goes beyond her general instrumental attitude toward others. It seems that she really hates the girl. She claims for herself all of Blume's achievements in the household and complains that the exploited, hard-working girl is nothing but a spoiled brat. When Blume first arrives at the Hurvitz home, she brings with her some cakes and offers them to the family. Tsirl—who actually is a glutton for rich food—scolds her: "'Thanks be to God',

13. Agnon, *Simple Story*, 36.
14. Gershon Shaked, *Omanut hasippur shel Sh. Y. Agnon* (Tel Aviv: Sifriyat Hapo'alim, 1976), 219–21 discusses the Romantic motif of the blind beggars and its connection to the subconscious in the novel.
15. Immanuel Kant, *Grounding for the Metaphysics of Morals*, trans. James W. Ellington (Indianapolis: Hackett, 1993), 36.

said Tsirl, her tone of voice changing, 'that we aren't cake eaters and pastry nibblers here. Plain ordinary bread is good enough for us'."[16] Later on, she gives
Blume worn-out dresses and shoes, and, when she uses the wearable garments
and discards the ones that are not usable, Tsirl again seizes the opportunity to
criticize her: "'I myself save everything,' Tsirl liked to say, 'Not like our Blume,
who throws out whatever she doesn't care for'."[17]

Why does Tsirl hate Blume so much? It is true that Blume is the daughter of
Mirl, who many years ago was engaged to Boruch Meir, but it seems that Tsirl
does not care about the deceased woman at all. It is Blume herself who com-
promises Tsirl's beliefs: she represents values that are incompatible with a social
order based on financial status. Blume is a bookish girl. After her father, Ḥayyim
Nacht, lost all his money and could no longer provide for his family, he called
her to sit with him and read books: "'I know' said Ḥayyim Nacht 'that I won't be
leaving you any riches, but at least I'll have taught you how to read a book. No
matter how black your life may be, you can always find a better one in books'."[18] In
his melancholy and passivity, Ḥayyim Nacht embodies the dichotomy between
books and the so-called real world, between the intellectual sphere and material success. Blume refuses to accept this romantic dichotomy. She has the inner
force and mental capability to combine hard work and intellectual interests. This
is exactly why Tsirl abhors her. Blume's education and values compromise the
exclusivity of financial success as a mark of merit.[19] Blume possesses virtues, abil-
ities, and knowledge that are far beyond Tsirl's reach, and it makes her presence
intolerable. Books frighten Tsirl for another reason. She "had had a brother who,
instead of turning out normal, had been driven mad by his academic studies."[20]
When his parents tore up his books, he found others, "and when they finally
threw him out of the house he took to the woods and lived there on berries and
plants like a beast until his vital powers failed him and he died."[21] Blume shares
her love for books with Hirshl; once a week he borrows one book for serious and

---

16. Agnon, *Simple Story*, 6. Shaked, *Omanut*, 203 claims that Tsirl's gluttony is simultaneously
for food and money, both part of bourgeois society.
17. Agnon, *Simple Story*, 9.
18. Agnon, *Simple Story*, 22.
19. Tsirl is ambivalent even about the independence of rabbinical authority. When the sev-
enteen-year-old Hirshl loses interest in religious studies, Tsirl thinks it is for the better: "Not
that she respected religion and its scholars any less than the average woman did; still, like any
occupation whose practical value was doubtful, it seemed to her less than ideal. Of course
there were rabbis who earned handsome living too, but how many of them could you point
to?" (Agnon, *Simple Story*, 16).
20. Agnon, *Simple Story*, 16. The theme of a former yeshiva student who turns to European
academic studied and loses his mind first appears in Mendele Mocher Seforim (S. Y. Abramovitch), "The Nag" ("Die Kliatshe") 1873.
21. Agnon, *Simple Story*, 16.

two for light reading for him and Blume. The content of the books is not speci-
fied, but the serious ones probably contain learning material while the light ones
probably describe the joys and sorrows of love. Tsirl is not afraid that reading
three books a week will, on its own, inflict madness on her son, but madness has
run in her family for generations. Her grandfather's grandfather had insulted
the town's rabbi by remarking that the latter is going out of his mind, and the
rabbi cursed him in retaliation: "From that day on there was not a generation in
Tsirl's family without its madmen."[22] Tsirl protects herself from madness by defying intellectual tendencies, stormy emotions, and romantic ideas. She restricts
herself and her family to the bourgeois social order of accumulating money and
devouring food as a defense against the devastating powers of madness.

When the army's draft board is about to come to Szybusz, Tsirl decides that
it is time for Hirshl to get married. She summons the town's matchmaker, Yona
Toyber, and discusses with him her choice for a future daughter-in-law: Mina,
the daughter of Gedalya and Bertha Ziemlich. Not only is Gedalya a rich man,
but his wealth also comes from growing food, as he is the count's estate manager
in the village of Malikrowik. His wife, Bertha, is an excellent cook, so money
and food will marry money and food. Tsirl tells her husband about the planned
shidukh, and he, as usual, accepts: "Boruch Meir was not in the habit of contra-
dicting his wife."[23] She is well aware of the historical change that is taking place
in Szybusz and knows that she needs to manipulate her son to accept her choice
of bride. The old days when parents simply decided their children's future in marriage are gone, and, in present times, modern young men and women have novel
ideas about falling in love and choosing their own spouses.[24] Tsirl invites Mina to
visit whenever she comes to Szybusz, and then, one day, when Hirshl goes down
to the cellar to fetch wine, Tsirl follows him and closes the door behind her. In the
intimacy and total darkness of the cellar, she tells him that Mina is an educated
girl, a daughter of a wealthy man and his only heir. Marriage, Tsirl lectures her
son, is a serious business and, like all other businesses, is based on money: "A
bachelor can be free to follow his heart, but what would the world come to if he
didn't put his romances aside when the time came to get married? A fine place
it would be if everyone followed their hearts!"[25] Blume is a good girl, but she has
not a cent to her name. They were kind enough to take her into their house and

---

22. Agnon, *Simple Story*, 17. The theme of a rabbi who curses a father that his son will lose
his mind (or his soul) appears in Mordechai Zeev Feierberg's *Le'an?* (*Whither?* 1899) and in
Agnon's "Hanidaḥ" ("The Outcast," 1919).
23. Agnon, *Simple Story*, 45.
24. See Seidman, *Marriage Plot*.
25. Agnon, *Simple Story*, 47.

provide for her needs, but now, says Tsirl, "I'm sure she knows her proper place and would never want to come between you and your good fortune."[26]

Hirshl does not answer his mother, neither on the spot nor in the following days. He needs Blume to fight this battle for him, but Blume needs him to stand up for himself. This does not happen. When Blume falls in love with Hirshl, she knows that she is heading toward great trouble; she does her work, but "Never once did she smile, while her mouth hung slightly open as if it has either given up talking in the middle of a sentence or else were about to scream."[27] When her fears are realized, she is deeply hurt and avoids Hirshl, and they both suffer greatly. "In a vague way Hirshl began to feel that, if he did not stand steadfast forever, this would only be because Blume had abandoned him."[28] When Blume leaves the house, Tsirl seizes the opportunity and manipulates Hirshl even further. While consoling him, she mispresents Blume's heartbreak as lack of love: "Better to marry a woman who respects you than to run after one who doesn't care."[29] Hirshl remembers that

> Once, when he had been a small boy, a friend had jilted him; seeing how hurt he was Tsirl took him in her arms, where her kisses and caresses soon put the friend out of his mind. And although Hirshl was now a young man, the same thing had happened again."[30]

The analogy to the childhood incident is significant. The memory evokes a very rare occasion of motherly warmth because, in general, Tsirl was a cold mother: "As soon as Hirshl was weaned, Tsirl went back to working full-time in the store [...] And though Hirshl was her only child, she was careful not to show him too much love in order not to spoil him."[31] When a baby, he never heard a lullaby, because Tsirl "had never sung to him," supposedly "because she knew her voice was unmusical."[32] Tsirl's reaction to Hirshl's disappointment with his childhood friend has a long-standing effect; he is very close to his mother even as a young man, and he has no friends, just some acquaintances for whom he does not really care.

All the same, Tsirl's demand from Hirshl to abandon the woman he deeply loves and marry a stranger he hardly knows is extreme. Why does he not refuse? In his words, "Why, Hirshl asked himself, do I put up with it?"[33] Indeed, why does he not ask Blume for her hand in marriage and present his parents with a fait

---

26. Agnon, *Simple Story*, 47–48.
27. Agnon, *Simple Story*, 35.
28. Agnon, *Simple Story*, 48.
29. Agnon, *Simple Story*, 52.
30. Agnon, *Simple Story*, 53.
31. Agnon, *Simple Story*, 11.
32. Agnon, *Simple Story*, 197.
33. Agnon, *Simple Story*, 52.

accompli? For sure, Tsirl and Boruch Meir would not have banished him, their only son, just because he wants to marry an honest and good girl like Blume. His mother undoubtedly would have been angry with him but not utterly surprised: "Tsirl was clever enough to know that she lived in an age when no parent could force a son to do anything, much less to marry against his will."[34]

Still, Hirshl complies with his mother's demands. He has no power to stand against her. According to A. B. Yehoshua and Amos Oz, the blame for his weakness lies with the women in his life, Tsirl and Blume. Yehoshua claims that, because Tsirl is a domineering and emotionally insufficient mother, Hirshl seeks motherly love from Blume, but Blume is subdued and irresponsive, *blumah* (closed, in Hebrew) by name and closed by nature.[35] According to Oz, Tsirl is like a beast, hardly human, and a castrating mother on top of it. Not only does she get rid of Blume, but she also creates a threat to his relationship with Mina. Oz claims that Hirshl loses his mind in order to free himself from his mother's grasp and be able to enjoy, behind her back, a blissful sexual relationship with his wife.[36] Blume, on the other hand, is frigid, actually not a real woman; if Hirshl had married her, he would have ended up in total misery. Oz's harsh description of Tsirl (or Blume) seems tendentious, and it does not appear to me that Hirshl's terrible psychotic crisis is a calculated act. Furthermore, he has no need at all to fight his mother in order to enjoy erotic bliss with his wife. The young couple lives in their own house, and Tsirl is very pleased with Mina, "for whom she felt a special affection for having agreed to become her daughter-in-law, thus saving Hirshl from the clutches of Blume."[37]

In my eyes, there are two reasons for Hirshl's inability to stand on his own and marry the woman he deeply loves. One is his melancholy; the other is his moral and psychological immaturity. At the age of nineteen, while his contemporaries in Szybusz, such as Getzel Stein, are adults—grown up men—Hirshl is still a child. He cannot evolve from childhood to manhood because no one has raised him properly. As mentioned before, his mother emotionally abandoned him at a very tender age, immediately when she stopped nursing him. From then on, she worked in the shop from early morning until late in the evening. Hirshl was put in the care of her servant, a morbid *'agunah* who did not waste her time on frivolous activities like singing to the baby; she "was too busy with the housework or with sewing the shrouds for her funeral to have any time for such things."[38]

34. Agnon, *Simple Story*, 52–53.
35. A. B. Yehoshua, "Nequdat hahattarah ba'alilah kemafteah leferush hayetsirah (hadgamah 'al pi *Sippur pashut* leShai Agnon)," *'Alei siah* 10–11 (1981): 74–88.
36. Amos Oz, *Shetiqat hashamayim: Agnon mitlonen 'al Elohim* (Jerusalem: Keter, 1993), 39–72.
37. Agnon, *Simple Story*, 65. Nitza Ben-Dov, *Ahavot lo me'usharot: Tiskul eroti, omanut uma-vet biytsirat Agnon* (Tel Aviv: 'Am 'Oved, 1997), 272–93 criticized Oz's "paranoid" (perhaps misogynistic) description of Blume.
38. Agnon, *Simple Story*, 197.

Near the end of the novel, when Hirshl comes back to Szybusz after his stay in Dr. Langsam's nursing home, he wishes for his baby son a better childhood than he had; he knows that there was no joy in his own childhood, and that it "was not blessed."[39]

The sudden and traumatic loss of the care and intimacy of the mother in his infancy rendered Hirshl melancholic in later years. According to Sigmund Freud, "melancholia too may be the reaction to the loss of a loved object [. . .] the object has not perhaps actually died, but has been lost as an object of love."[40] Hirshl's melancholia precedes his heartbreak over Blume. At the age of sixteen, he reflects that, "There were those who claimed that the whole problem with the world was its being divided into the rich and the poor. Indeed that was a problem. Certainly, though, it was not the main one. The main problem was that everything came about with so much pain."[41] The loss of Blume three years later repeats the childhood trauma. Hirshl's melancholia deepens; the world seems to him to be devoid of meaning and interest: "How worthless is the human being. Sleeps only to wake up, wakes up only to go to sleep. And between waking and sleeping his lot is only trouble and misery, injury and insult."[42] Reminiscent of Freud's description of the melancholic, Hirshl feels "profoundly painful dejection, cessation of interest in the outside world, loss of the capacity to love, inhibition of all activity, and a lowering of the self-regarding feelings"; he is ambivalent toward his lost love object (Blume), rejects food, and finds it difficult to sleep.[43] "The sleeplessness in melancholia testifies to the rigidity of the condition," says Freud, and when Hirshl's sleeplessness worsens, his mental state deteriorates to psychosis.[44]

Not only Hirshl's relationship with his mother but also that with his father is to blame for his lack of stamina. He feels that both of them render him powerless: "[A]s long as I am dependent on my father and mother I cannot amend anything." Later he says, "Nevertheless, as long as I am under the control of my father and my mother, I cannot change my ways."[45] Unlike his wife, Boruch Meir is a warm parent. When Hirshl is born, he loves him "to excess,"[46] "holds him

39. Agnon, *Sippur pashut, Kol sippurav shel Shmuel Yosef Agnon*, vol. 3, *'Al kappot haman'ul* (*On the Handles of the Lock*) (Schoken, Tel Aviv, 1962), 246 (my translation).
40. Sigmund Freud, "Mourning and Melancholia," in *The Standard Edition of the Complete Psychological Works of Sigmund Freud*, trans. James Strachey, 24 vols. (London: Hogarth, 1961), 14:246.
41. Agnon, *Simple Story*, 9–10.
42. Agnon, *Sippur pashut, Kol sippurav* (1962), 196 (my translation).
43. Agnon, *Sippur pashut, Kol sippurav* (1962), 243 (my translation).
44. Freud, "Mourning," 253.
45. Agnon, *Sippur pashut, Kol sippurav* (1962), 129, 132 (my translation). "Father and mother" is the expression for "parents" in Yiddish, but the use of it in Hebrew underscores Hirshl's dependency on both of his parents.
46. Agnon, *Simple Story*, 11.

in his hands, presses him to his heart and plays with him even when his wife is not around."[47] Boruch Meir is a loving parent and husband, a nice person in general, and a very successful shopkeeper. His only flaw as a father figure is his weakness. In the words of Baruch Kurzweil, in his relation to Tsirl, he is "a small passive type."[48] Boruch Meir comes from a humble origin. He marries high above his class to the daughter of a rich man, Shimon Hirsh Klinger, only because the wealthy families in Szybusz would not wed their sons to a girl who comes from a house plagued with lunacy. Boruch Meir works in Klinger's shop for six and a half years and looks up to him in awe. When Klinger offers him his daughter's hand in marriage, he accepts immediately and transfers his obedience and servile attitude from the father to the daughter. Boruch Meir always agrees with Tsirl and never thinks or says anything that Tsirl has not thought or said before.

Quite a few obstacles stand in the way of life as a couple for Boruch Meir and Tsirl. The marriage is an arranged affair, Boruch Meir breaks his promise to his beautiful cousin Mirl, he never feels equal to his wife, and Tsirl has to marry one of her father's servants instead one of the sons of the respectable families in Szybusz. Nevertheless, the bond between the two is a very happy one. It is true that the climax of their intimacy is when they sit in the evening together in the half-closed shop and count the money they made during the day. Some people, says the narrator, "insisted that only the man driven out of his senses by passion could claim to be love's acolyte," but he adds, "the passion for love misled them about love itself." Boruch Meir and Tsirl "had no time for such diversions," and they did not drive each other out of their senses, yet "He simply was as happy with her as she was with him."[49] Not only are they good partners and very fond of each other, but they also maintain a strong physical attraction. The narrator does hint that Tsirl has lost her sex drive: she "had reached the age when what concerns a woman most is eat and drink," but it seems that his remark is misleading.[50] Undoubtedly, Tsirl loves her food, but, until Hirshl's mental breakdown, she keeps both her appetites, for food and for her husband: "As for Tsirl, she kept her eyes on Boruch Meir. Other wives might not have spent their son's engagement party looking at their husband [like this,] but Boruch Meir was no ordinary husband. At the age of forty-seven he was still young in body and mind,"[51] and Boruch Meir reciprocates: "Boruch Meir looked lovingly at Tsirl. Her round,

47. Agnon, "Sippur pashut," *Kol sippurav* (1962), 64 (my translation).
48. Kurzweil, *Masot*, 40.
49. Agnon, *A Simple Story*, 45.
50. Agnon, *Sippur pashut, Kol sippurav* (1962), 74 (my translation). It is true that Tsirl is a glutton for food, and that food plays a major role in the novel; see Shaked, *Omanut*, 197–227.
51. Agnon, *Simple Story*, 64.

rosily tinged face, with its head of dark hair seemed suddenly changed to him. Indeed, each time he looked at her he discovered something new."[52]

Boruch Meir's subservience to his wife does not compromise the happiness of his marriage, nor does it interfere with his love for his son, but it is a symptom of his moral weakness, and it has a devastating effect on his son's psyche. According to Freud, in the process of the dissolution of the Oedipus complex, "The object-cathexes are given up and replaced by identifications. The authority of the father or the parents is introjected into the ego, and there it forms the nucleus of the super-ego."[53] The problem is not that Boruch Meir has wrong values, but that he is too weak to hold to his own values, is happy to adopt his wife's views, and always affirms her moral conduct.[54] Because the father with whom Hirshl identifies, whose authority he internalizes, is morally weak, his emotional maturity is undermined. The text criticizes Tsirl's base materialistic values, but it is not clear what Boruch Meir's values are. It is clear, though, that, whatever they were, he gave them up when he decided to abandon Mirl and marry Tsirl for the sake of money: "Tsirl's silver and gold blinded Boruch Meir's eyes, so he deserted his relative and married her."[55] When Blume comes to his house, he has an opportunity to make a symbolic amend and marry his son to Mirl's orphaned daughter, but it seems that this kind of recognition of his fault and wish for atonement does not cross his mind.[56] Unlike his wife, Boruch Meir is kind to Blume, but his kindness is weak and limited: he does not seem to mind that his poor relative works in his house for years without pay. Boruch Meir never opposes his wife; it is little

52. Agnon, *Simple Story*, 125.

53. Sigmund Freud, "The Dissolution of the Oedipus Complex," in *The Standard Edition of the Complete Psychological Works of Sigmund Freud*, trans. James Strachey, 24 vols. (London: Hogarth, 1961), 19:76.

54. The Freudian theory of the superego excludes ethical distinctions between so-called right and wrong values: "Freud's explanation of morality in terms of the superego ostensibly embraces an ethical relativism"; see Ernest Wallwork, "Ethics in Psychoanalysis," in *Textbook of Psychoanalysis*, ed. Ethel S. Person, Arnold M Cooper, and Glen O. Gabbard (Washington, DC: American Psychiatric Publishing, 2005), 281.

55. Agnon, *Sippur pashut, Kol sippurav* (1962), 68 (my translation). Kurzweil, *Masot*, 43 claims that Boruch Meir does Mirl injustice and does not care. In the next generation, his son Hirshl takes after his father and does Mirl's daughter Blume injustice, but, unlike his father, he is well aware of what he did.

56. In *In the Prime of her Life*, the young protagonist, Tirtza, supposedly tries to make amends by marrying her mother's old love, Akavia Mazal, but her motives are complex and unclear; see Adi Zemach, *Qeri'ah tamah basifrut ha'ivrit bat hame'ah ha'esrim* (Jerusalem: Mossad Bialik, 1990), 11–24 and Michal Arbell, *Katuv 'al 'oro shel hakelev: Tefisat hayetsirah etsel Sh. Y. Agnon* (Jerusalem: Ben-Gurion University and Keter, 2006), 41–46. In *A Simple Story*, when Blume has to leave the Hurvitz's house she moves to the home of Akavia and Tirza and works there as a servant.

wonder that his son cannot find in himself the strength to defy her in the morally charged and extremely sensitive issue of marrying Blume.

There is another important sense in which ethical issues affect Hirshl's psyche. Tsirl's crude egotism and Boruch Meir's subservience to her represent the moral decline of Szybusz as a whole. The abandonment of the old world of the Torah creates a society devoid of moral values, of solidarity or compassion. Hirshl's melancholia stems from the loss not only of the care of his mother when he was an infant, but also of the moral order of the community in which he grows up. Freud claims that melancholia, like mourning, can be the reaction "to the loss of some abstraction [...] such as one's country, liberty, an ideal and so on."[57] At the age of sixteen, when Hirshl reflects, as quoted before, that "everything came about with so much pain," he has an intuition about the source of his grievance:

> Hirshl himself could not explain this pain. From the moment he first saw the light of day he never lacked for food or clothing, nor for the attention of good people who lavished him with kindness and lovingly fulfilled his every wish. Perhaps he had eyes to see that the same people who were so good to him were not always as good to others, which grieved him.[58]

In the minds of Tsirl and Boruch Meir, to be good parents means to keep for their son all they have and can achieve. This seemingly devoted behavior turns, against their good intentions, into a parental failure. The norm of egotistic selfishness deprives Hirshl of an upbringing in a supportive and caring community. Moreover, the habitual moral egotism of his parents diminishes their emotional amplitude. Not only can Tsirl not feel motherly compassion toward an orphaned girl who comes to her house, but she also cannot find in herself real empathy for her son's broken heart. Parental love is limited; as a result (and also as a kind of symbol), the families that stand in the center of the novel are very small. In the Eastern European Jewish society of large families, the Hurvitz, Nacht, and Ziemlich families consisted of a father, a mother, and only one child.[59] After having Hirshl, Tsirl "was not expecting more children [...] neither was she anxious to have them."[60]

Tsirl's base "shopkeeping logic"—namely, get as much as you can and give as little as you can—plays an important role in another story by Agnon, "Panim Aherot" ("Another Face"). In "Another Face," as well as in *A Simple Story*, the implementation of the shopkeeping logic in the emotional sphere triggers a disaster. In "Another Face," Michael Hartman ruins his marriage to Toni because he tries to manage all the aspects of his life according to these commercial principles:

---

57. Freud, "Mourning," 242
58. Agnon, *Simple Story*, 10.
59. This is also the case in *In the Prime of her Life* and "In a Single Moment."
60. Agnon, *Simple Story*, 11.

"Michael Hartman was a merchant, and sold his commodities in exact measures, and he knew that he who wastes one measure is short that same measure."[61] Not only is Michael angry with Toni because she "wastes" her kindness by talking to other people or playing with their babies, but he also stingily refuses to give any measure of kindness to his own family. After the divorce, when Michael and Toni stroll aimlessly in the streets, he buys flowers from a little peddler girl. Through this trifle encounter, Toni can, for the first time, show him that the shopkeeping logic is incongruent with the logic of love; in the latter, "wasting" a measure might be a gain, not a loss. From this point on, Michael can start a therapeutic process that will culminate in a meaningful insight at the end of the story.[62] When Hirshl falls in love with Blume, he tries childishly and halfheartedly to defend himself from the pain of the situation by using the familiar shopkeeping logic in regards to her:

> I see you're keeping accounts, thought Hirshl. If you mean to give me the silent treatment, two can play at that game: I can be as silent as you. And yet the fact was that it was Hirshl, the son and grandson of shopkeepers who were used to weighing and measuring, who was keeping accounts."[63]

Nevertheless, when Hirshl sees how anguished Blume's eyes are, his attitude of "keeping accounts" dissipates.

It is important to note that, in the passage I quoted before, "people"—not just Hirshl's parents—were good to him but not to others. In a sense, Szybusz as a whole (although, for Hirshl, this mainly means his family's social stratum) functions as an overarching parent. In many works by Agnon, the hometown of Buczacz (or Szybusz) is figured as a "big mother." Various texts portray the town as a nurturing entity, and it has a signature smell of the beloved food. In the novel *A Guest for a Night*, the narrator comes to visit his old hometown after the terrible devastation inflicted on it during World War I and its aftermath. Even in its state of ruin and decay, still "the odor of Szibusz had not yet evaporated—the odor of millet boiled in honey, which never leaves the town from the day after Passover until the end of November, when the snow falls, covering all."[64] According to Mintz, in *A City In its Fullness*, in the earlier period, "when Buczacz was a fragile band of survivors in the throes of recovering from the 1648 massacres," the *qehilah*, the community, was united and protected its traumatized sons and

61. S.Y. Agnon, ʾAl kappot hamanʾul (At the Handle of the Lock), vol. 3 of *Kol sippurav shel Shmuel Yosef Agnon*, 8 vols. (Tel Aviv: Schocken, 1962), 445 (my translation). The first version of the story was published two years before *Sippur pashut* (*Davar*, December 12, 1933) and the final version in 1941 (*Kol sippurav*, vol. 8).
62. Michal Arbell, "'Panim aherot': Haheshbon hakalkali vedahaf hamavet," *Maʿasei sippur* 4 (2018): 323–44.
63. Agnon, *Simple Story*, 34.
64. S.Y. Agnon, *A Guest for the Night*, trans. Misha Louvish (New York: Schocken, 1968), 2.

daughters, but, as the moral order declines after the partition of Poland, its positive parental functions diminish.[65] In a story like "Haneʿelam" ("Disappeared,") which describes the city in times of modernization under the rule of Austria, the terrible injustice toward the most vulnerable members of the *qehilah* exemplifies that "the world of Buczacz is bereft of human feeling and communal responsibility."[66] The city becomes a cruel mother that eats her weakest young.[67] In *A Simple Story*, "Szybusz has a pledge that he who eats her dishes will stay with her forever."[68] She is the mother who swallows her sons by feeding them.[69]

Ultimately, Hirshl is pushed into announcing the engagement to Mina by the city itself; namely, by the society of the well-to-do, modern Jews in Szybusz. It happens at a party thrown by Mina's friend, Sophia Gildenhorn. The gathering is almost hellish. It is vulgar and crude; the guests play cards, crack jokes, and exchange insults, and the mix of cigarette smoke and oil fumes from the kitchen causes Hirshl nausea and dizziness. In one of his somber moments, the narrator claims that Yitzchok Gildenhorn's parties and his friends' demeaning behavior was to blame for the moral deterioration of the city: "Indeed the decline and fall of Szybusz's old patricians had begun on the day that Gildenhorn moved into town."[70] In this depraved environment, Hirshl, who finds refuge in talking to Mina, takes her hand in his, and Yitzchok Gildenhorn seizes the moment and congratulates him (in snobbish Germanized Yiddish) for an engagement that did not yet exist. Later on, the couple's parents join the party, and Boruch Meir rubs his hands in pleasure, observing that the party brought about his son's engagement: "khevre, khevre" he exclaims, "like a man who says, it is not my doing, the responsibility for this stays with the *khevre*."[71] In Yiddish, the word *khevre* means both "friends" and "society."

It seems to bother Hirshl that immoral and cynical people like Yitzchok Gildenhorn and his friends announce his engagement to Mina. When he meets with her after the party, in a family gathering in Malikrowik, he decides to tell

65. Mintz, *Ancestral Tales*, 338.
66. Mintz, *Ancestral Tales*, 337.
67. Shaked, *Omanut*, 205–6 claims that, in *A Simple Story*, Szybusz sees the world as a "big mother" who provides her goods to her successful children, and that it is necessary to be "orphaned," literally or metaphorically (from the Jewish society), in order to become an independent adult like Blume or her suitor Getzel Stein.
68. Agnon, "Sippur pashut," *Kol sippurav* (1962), 99 (my translation).
69. On the great mother who swallows her sons, see Erich Neuman, *The Great Mother: An Analysis of the Archetype*, trans. Ralph Manheim (New York: Pantheon, 1954), 10.
70. Agnon, *Simple Story*, 55–56.
71. Agnon, *Sippur pashut*, 109 (my translation). It seems that not only the Hurvitzes' social stratum but also the city as a whole approves of the bond between the two rich families. Unlike the public uproar that follows the abandonment of the bride in "In a Single Moment," the harsh injustice done to Blume remains private, and "the whole town was as happy for the Hurvitzes as it always was" (87).

her, totally out of context, a historical anecdote about the immorality and cruelty of Jewish society, about the misuse of power by the rich and mighty. The story took place in Stanislaw, the city where Mina was staying while she was studying in a boarding school for educated Jewish girls. It is

> about a party of Jewish refugees from Rumania who appeared one day before you were born in Stanislaw, where the bailiff of the community refused to take them in for fear of them becoming a burden, so they were forced to squat in squalor with their wives and children before the city gates, until their cries for help reached the heavens.[72]

Mina is fascinated:

> How curious, she marveled, thinking about the hard-hearted bailiff: I've been in that man's house to visit his granddaughters and never found him cruel at all. In fact, he once gave me a friendly pat on the back. And even if his cheeks are blue and he always looks unshaven, what sort of proof for cruelty is that?[73]

Mina is mildly puzzled by the revelation of the immanent cruelty of her social stratum; Hirshl is deeply disturbed by it. His misgivings and dark premonition hang heavily over him during the wedding ceremony, and his melancholia deepens over the following days and weeks. The loss of Blume, whom he still deeply loves, is unbearable, and his surrender to his mother and to the degraded social order he despises is insufferable.

Psychosis and Treatment

The heart-rending and overwhelming description of Hirshl's mental breakdown is one of Agnon's greatest literary achievements. It is not in the scope of this article to do it justice, but I would like to refer to one aspect of it; namely, Hirshl's rejection of the social order and consequently its total disintegration in his mind. As Hirshl's depression deepens, he thinks more and more about his uncle who lost his mind and perished. In the beginning of the novel, the uncle's madness is explained as stemming from an old curse or a hereditary mental illness that plagues the family, but, in Hirshl's tormented mind, in his horror and rage, the uncle appears as a romantic rebel:

> It was storming violently outside. The trees swayed in the wind. The birds and beasts of the forest hid as best they could, and not even a bug showed its face. One man alone was out on such a night, because he had no house to call his own. Who was he? Why, Hirshl's uncle, who had been banished by his parents for [he had crossed the line]."[74]

72. Agnon, *Simple Story*, 78.
73. Agnon, *Simple Story*, 79.
74. Agnon, *Simple Story*, 162.

In his fantasy, his uncle is not dead but alive, and he is not crazy but an intellectual rebel. In Hebrew, the expression *yatsa ḥuts lashurah* ("crossed the line") suggests that the uncle broke religious norms and educated himself in European culture. During the decades before Hirshl was born, the vast majority of the Jewish community in Szybusz was orthodox and would have considered reading non-Jewish books of science, philosophy, or literature a form of heresy, with the transgressor ostracized as an *apikores*. Nothing in the novel except Hirshl's fantasy suggests that this was the case with his uncle. Hirshl's next fantasy imagines an idyllic return to nature, which renders society, with its oppressive rules and restrictions, escapable. In Hirshl's imagination, his uncle lives in a prelapsarian world in which he does not have to work to provide for himself. While Hirshl's parents invest their entire energy in pursuing material success, the uncle embodies an alternative reality:

> Sometimes the trees stood quietly at peace while a mild sun shone down on them and the birds flew chattering among their branches, a good smell of grass and mushrooms filled the air, and Hirshl's uncle lay on his back, happy to be alone and unbothered. When he was hungry, he picked and ate berries. When he was thirsty, he drank from the spring, [unlike all other people, who fictionally created for themselves fictional houses, shops, customers and wives.][75]

When psychosis takes over, Hirshl runs from the morning prayer in the house of study to the woods, following the footsteps of his uncle. Civilization should protect its members from the lawlessness and dangers of the wilderness, but, when the moral order in the city disintegrates, when there is no justice or value except the ruthless rule of power, when society kills the hearts of her sons inside their bosoms, the woods become a refuge.[76] Hirshl casts off the external signs of social order. He throws his hat, he takes off his shoe and puts it on his head, he lies on his back and spits, and the spit falls back into his eyes. Before his breakdown, during the long and tormenting nights of insomnia, Hirshl develops an obsessive hatred toward the town's roosters who disturb his sleep. As Gershon Shaked points out, the rooster is a central figure in the novel.[77] Tsirl devours poultry dishes that Blume cooks for her; in the engagement feast in Malikrowik, Hirshl avoids eating the fatty gravy served in a china pot shaped like a duck and ponders whether his uncle was a misunderstood vegetarian.

> If my mother would not have her heart set on Ziemlich's money, thought Hirshl, I would not have to be sitting here right now with all this cooked dead

75. Agnon, *Simple Story*, 162.
76. For kiling hearts inside their bosoms, see Agnon, *Sippur pashut*, *Kol sippurav* (1962), 173
77. Shaked, *Omanut*, 222–23.

flesh in front of me. He looked up to see if anything was left of these abominations, whose smell [arouse his appetite] and caught sight of Mina."[78]

In Hebrew, one of the names of the cock is "man" (*gever*) and its crowing is the "call of the man" (*qeri'at hagever*). The rooster symbolizes Hirshl's manhood, which was fractured by his mother. On the morning of his breakdown, the people in the house of study discuss a special kind of poultry. The question is whether one should check, after slaughtering the birds, if they have cavities in their skulls that would render them unkosher. The discussion agitates Hirshl. He is frightened that he is about to crow like a rooster, that people might think that he is mad. "I'm glad," he thinks, "that I scream like a man and do not crow like a rooster."[79] In the Hebrew, "and do not crow like a rooster" (*ve'eini qore kegever*), also means "and I do not call like a man." Hirshl runs away from the house of study to the woods, feeling "as light as a feather."[80] He is preoccupied with both the wish to be a rooster and the fear that being a rooster means losing his mind. He thinks that if he had hung himself from a tree, he would have heard not the crowing of the rooster but the croak of the frogs in the river. In mock talmudic fashion, he argues confusedly that one might think that he is crazy because he crows like a rooster, but, because he accepts this argument, and because he is not crazy, he does not crow like a rooster but only quacks like a duck, *ga ga ga*. At sundown, some townspeople find him in a field, "with one shoe on one foot and the other on his forehead, an expression of great anguish in his eyes. It was hard to look at him." Hirshl cries to them: "'Don't cut my throat! I'm not a rooster! I'm not!'"[81] The men bring Hirshl home; when Mina tries to stroke his hair, he pulls his head away and calls her by the name of his lost love: "'Blume I didn't go cockle doodle do, I just went *ga ga ga*.' Mina fainted dead away and was put to bed at once."[82]

The rooster symbolizes for Hirshl not only his robbed manhood but also his sense of the lost order of time. The rooster's crowing at the crack of dawn marks the beginning of the day. For Hirshl, as for Hamlet, "The time is out of joint."[83] When he leaves his house in the morning, his watch stops, is out of order, and Mina tells him that the time is half past seven. From then on, the time for him remains half past seven. When examined by a doctor, he responds to all his questions with the same answer: half past seven. Likewise, Hirshl's language is out of proper order. His deranged talk marks him as someone who drifts away from normal discourse. It is interesting to note that the language of his insanity has its

78. Agnon, *Simple Story*, 83.
79. Agnon, *Sippur pashut*, 215 (my translation).
80. Agnon, *Simple Story*, 178.
81. Agnon, *Simple Story*, 180.
82. Agnon, *Simple Story*, 181.
83. William Shakespeare, *Hamlet*, act 1, scene 5 (Signet Classic, New York: Penguin, 1986).

own beauty and poetic impact. In the chapters that describe his acute melancholia and psychosis, the mad figurative imagination becomes the poetic language of the text itself. Moreover, Hirshl's cock-a-doodle-dos and *ga-ga-ga*s, as well as his inability to walk on his hind legs, render him, in the words of Noam Pines, "infrahuman."[84] Hirshl turns into a hybrid, a scared and bewildered rooster-man, although he denies it vehemently and claims that he is just a duck-man or a frog. Animal-human hybrids play a central role in some of Agnon's major works, in the novel *Temol shilshom* (*Only Yesterday*) and in his long stories "Shevu'at emunim" ("Betrothed"), "Mazal dagim" ("Pisces"), and "Hadom vekhise" ("Stool and Chair").[85] The presence of hybrids in Agnon's works is always ominous, and it evokes the presence of the unconscious and of death.[86]

After two days, Hirshl's parents take him to Dr. Langsam's sanatorium in Lemberg. Leaving Szybusz, his wife, his parents, and everyone in Szybusz is good for Hirshl. Dr. Langsam does not ask him or his parents any questions. He lets him rest, he gives him his late wife's books to read and talks to him about them, tells him stories about his own old hometown, and sings to him the endless, sad songs of the blind beggars who used to come to his old town. Langsam's unorthodox and especially non-Freudian methods have puzzled Agnon's critics and inspired insightful interpretations.[87] For example, Shaked claims that Langsam exposes Hirshl's romantic ideas about life, literature, and love as false and thus diminishes his fascination with the irrational and imaginary aspects of the psyche. The disillusioned Hirshl can now accept his mundane life in the bourgeois society in Szybusz.[88] According to Dan Miron, by describing Langsam's treatment, Agnon reflects on his own way as a writer. Should he, as his body of readers may have expected at the time, provide them, like the good Dr. Langsam does, with a literary remedy, offer them aesthetic sublimation by telling them in a naïve mode (to use Friedrich Schiller's term) stories about their old, lost hometowns? Or maybe he should refrain from such literary practices and make them see the harsh reality of present times as he does, for example, in his next novel, *Oreah natah lalun* (*A Guest for the Night*)?[89]

84. Noam Pines, *The Infrahuman: Animality in Modern Jewish Literature* (Albany: SUNY, 2018), xi–xxix.
85. See Arbell, *Katuv*, 132–52, 198–254; Michal Arbell, "Shirat hayam: 'al Shevu'at emunim uBilvav yamim," *Ot: A Journal of Literary Criticism and Theory* 6 (2016): 215–55; and Pines, *Infrahuman*, 103–30.
86. Only when Hirshl comes back to Szybusz and plays with his baby son can he "hop like a frog, and whistle like a bird for him" (212) without becoming an animal and crossing the line of what is accepted as normal behavior.
87. On Agnon's growing interest in psychoanalysis during the 1930s, see Miron, *Harofe*, 175–83.
88. Shaked, *Omanut*, 222–25.
89. Miron, *Harofe*, 190–95.

I argue that Dr. Langsam heals Hirshl by way of two acts. First, he reconstructs his lost and damaged childhood. Second, he evokes for him the historical
memory of moral order. The old and lonely doctor finds in himself fatherly love
for Hirshl: "The combination of meekness, resignation and sadness that he saw in
Hirshl's face made the old doctor take an instant liking to him."[90] With this love,
he, as it were, rears him again from babyhood to childhood and from adolescence
to manhood. In the first days, Dr. Langsam puts Hirshl in bed like a baby and
brings him food and drink. After three days of sleeping off his fatigue, the psychosis subsides. The melancholic Hirshl talks ceaselessly and confusedly. Instead
of examining him, Dr. Langsam comes every day, sits down by his bed, and tells
him stories about his own old hometown, which he left forty years earlier. "Had
anyone asked Hirshl how Dr. Langsam was treating him, he might have replied
in surprise: What? Is he a doctor? Still, he could feel he is being healed."[91] Hirshl
never mentions Blume to the doctor, and he is very grateful for the consoling
touch when Dr. Langsam holds Hirshl's hand in his own firm hand.[92] In the next
stage, the doctor treats Hirshl not like a baby but like a little boy. Every day,
Schrenzl, the "fatherly orderly," helps Hirshl dress, takes him to the garden, and,
after a couple of hours, helps him undress again and puts him to bed.[93] Hirshl
knows that he is an inmate in the sanatorium, not free to leave the place, but it
does not make him angry. "If anything, he felt grateful, as a homeless child might
be expected to feel towards someone who has taken him in. Indeed, Hirshl had
good reasons for feeling this way, because he had never been better off."[94] Langsam talks to Hirshl every day. "These chats must have stimulated the doctor too,
for the more he said the more he had to say." Although Dr. Langsam has lived in
big cities and studied in famous universities, "nothing had remained in his memory, it seemed, but the little town he grew up in."[95] Two stories stand out in the
doctor's reminiscences. One is about the town's values, those of the Torah rather
than of money. According to what he remembers, scholars in his old hometown
studied day and night out of their love of the Torah, not caring about food, drink,
or sleep, not wanting anything except the light of the Torah. Only the old local
rabbinical judge wished for something—for the book, *Maḥatsit hashekel*, which
he could not afford to buy. This *dayyan* used to write his comments on the Talmud with a feather, and when he did not have even that, he used his fingernail to

90. Agnon, *Simple Story*, 185.
91. Agnon, *Simple Story*, 191.
92. Ben-Dov, *Ahavot*, 208–38 discusses the figure of the hand and its importance in Hirshl's
treatment.
93. Agnon, *Simple Story*, 191.
94. Agnon, *Simple Story*, 195.
95. Agnon, *Simple Story*, 196.

scratch signs on the paper. The other story Dr. Langsam tells is about the mysterious beauty of art, which always stems from a great loss:

> Sometimes Dr. Langsam told Hirshl about the blind musicians who sat on empty sacks in the marketplace of his town and coaxed from their instruments such boundlessly sweet music that it could put one into a trance. And though the doctor's voice was that of an old man, Hirshl was as entranced by the sweet, gruff sadness of it as he might have been by a lullaby, had he ever heard one when he was a child.[96]

Meanwhile, Hirshl receives a message that Mina has borne him a son. His insomnia returns as a result, but, after some time, it once again subsides. Hirshl thus reaches the third stage of therapeutic maturation. Like a grumpy adolescent, he rebels somewhat against Dr. Langsam, who supposedly holds him captive. Hirshl begins to think about the duties he needs to assume, such as appearing before the army recruiting committee, participating in his son's *pidyon haben* ("redemption of the firstborn") ceremony, and resuming his work in the shop.

Soon after this, Hirshl returns home to Szybusz. It helps that most people in town assume that his madness was a trick to avoid recruitment into the army. Hirshl's fears that he would not be able to love his son prove wrong; as time passes, he wishes less and less for Mina to disappear and for Blume to return and put him under her protective wing. The baby, Meshulam, is sickly and does not develop well, so his parents send him to his grandparents in Malikrowik. In a symbolic way, Hirshl aspires through this act of sending away his child to make the sickly, underdeveloped, childish parts of his psyche disappear.[97] Ostensibly, from then on, everything seems to be alright. Hirshl and Mina are very happy together, enjoying marital life and sexual bliss and having another son, this time a strong and happy baby. Both Hirshl and his father, Boruch Meir, gain weight, while the traumatized Tsirl, who has learned that the ruthless exercise of power can in some cases work against her, loses her famous appetite. All in all, Hirshl appears well adjusted and content with his lot in life. When he walks with Mina in the snow in Malikrowik, they come across a blind beggar who sits and plays his sad song, which seems to have no beginning or end. Suddenly Hirshl turns away and then comes back and tosses the singer a coin, bigger than was ever given to him. Shaked claims that, through this act, Hirshl concludes all his dealings with the dark world of the imagination.[98] Hirshl is cured by Dr. Langsam, Shaked argues, but he loses his soul in the process. I am not sure that this is the case. The second childhood that Dr. Langsam gave to Hirshl enables him to be a good

---

96. Agnon, *Simple Story*, 196–97.
97. See Yehoshua, "Nequdat hahattarah," 86.
98. For another discussion of this scene, see Wendy Zierler's "Breaking the Idyll" in this volume.

partner to his wife and a good father to his second son, but, as Shakespeare's Iago rightly observes, "What you know, you know."[99] One cannot dis-know. Hirshl can be as bitter as he likes about Blume, but he will always remember the enormity of what he has lost, of what he has given up.

A Simple Story ends with the narrator's remark that the tale about Hirshl and Mina has ended, but not the one about Blume or Getzel Stein. It seems to me that this half-promise to write about Blume and Getzel in the future not only ironically refers to the traditional convention of the novel to tie together all the loose ends and marry off all the single young characters but also functions as a sort of consolation. Perhaps a later tale about Blume, the paragon of true virtue, independent mind, and strong character, and about Getzel Stein, the ardent activist of Po'ale Tsiyyon, the ideological Zionist and socialist movement, will offer a hope for a future Jewish society that is not devoid of moral values.

Even in this respect, "In a Single Moment" and *A Simple Story* mirror one another. "In a Single Moment" ends with a virtuous deed that unites an entire city in joy. Nevertheless, as Mintz claims, it offers but a momentary redemption. Buczacz's prospects for a spiritual future are bleak; the moral debasement of the community seems inevitable. On the other hand, *A Simple Story* ends with Hirshl's surrender and acceptance of an unjust social order that he knows causes so much suffering. He might remember his moral resistance as a younger man, but, alas, he has given it up. He might try to be a good father to his second son, but this does not take away the fact that he has already sent his first and weaker child away. In this bleak social present, the novel's conclusion with the narrator's promise to tell a different story about different characters who hold different values brings but a flicker of hope for the future.

Dr. MICHAL ARBELL is an adjunct lecturer in the Department of Literature at Tel-Aviv University. Her first book, *Katuv 'al 'oro shel hakkelev: 'al tefisat hayetsirah etsel Agnon Written on the Dog's Skin* (2004) offers an analysis of the metapoetic concepts of creativity and art in the writing of S.Y. Agnon. Her second book, *Tam venishlam? 'al darkei hasifrut All's Well that Ends Well?* (2006) deals with narrative closure in Hebrew literature. Her forthcoming book explores the different concepts and manifestations of desire in the work of Agnon. Dr. Arbell is one of the editors of *Ot: A Journal of Literary Criticism and Theory*.

---

99. William Shakespeare, *Othello*, act 5, scene 2.

15 "Our Town": Mr. Stern and Buczacz In Mr Lublin's Store

Glenda Abramson

In 1912, s.y. Agnon left Jaffa for Germany. He first lived in Berlin and then moved to Leipzig in 1917, where he remained for various short periods in 1917 and 1918. According to Gershom Scholem, Agnon wished to dissociate himself from Galicia and Palestine and sought a place for further artistic development.[1] "Living in Leipzig is pleasant. It doesn't impose much on its citizens and even a person like me finds his way around." So writes Agnon's narrator in *Beḥanhuto shel Mar Lublin* (*In Mr. Lublin's Store*), echoing Agnon's own comment in a letter to Zalman Schocken in 1917: "I like Leipzig very much."[2]

Classified as a foreigner, Agnon was obliged to register daily with the police despite being a national of an allied country. Generally, imperial Germany made it difficult for foreigners to settle within its borders, and few of them could evade its tight residency permit system.[3] Once military rule had been established in German cities, including Leipzig, the restrictions for foreigners increased, and Agnon was eventually required to leave Leipzig permanently without having been able to obtain a residence permit, unlike his narrator in *In Mr. Lublin's Store*. He moved to Bad Homburg and left in 1924 to return to Palestine after a fire had destroyed his house and his library, including unpublished manuscripts, among them an autobiography.

Throughout the years he lived in Germany, Agnon did not neglect his literary activities but wrote, revised, and published his work. However, none of the works written between 1912 and 1924 dealt with his life in Germany, his attitude to German Jewry and Germans in general, or indeed with World War I. His literary preoccupation during the war years, as it had been for some years previously, was the life and culture of Eastern European Jewry. In the mid-1950s, he began to publish a series of stories about Buczacz, which appeared in newspapers and

---

1. Gershom Scholem, *On Jews and Judaism in Crisis* (New York: Schocken, 1976), 100.
2. See Yaakov Shavit, "Be'iro shel hasoḥer miLublin," *Masa'aḥer* (October 18, 2014), https://www.masa.co.il/article/לייפציג-בעירו-של-הסוחר-מלובלין.
3. Tobias Brinkmann, "From Green Borders to Paper Walls: Jewish Migrants from Eastern Europe in Germany Before and After the Great War," *History in Focus*, Autumn 2006, http://www.history.ac.uk/ihr/Focus/Migration/articles/brinkmann.html.

Building a City: Writings on Agnon's Buczacz in Memory of Alan Mintz (2022): 229–248
DOI: 10.2979/BuildingaCityWriting.0.0.16

literary supplements in the 1950s and 1960s and culminated in the publication of 'Ir umelo'ah (*A City in its Fullness*) in 1973.[4]

More or less at the same time, beginning in the 1950s, he also turned his attention to Germany, to write his impressions of the country in wartime and what is considered to be his valediction to prewar German Jewish life.[5] Two major novels, 'Ad henah (*To This Day*), published in two sections in 1952 and 1953; *In Mr. Lublin's Store*; and a handful of short stories were based on his impressions of Germany gleaned from 1912 to 1924.[6] *Mr. Lublin* deals not only with the German Jewish communities but also with Germany, its history, its people, and, of course, the war. It is not inconceivable that parts of it were written concurrently with *A City in its Fullness*, for some of the anecdotes and stories, similar in style to those in *A City*, seem to have spilled over, together with the narrator's elegiac memories of his hometown.

Yet *Mr. Lublin* is a novel of modernity, set within a mechanized war and in a modern city where all the buildings are new, "for there is no building more than forty or fifty years old."[7] The novel's narrator is engaged in an internal struggle with the encroachment of urban modernity upon traditional Jewish practice and study. In terms of composition, the novel is something of a mystery. We do not know the circumstances of its creation, why Agnon put it aside, whether he intended its various parts to form a coherent whole, or whether he intended it to be a parallel narrative to *To This Day*, which is set in the same space and time. Alan Mintz, writing about the unfinished *A City in its Fullness*, consoles us:

4. See Alan Mintz, "I Am Building a City: On Agnon's Buczacz Tales," in *A City in Its Fullness*, by S.Y. Agnon, ed. Alan Mintz and Jeffrey Saks (New Milford, CT: Toby, 2016), xv–xxxi
5. For comments on Germany and Germans in the novel, see Ya'akov Ariel, "Good Germans, Confused Jews, and the Tragedy of Modernity: S.Y. Agnon Remembers Leipzig," in *Leipziger Beiträge zur Jüdischen Geschichte und Kultur* 3 (2005): 275–92; Avraham Aderet, "Taḥat mo'aqat shtei 'aqirot," *'Alei siaḥ*, ed. Yedidya Yitzḥaqi (September 1976), 9–28; and Dan Miron, "German Jews in Agnon's Work," *The Leo Baeck Institute Yearbook*, vol. 23, no. 1 (1 January 1978): 265–280.
6. For a recent edition of the first work, see S.Y. Agnon, 'Ad henah (*To This Day*), trans. Hillel Halkin (London: Toby, 2008). *In Mr. Lublin's Store* consists of eight chapters. The first four and the last were published during Agnon's lifetime, in 1964, 1966, and 1967, while chapters five, six and seven (about half the book) were reconstituted by Emuna Yaron from material in four large boxes that contained manuscripts connected to Lublin. The boxes also contained many drafts of chapters already published with new corrections in Agnon's handwriting, as well as chapters and fragments of chapters that were not yet published, some of them from an earlier period and others that Agnon had written during the last years of his life. Because Yaron copied and recopied the chapters, she was familiar with the material and had a good idea of her father's intentions for the novel. It was published as a whole in 1975. Citations from *Mr. Lublin* are from S.Y. Agnon, *In Mr. Lublin's Store*, trans. Glenda Abramson (New Milford, CT: Toby, 2016).
7. Agnon, *In Mr. Lublin's Store*, 6.

For readers and scholars alike, this situation is both bad and good. We are deprived of the perfection that adequate time for revision would have provided; however, at the same time, we are granted access to the writing as it flowed from Agnon's pen, and we feel the master's imagination in the process of origination.[8]

As I have said, Agnon was preoccupied with the writing of *A City and its Fullness* from the 1950s to his death in 1970, the time when he was also publishing *Mr. Lublin* chapter by chapter. Yet *A City* is a celebration of the richness of Jewish life in Buczacz in all its greatness and baseness, a reconstruction, consecration, and memorial, whereas *Mr. Lublin* is largely a lament. There Buczacz is lost, relegated to memory, its metonym being a *revenant,* the ghost of one of its greatest sons, Mr. Jacob Stern. In fact, within its mixture of history, autobiography and fantasy, *Mr. Lublin* is a commemoration of the lost, beloved "our town" whose metaphorical and actual significance Mintz so brilliantly explored throughout his career. Agnon's dedication in *A City* can easily refer to both wars: "This is the chronicle of the city of Buczacz, which I have written in my pain and anguish[....]" *Mr. Lublin* reveals no less pain and anguish at the destruction of the Eastern European Jewish communities in the second decade of the twentieth century both by the exigencies of wartime and the malevolence of the czar's armies.

This article will examine the section of *Mr. Lublin* Agnon called "The Last Chapter," which was published in a literary supplement of the Writer's Union the same year, 1964, that the first chapter was published in *Ha'aretz*. It recalls not only World War I with its corollary, the destruction and displacement of Jewish communities throughout Eastern Europe, but also the narrator's dilemma within his confrontation with modernity. I discuss the figure of Mr. Stern as a metaphor and metonym of these elements and their significance in the narrator's life. Through his monologues to the ever silent Mr. Stern, the narrator also exposes his deep love of and nostalgia for their shared hometown. Mr. Stern, who was the living embodiment of the town, who "almost crossed the city limits, but his shoes led him back, because they knew that he didn't want to overstep our town's border," represents the narrator's valediction to Buczacz and its vanished inhabitants.[9]

The Framing Story

In *Mr. Lublin*, the narrator, who is referred to once in the novel as "Agnon," has moved from Berlin to Leipzig. Unable to leave Germany because of wartime restrictions, he has settled in Leipzig, a city he enjoys. On his way one Sabbath eve to buy his requirements for his Sabbath meals, he runs into his friend

---

8. Alan Mintz, "I am Building a City," in *Ancestral Tales: Reading the Buczacz Stories of S.Y. Agnon* (Stanford, CA: Stanford University Press, 2017), 25.
9. Agnon, *In Mr. Lublin's Store*, 204.

Mr. Lublin, the wealthy proprietor of a mail-order company.[10] Through his important connections, Mr. Lublin has been able to obtain the right of residence for him. On meeting the narrator, Mr. Lublin tells him that he has an urgent appointment and has no one to mind his office. The narrator agrees to sit in the store until Mr. Lublin returns. We do not know whether he ever leaves the store or whether Mr. Lublin returns. The novel ends abruptly, presumably unfinished—or perhaps this is an intended ending, a suitable one for an enigmatic story.

The narrative is set in a series of frames, both real and conceptual, the central one being Mr. Lublin's store and the other, the date on which this episode takes place, Friday, the 20th of Tevet.[11] Another significant frame surrounds a portrait of Field Marshal Hindenburg, commander of the German military, that hangs on a wall in the narrator's room. This metonymic picture encapsulates the entire narrative: the war rages, the cannons rumble, submarines infest the seas, and menfolk are dying. Life in Germany is increasingly difficult, food is scarce, Leipzig suffers social unrest, and grief overtakes the home front. Elsewhere, Jewish communities are being decimated. The war is therefore an additional frame around the events being played out within it. In spite of all this, the narrator lives a pleasant life meeting friends, dining out, visiting the theatre, and working in a publishing company, a job he enjoys.

While in Mr. Lublin's store, the narrator has nothing to do. There are no books or magazines, and Mr. Lublin has taken the newspapers, which signify temporal specificity, with him. The absurdity of the situation is signaled from the start: Mr. Lublin not only inexplicably removes all the newspapers, but he also disconnects the telephone, ostensibly not to disturb the narrator and, less likely, because of the advent of the Sabbath. The point of having someone mind an office is to take calls, but we are not in the real business world: here the empty office signifies an anticipatory space, a stage on which many dramas and tragedies, and a few comedies, will play out. The narrator is confined to sitting in a vacant room within four walls, so all he can do is allow his imagination to range far beyond them, without boundaries of time and space.

He reflects on his life and the people he has encountered in the past both in Germany and in Galicia, his birthplace. He re-creates a world in memory, from the distant past to the present, through authentic historical events in a modern European metropolis to fantastical happenings, dreams, and adventures. Through his memories we receive a detailed account of the narrator's life in wartime Germany; the German Jewish communities before and during the war; Leipzig, where he lives; his friends and acquaintances; and, in particular, all the

10. Mr. Lublin's name is ironic because he represents the opposite of Lublin, the spiritual center of Polish Jewry, which was completely destroyed in the Second World War.
11. There was no Friday, 20th of Tevet during the war years.

pressures of wartime. He also devotes much of his reflection to his hometown, which he does not name, although it is clearly Buczacz.

Because of the fragmentary, "decoherent" nature of the text, there is no continuous, cogent narrative, although the book's separate sections are bound together by an inner logic, however disparate they may seem to be.[12] In any case, even as a completed whole the novel would have retained its episodic nature, as indicated by each of its component parts. Not only this, but it possesses the characteristically Agnonic temper of many of his stories, particularly those in *Sefer hama'asim* (*The Book of Deeds*): a man sets out to undertake a mission, to celebrate a festival or reach a destination, and is waylaid or misdirected by meeting an acquaintance, whether by happenstance or by his own physical needs, such as hunger. His failure to complete the undertaking, which in many cases is to ensure his own personal or metaphysical redemption, is the underlying premise of these stories. In *Mr. Lublin*, the narrator, on his way to fulfil the laws of the Sabbath, meets Mr. Lublin, who, perhaps unwittingly or perhaps deliberately, leads him to flout them. In *Mr. Lublin* and other stories, the distraction from a religious obligation or an important task may appear to come from an outside force, but it is the protagonist who ultimately makes the choice.

While in the store, the narrator also reflects on his present environment, Mr. Lublin's compound on Böttcher Street in an historic area of Leipzig, the Brühl, still known for its shops and markets. This area houses four old workshops belonging to a quartet of non-Jewish artisans all of them incredibly ancient and representative of the local culture of the past. The workshops belong to Götz Weigel, a knife sharpener, Jakob Weinwurzel, a beltmaker, Adam Isba, a puppeteer, and Joachim Hermann Witzelrode, an antique dealer who rarely bothers to open his shop. They represent Agnon's portrayal of the world of unadaptability to modern life. As Dan Miron writes, they are the remnants of the German Middle Ages, the guild culture trained by generations of artisans, evoking the tradition in Richard Wagner's *Der Meistersinger von Nürnberg*.[13] This section of the story is the consolidation of the narrator's observations about the prewar German world, reflected mainly in these four characters. Their stories constitute the core of the book, reflections of Agnon's intention to emblematize these storekeepers as a Germany that has disappeared, where the builders of modern Leipzig, in addition to the war, have wiped out the traces of the past.

The narrator's friend Mr. Arno (né Aaron) Lublin is tall, blond, and blue-eyed, and, in the nature of his business and his philanthropy, very likely to be have been modeled on Schocken, Agnon's patron. He represents the assimilated, acculturated Jew, as well as the economic prosperity and social integration that

12. The term "decoherent" is used in Gershon Shaked, *Hasiporet ha'ivrit 1880–1980. Ba'arets uvatefutsah*, 5 vols. (Tel Aviv: Hakibbutz Hameuchad 1983), 2:111.
13. Miron, "German Jews."

many German Jews enjoyed before the war. Lublin is honorable, well-liked, and respected even by the city authorities. Although he seems to have completely rejected his origin in the same unnamed town as the narrator, he has befriended the devoutly Jewish narrator who struggles against his admiration of him, the ex-Galician, secular, assimilated Jew.

At the opposite pole stand two figures, both antitheses of Mr. Lublin: the learned and rigidly prescriptive Rabbi Jonathan, whom the narrator has followed from Berlin to Leipzig in the hope of studying Talmud with him, and Mr. Jacob Stern, his mentor from their native Galician town. Rabbi Jonathan is thought to be a reference to Rabbi David Feldman, a Torah scholar who was appointed as a rabbi in Leipzig in 1910. Somehow the narrator never manages to "run through the Gemara" with the rabbi, and one wonders whether his obsessive desire to do so stems rather more from form than substance.[14]

The narrator is suspended between these two poles of Jewishness in Leipzig; he attempts to study with the rabbi but is thwarted, or thwarts himself, at every turn, signaled mainly by his continuing to sit in Mr. Lublin's store. Moreover, even though that Friday is the anniversary of the death of the narrator's much admired rabbinic and intellectual master, Maimonides, he does not have his books to read, as is his custom on this annual anniversary. The narrator's dedication to Maimonides is undoubtedly derived from the devotion and erudition of Agnon's father. Dov Sadan writes that Shalom Mordechai Czaczkes knew the work of Maimonides almost by heart, and he relates the story of an old rabbi who was advised to consult Shalom Mordechai if he wanted to understand a difficult portion of Maimonides's text. Sadan argues that the emphasis on Maimonides is the authentic seed from which the story of *Mr. Lublin* grew.[15] Yet, in a brief statement that seems to tilt the balance away from the pursuit of traditional learning, the narrator wonders why he has become "closer to [Mr. Lublin] than to anyone else in Leipzig."[16]

Mr. Stern

Mr. Jacob Stern, the narrator's old friend from his hometown, suddenly appears in Mr. Lublin's store shortly after the narrator imagined that he was walking with him through the streets of their town, discussing the events of the day. The town is never named but is clearly modelled on Buczacz, with the Strypa River—the town's "living soul [...] which invigorated us every year from the eve of Shavuot in the spring to September"—running through it.[17] Mr. Stern had been

14. Agnon, *In Mr Lublin's Store*, 29.
15. Dov Sadan, "Zimun, ofyo ve'inyano. 'Al Beḥanhuto shel Mar Lublin," in *S.Y. Agnon kerekh masot uma'amarim* (Tel Aviv: Hakibbutz Hameuchad, 1978), 184.
16. Agnon, *In Mr. Lublin's Store*, 190.
17. Agnon, *In Mr. Lublin's Store*, 228.

the narrator's mentor, a man of great knowledge and intellect, also wealthy and prominent, who always enjoyed a good cigar. A descendant of generations who lived there, Mr. Stern was devoted to his town and its inhabitants, customs, and history to the extent that his feet resist the very attempt to cross the city limits. Only the war has shifted him from his birthplace. Now an exile, he is weary and old. When he enters the store, he sits down wordlessly and removes his hat. The narrator is pleased to see him.

Throughout Mr. Stern's visit, during which he seems to wither away as he sits opposite the narrator, his skin assuming the color of clay, Stern does not speak. His silence becomes increasingly oppressive to the narrator, who tries to arouse his interest and elicit some words by talking about their hometown. Yet there is no dialogue with Mr. Stern. The narrator strives to retain the memory of his town by summoning its stories, characters, and events while his visitor and their town fade away. Without surprise at Mr. Stern's presence in the room, the narrator tells him that once, when visiting their town, he asked about a wise man who had been buried there. The townspeople replied,

> There was a certain Jacob Stern who had expert knowledge of our town and knew everyone, living and dead, and if he were here he would tell us who this righteous man is. ... "If Jacob Stern had known that you were about to come here he would have tried to stay alive for another three or four days to tell you all about our town." Please, Mr. Stern, what do you think about this?[18]

Of course, Stern does not reply. and this constitutes the structure of the entire chapter: the narrator appeals to Mr. Stern, tells him a story or recalls fellow townspeople, and becomes increasingly agitated as he receives no reply. He recounts the histories of sages and various ancestors, including those of Mr. Stern and Mr. Lublin, and some communal controversies. He adds anecdotes, some of them humorous, about ordinary folk, each tale ending with a moral. As the time passes, Mr. Stern sinks even deeper into vagueness to become a kind of ghostly presence, while the narrator exhausts himself by talking. "I was deeply troubled so I stopped thinking about time and I began again to tell stories about our town which is blessed with stories. People like us can talk about our town all week long and not complete our telling."[19]

Mr. Stern is a refugee, having been forced to abandon his beloved home together with millions of other Eastern European Jews. He represents not only his and the narrator's shared and lost hometown but also the displaced Jews whose lives, homes, and communities were destroyed in the conflict. In addition to his personification of the town, Mr. Stern appears to be a matrix of sadness, both his and the narrator's:

18. Agnon, *In Mr. Lublin's Store*, 232–33.
19. Agnon, *In Mr. Lublin's Store*, 231.

I clothed this sorrow in skin and bone and flesh and sinews and found words in my mouth that I didn't say, I said them in my mind, not quite aloud. He and his father's and mother's families had been rooted in our town for ten generations, then the war came suddenly and forced him out of his town, he wandered through the world.[20]

Earlier in the novel, the narrator meets a fellow Galician whose tale encapsulates the Eastern European Jewish experience, including Mr. Stern's, in World War I:

Wilhelm, the German Kaiser, wanted to declare war on the Czar of Russia. He said to our Emperor, join me and we shall fight Russia. Our Emperor agreed and followed him, but the Russian Czar heard about this and anticipated him. He moved into Galicia and committed widespread slaughter, destroyed its cities and burned down their houses. Those who were not killed were captured. Those who were not captured fled. Some of them fled to their relatives or relatives' relatives in Hungary, Bohemia, or Moravia, and some of them were trapped where they were, weakened, with legs that would not carry them. Some of them reached the cities of Germany and among them was I, who came here because I had heard that a number of Jews like me had fled here. When a man has been uprooted from his home every other place is the same to him.[21]

The identity of the fictional Mr. Stern is difficult to determine. "Stern" was a respected name in Buczacz. Berish Stern was one of the leading citizens of the town, serving as its mayor from 1879 to 1921.[22] Scholars have suggested a variety of possibilities, one being that Agnon's Mr. Stern is the narrator's alter ego and that the encounter is an internal one.[23] He may also be a symbol of the narrator's guilt for having left the town he loved and of the waning of this love as time passed and other places claimed his affection or a projection of the narrator himself or the narrator's reproachful father. Alternatively, the narrator and Mr. Stern may both be dead and sitting in a tomb, or Mr. Stern is his judge and the narrator's nemesis. Perhaps Mr. Stern is more like a psychiatrist listening to a patient's long confession, or he may serve as the narrator's memory, compelling him by his silence to dig deep into his mind not only to recall the town and its present and past inhabitants but also to confront his own abandonment of them. According to Avraham Aderet, Stern's silence allows the narrator a chance to repent of what

20. Agnon, *In Mr. Lublin's Store*, 227.
21. Agnon, *In Mr. Lublin's Store*, 39.
22. Dan Laor, *Ḥayyei Agnon* (Jerusalem: Schocken 1998), 17. See also Sadan, "Zimmun," 188–89.
23. For discussion about the identity of Mr. Stern, see Sadan, "Zimmun," 180–89; Ariel, "Good Germans"; Sarah Katz, "Hit'asquto shel Agnon baḥanut hareqah," *Moznayim* 40, no. 3 (1975): 171–77; and Aderet, "Taḥat moʻaqat".

he has done.[24] Sadan suggests that the story of Stern is the narrator's dream and adds that Stern and Lublin are two sides of the narrator.[25]

Mr. Stern embodies a mystical element associated with the most prosaic of articles: a cigar. His name, "star," could be derived from Numbers 24:17: "I see him, but not now. I see him, but not near. A star will come out of Jacob. A scepter will rise out of Israel, and shall strike through the corners of Moab, and break down all the sons of Sheth."[26] The narrator regards Stern as man possessed of singular qualities. "As I remembered him with a cigar in his mouth I also remembered that fiery eye gleaming within the cigar's ash that I imagined was leading me and I was following it."[27] The burning cigar tip glimmers like a star, also, he writes, adds the narrator, like an all-seeing eye, that of the Jewish martyrs glaring at the Jews on the first night of *Seliḥot* to see if they had repented.[28] This is a frightening image of Mr. Stern's power to trigger the narrator's multilayered guilt. It is not only the war that has destroyed the town—he has done so himself by leaving, as if the town's image disappears once has turned his back on it. "I was sitting in Mr. Lublin's store. For that reason, the events of the day are engraved in my heart because of what was missing on that day."[29]

The narrator tells Stern about Mr. Lublin, who left their town and never returned. The term "left our town" recurs frequently in the text.

> [W]e can assume that he [Stern] was not at ease with Mr. Lublin, for even gentiles who left our town usually went back, and worst of all Mr. Lublin had left our town while still a child and never returned for all those years. Mr. Jacob Stern was not at ease for another reason, because I had reminded him of Mr. Lublin and his ancestors, for Mr. Jacob Stern used to say, "If you come across the errant son of distinguished people do not mention his ancestors," but I had mentioned Mr. Lublin's two forefathers Rabbi Neta Netsaḥ and the sage Rabbi Israel Netsaḥ, the author of *Netsaḥ Israel*.[30]

24. Aderet, "Taḥat mo'aqat," 22.
25. Sadan, "Zimmun," 186.
26. The sages comment: "Israel declared before the Holy One blessed be He, 'Master of the World, how long shall we be oppressed at his [the non-Jewish] hand?' He replied, 'Until that day about which it is written: A star rises from Jacob, and a scepter comes forth from Israel—when a star arises from Jacob and ignites the kindling of Esau" (Deuteronomy Rabbah 1:20, following Obadiah 1:18). See Haim Be'er, afterword to *In Mr. Lublin's Store*, by S.Y. Agnon, trans. Glenda Abramson (New Milford, CT: Toby, 2016), 237–49.
27. Agnon, *In Mr. Lublin's Store*, 229.
28. The passage actually reads: "They didn't know that this was the eye of the Jewish martyrs who had drowned glittering at the Jews to see if they had repented [...]" (211). This may refer to some Ashkenazic women who drowned themselves rather than endure baptism. Echoing BT Gittin 57b, the eleventh-century chronicle ascribed to Solomon bar Simson connects Psalm 68:23 to these women and others like them who died by drowning.
29. Agnon, *In Mr. Lublin's Store*, 209.
30. Agnon, *In Mr. Lublin's Store*, 215.

He continues,

> So you see, even a gentile who was born in our town and left it, couldn't live in peace until he returned. However, Aaron Lublin whom you call Mr. Arno Lublin and his forefathers and their forefathers were born in our town but he never returned from the day he fled, as if his feet had never stood in our town, as if he had never smelled its earth.[31]

The narrator has no idea what Mr. Stern is thinking, but he projects onto him his own discomfiture at Mr. Lublin's desertion, expressing his *own* unease and using Mr. Stern's presumed admonition to admonish himself. He attributes attitudes to other townsmen that apply more appropriately to himself, referring to one who was happy and lighthearted for all the years he had lived there but seemed to have become lifeless since leaving it.[32] In addition, Mr. Stern avoids mention of the ancestors not only because he thinks their sons are errant, but also because he finds the ancestors themselves to be equally so. One of the earliest *maskilim*, Israel ben Moshe Halevy of Zamosc, whom Agnon calls Rabbi Israel Netzah (1700–72), was born and educated in Galicia. One of the most important Jewish intellectuals of the eighteenth century, he represents the advent of rationalism and science within central European Jewry during the early Haskalah period. His *Netsah Yisra'el* (*The Eternity of Israel*, ca. 1737) interprets numerous passages from the Talmud dealing with astronomy and geometry from a rationalist and scientific viewpoint.[33] In the novel, his fictional descendant, Mr. Lublin, appears to have taken Rabbi Israel's intellectual rebellion to one of its regrettable conclusions, defection from Judaism and Jewish community and assimilation.

The narrator comments, "I stopped talking, unable to find a way to defend Mr. Lublin who had escaped from our town and never returned."[34] He confesses,

> I had meant to defend Mr. Lublin for not bothering to visit our town, for not having been there since he had left, for we knew that he had run away at age eleven because of his father and he never again showed his face in our town. In the end I told the stories of all the others who had done the same thing."[35]

The narrator feels a compulsion to support Mr. Lublin, whose major transgression seems to be less his Germanization and secularism than his abandonment of his town. "Even a gentile who left our town usually returned," says the narrator and substantiates his statement by telling Mr. Stern a long story about a gentile murderer who escaped from the town but returned decades later only to meet retribution there. Mr. Lublin's total desertion is therefore not a geographical

31. Agnon, *In Mr. Lublin's Store*, 217.
32. Agnon, *In Mr. Lublin's Store*, 226.
33. Agnon, *In Mr Lublin's Store*, 215.
34. Agnon, *In Mr. Lublin's Store*, 217.
35. Agnon, *In Mr. Lublin's Store*, 219.

but a philosophical one. Yet the narrator forgives Mr. Lublin without forgiving himself.

The town, or "our town," is one of the central themes of the novel, weaving through the assorted stories, ironically even in the life of assimilated Mr. Lublin. As the narrator recollects each inhabitant of the town, "he immediately appears before me and does not leave me alone."[36] He searches for the names of fellow townsmen in a telephone directory he has found in the store, and he imaginatively relives the pleasant conversations during which Mr. Stern, not only a denizen of the town but also its historian, taught him about the town, its inhabitants, and its heritage. In *Mr. Lublin*, Agnon avoids enhancing the town's fictitiousness by naming it, as, for example, Mendele and Sholem Aleichem did when constructing their imaginary towns. In other works, notably in *Oreaḥ natah lalun* (*A Guest for the Night*, 1939), Agnon gave the town an inventive name, Szybusz or Shibush, meaning "blurred" or "unclear," a play on its real name of Buczacz. He did not do so in *Mr. Lublin* because the hometown there is not entirely a construct but contains elements of the real heterogeneous city, including shared Christian spaces and their inhabitants. The hometown in *Mr. Lublin* also demonstrates a selection of the common tropes that illustrate the literary shtetl: the cemetery, the market places, the synagogues, the bathhouses, and the *batei midrash*. While many of the shtetls and towns in the modern Yiddish and Hebrew classics are to a large extent fabricated, the Galician town in *Mr. Lublin* is more real than imagined, as elements of Buczacz are incorporated in the story, such as the Strypa and the tailors' synagogue.[37] We learn a little about the town's layout through a few authentic street and synagogue names and other landmarks, and we are told that it has a large well-educated Jewish population that produced many notable scholars, many of them historical personalities, and that it also tends toward rationalism: "I know that Mr. Jacob Stern retains our town's custom of disliking things that are not rational, meaning that the intellect cannot prove them, and I am also a little like that."[38]

When, after the Haskalah, the Jewish writers born in Eastern Europe moved away from their towns and shtetls physically and psychologically, their sense of guilt and betrayal and their nostalgia, real or imagined, led them to idealize their birthplaces and offer romanticized memories of them in their fiction while benefiting from life in their European cities. "They recall the dust of our town as if

---

36. Agnon, *In Mr. Lublin's Store*, 147.
37. Arnold Band, "Agnon's Synthetic Shtetl," in *The Shtetl: New Evaluations*, ed. Steven T Katz (New York: New York University Press, 2007), 234.
38. Agnon, *In Mr. Lublin's Store*, 214. One of Agnon's facts is erroneous: the birthplace of the poet Adam Asnyk, after whom a street was named, was Kalisz rather than Buczacz. It seems unlikely that Agnon would have made such an egregious mistake, so perhaps this is his way of suggesting the synthesis of fiction and reality in "our town."

it were gold dust," the narrator of *Mr. Lublin* relates.[39] Sadan says of Agnon, "He is not the only son who reconstructs his town in its entirety when he's far away from it."[40] After the Holocaust, memorial volumes for destroyed communities tended to present an idealized picture of a vanished way of life.[41] Yet Agnon, too, much the ironist, does not maintain any pattern of condemnation or idealization. Within his loving emphasis throughout the novel on the hometown, his narrator speaks of the renegade Mr. Lublin with affection, he expresses his regard for Leipzig and his gratitude at being allowed to remain there, he recounts its real history almost as much as he records the features of his semifictional town. He extols the visually observant Galician Jews in Leipzig and describes their manner of dress, he discusses the variety of Leipzig's synagogues and stiebels, he recounts the history of the Leipzig Jews, and he also observes that many Jews who left his home town succeeded in their lives.

Agnon's description of Buczacz in his short piece "Betokh 'iri" ("In My Town"), part memoir, part fiction, contrasts strongly with the generic towns of Yiddish and Hebrew literature, with their houses crowded higgledy-piggledy in narrow streets. Despite writing more about the notable persons who inhabited the town than about its geographical reality, he does offer a paean to its

> mountains surrounded by rivers and lakes. Waterfalls flow down to forests filled with trees that are alive with birdsong. Some of the birds are natives of the forests around my city; others have come from faraway lands and have chosen to stay, for it would be folly to leave as delightful a place as this.
>
> The streets and avenues in the town lie against the mountains. They were made by both man and nature, each harmonizing with the other. This is one example of God's creations and those of man residing together peacefully, complementing each other. It is easy to imagine that those same streets and avenues go back to the earliest times when people's hearts were pure and uncorrupted.[42]

This idyllic picture of Buczacz may be an example of "imagined geography" or irony in the implication that, even in this paradise, people's hearts are no longer pure.[43] Agnon does not eschew irony in "In My Town," stating that, along with wisdom, Buczacz also boasts humility: "In all of its history, Buczacz never

39. Agnon, *In Mr. Lublin's Store*, 151.
40. Sadan, "Zimmun," 186.
41. See Mintz, "I Am Building," xvi.
42. S.Y. Agnon, "Betokh 'iri. Pereq eḥad shel sippur eḥad." http://www.buchach.org/book /mytown.htm (my translation). This piece does not appear in the translated version of *A City in Its Fullness*, but a translation can be found at "In My Town: One Chapter of One Story," trans. Adam Prager, http://www.buchach.org/book/in my town.htm.
43. Israel Bartal, "Imagined Geography: The Shtetl, Myth and Reality," in *The Shtetl: New Evaluations*, ed. Steven T. Katz (New York: New York University Press, 2007), 179.

appointed a rabbi from among its own citizens even if he were knowledgeable in all matters of Torah and Jewish law."

In *Mr. Lublin*, Agnon writes less about the town itself than about his and others' attitudes toward it, oscillating between disdain (Lublin) and nostalgia (the narrator). The narrator's memory involves the town's intellectual prowess rather than its topography. Therefore, the town's presence in the lives of the narrator, Mr. Lublin, and Mr. Stern, is more *something left behind*, something never to be regained and confined to memory alone. For Agnon as a young man encountering the bright lights of central European cities for the first time, Buczacz felt dull and small.[44] In a postscript to a letter to his publisher, Fischel Lachover, he wrote: "Actually if you do not send me [the sum of 150 marks] God forbid I shall sink into the mud of Buczacz."[45] Agnon's attitude toward Buczacz might have been ambivalent in his early years, but it became a literary subject through which he expressed his love of Jewish tradition, scholarship, and folktales and his response to their loss in the modern world. In this sense, it was preserved forever in its classical distinctiveness, a kind of innocence and purity unspoiled by modernity.[46]

In *Mr. Lublin*, the narrator's nostalgia for his birthplace is a kind of expulsion from Eden.[47] In *A Guest for the Night*, which resulted from Agnon's visit to Europe—including Leipzig—in 1930, the narrator visits his home town of Szybusz, which has been ruined by the conflict of the World War I and the dispersal of the Jewish community in its aftermath. Streets are empty and filled with rubble, the Jewish population is sparse, and those who are left mourn their dead. Only the river is unchanged. The decay is accentuated by the narrator's childhood memory of the town. He asks, "Did the pictures in my memory precede what I saw with my eyes or did the sight of my eyes come before the pictures my memory drew? ... At those moments the pictures in the soul were stronger than the sight of my eyes."[48] It is likely that the picture in his memory came first. In *Mr. Lublin*, the town remains uncorrupted by the war and death that surrounds it. It is preserved in its innocence and purity in the timeless museum of the narrator's memory.

The Dream

It is ultimately more than the town itself or Mr. Stern's perplexing evanescence that brings about the narrator's great unease. He is compulsively driven to

44. See Laor, *Ḥayyei Agnon*, 99.
45. Laor, *Ḥayyei Agnon*, 99.
46. Arnold Band, *Studies in Modern Jewish Literature*, JPS Scholar of Distinction Series (Philadelphia, PA: Jewish Publication Society, 2004), 221.
47. See Rachel Sebba, "The Landscapes of Childhood: The Reflection of Childhood's Environment in Adult Memories and in Children's Attitudes," in *Environment and Behavior* 23, no. 4 (1991): 415.
48. S.Y. Agnon, *A Guest for the Night*, trans. Mischa Louvish (New York: Schocken, 1968), 411.

treat the silent Mr. Stern as his confessor and tell him about his abandonment of his mission to study Torah and all that emanates from that.

> I said to Mr. Jacob Stern, "Mr. Lublin is delayed and won't return and I haven't managed to buy what I need for the Sabbath and I'll suffer the same fate as that of those sharp and learned scholars on the eve of Yom Kippur who were so immersed in their studies that they forgot to buy food for the final meal before the fast. The circumstances are the same but the reasons are different."
>
> I was deeply troubled so I stopped thinking about time and I began again to tell stories about our town which is blessed with stories.[49]

He refers to Maimonides, whose books he has neglected to study, as he always does on this day, the commemoration of the great master's death. He makes an apparently casual observation, a non sequitur that is, in fact, laden with significance: "I have heard it said that the course of our Strypa has changed because they diverted the river."[50] The narrator's words are not a pleasantry; they indicate that he is aware of his own divergence from one course to another, from Rabbi Jonathan to Mr. Lublin. Agnon himself gives us a clue to the meaning of this divergence. Meir Hovev reports on a conversation between Agnon and Dr. Yehuda Even Shmuel in 1960 regarding national redemption, in which they compared the exceptionality of Baal Shem Tov and Maimonides. After a long thoughtful silence, Agnon declared, "Actually there were three significant personages in Jewish history, Moses, Maimonides and Herzl." Hovev describes the consternation in the room in which the conversation took place: Agnon's words came across as blasphemy. Yet, in another conversation, Agnon said, "The redemption of the Jews will not be brought about by America or the United Nations, but the Lord God. Faith and religion are the only means by which the nation can survive."[51] These contradictory ideas became the lining within the fabric of *Mr. Lublin.*

Within the context of national revival, or to cheer Mr. Stern who is gradually disappearing, the narrator tells him about the foundation of the Hebrew University in Jerusalem and the future use of modern Hebrew by all the Jews in the Land of Israel. Inexplicably, perhaps because of his efforts to engage Mr. Stern, the narrator falls asleep and has the dream that is central to his spiritual struggle. Both *To This Day* and *Mr. Lublin* display "divided intentionality"; that is, something

---

49. Agnon, *In Mr. Lublin's Store*, 231.

50. Agnon, *In Mr. Lublin's Store*, 228.

51. Meir Hovev, "Beḥanhuto shel Mar Lublin," *Maʾariv* 1, no. 11 (1974): 39. Hovev ends his comments with the suggestion that Mr. Stern represents a new chapter in Jewish history, that of Theodor Herzl, the "star of Jacob." It is another possible interpretation of one of the most enigmatic of Agnon's creations, although an erroneous one in my opinion.

left unsaid in the text is said in a dream.[52] Agnon intentionally placed dreams throughout the texts of both novels to provide their psychological substrata and theoretical commentary on the events. In *Mr. Lublin*, the narrator dreams that his father is mourning his death, surely the most horrifying indictment of a child in all Hebrew literature. The dream follows the observation about the founding of the Hebrew University in Jerusalem and the dissemination of modern Hebrew. "Is there a better vision that this in all the world?" asks the narrator. Shortly afterward:

> My eyes filled with tears because I dreamt that I had seen my father, my teacher. I greeted him but he didn't return my greeting because he was in mourning. I asked him, "Father, who are you mourning?" He said, "You, my son, I mourn for you." I said to him, "This mourning is over. Even I have forgotten when I died." He replied in amazement, "Over? If this is so, we are allowed to study Torah." He stretched his hand towards the bookcase and took down a volume of Maimonides's code of law.[53]

Fathers mourning dead sons in wartime are not unusual in *Mr. Lublin*. In the narrator's dream, the son is not a war casualty but a spiritual one. Mourners are forbidden to study Torah during the *shiva* in accordance with the precept that the study of Torah is joy that the mourner may not experience. The son's unilateral decision not indicates not the seven days of mourning but some time since his death. It seems that, to the father, studying the Torah is more important than continuing to mourn his dead son despite not knowing whether or not the prescribed period is over. Or perhaps the father's insistence on the Torah is a prescient admonition to his son that, in the joy of creating a Hebrew University, the true [religious] source of or reason for study should not be forgotten. On the other hand, perhaps, the father is lamenting the generational divides, the son confident in the future while the father will not enjoy the growth of Jewish culture on its own soil.

All the central spiritual preoccupations in the novel, and indeed in many of Agnon's works, are united in the narrator of *Mr. Lublin*. The symbolism of his dream reinforces Agnon's search for a via media: Jonathan or Lublin, Baal Shem Tov or Herzl, Buczacz or Leipzig. Through its convoluted irony the dream evokes the guilt that pervades the entire text. It is as if the son is dead to his father and to himself because he has abandoned his Torah studies, has failed to maintain his Jewish practice, visits the theatre, dines in fine restaurants, makes friends with assimilated Jews and non-Jewish women, and sits in a place of commerce on the Sabbath. In a book that, despite its humor

52. See Lawrence M. Porter, "The Dream: Framing and Function in French Literature," in *Dreams in French Literature: The Persistent Voice*, ed. Tom Conner (Amsterdam: Rodopi, 1995), 107.
53. Agnon, *In Mr. Lublin's Store*, 230–31.

and irony, largely deals with death and loss, the loss of the *self* in this dream is perhaps the most terrifying. The dreamer is questioning his own identity and recalling the time when he lost sight of himself and realized the need to recover what can only be called his soul. His claim in the dream, "Even I have forgotten when I died," reads as a little flippant, and the father stretching out his arm to take down Maimonides's book is an obvious remonstration. While in the store, the narrator has been deprived of Maimonides's work, which his dream father consults; he is immediately permitted to after the period of mourning. Yet, despite his mourning garb, the father is quite impassive, unamazed and unmoved at encountering his dead dream son who is also dry eyed. It is the waking son who weeps.

Carl Jung's idea of the personal unconscious includes both memories that are easily accessed and those that have been suppressed. In an often quoted passage, Jung states,

> The dream is a little hidden door in the innermost and most secret recesses of the psyche, opening into that cosmic night which was psyche long before there was any ego-consciousness, and which will remain psyche no matter how far our ego-consciousness may extend... in dreams we put on the likeness of that more universal truer, more eternal man dwelling in the darkness of primordial night... There he is still the whole, and the whole is in him, indistinguishable from nature and bare of all egohood. Out of these all-uniting depths arises the dream, be it never so immoral.[54]

The narrator's dream signals the well-known "dark night" during which, unable to offer himself a cure for his defections and his helplessness, he evaluates his life. It is his dream that compels him to confront the crisis that has dogged him since his arrival in Leipzig, hidden under the surface of his willed memories, social activities, and minding Mr. Lublin's store. His attempts to study with Rabbi Jonathan rather than following the attractive tempter figure of Mr. Lublin have not materialized.[55] The dream about the death of the self or ego may account for his passivity about continuing to sit in an empty room with no diversions. There may be an echo of past activities in that room, the bustle of a modern office symbol-

---

54. C. G. Jung, *Civilization in Transition: Collected Works*, 20 vols. (Princeton, NJ: Princeton University Press, 1964), 10:67.

55. The question is whether Agnon conceived Mr. Lublin to be a tempter figure like Mr. Gressler in his short story "A Whole Loaf," ("Pat sheleimah") or the various tempters of the tailor in "The Garment." ("Hamalbush"). Stories that involve a temptation motif frequently focus on internal conflict or psychological drama in addition to any external plot lines. The protagonist in "A Whole Loaf" oscillates between the scholar Dr. Yekutiel Ne'eman (thought to be a symbol of Moses) and Mr. Gressler, the embodiment of evil urges who tempts him away from his task. The tempter's task is to lead a person away from God and toward other desires, either of the flesh or for some form of aggrandizement.

ized by the telephone and newspapers, but now it is suspended and void of activity and energy except the narrator's reckoning with himself.

This dream has its origin in reality: Agnon arrived in Buczacz too late for his father's funeral.

> My father became ill and died and I did not manage to honour his pure soul nor did I arrive at his funeral in time, only after his burial... I tried to study some verses of Mishna to honour his soul... when I came to one of them I remembered what my father had written in his commentary to Maimonides. Then I wept for the first time and could not even say the Kaddish.[56]

As Mintz comments, in light of the proliferation in Agnon's fiction of themes of lateness and delay in fulfilling important obligations, his failure to arrive in time for his father's funeral takes on a dramatic resonance.[57]

Immediately after the seven days of mourning Agnon returned to Berlin.

The dream is the climax of the narrator's misery, and, when he awakens, weeping, he decides to redeem the day and himself by studying Maimonides's work: "'I thought (not in a dream but awake while I was sitting in Mr. Lublin's store), 'If this is the case the day hasn't been wasted. I'll study one or two laws from Maimonides's book'."[58] However, the text of Maimonides is not available to him, and his symbolic death continues. Yet his failure to study or his guilt at having sought intellectual rather than spiritual growth in a foreign city only partially explains the narrator's disquiet and the physical waning of Mr. Stern. There is still something more. Rather than being affected by his nostalgic memory of the *physical entity* of the town, the crucial element to him is that which it represents, the Jewish universe of cohesion that eludes almost every protagonist in Agnon's work. Rather than religious practice and scholarship, the narrator yearns for the sense of a community and the interrelatedness that defined Jewish distinctiveness in the Eastern European towns.[59]

It does not matter whether the narrator's, Lublin's, and Stern's "our town" is an accurate representation, "a metaphor frozen in time," or a synthesis of both.[60] It was not only the religion or religiousness but also the sense of community and cohesiveness, of "peoplehood," that afforded the Eastern European Jews an identity and a sense of belonging that was not possible in the melee of Central European cities. The life and culture of the nonurban Jewish communities were anchored in tradition. What Agnon saw in prewar Buczacz

---

56. Laor, *Ḥayyei Agnon*, 100.
57. Alan L. Mintz, *Translating Israel: Contemporary Hebrew Literature and its Reception in America* (Syracuse NY: Syracuse University Press, 2001), 91.
58. Agnon, *In Mr. Lublin's Store*, 231.
59. Samuel Kassow, introduction to *The Shtetl: New Evaluations*, ed. Steven T Katz (New York: New York University Press, 2007), 12.
60. Bartal, "Imagined Geography," 180.

was a "variegated vitality bubbling up from an organically Jewish life."[61] He was unable to reproduce this life anywhere else or by any means other than words on the page. Even in Israel the organic amalgamation of Torah and life was absent in the Zionist reality of the modern state.[62] It might have been easier at the time to attain in Leipzig with its large and traditional Galician Jewish community and the associated synagogues and study houses. Yet the narrator does not attain it.

Despite the metaphorical link with the narrator's father, Mr. Stern does not represent Jewish observance, religiousness, or scholarship, or Buczacz itself, but the essence of cohesive Jewish life in this idealized, somewhat mythical framework of the Galician town, the city in its fullness. This is the central topic of their encounter. The town is a metonym for an encompassing Jewish life, and Mr. Stern is the metonym for the narrator's inability to retain his fidelity to it.

In the end, while Mr. Stern is still present, the exhausted narrator decides to call Mr. Lublin's storeman, Lemke, to take over the vigil in the store until Mr. Lublin's return. "The day is ending and the company's director is still away and I haven't prepared food for the Sabbath. I'll go and call Lemke to come and sit in the store."[63] With a sense of relief, he tells Mr. Stern that Lemke is about to arrive, and that they are now free to go wherever they would like to, and then Mr. Stern vanishes as suddenly as he had arrived. The strange ending invites a number of interpretations. The most obvious is that the room has indeed served as a psychiatrist's couch, that the narrator has made his confession, unburdened himself to Mr. Stern, whoever or whatever he may be, and is now free to redress the errors he has made and return his life to its correct course. The indication of this course is in the dream, where his dream father takes down the volume of Maimonides's work and, when the narrator awakens, decides to continue his studies. This is a satisfying ending with the problems resolved, the dark night banished by illumination and the path ahead clear. But we are in Agnon territory, where paths are generally not smooth and happy endings are rare. There is no doubt that the narrator felt an easing of his conscience—or soul, perhaps—and that, when Mr. Stern was no longer required to be therapist, judge, father, or avenging angel, he vanished. Yet there is a slight anomaly in this paragraph: Agnon writes "kevar Lemke ba." This means both "Lemke is already here" or "Lemke is just coming." He continues: "We can go anywhere we want to." The narrator has not yet left the store, and there is still the liminal position of decision one way or the other. If Lemke is only on his way, the narrator may sit down again and wait for Mr. Lublin. If Lemke has arrived, the narrator may leave and seek Rabbi Jonathan. Whether the Hebrew University has triumphed over *beit midrash* is left undecided.

61. Mintz, "I Am Building," xvi.
62. See Mintz, "I Am Building," xxi.
63. Agnon, *In Mr. Lublin's Store*, 233.

Conclusion

"The Last Chapter" appears to have little narrative relationship to the rest of the novel. After many queries from readers who had read the published chapter, Agnon's daughter confessed that she was unsure whether it belonged in the book. She then found a page in her father's handwriting:

> I sat in silence, filled with wonder at the amazing things I had seen. A man sits in a housewares store not far from the Leipzig crowds, thinking about his town, and suddenly a miracle happens and his entire town and its surroundings, its markets and its houses, all of them together, come into view, as close as if they were a few yards away. If I were not a modest man and aware of my low value I would see myself as important in heaven, which takes so much trouble on my account. Inasmuch as there is no man so self-assured that he avoids pride I said to myself, "This is only a dream," and to make certain I was not deceiving myself I looked around to see where I was, and I realized that I was sitting in Mr. Lublin's store after he had gone out and left me alone.

Emuna Yaron added this passage to the end of chapter 7, the one immediately preceding the Stern chapter. At the end of this page, Agnon had penciled in two words, "niftehah hadelet" ("the door opened") the first words of the Stern chapter, indicating that this chapter was to follow.[64] The Stern chapter is therefore integral to the rest of the novel.

At the end of *To This Day*, the narrator, having lived in Berlin, resolves to return to the Land of Israel. He had dreamt of Voltaire and the best of all possible worlds. Ultimately, therefore, despite their similarity, the two novels reach different conclusions. *Mr. Lublin*, which rarely mentions the Land of Israel in modern times, is Agnon's valediction to Buczacz and its memorial.

Contrary to those who argue that *Mr. Lublin* represents Agnon's nostalgia for the old Germany with its sense of intercommunal cooperation and even affection, I believe that the novel emphasizes the death throes of two cultures. In addition to his other symbolic roles in the novel, the fading Mr. Stern also provides a sense of finality. Ultimately, he represents the multivalent facets of the narrator's life and times. Written after the Holocaust, *Mr. Lublin* presents its people as the last vestiges of a community that flits across the stage like a phantom. World War I was the beginning of the end for the German Jewish community. Every small narrative of deprivation in the novel, even if unrelated to the war and even if within a humorous context, adds up to a devastating whole, a novel about loss and pain.

64. Emuna Yaron, "Kakh hutqan hasefer," *Ha'aretz* February 21, 1975, 18.

Born in Johannesburg, South Africa, GLENDA ABRAMSON now holds the titles of Emeritus Professor of Hebrew and Jewish Studies and Emeritus Fellow of St Cross College and of the Oxford Centre for Hebrew and Jewish Studies. Her publications include *Modern Hebrew Drama, The Writing of Yehuda Amichai* (SUNY 1989), *Drama and Ideology in Modern Israel* (Cambridge 1998), *Hebrew Writing of the First World War* (Vallentine Mitchell (2008), *Soldiers' Tales: Two Ottoman Jewish Soldiers in the First World War* (Vallentine Mitchell 2013). Translation and Introduction: S Y Agnon, *In Mr Lublin's Store.* (Toby Press, 2016). She is the founder and now co-editor of *The Journal of Modern Jewish Studies* (Routledge UK).

A Revolutionary Traditionalist

16 *"New Faces": A Study of* Sippur pashut

Haim Be'er
Translated by Deborah Greniman

THE RELATIONSHIP OF Agnon's work to Judaism's ancestral texts — its intertextuality — is neither literary device nor mere turn of phrase, but the very wellspring of his creativity and perhaps also its principal theme — so argues Gershon Shaked; to plumb the depths of the narrative, one must be both broadly
and deeply conversant with the "Jewish bookshelf."[1] Such familiarity is required,
in his view, not only in order to discern the traditions embedded in the text, but
also, principally, for the sake of creating the encounter between the "tale that's
told" and the sacred canon, as it emerges from the relationship between the overt
and covert texts. Or, as Shaked subsequently fine-tuned his formulation,[2] Agnon
the writer is characterized by his two faces; he was, in Shaked's oxymoronic definition, a "revolutionary traditionalist," with his roots planted in tradition and his
crown in modern reality.

Agnon did develop this tension throughout his oeuvre, but not quite in the
way Shaked put it: Time after time, he highlighted the unbridgeable gap between
the glories of the past and the wretchedness of the present, a gap summed up in
the Talmud by Rabbi Zeira, quoting Raba bar Zimuna: "If the earlier [scholars]
were sons of angels, we are the sons of men; and if the earlier [scholars] were sons
of men — we are like asses."[3] For our purposes, suffice it to recall the unforget-
table opening words of the novella *Two Scholars Who Were in Our Town*, which
recur almost verbatim at the story's end:

> Three or four generations ago, when the Torah was beloved by Israel and the
> entire glory of a man was Torah, our town was privileged to be counted among
> the most notable towns in the land on account of its scholars, who endowed
> our town with a measure of grace through the Torah that they learned. ... But,

---

1. Gershon Shaked, *Other Aspects of Agnon's Oeuvre* (Panim aherot biytsirato shel S.Y. Agnon),
Tel Aviv: Hakibbutz Hameuchad, 1989, 11.
2. Idem, "Shmuel Yosef Agnon, Revolutionary Traditionalist." (Shmu'el Yosef Agnon, hama-
hapekhan hamesoreti), in Emuna Yaron, Raphael Weiser, Dan Laor and Reuven Mirkin (eds),
Kovets 'Agnon (Jerusalem: Magnes Press, 1994), 308–318. See also, Gershon Shaked, *Shmuel
Yosef Agnon: A Revolutionary Traditionalist* (New York: NYU Press, 1989).
3. BT *Shabbat* 112b, Soncino translation.

Building a City: Writings on Agnon's Buczacz in Memory of Alan Mintz (2022): 249–270
DOI: 10.2979/BuildingaCityWriting.0.0.17

now let us leave aside these matters that will not reappear until the coming of the Redeemer, and tell a little something of what our elders used to tell, about two great scholars who were in our town back in the days when everyone made Torah the essence of their being, because they understood that the saying "the joy of the Lord is our Fortress" refers to the Torah.[4]

Did Agnon really believe the past was so glorious? Reading the story, even glancingly, suffices to convince us that this talk of a harmonious, idyllic past rings hollow and dissembling, that it has nothing to do with the harsh and cruel reality described in *Two Scholars*.

One way or another, this basic binary of tradition and revolution, in Shaked's view, is the key not only to understanding Agnon's world, but also to understanding the tension in his work between text and anti-text, between the original meaning of the sources embedded in the story and the new meaning with which Agnon endowed them.

Haim Weiss, a scholar of rabbinic literature, has recently challenged Shaked's rigid conception,[5] arguing that Agnon's presentation of the past as harmonious is but a romantic pretense, and so his use of "quotes" from the sources does not necessarily create a binary tension between tradition and revolution. Suffice it to say, as Weiss goes on to contend, that Agnon's continuous subversion of the overt meaning of the sacred canon, and his innumerable efforts to elicit new meanings from it, is not so much a modern stratagem as a classic interpretive technique, with its roots in rabbinic literature and its topmost branches in Hassidic teachings. In his genius, Agnon broadened and deepened the range of the text's meanings with his daring usage of these "quotes," setting them within a multivalent framework.

Whether right is on the side of Shaked or of Weiss, Agnon's finely crafted, subtle, nuanced and sophisticated use of intertextuality is incontestable. His ideal addressee is asked not only to identify the allusions to textual tradition embedded or implicit in his text, but also to attend above all to the question of how the narrator is using that stub of a verse, halakhic term or rabbinic coinage. Is the "quote" invoked merely as a linguistic convention, a reusing of the text as a continuous link in the chain of sacred literature, not to be interpreted as substantive? Or is it significant — to be taken as an anti-text of the literary tradition within which it emerged and from which it was drawn, as Shaked would have it, or as broadening and enriching the range of its reading possibilities, as Weiss would have it? At any rate, the "quote" leverages the work and endows it with a new dimension that would at the outset be concealed from the eyes of the average reader.

---

4. In: S.Y. Agnon, *Samukh venir'eh* (Jerusalem–Tel Aviv: Schocken, 1946), 5. English transl. by Paul Pinchas Bashan and Rhonna Weber Rogol, in S.Y. Agnon, *Two Scholars Who Were in Our Town and Other Novellas* (New Milford, CT–London: Toby Press, 2014), 3.
5. Lecture delivered in a seminar at Ben-Gurion University, January 2016.

As an example, let us look at the phrase "new faces" (*panim ḥadashot*), which Agnon reiterates over thirty times in his oeuvre, from *The Bridal Canopy* (*Hakhnasat kallah*) and *A Simple Story* (*Sippur pashut*), through *A Guest for the Night* (*Oreaḥ natah lalun*) and *Two Scholars* (*Shenei talmidei ḥakhamim*), and on up to *Only Yesterday* (*Temol shilshom*) and *A City in Its Fullness* (*'Ir umelo'ah*).

"New faces" is a halakhic term first used in three different contexts in rabbinic literature, beginning with the Tosefta and then in the Jerusalem and Babylonian Talmuds, from which it was taken up into all the multiple genres and branches of rabbinic literature.

One use of "new faces" relates to the wedding ceremony and its addenda. On each of the seven days of the wedding, the custom is for the chief celebrants to hold a *se'udat mitzvah*, a religious feast, in the presence of the groom and bride and at least ten more invitees. In modern Jewish parlance, this meal, referred to in rabbinic literature as *birkat ḥatanim*, a "wedding benediction," is called *sheva berakhot*, for the "seven blessings" recited under the *ḥuppah* at the wedding ceremony and at the end of the Grace after each of the festive meals. In order for the meal to take place, its participants must include "new faces" — people who had not met the groom and bride at the wedding or since. "Our Rabbis taught: The blessing of the bridegrooms [*birkat ḥatanim*] is said in the presence of ten [persons] all the seven days. Rab Judah said: And that is only if new guests [*panim ḥadashot*] come."[6]

The second context in which the concept of "new faces" appears is associated with the laws of mourning. The Rabbis concur that the (male) mourner is not to don *tefillin* (phylacteries) on the first day of the *shiva*, the seven days of mourning. Instead of *tefillin*, which are considered his "glory" (*pe'er*, .ר.א.פ), he puts a pinch of ashes (*efer*, .ר.פ.א) on his head — reversing the order of the word's first two letters. However, there is some disagreement among the Rabbis regarding the rest of the *shiva*. In our context, the view of R. Eliezer (Liezer) in the Jerusalem Talmud and the concurring view of R. Joshua in the Babylonian Talmud are of interest. According to R. Liezer in the Jerusalem Talmud, "A mourner on the first day does not put on phylacteries; on the second day he puts on phylacteries, but at the entry of fresh personages [*panim ḥadashot*] he takes them off throughout the seven days."[7] Similarly, in the Babylonian Talmud, R. Joshua states: "A mourner is forbidden to put on phylacteries [during] the first two days. From the second day onward, the second day included, he is allowed to put on phylacteries; but at the entry of fresh personages [*panim ḥadashot*] he takes them off."[8]

Nor should the parallel here between wedding and mourning customs surprise the reader. Shmuel Glick has shown that, notwithstanding the obvious

---

6. BT *Ketubot* 7b, Soncino translation. Cf. Tosefta *Megilah* 3:14.
7. JT *Mo'ed qatan* 13b, 3:5.
8. BT *Mo'ed qatan* 21b; Soncino translation.

opposition between the two realms, they are discussed alongside each other in the halakhic literature, and rabbinic scholars through the ages have consistently sought either to analogize or to contrast the reasons for these customs.[9]

At any rate, the idea that underpins both of the above rules and fastens them together, notwithstanding their polar opposition, is that the appearance of "new faces" — the entrance of persons who up to now have had no part either in the mourner's sorrow or in the rejoicing of the bride and groom — results in things returning to their former state. The mourner's sorrow, which, as it were, had begun to dull, wells up anew as a consequence of meeting someone who had not seen him in his hour of bereavement; and the rejoicing of the new couple, which might seem to have dimmed since the wedding ceremony, is rekindled upon meeting someone who has not yet had a chance to take part in their celebration.

The third context in which the concept of "new faces" appears is borrowed by the Sages from the laws of impurity. It rests upon rules concerning changes or repairs made to an implement that create in it a new halakhic state. For example: an impure sandal that has had both its "ears" or flaps repaired, first the one and then the other; or, as the Talmud puts it: "If one of the ears of a sandal is broken and he repairs it … if the second is broken and he repairs it."[10] The two repairs cancel the sandal's former impurity and create a new halakhic state for it; as the Talmud says, "a new face has arrived here," and the sandal can now again be considered pure.[11]

The question, then, is: Which of the "new faces" that peep out at us from Agnon's page are no more than turns of phrase that occurred to the writer by the by, so that we needn't dwell too much upon them or seek more in them than what there is; and which are not chance utterances but rather, constitute a form of "epiphany," that literary miracle characterized by James Joyce as a glowing moment, singular and rare, wherein the writer, and consequently the reader, arrives at a sudden comprehension of some phenomenon of reality, whose essence or inner nature is now laid bare to the public eye, perfect in its magnificence and bathed in brilliant light.[12]

9. Shmuel Glick, *Or nagah 'aleihem: Marriage and Mourning Customs in Jewish Tradition* (Efrat, Israel: Keren Uri, 5757/1997).
10. BT *Shabbat* 112b, Soncino translation.
11. *Ibid.*, Davidson translation. In the same place, the Talmud adduces an additional example of a utensil that had been perforated several times and was repaired each time, as a result of which the Sages view it as a new vessel that no longer bears its former impurity. See also BT *Baba kama* 96b, which deals with the ritual fitness of a brick that someone has made out of earth obtained from a brick he had stolen from someone else and crushed, so that, from here on, it is considered a "new face."
12. See my essay, "The Hunt for Epiphanies" (*Tseid ha'epifaniyot*), in: Ruth Kartun-Blum (ed.), *From Where Did I Get My Poem: Writers and Poets Talk about Sources of Inspiration (Me'ayin nahalti et shiri: Sofrim umeshorerim medabberim 'al meqorot hashra'ah)* (Tel Aviv: Yedi'ot Aharonot, 2002), 195–220.

It's almost impossible to give a precise answer to that question, because the answer is as elusive as Agnon's intertextuality itself. However, in some places it can clearly be seen that the linguistic fragment drawn from the sacred canon and fitted into the text is not "alone in its times."[13] Rather than standing on its own, independent of the context, it resurfaces time after time, each time in a different variation, like a musical theme, and its reverberations and their own reverberations are associated each time with different situations, forming mutual ties with the plot. It is in this that the reader may witness the magic touch of the artist, as he transfigures the "quote" — in our case, the "new faces" — and uses it to leverage the story, while simultaneously carrying out a multivalent dialogue with the source, replete with voices and echoes.

The phrase "new faces" appears four times in *A Simple Story*. It confronts the reader already in the opening scene, when Blume Nacht arrives in Szybusz, lost and desperate after her mother's death, and waits in the Hurvitzes' entrance hall for the return of the house's owners:

> Blume boarded the wagon and left for Szybusz. When she reached her cousin's house she sat down on a chair in the entrance hall with her belongings beside her.
>
> On coming upstairs from the store that evening, Tsirl Hurvitz saw a new face. She took it by the chin between her fingers and asked:
>
> "Who are you, my dear? And what are you doing here?" (*Sippur pashut*, 55; *Simple Story*, 4)[14]

The reader's attention naturally is principally drawn to the lordly way in which Mrs. Hurvitz grasps the chin of the lone girl seeking a roof in her home, inspecting her as one would the quality of a slave girl in the market, and one scarcely notices the words "a new face," behind which, as it were, the intimated image of the writer pops out for a moment, whispering in Tsirl's ear: "See, Mrs. Hurvitz, it's now in your hands to determine whether Blume, who has arrived in your home, is to become a 'new face' for the purpose of rejoicing or rather of pain and sorrow." In other words, this innocent phrase enfolds within it in miniature the whole theme of *A Simple Story*.

But already on the day after Blume's arrival, as the home's denizens dine on the breakfast that the girl has prepared for them, Agnon's ideal addressee will know for certain which of the two possibilities Mrs. Hurvitz will choose. As she sets the table, Blume puts on the serving dish some cakes that she had taken out of her bags. The cakes, to which the Hurvitzes are unaccustomed, immediately

13. See Isaiah 14:31.

14. S.Y. Agnon, *Sippur pashut*, in: idem, *Al kappot haman'ul* (Jerusalem–Tel Aviv: Schocken, 1953); English translation: S.Y. Agnon, *A Simple Story* (English transl. by Hillel Halkin; New Milford–London: Toby Press, 2014). All the citations are from these editions. Unless noted otherwise, the translations are Halkin's.

attract the notice of the diners. Boruch Meir, the father, "regarded his cousin and the cakes she had brought with approval" (*Sippur pashut*, 58; *Simple Story*, 6). His son Hirshl, coming in after him, remarks: "'Those cakes look awfully good!' He took one of them, ate it, and said, 'These deserve a special blessing.'" Only Tsirl, who tastes just a little piece, changes her tone of voice and declares: "Thanks be to God … that we aren't cake-eaters and pastry nibblers here. Plain ordinary bread is good enough for us."

This scene takes on its full significance only if the reader directs his attention to the weighty burden of female eroticism with which bread and other kinds of baked goods are encumbered by the classical Hebrew canon, beginning with the Bible.[15] By way of her cakes, we learn what each member of the household feels about the girl. She is viewed with favor by both the father and the son, the latter not only tasting her cakes with relish but also manifesting his opinion that they are worthy of a blessing — that is, that he sees her as a worthy candidate for marriage. But the wife and mother, by contrast, is repelled by this burst of eroticism that has instantly overcome both men and declares that she will not allow it to penetrate.

The writer sums up the abashed girl's response to Tsirl's unexpected attack with the following words: "Blume looked down at the table. The munching of cake did not stop" (קול לעיסת העוגות מפוצץ והולך.) In rabbinic literature, the word *mefotsetset*, used by Agnon here to describe this "munching," is attached to the miraculous apparition of a heavenly voice, as in שמעתי בת קול מפוצצת ואומרת —"And I heard a heavenly voice rumbling" (*Ruth rabbah* 6:4); עתידה בת קול להיות מפוצצת באוהלי צדיקים ואומרת—"A heavenly voice shall rumble through the tents of the

---

15. For example: "Stolen waters are sweet, and bread eaten furtively is tasty" (Prov. 9:17). Cf. Rashi's commentary on Gen. 39:6–7: "[Potiphar] left all that he had in Joseph's hands and, with him, he paid attention to nothing save the food [lit.: bread] that he ate. Now Joseph was well built and handsome. After a time, his master's wife cast her eyes upon Joseph and said, 'Lie with me.'" On the words "nothing save the bread," Rashi, alluding to *Genesis rabbah* 86:6, remarks: "That is, his wife, but the text used clean language." Cf. also Rashi's comment on Ex. 2:20–21: "[Jethro] said to his daughters, 'Where is he then? Why did you leave the man? Ask him in to break bread.' Moses consented to stay with the man, and he gave Moses his daughter Zipporah as wife." Citing his comment on Gen. 39:6, Rashi interprets the words "Ask him in to break bread" as meaning "Perhaps he will marry one of you." In BT *Ketubbot* 62b, sexual satisfaction is defined using the metaphorical expression "one who has bread in his basket" (Soncino translation). On this see the extensive discussion in Jacob Nacht's *Symbols of Women in Our Ancient Sources, in Our New Literature and in the Literature of Other Peoples (Simlei ishah bimekoroteinu ha'atikim, besifruteinu hahadashah uvesifrut ha'amim)*, Tel Aviv: Studies in Torah, Beliefs, Customs and Folklore, 5719/1959, s.v. *Lehem* (Bread), 140–144. The first to observe the centrality of cakes as a metonymy for female eroticism in Agnon's writings was Dov Landau, in *From Style to Meaning in the Stories of S.Y. Agnon (Mesignon lemashma'ut besippurei Sh.Y. Agnon)*, (Tel Aviv: Eqqed, 5748/1988), 91–94.

righteous" (JT *Shabbat* 6:8); ‏וֹשמעתי בת קול יוצא מבית קודש קודש הקודשים מפוצצת ואומרת‎—
"And I heard a heavenly voice rumbling from the Holy of Holies" (*Yalkut Shim'oni*, Kohelet, 974). In the breakfast scene, the sound of chewing on the cakes takes the character of a feminine heavenly voice, a kind of mini-prophecy or notice of future events dispatched straight down from heaven, with the intention of clarifying both to Blume and to Agnon's addressees the ultimate fate of the relations that will emerge between the protagonists.

The story's plot, as we know, is quite simple. Hirshl, the only son of Boruch Meir and Tsirl Hurvitz, falls in love with Blume as soon as she arrives at their home, but his mother, for reasons of money and class status, nips the relationship in the bud and marries her son off to Mina. His pining for Blume, strengthening by the day, not only undermines his fresh marriage but also conflicts his soul, culminating in the dramatic scene that commences during the morning service for the New Moon in the Little Synagogue and climaxes in his outburst of madness in the forest. Consequently, Hirshl is sent off for a lengthy stay in a sanatorium for the mentally ill in Lemberg. But even after he returns to his home and his wife, the reader doesn't know for sure whether he has really been cured of his madness, or whether he has merely acquired the ability to behave like a sane person, though his heart is still hollowed out from within.

Those "new faces" that greeted us at the outset of *A Simple Story* were a harbinger of the great conundrum that accompanies the reader throughout the first part of the story: Does Blume's entrance into the Hurvitz home herald the onset of family celebrations or a series of traumatic events? As the story continues, the phrase also becomes an aperture through which the reader may follow the process of Hirshl's derangement, over which hovers the threatening shadow of the congenital mental illness that has passed down through the generations in his mother's family, from his great-grandfather to his uncle, Tsirl's brother, and on to him.

****

Before continuing, it is worth setting aside briefly the discussion of "new faces" to direct our gaze to the hidden deep structure upon which the plot of *A Simple Story* was built. At the base of Agnon's story, which takes place at the beginning of the twentieth century in a Galician shtetl, lies a reversal of the classic structure of the Book of Ruth, anchored in the agricultural scenery of Judea at the time of the biblical Judges. The biblical story, threaded throughout with a ‏חוט של חסד‎ — a thread of compassion — is the hidden deep text of the merciless realistic story woven by Agnon; Bethlehem, and Boaz, the "man of substance of the family of Elimelech," are the converse reflections of Szybusz and the Hurvitz family of shopkeepers. Or, to use a term coined recently by Daniel Blanton of the University of California at Berkeley, the Book of Ruth serves as a kind of "shadow-text" for *A Simple Story*.[16]

The openings of both stories are identical: the unplanned entrance of a girl from a low socioeconomic class, forlorn and destitute, into the bounds of the story as set out by the author. In *A Simple Story*, this is the orphaned Blume, who arrives in Szybusz after the death of her mother to seek the help of her wealthy relative, the shopkeeper Hurvitz, having received several recommendations in this regard. "When I die, go to our cousin Boruch Meir. I'm sure he'll have pity and take you in," counsels her dying mother, and the neighbors, too, urge her: "There's a cousin named Boruch Meir Hurvitz who's a wealthy storekeeper in Szybusz. He certainly won't turn her away." In the biblical book, too, a destitute young widow arrives from the "field of Moab" into the plot scene and decides, on the advice of her mother-in-law Naomi, to try her luck with Boaz, a family acquaintance, in the hope that she might find favor with him and gain his protection.

At this point the stories diverge, each pulling toward the opposite pole of the other.

Boruch Meir, despite the natural affection he feels toward the girl already from first sight, submits wordlessly to his wife's merciless dictates. Not only does he dare not stand up for her or for his son, who has fallen in love with her, but no moral scruple arises in him either. No natural feeling instructs him to aid his relative and rectify the wrong he had done her mother a generation ago, when he cancelled their wedding, preferring instead the daughter of his wealthy employer.

The foundational event takes place on the first night of Blume's stay in the house. All the members of the family are fast asleep; none is attentive to the distress of the guest lying awake, her thoughts of what the morning might bring allowing her no rest.

The events of that biblical night beside the grain pile on the threshing-floor during the barley harvest in Bethlehem, and everything that transpired from them, are as it were a mirror image of the sleepless night in Szybusz — the town whose name, in Hebrew, means defect or mistake — in which the local worthy gives his relative no succor, nor saves her from her distress. Boaz, who, as Naomi says, is "related to us; he is one of our redeeming kinsmen" (Ruth 2:20), "gives a start and pulls back" (3:8) when he discovers the young woman lying at his feet, asking him to "spread your robe over your handmaid, for you are a redeeming kinsman" (3:9). He responds without hesitation, promising:

> And now, my daughter, have no fear. I will do in your behalf whatever you ask .... But while it is true that I am a redeeming kinsman, there is another

16. C.D. Blanton, *Epic Negation: The Dialectical Poetics of Late Modernism* Oxford–New York: (Oxford: Oxford University Press, 2015), 10, 18.

redeemer closer than I. Stay for the night. Then in the morning, if he will act as a redeemer, good! Let him redeem. But if he does not want to act as redeemer for you, I will do so myself, as the Lord lives! Lie down until morning. (Ruth 3:11–13)

Ruth's entreaty and Boaz's response have a single source: the ancient law that prevailed among the Hebrews in biblical times:

When brothers dwell together and one of them dies and leaves no son, the wife of the deceased shall not be married to a stranger, outside the family. Her husband's brother shall unite with her: he shall take her as his wife and perform the levir's duty. The first son that she bears shall be accounted to the dead brother, that his name may not be blotted out in Israel. (Deut. 25:5–6)

If the designated levir refused, for some reason, to do his duty and obey the sacred command, a public ceremony would take place at the city gate, before the elders, in which he was humiliated and scorned for his resistance:

His brother's widow shall go up to him in the presence of the elders, pull the sandal off his foot, spit in his face, and make this declaration: Thus shall be done to the man who will not build up his brother's house! And he shall go in Israel by the name of "the family of the unsandaled one." (*ibid.*, 9–10)

It's no coincidence, of course, that none other than the shoe was chosen as the symbolic object used in the ceremony of *halitsah*, by which the widow releases her dead husband's brother and frees him of her obligation to her. In many cultures, including that of the ancient Hebrews, the shoe is a tangible symbol of woman and her sexuality. For example, Bruno Bettelheim has interpreted Cinderella's slipper in the well known folktale as symbolically representing the female vagina.[17] The same is true in the Hebrew sources. Thus, in the *Zohar*, we find: "Rabbi Yehuda said in the name of Rabbi Ḥiyya: It is written: "Do not come closer. Remove your sandals from our feet" (Deut. 3:5). ... Rabbi Abba said: This teaches that the Holy One, Blessed Be He, commanded [Moses], in a dignified way, to withdraw completely from his wife."[18] According to R. Menahem Recanati's commentary on the Torah, "From the mystery of the levir you may understand the matter of *halitsah*, for the woman is the footwear of her husband, and now he is free of them."[19] Jacob Nacht treats this subject extensively in his book *Symbols of Women*.[20]

17. Bruno Bettelheim, *The Uses of Enchantment: The Meaning and Importance of Fairy Tales.* (New York: Alfred A. Knopf, 1989), 269–271.
18. *Zohar ḥadash, Ki tetse*, 59a.
19. R. Menahem Recanati. *Commentary on the Torah*, *Vayeshev*, Venice edition, §283 (n.p.).
20. Nacht, *Symbols of Women* (above, note 15), s.v. Na'al (*shoe*), 166–167.

We may note parenthetically that in the work of Agnon himself, shoes and sandals are manifest symbols of women's sexuality.[21] For example, Sonia, the female protagonist of *Only Yesterday* (*Temol shilshom*), had shoes made for her by the cobbler from Homel, which accented her erotic appearance and gave her "an upright body and a fine posture," a secret she took care to conceal from her girl-friends.[22] Sandals also play a key role in the novel *Shira*: in the dream that recurs to Manfred Herbst several times, where the nurse Shira and the blind Turkish beggar both disappear into a sandal — "until nothing was left of Shira except her left sandal";[23] in the shoes on her dainty feet, made by a skilled craftsman, so that they give her an elegant bearing;[24] in the pair of sandals that Manfred buys for his wife Henrietta, putting them on her feet himself, to the astonishment of his little daughter Sarah;[25] and, finally, in the lovely, graceful shoes, rather like sandals, that Shira buys for herself in Herbst's presence, which will reappear powerfully in the novel's dramatic final scene, when he is united with his beloved in the leper hospital.[26]

The "redemption" at the center of the nocturnal interchange between Ruth and Boaz is an extension of the commandment of levirate marriage. The obligation to take responsibility for a childless widow did not stop with her late husband's brother; in the absence of a direct levir, it passed on to wider kinship circles. Thus, Boaz sees himself as obligated to look after his relative, and on the very next day, without delay, he gathers ten elders at the city gate and calls in their presence upon the nearer redeeming kinsman, who ought by right to redeem Ruth, to ascertain whether or not the latter was indeed interested in taking on this task: "If you are willing to redeem it,[27] redeem! But if you will not redeem, tell me, that I may know. For there is no one to redeem but you, and I come after you" (Ruth 4:4). This closer redeemer, whose name seems intentionally to be concealed by the scriptural text, rejects the invitation and proposes to Boaz: "You take over my right of redemption, for I am unable to exercise it" (4:6).

As soon as the barrier is lifted, opening the way for Boaz, the ritual of redemption takes place, and, as with the *ḥalitsah* ritual, the shoe is its central symbolic object: "Now this was formerly done in Israel in cases of redemption

21. Adi Zemach, "For the Sake of a Pair of Shoes" (*Ba'avur na'alayim*), in: idem, *Plain Reading in Twentieth-Century Hebrew Literature* (*Keri'ah tamah besifrut 'ivrit bat hame'ah ha'esrim*), (Jerusalem: Mossad Bialik, 5750/1990), 62–70.
22. Agnon, *Only Yesterday* (English transl. by Barbara Harshav), (Princeton: Princeton University Press, 2000), 117.
23. Agnon, *Shira* (English transl. by Zeva Shapiro), New Milford, (CT: Toby Press, 2013), 5, 510 and 574.
24. *Ibid.*, 63.
25. *Ibid.*, 509.
26. *Ibid.*, 756.
27. The property of Elimelech's family, along with the widowed Ruth.

or exchange," the narrator informs his readers, "to validate any transaction, one man would take off his sandal and hand it to the other. Such was the practice in Israel" (4:7). The closer redeemer says to his surrogate, Boaz: "Acquire for yourself," and he draws off his sandal (4:8); and Boaz thereupon declares publicly before the elders: "You are witnesses today that I am acquiring from Naomi all that belonged to Elimelech and all that belonged to Chilion and Mahlon. I am also acquiring Ruth the Moabite ... as my wife, so as to perpetuate the name of the deceased upon his estate" (4:10).

The many similarities connecting the Book of Ruth with *A Simple Story*, on the one hand, and the yawning chasm between them, on the other, together endow this division of Agnon's prose with a new dimension. Boaz's moral undertaking on Ruth's behalf served as the point of departure for the story of the eternal flourishing of the Kingdom of David, from then until the end of days. By contrast, Boruch Meir's indifference to Blume's distress and to his own moral obligation toward her, and his submission to his wife's dictate, lead to the family tragedy surrounding Hirshl's married life, the debility and sickliness of his firstborn son, and above all the hereditary mental illness that rears itself anew, and whose cure, following the lengthy course of treatment in Lemberg, is left in doubt.[28]

****

Let us return, then, to the "new faces." The first appearance of this halakhic term, in association with the wedding benediction, points to the direction in which the life of the Hurvitz family might have developed as a consequence of Blume's entrance into their lives, had Tsirl not adamantly and firmly thwarted this process. By contrast, its other two appearances, the one connected with the mourner taking off his phylacteries and the other with the "ears" of the sandal, point to the direction in which Hirshl's life will be tugged from here on. It will suffice us in this regard to track the appearance, throughout the novel, of the key words *tefil-*

28. In the novel *Only Yesterday* (*Temol shilshom*), too, the Book of Ruth serves as a deep antithetical story to that of Isaac Kumer and his second-aliyah comrades. I shall not discuss this at length here but will suffice with a few details: The story's title, *Temol shilshom*, is drawn from Ruth 2:11, the only place in the Bible where this pair of words appears with no addition. The title of *Sefer ḥelkat hasadeh* — the Book of the Piece of Land — which, as the author promises at the end of *Only Yesterday*, is to be the novel's sequel, is also taken from the Book of Ruth. That phrase ḥelkat hasadeh, too, appears just five times in the Bible, two of them in the Book of Ruth, in the context of Boaz's act of redemption. Moreover, the writer refers to the members of the Second Aliyah (the second wave of Zionist immigration to Palestine/Erets Israel, 1904–1914) at the outset of the book as ' the people of our redemption," while by the end they are called "our chosen people" as an expression of his disappointment with them for not fulfilling their obligation to Isaac Kumer, not giving him their protection and not caring for him at a time of crisis, unlike Boaz's behavior toward Ruth.

lin (phylacteries), shoe or sandal, and the verb *ḥalats,* "to remove a shoe" (*ḥalats*), up until the pivotal scene of Hirshl's madness, in which the three come together in a chilling episode of casting off and getting free.

In Hirshl's mind, a secret plan gradually and almost unconsciously takes shape for casting off Mina's hold. One of the best means at his disposal to do so, a means of breaking out of his marriage, will be to put on a performance of madness, by way of defiling and desecrating his phylacteries. In *A Simple Story,* the *tefillin,* perhaps more than any other object, symbolize the home in which Mina was raised and the values by which her father, Gedalia Ziemlich, had educated her: modesty, caring for others, piety and humility:

> Becoming the count's manager, therefore, had not gone to his head. His house was still open to rich and poor alike and he himself waited on each guest. Whenever he had a free moment he read Psalms to himself, while each Monday and Thursday he journeyed to Szybusz to hear the Torah read in the synagogue. Far from a jealous man by nature, his only envy was of those Jews who could double their merit by putting on two pairs of tefillin each morning, one according to the formula of Rashi and one according to that of Rabbenu Tam—and if he did not emulate them it was not for lack of time but because he feared that, since many pious and learned Jews made do with one pair, it would be vainglorious of him to insist on two. As it was, he took great care of his tefillin, inspected them constantly to see that they were in order, and made sure never to engage in unnecessary conversation while wearing them. It was his custom too to buy a new prayer shawl before each holiday and exchange it for the torn one of some poor but God-fearing scholar—and indeed, his tongueless tefillin and torn prayer shawls were apt symbols for the man himself, who never said a word to anyone about how torn he felt inside. (*A Simple Story,* 92; *Sippur pashut,* 137)

Hirshl has two models for how to go about fulfilling his plan: The one is his mother's grandfather, and the other the compiler of a dictionary, a copy of which is found in Hirshl and Mina's home.

His maternal great-grandfather arises in Hirshl's thoughts three times, always at significant junctures in the story, and always in connection with the grandson, Hirshl's uncle. As he seeks an escape route from his marriage, the regular appearance of his mother's brother in Hirshl's consciousness sharpens his perception that he ought to follow in his uncle's path, and that this is to be his path of choice, given the deep-rooted, time-honored Jewish folk belief, cited already in rabbinic literature, that "Most sons resemble the mother's brothers."[29]

The first time his mother's grandfather and brother are mentioned in the story is on Hirshl and Mina's wedding day:

29. BT *Bava Batra* 110a; JT *Qiddushin* 4, 66.

If anything, he thought of his mother's family, that is, of her brother who went mad and of her grandfather, who was said to have once put a chamber pot on his head and worn it in place of *tefillin*.[30] (*A Simple Story*, 106; *Sippur pashut*, 149)

The second time, they burst into Hirshl's thoughts as he lies awake in bed at night:

Whatever he saw or heard that day came up for review at night. Things he had never understood before were suddenly clear to him. Though he had never, for example, seen a photograph of his mother's crazy brother or of her grandfather who drank tea through a hole in a sugar cube and wore a chamberpot where one would don *tefillin*.[31] he saw them as clearly in bed at night as if they were standing before him. (*A Simple Story*, 162; *Sippur pashut*, 201–202)

And the third time is at the conclusion of the scene of madness in the forest:

As bizarrely as he was acting, Hirshl had his wits about him. He knew that, unlike his mother's grandfather who wore a chamberpot in place of *tefillin*,[32] he could not make a hat of a shoe, and that, unlike his maternal uncle who ran off to the forest for good, he would have to go home in the end. Why didn't he, then? Because he had lost his hat, and one did not go hatless in the hot sun.

His mother's progenitor, from whom generation after generation of hereditary mental illness goes down through the Klinger family, delineates the path for his great-grandson — casting off and desecrating his *tefillin* — and in the former's case, also by casting the *tefillin* off his head and wearing a chamberpot instead. Although the word rendered here as "chamberpot," *qiton*, commonly appears in rabbinic literature in the phrase *qiton shel mayim*, "a pot of water," the Hebrew reader will surely hear between the lines the expressions used more often in modern Hebrew literature: *qiton shel shofkhin*, "a pot of sewage," *kiton shel rothin*, "a pot of boiling water," or *shafakh 'al peloni qiton shel buz/harafot/'el-bon*, "poured a potful of scorn/curses/insults on X" — that is, cursed, mocked, insulted or defamed him. These expressions would appear to derive from a passage in Mishnah *Sotah*:

During the whole seven days [of the festival], one makes his sukkah [his] permanent [dwelling], and his house [a] temporary [dwelling]. If rains fell, starting when is one permitted to clear out [of the sukkah]? When a stiff dish [of food] would be spoiled. They [the elders] illustrate this with a parable: To what

---

30. Halkin's translation: "instead of a skullcap."
31. Halkin's translation: "instead of a skullcap."
32. Halkin's translation: "on his head."

can this matter be compared? To a slave who came to pour a goblet for his master, and he [the master] poured a bowl-full [*kiton*, i.e., of water] in his face.[33]

Incidentally, just as the symbolic meaning with which the *tefillin* are invested in Hirshl's childhood home is entirely different from their meaning in Mina's childhood home, so, too, with the meaning of the *kiton*. While for Hirshl the *kiton* is a symbolic expression of the primal madness of the family's progenitor, for Mina it expresses the healthy normalcy of her family, a health with which she flatters herself in one of the tensest conversations between herself and her husband, to which we shall immediately turn. "I come from an honest family that's earned its keep by hard work, not by flattery," she upbraids him. "Why, when I think of how my father started out as a milkman with a route, I feel proud of him!" (*A Simple Story*, 132; *Sippur pashut*, 172–173)

In this conversation, which takes place between the couple as they await the arrival of Mina's friend Sophia Gildenhorn, Hirshl not only reveals to his wife for the first time the existence of his mad uncle, a deep secret that the family had up to then endeavored to conceal from her, but he also takes the trouble to share with her his own interpretation of how the madness of his mother's brother is really to be understood, giving her a glimpse of the mechanism that he will use to free himself of their failed marriage and clear the path for Blume's return to his life:

> He soon got onto the subject of his mother's brother, whom his surprised wife had never heard of, so that he said to her:
> "If you ask me, my uncle was perfectly sane and just pretending to be crazy, because otherwise his father, that is, my grandfather Shimon Hirsh, whom I'm named after, would have married him off to some woman he didn't love and made him waste the rest of his life on her, raising a house full of her little darlings, and making lots of money, and getting filthy rich, and being disgustingly respectable. There may be nothing wrong with all that, but I tell you, it would have left him an empty shell of a man. If my uncle had managed to make something of himself on his own, everyone would have said how clever he was. Since he didn't, everyone thought he was crazy. ... I will say this, though, and that's that if I feel empty inside, what does anything else matter? You look so sad, Mina. I swear I didn't mean to make you feel that way. It makes me sad to think of my uncle too, even though it happened years ago. Well, let me tell you something funny, then. ..." (*A Simple Story*, 131–132; *Sippur pashut*, 173–174)

At this point, when the image of his uncle turns up in Hirshl's mind, one would think that the image of his mother's grandfather, who always appears together with him, would turn up as well. But Hirshl, apparently not wanting Mina to draw the self-evident conclusion that there were serial cases of madness in his

33. Mishnah *Sotah* 2:9.

family, presents a double of his grandfather, a kind of replica of a man who desecrated his *tefillin* — a distinguished composer of a dictionary, who was not a
family member:

> "Well, let me tell you something funny, then. Do you see that fat volume in the
> bookcase? It's a Hebrew dictionary. The man who compiled it was married off
> when he was young to some woman he didn't even know, as was the custom in
> those days. Do you know what he did? When he grew a little older and decided
> to get rid of her, he took the cat one morning and put his tefillin on it. Just
> imagine it, Mina: his wife and her parents were so frightened that they agreed
> to a divorce at once. After that he married a woman of his choice and lived
> with her happily ever after. I don't know if he still puts on tefillin every day,
> but I'm sure he leaves the cat alone." (*A Simple Story*, 132; *Sippur pashut*, 174)

Consciously or not, Hirshl has just revealed his future actions to Mina, but she,
on her part, prefers to suppress and deny them, as expressed metaphorically in
the way she treats the dictionary when she comes across it again:

> Mina ... had no interest in Hebrew dictionaries. One day, in fact, when the
> dictionary fell by mistake while she was taking down a book from the shelf,
> she nudged it along the floor with her foot until it vanished beneath the book-
> case. (*Ibid.*)

****

Let's hang up the *tefillin* for a bit and turn our gaze to Hirshl's shoes. The shoes
come into the frame of the story for the first time on that oppressive, rainy night
when Hirshl, broken-hearted, stands as is his wont, before the home of Akavia
Mazal, watching Blume's room. He finally sees her when she goes down to close
the garden gate, which had been blown open by the wind, but she recoils at hearing his voice and runs back in:

> The rain fell noiselessly. Through a curtain of mist so thick that he could not
> see his own self the image of Blume appeared as brightly before him as it had
> on the day she had stroked his head in her room after walking out and return-
> ing. Hirshl rested his head on the latch of the gate and began to cry.
>   The tears kept coming. Rain collected in his shoes. He let the umbrella
> slip from his hands and soon was wet all over. (*A Simple Story*, 153; *Sippur
> pashut*, 193)

At midnight, after going home and holding an imaginary, revealing and unin-
hibited conversation with Mina, who has been fast asleep for hours,

> Hirshl took off (*ḥilets*) his shoes and wet socks and tiptoed to his bed. The
> windows were shut tight, and a warm, somnolent smell came from Mina. (*A
> Simple Story*, 155; *Sippur pashut*, 195)

But if, in real life, Mina's bed gives off a warm and somnolent smell — a perfect expression of domestic calm and marital harmony — in Hirshl's consciousness, exactly as in the ancient Hebrew traditions that we saw above, the shoes are a symbolic expression of Mina's femininity and sexuality. For Hirshl, however, the trouble is that Mina is like the wet, cold, rain-soaked shoes: a hindrance that he wants only to cast off his feet, to rid himself of its punishment.

Actually, the verb *h.l.ts* has already served the author of *A Simple Story*, and not unintentionally, in a passage where he intimates to his readers what goes on in Hirshl's heart after his engagement to Mina:

> Whereas until now Hirshl had tried thinking of everyone but Mina, now he could think of no one else. As detached as he felt from her, there was no escaping her existence. And yet—though he did not, God forbid, wish her any harm—to escape it was what he most wanted. He prayed for something to save him (*veyehaltsenu*), such as his family losing its fortune overnight, which would force Ziemlich to call off the wedding and himself to go to work as a shopboy in another town. One night, without knowing how Mirl's dead parents, Blume's grandparents, had sat reading Boruch Meir's letters to them before Boruch Meir became engaged to Tsirl, Hirshl dreamed that he had written them. If worse comes to worst, he thought, I can always run away to America. Though he knew that an only child like himself could do nothing of the sort, imagining it kept him from despair. (*A Simple Story*, 72; *Sippur pashut*, 117–118)

****

The key words *tefillin*, shoe/sandal and the verb *h.l.ts*, which have slowly but surely commandeered their place in the first twenty-five chapters of the story, following their debut on the opening page, where they were implicitly encoded in the phrase "new faces," play their peak dramatic roles in the pivotal scene that begins at the end of Chapter Twenty-Six and concludes in the first part of Chapter Twenty-Seven. In this scene the narrator relieves Hirshl of his *tefillin* and his shoe and provocatively ties them together, even as the protagonist fantasizes that he has finally shed his bonds and momentarily achieved a chimerical freedom — the liberation bestowed by madness upon its sufferers.

The scene begins during the morning prayers:

> Hirshl stepped into the Little Synagogue, donned his prayer shawl and tefillin, and joined the prayer. (*A Simple Story*, 176; *Sippur pashut*, 214)

The day wasn't an ordinary weekday, but one with a special character:

> It was the day of the New Moon, and the Torah scroll was taken out to be read. (*Ibid.*)

Incidentally, when Hirshl first saw Blume and was swept away by her magical charm and cakes, it was also the New Moon:

> It was a day in May, the first of the Hebrew month of Iyyar, when servants and household help renewed their annual contracts. Not long before Blume's arrival the Hurvitzes' maid had given notice and a new maid had yet to be found. When the employment agent came to Tsirl with a replacement, Tsirl said to her:
> "Just where, please tell me, am I supposed to put her? A cousin of ours is staying with us and sleeping in the maid's bed." (*A Simple Story*, 7; *Sippur pashut*, 59)

Since then, the New Moon has borne an emotional charge for Hirshl, which comes to crashing expression in the events of this morning.

The indications of his breakdown, already evident in his conversation with Mina before his departure for the morning service and intensifying throughout the prayers in the Little Synagogue, revolve again and again around his head, finally concentrating on the spot upon which the worshipper sets his phylactery.

The sensations in Hirshl's head appear as soon as he arises:

> Nor was [his good mood] affected by the headache he had, which merely proved to him that, while he might not feel well physically, there was nothing the matter with his mind. Indeed, a sound mind was needed to realize that there was something wrong with his body. (*A Simple Story*, 172; *Sippur pashut*, 210)

Mina, waking up, immediately notices this:

> "Does your head hurt, Heinrich?" asked Mina.
> "Come, Mina," he answered. "Where would I be if my head didn't hurt? It's my way of knowing I'm alive." (*Ibid.*)

After he enters the small Beit Midrash, wraps himself in his prayer shawl and dons his *tefillin*, his problems still center on the spot on his head where his phylactery lies:

> Midway through the service he felt a jolt in his head as if it had been banged against a wall. A moment later he felt another jolt as if it were being blown right off. He bent to look at the floor, then felt his forehead to see if his tefillin had been knocked to the ground. (*A Simple Story*, 176; *Sippur pashut*, 214)

With a thousand thoughts racing through it, his mind wanders from his prayer book, whose pages are riffled by a breeze, to the sneeze of a snuff-taker and from there to a couple of couple of men discussing a talmudic text. Listening to their conversation brings his thoughts back again to the same spot where the phylactery rests on the head, the spot upon which all his yearnings were concentrated:

Two men who had prayed already were discussing a Talmudic text that dealt with birds with upright feathers on their heads, and whether there is a need, after their slaughter, to check for a piercing of the skull. (*Ibid.*)[34]

But only with the conclusion of the service, after he has departed "as light as a feather" from the heart of Jewish civilization — the study house — and gone out to the unencumbered space of the forest, by way of the intermediate stages of the cattle and spirit markets, will his lunatic episode reach its apex. Everything that has been fermenting within him since the day that Mina straddled his path, and he was compelled by his mother's command to relinquish Blume, bursts out in momentary illusion of relief and liberation.

Taking off his *tefillin*, which in Hirshl's eyes symbolize accepting the yoke and authority of community tradition and his subjection and submission to his father's discipline and his mother's instruction, opens the way to taking off something else — his shoes. At the height of this outburst, Hirshl will hold an alternative ritual of *ḥalitsah* for himself, in which he will symbolically free himself of his wife and his obligation toward her.

To conceal his madness, which is about to break out, and so as not to draw the attention of anyone who might block his way, Hirshl sticks to the conventional comportment of east European Jewish householders, with their old-fashioned ways:

[H]e made himself walk slowly, for a man in full possession of himself, he thought, should do nothing that might appear unseemly.

He made his way with a modest air of deliberation, clutching the velvet bag that contained his prayer shawl and tefillin. Anyone happening to see him just then would have thought he had much on his mind ....

Holding his bag in his left hand, Hirshl tipped his hat with his right as if passing before a reviewing stand, though there was no one there but him and the trees. (*A Simple Story*, 178; *Sippur pashut*, 215)

And here, in the depth of that isolated spot, the decision to hold a *ḥalitsah* ceremony for himself rises to the threshold of his consciousness:

What a fool you were, Hirshl, not to have thought of that in front of Blume's house. There's nothing like tipping your hat for staying out of trouble—unless it's taking off your shoes so that Mina won't hear you when you come home late at night. I had better take them off right now. (*A Simple Story*, 178–179; *Sippur pashut*, 215)

The original *ḥalitsah* ritual as it was carried out in east European Jewish communities looked something like this: The ceremony took place in the morning, right

---

34. Halkin's translation: "Two men who had prayed already were discussing a Talmudic text that dealt with the head feathers of slaughtered birds."

after the morning service, usually in or near the synagogue. The brother-in-law donned a special type of footwear on his right foot, something between a shoe and a sandal, made of black leather, with two flaps sewn onto its edges. Through these loops the wearer threaded two strips of black leather, bearing no trifling resemblance to *tefillin* straps, which he bound around his calf just as a male Jewish worshipper binds *tefillin* straps around his arm. The sister-in-law untied the straps and pulled the shoe off the foot of her dead husband's brother, after which she spat in his face and repeated word for word the verse read to her by the rabbinic judges: "Thus shall be done to the man who will not build up his brother's house! And he shall go in Israel by the name of 'the family of the unsandaled one' (Deut. 25:9–10), 'the family of the unsandaled one,' 'the family of the unsandaled one.'"[35]

Hirshl reenacts this ritual almost precisely in the forest, and he, too, takes off just one shoe:

> As he was about to remove his second shoe, though, he stood up anxiously and thought, Why, I said I couldn't feel my own body, but now I see that I can. Or is it just something I imagined .... Suddenly Hirshl struck his head and cried aloud, "I am not crazy, I am not!" (*A Simple Story*, 179; *Sippur pashut*, 216)

Note the words that are put into his mouth: "I said I couldn't feel my own body, but now I see that I can." When Hirshl says *besari*, my body or my flesh, it is clear to anyone versed in the sacred canon that the reference is not to himself but to his wife. Suffice it to cite just two sources: "Hence a man leaves his father and mother and clings to his wife, so that they become one flesh (*basar ehad*)" (Gen. 2:24); "and do not ignore your own kin (*besarekha*)" (Is. 57:7). The Sages interpret the latter verse: "Your kin — this is his ex-wife,"[36] speaking admiringly in this connection of Rabbi Yossi Hagelili's concern for his ex-wife after their divorce, though she had made his life miserable during their marriage.[37] Agnon himself would again invoke this meaning of *besarekha* in his unfinished novel *Shira*. In what was to have been its concluding chapter, as Manfred Herbst tries to persuade Shira, who is confined to the leper hospital, that he must stay with her forever, he declares: "...How can I tell you? I once read a poem, and I found a line in it that sticks to my tongue." "What is it?" "'Flesh such as yours will not soon be forgotten.'"[38]

---

35. See Shlomo Yosef Zevin (ed.), *Entsiklopediyah talmudit*, (Jerusalem, 1976), XV, cols. 615–816, s.v. *Halitsah*.
36. *Yalkut Shim'oni*, Behar, §665.
37. JT *Ketubot* 11:3; *Genesis rabbah* 17:3; *Leviticus rabbah* 34:14.
38. Agnon, *Shira* (English transl. by Zeva Shapiro; above, note 22), 757. The quote is from the poem "Woman" by S. Shalom, *Sefer hashirim vehasonetot*, (Tel Aviv, 1943), 191.

Nevertheless, despite the surprising awakening of his feelings for Mina, Hirshl does not desist from the *halitsah* ritual that he is conducting for himself:

> He took out his stopped watch and studied it, then lay down in the grass with it hanging out of his pocket, one shoe off and one shoe on, happily laughing and ga-ga-ing to himself. He could not remember ever having felt so at peace. (*A Simple Story*, 179; *Sippur pashut*, 216)

Like the original *halitsah* ritual, this solipsistic, self-devised ritual finishes with expectoration. And since the widow is supposed to spit in the face of her brother-in-law, Hirshl must lie on his back and spit upwards in order for the spittle to hit him. By means of this bodily pose, the narrator achieves two bold effects that are missing from the original ritual: defamation of God and defiance of heaven, on the one hand,[39] and self-abasement, on the other:[40]

> Oh nice oh nice, he thought, staring joyfully up at the sky with a hallucinatory smile on his lips. All at once he leaped up in dismay and exclaimed, "Half past seven!"
>
> In an instant his smile vanished and a turbid froth appeared in its place. He spat it into the air and it fell back into his eyes. Again he spat it upward and again it rained down on him. (*Ibid.*)

At the end of the ritual, the *tefillin*, which were briefly set aside, return to the center of the story, again taking their place in Hirshl's consciousness, this time in the form of a shoe, which he puts on his head in the spot where one would set a phylactery, in a kind of reincarnation of the pot bound by his great-grandfather in place of a phylactery:

> Then he turned and ran, the hat toppling from his head. The sun beat down on him. The veins stood out hotly in his brow. He drummed on them with his fists, then removed his other shoe, placed it on top of his head, and began to hop on one foot until a stone sent him sprawling.
>
> As bizarrely as he was acting, Hirshl had his wits about him. He knew that, unlike his mother's grandfather who wore a chamberpot on his head, he could not make a hat of a shoe, and that, unlike his maternal uncle who ran off to the forest for good, he would have to go home in the end. (*ibid.*)

Hirshl remains lying in the place where he performed his *halitsah* for hours, until a member of the search party finds him there at the end of the day:

39. It is said of Titus that upon his entrance into the Temple, he set his face defiantly, "drew his sword and cut into the curtain ... And not only that, but he seized a whore and brought her into the Holy of Holies, and began to curse and revile and blaspheme and spit upwards" (*Avot deRabbi Natan*, B, 7).
40. See, e.g., Num. 12:14, where, after Miriam is smitten with leprosy for her untoward words, "The Lord said to Moses: If her father spat in her face, would she not bear her shame for seven days? Let her be shut out of camp for seven days, and then let her be readmitted."

At sundown Hirshl was found in a field with one shoe on one foot and the other on his forehead, an expression of great anguish in his eyes. It was hard to look at him, though he himself stared straight back at his finders without saying a word. At last he cried out to them, "Don't cut my throat! I'm not a rooster! I'm not!" (*A Simple Story*, 180; *Sippur pashut*, 219)

From here on, from when Hirshl is brought back home until the end of the story, the key words *tefillin*, shoe (*na'al*) and *ḥalitsah* vanish from the textual scene. Now that they have finished their roles, the narrator takes them off the stage and places them behind the scenes for safekeeping.

***

At the outset of this essay, I argued that Agnon's intertextuality is finely and artfully crafted, subtle, refined and sophisticated, demanding of the reader not only identification of the allusions to traditional passages embedded in the text, but also a response to the question of what type of use the narrator is making of them.

I believe I have demonstrated here that the "new faces" peeping out at us from the opening scene of *A Simple Story* become, by virtue of the author's creative genius, not only a foreshadowing of the story's central theme, but also a kind of inverted reflection of the narrative tradition from which this phrase sprang and is taken. The meeting of the two texts, ancient and new, leverages the work and gives it a profound dimension that otherwise would be concealed from the eyes of the ordinary reader.

Apart from that first occurrence at the beginning of *A Simple Story*, the phrase "new faces" recurs thrice more in the course of the story, once on p. 137[41] (*Sippur pashut*, 178) and twice on 236 (*Sippur pashut*, 269). But even a cursory inspection of its role in these passages will show that the phrase is used in these cases in its simplest sense, no more than a turn of phrase by a Hebrew author writing in the holy tongue, and if readers, for reasons best known to themselves, should seek in these usages something more substantial, they may run a risk of seeing something that isn't there.

* My thanks to Batya Be'er, Dr. Roni Be'er-Marx, Raphael Weiser, Dr. Haim Weiss, Dr. Gideon Tikotsky, Rivka Pilser and Edna Zahor, who read the manuscript of this essay, and whose deep and broad-ranging knowledge helped me to improve it greatly. I, of course, bear exclusive responsibility for any mistakes or shortcomings that may be found in it.

41. Where it is rendered "its only visitor" in Halkin's translation.

HAIM BE'ER is a celebrated Israeli novelist, literary critic, and professor of Hebrew literature at Ben-Gurion University. He has authored works of literary criticism, among them *Gam ahavatam, gam sin'atam* (*Their Love and Their Hate*) on the relationship of Bialik, Brenner, and Agnon, and most recently *Ḥadarim melayim sefarim* (*Rooms Full of Books*), which explores Agnon's *To This Day*. He is the recipient of the Bialik, Brenner, and Agnon literary prizes, which recognized his many novels, among which *Feathers* and *The Pure Element of Time* have been translated to English. His most recent Hebrew novel, *Tsel yado* (*The Shadow of His Hand*), appeared in 2021.

17   The Source and the Depth of Oblivion: Story and Folktale in Two Stories by Agnon

Ariel Hirschfield
Translated by Deborah Greniman

AGNON, NO LESS than Y.L. Peretz, sought to embed his literary work in the essence of the *volk*, as embodied in "folksongs" and "folktales." The idea of the "folk," in the Romantic, ethnic sense of the term, was felt to bear within it a life-truth embodied in a distinctive character — that of a particular people. From the end of the eighteenth century through the middle of the twentieth, this notion enjoyed the status of a primal truth, and it was shared by the Jewish writers active in the late nineteenth and early twentieth centuries. The use of folkloric elements by Bialik, Tchernikhovsky, Peretz and Agnon is well known and has been the subject of not a few scholarly treatments.

But Agnon, from the very outset of his career, worked in the field where folk literature meets *belles lettres* in a way all his own, one that was quite remote from any simple faith in the "innocent" creations of the "folk," and even more remote from any desire to generate an impression of "authentic folklore" in his modern writings. Between his own writings and the creations of the "folk," Agnon wove a complex web of tensions, paradoxes and uncertainties, to the point that his work appears at times intentionally to subvert the traditional story, to wreck its credibility or its basic notions of aesthetics and value, no less than it is sustained by the story's vitality and its ability to constitute an identity and a sense of the genuine.

It was clear to the audiences of the writers of that generation that folk elements, where they served as material for an artistic work, had undergone extensive adaptation. The very notion of this kind of reworking and the various methods of accomplishing it were already a ramified literary tradition, and the "artistic" tale or folksong had evinced the burnish of a glorious heritage since the days of Herder, Goethe, Hoffman, Pushkin and Andersen.[1] Agnon's works, too, based as they were on folkloric elements, were widely viewed as traditional artistic

---

1. See especially the distinction made between "literary" and "artistic" tales in M. Luthi, *The European Folktale* (English transl. by J.D. Niles) (Philadelphia: Institute for the Study of Human Issues, 1982); and see M. Thalmann, *The Romantic Fairy Tale: Seeds of Surrealism* (English transl. by M.B. Corcoran) (Ann Arbor: University of Michigan Press, 1963). On the gaps between these genres see the interesting discussion of J.D. Zipes, *Breaking the Magic Spell: Radical Theories of Folk and Fairy Tales* (Austin, TX: University of Texas Press, 1979).

Building a City: Writings on Agnon's Buczacz in Memory of Alan Mintz (2022): 271–292
DOI: 10.2979/BuildingaCityWriting.0.0.18

reworkings of folkloric "material."[2] However, many of Agnon's readers well sensed that what he was doing broke with the usual notions of adaptation, that he was going far beyond other writers of his generation in interacting with his various sources, and in that distance seethed a painful drama of destruction and loss.

In the following pages I shall train my gaze on two major signposts in Agnon's work that touch upon his treatment of "folkloric" elements and upon the concept of the "folk" itself, for the sake of learning something about the complex synapse that connects these bodies of literary knowledge in Agnon's writing. The idea of a synapse, drawn from the field of anatomy, defines the strong connection formed by the transmission of energy between two entities — not by means of a simple, direct transfer, but by bridging a gap between the nerve cells that have no direct connection between them, so that the energy must move in a different medium. In other words, the connection bridges a discontinuity, over which the message is passed in a different mode, to be "reinterpreted" by the arms of the next cell, awaiting it beyond the discontinuity. The energy passing between the nerve cells in the form of an electric current is converted in the synapse, for a very tiny fragment of time, into a movement that transpires in chemical form, and only at the end of the passage does it turn back into an electric current. This notion seems to me a useful simile for defining the tension between the transmission, transfer, discontinuity and rectification that take place in the course of cultural transitions in general and in the contact between Agnon's writings and their folkloric elements in particular.

In the first story that Agnon published in Erets Israel — the story from which he took his pen name, and which he saw as his literary debut — "'Agunot" or "Abandoned Wives" — he implanted a fascinating, complex signpost that points to his basic attitude toward the entire heritage of the "folk." That signpost stands at both ends of the story — at its beginning and at its end. Here are the opening lines:

> It is said [in the writings[3]]: A thread of grace is spun and drawn out of the deeds of Israel, and the Holy One, blessed by He, Himself, in His glory, sits and weaves — strand on strand — a tallit all grace and all mercy, for the Congregation of Israel to deck herself in. Radiant in the light of her beauty she glows, even in these, the lands of her exile, as she did in her youth in her Father's

---

2. Abraham Yaari and Fischel Lachover pioneered the discussion of Agnon's adaptation of folkloric materials in short essays published in the 1930s. Some important remarks on this are to be found in Gershom Scholem's article, "The Kabbalistic Sources of 'The Tale of Rabbi Gadiel the Infant,'" in D. Sadan and E.E. Urbach (eds.), *Le'Agnon Shay* (Jerusalem: The Jewish Agency, 1959), 289–305 (Hebrew). The systematic studies in this field are: Aliza Shenhar, "Folkloric Elements in S.Y. Agnon's 'A Lovers' Bridal Canopy,'" *Jerusalem Studies in Jewish Folklore*, 4 (5743/1983), 27–62 (Hebrew); and especially Shmuel Werses, "Folk Narrative Processes in the Work of Agnon,'" *Jerusalem Studies in Jewish Folklore*, 1 (5741/1981), 101–126 (Hebrew), and his book *S.Y. Agnon Literally: Studies of His Writings*, Jerusalem 2000, 93–105 and 123–189 (Hebrew).

3. *Bikhetavim*. This word is not rendered in Hochman's translation (below, note 4).

house, in the Temple of her Sovereign and the city of sovereignty, Jerusalem. And when He, of ineffable Name, sees her, that she has been neither sullied nor stained even here, in the realm of her oppressors, He — as it were — leans toward her and says, "Behold thou art fair, my beloved, behold thou art fair." And this is the secret of the power and the glory and the exaltation and the tenderness in love which fills the heart of every man in Israel. But there are times — alas! — when some hindrance creeps up and snags a thread in the loom. Then the tallit is damaged: Evil spirits however about it, enter into it, and tear it to shreds. At once a sense of shame assails all Israel, and they know they are naked. Their days of rest are wrested from them, their feasts are fasts, their lot is dust instead of luster. At that hour the Congregation of Israel stays abroad in her anguish, crying, "Strike me, wound me, take my veils from me!" Her beloved has slipped away, and she, seeking him, cries, "If ye find my beloved, what shall ye tell him? That I am afflicted with love." And this affliction of love leads to darkest melancholy, which persists — Mercy shield us! — until, from the heavens above, He breathes down upon us strength of spirit, to repent and to muster deeds that are price to their doers and again draw forth that thread of grace and love before the Lord.

And this is the theme of the tale recounted here ...[4]

The tale of the Holy One weaving a tallit out of a "thread of grace ... drawn out of the deeds of Israel," for "the Congregation of Israel to deck herself in" before Him as he proclaims to her the words of the lover in the Song of Songs — "Behold thou art fair, my beloved" — is a chapter in the Jewish story of redemption, stretching from the creation of the world to the End of Days. That story is told here in an allegorical form that has its source in rabbinic midrash ("See how the Holy One, Blessed be He, sings the praises of Israel: 'Behold thou art fair, my beloved, behold thou art fair'"—Song of Songs *rabbah* 1, et *passim*) and is retold in many ways in the kabbalistic literature.

However, this particular story is not told in any "writings," as the narrator says of it in the opening words (a matter to which I shall presently return), though it is in the style of the midrash and merges completely with the midrashic spirit, and its characteristic progression — from the primal wholeness ("as she did in her youth in her Father's house, in the Temple of her Sovereign and the city of sovereignty") through to the final rectification, in which "that thread of grace and love before the Lord" is once more drawn down — is the whole abstracted progression of the redemption story. Chapter 5 of the Song of Songs — the same chapter from which Agnon took the phrase "at the handles of the lock," which he used in several of his stories and eventually took as the title of his volume of "love stories" — serves him here in his complete reconstruction of the allegory.

4. S.Y. Agnon, "Agunot" (English transl. by Baruch Hochman), in idem, *A Book That Was Lost: Thirty-Five Stories*, ed. Alan Mintz and Anne Golomb Hoffman (New Milford, CT: The Toby Press, 2008), 39–40

In Agnon's hands, the episode of the lover "slipping away" (Song of Songs 5:6), leaving the beloved to wander in the night until the guards of the walls tear away her veil (vv. 6–7), becomes the episode of the "tearing" of the "tallit" — that is, the phase of the historical present, remote as can be from redemption. What is fascinating about this story, crafted by Agnon from his midrashic sources, is that the tearing of the tallit — the phase of hindrances, shame and losing the way — parallels not the destruction of the Temple and the exiling of the Jews, as it is customarily interpreted, but rather a later process of corruption or debasement that occurs with the people, breaking the continuity of the thread from which the cloth of the tallit, or the wedding canopy joining the God to the people, is woven. In other words, Agnon points here to a further chapter in the redemption story, not necessarily bound up with historical events of mythological status, like the destruction of the Temple, one that pushes the redemption yet further away, implying, perhaps, that this eternal Jewish story faces a rupture that may no longer have a chance of rectification.

This further chapter of rupture that is added to the Jewish redemption story has a fundamental meta-literary significance that touches upon the young Agnon's attitude in setting out to be a Hebrew writer. The rupture is not identified with any particular moment of crisis in Jewish history (such as the Shabbatean heresy, the Chmielnicki massacres of 1648–1649, the schism between Hasidism and its opponents, the Enlightenment, or Zionism and secularization), because it is not a historical moment, but a literary state: The rupture transpires in the present moment, whenever that is. That is to say: A story of mythological status, by its very exalted nature, can take place only in the past; while the authentic perspective of a down-to-earth look at the world, one that demands realism (where "realism" here is opposed to "idealism"), by its very nature destabilizes any generalizing view from above; it sees the human, Jewish, reality, and that reality, it will disclose, contains elements that subvert any causative or directional sequence in the apprehension of events and of history. At the same time, let us not err by ascribing a secular nature to this Agnonian realism, and especially to the lack therein of a directionality of cause and effect. This realism is the concept of "truth" so often invoked by Agnon, to which he was committed above and beyond any other value. Agnon's concept of truth appeared to him not as a secular domain but rather as an embodiment of divinity — in the complex and radical way that Agnon understood that concept. The most broken-down, secular, worldly present, in his eyes, is a divine revelation, not in its being wondrous or exalted, but in its being random, chaotic, abysmal and incomprehensible.

This rupture, then, is what is happening in the present, and it is the symbolic embodiment of the historical present in which the story taking place within it — "Abandoned Wives" — occurs. Moreover, this opening invites the reader to read "Abandoned Wives" as a whole as an allegorical continuation of the redemption story on a new level — not on the level of sweeping generalization, as in the opening, in which a brief moment in the Song of Songs grasps the entire historical present, but in a more complex and detailed form, in which, too, the story's protagonists and progression are understood to represent, symbolically and allegorically, the rupture of the "thread of grace" between the people and its God — the rupture of the redemption story itself. The "nakedness" eventuating from the rupture is also an exit from the domain of the protective force of the plot of the spousal relationship between the people — the "Congregation of Israel" — and the Lover — its God. In other words, the story is not only about Jews situated in the world and in history; it is also part of the singular Jewish story, and it is to be understood as a story about the relationship between the people and God. Of course, one shouldn't try to find a figure in the story that represents God, or the like; the stories should be seen, rather, as two spheres describing reality, superimposed one over the other.

In this way Agnon contrived a complex and unique literary setting: He created a notion of a distinctively Jewish story, a story whose Jewishness is not made out of any one language or out of a literary tradition of Hebrew prose-writing — a tradition that was then, as we know, rather poor, fragmentary and lacking any clear distinctiveness. It is made, rather, in conjunction with an existing story, ancient and all-embracing, existing, indeed, as a story of the Jewish people. He fashioned here a finely honed literary possibility, in which the "rupture" — the historical setting into whose "midst" the new story will be inserted — creates a situation that is already chaotic and breached, making it capable of receiving foreign elements, "evil spirits" of various kinds, and of serving as a vessel for joining together a great wealth of literary modes. In this way, any story will stand simultaneously in a relationship both of belonging and of "rupture" with the one Jewish story.

At the end of the story, Agnon created a parallel but converse structure, one that joined the story from a different direction to the "folk": Ben-Uri and Dinah, the story's protagonists, are left separated and lost in the world. Dina has been divorced from her husband, Rabbi Ezekiel, following a marriage that was empty of content — both because of her love for Ben-Uri and because of Ezekiel's love for Freidele. The rabbi who had officiated both at Dinah's wedding and at her divorce sees in a dream "the Shekhinah in the guise of a lovely woman, garbed in black, and without adornment, nodding mournfully at him" ("'Agunot," p. 50). From that dream, he goes out to search for Ben-Uri in "exile," calling to his wife: "seek not after me in my going forth, for the doom of exile has been levied upon me, to redeem the forsaken in love" (*ibid.*). But his departure brings no rectification to the story or to the "forsaken"; instead, the rabbi himself, who, in the story, represents the laws of Jewish practice and the tradition of Judaism, disappears as well, and his wife is left forsaken as well: "He kissed the mezuzah and slipped away. They sought him, and did not find him" (*ibid.*, alluding to the same chapter of the Song of Songs to which the beginning of the story alludes, only now it refers to the figure of the rabbi!). But this, too, is not the end of the story; from here on, it continues to disintegrate. To start with, the narrator offers different versions: "They say he wanders still" (*ibid.*). First comes the version of an emissary who sojourned in the Diaspora and perhaps, perchance in a dream, saw Ben-Uri fashioning an ornament, with an old man at his side. "Since that time," continues the narrator, "innumerable tales have been told," but their narrative becomes more and more incredible, turning into "awful and fantastic tales," like the Hasidic stories that are in part contrived and in part utterly false. Finally, they arrive at the present day:

> At the present time it is said that he has been seen wandering about in the Holy Land. The world-wise cavil and quibble, and even—some of them—mock. But little children insist that at times, in the twilight, an old man hails them, and peering into their eyes drifts into the gathering dusk. And whoever has heard the tale here recounted surely knows that the man is that rabbi, he, and no other. But God alone knows for a fact. (*Ibid.*, p. 51)

The protagonists of "Agunot" disappear into the world. Their presence passes to other planes — to dreams, and then to baseless folktales, and finally to fragmentary impressions of children that no longer have in them anything that attests to their belonging to the story, but one who knows the tale says something about their belonging to it. Moreover, at the end of the story, it revolves not around the protagonists but around the rabbi, the last link to them, who follows a dream to which he gave this interpretation — but perhaps he was wrong? And he, too, disappears. This disappearance into a fog of unknowing creates quite a complex impression: The protagonists, brought close and illuminated by the story on account of their love, have become "forsaken" and receded into the murk of solitude, in which there is no story — but that murk is the "folk" and its stories. Those stories differ essentially from the strong, cohesive story told by the narrator; they are multiple and lack the authority of truth, but they well up within the folk and in life. And so the story melts into the "folk." To be sure, the story fails in the reestablishment of a "mini-sanctuary" in Jerusalem, because of that forsakenness within that vanquishes anything good in its world, but it finds its place in a kind of transpiring of life and story that continues unfolding outside of it. But, no less than this: It is clear that the "folk" story transpires in parallel with the vanishing and disembodiment of the protagonists after their separation. Disconnected from time and place, they float in a twilight zone between fact and fiction.

In this way, Agnon created a kind of double belonging — to the overarching Jewish story, the redemption story, and to the "folk" story in which "Agunot" is embedded. This is obviously a completely original move: There is no Jewish-Hebrew literary precedent for a story that is a work of fictional art joining itself to the people's history in the rigorous, religious-messianic sense of the concept, while so sophisticatedly constructing an entirely different association — with the folk legends circulating in various, shifting forms in every Jewish locale. The kind of association that Agnon devised in the story "Agunot," formed by way of a "rupture," creates an entirely free artistic space within it. But, pointedly, Agnon in "Agunot" swore an oath of loyalty to this framework of belonging and to the full scope of its significance, and so posed himself as a national writer in the profoundest sense. It wasn't the Zionist idea that did this, but the great "subject" from which he never wavered: the historical unfolding of the "folk."

We must still take a close look at the opening words of the story: "It is said in the writings." Bringing evidence from the "writings" is, as we know, the accepted way of establishing or proving something throughout all the many branches of Jewish literature. What's "written" is the source for all interpretation, and it is also the basis for the literary edifice that has grown up over the course of history. What's "written" is primary. It is primary in time and in value, and it is grasped as more written than anything written after it or about it. It is inscribed, as it were, on the hard rock of time. For the Sages of the Talmud, the "writings" were the Holy Scriptures, but for the medieval sages, the words of the talmudic sages became "writings," and for those who came later still, their predecessors became "writings" — and so on up to the present day, in which Agnon and Bialik have become "writings." This cultural mechanism by which the earlier becomes superior from the point of view of its spiritual authority, so that the very earliest becomes the highest spiritual authority, is universal, but the specific attitude toward the "writings" as marking an authoritative text, and the ways of marking them — "as it is written" (in its various forms) — is Hebrew, and it is bound up with the history of Hebrew as the unfolding of a language and a faith. The "writings" are the underpinning. They are like a fixed construction in the world; they are a Place. From them one goes out and to them one comes. They are firmer than the earth, and they are maintained in time in the way that only writings are maintained — by that mode of transcription that Agnon devoted himself to explicating in "The Legend of the Scribe." The writings, in being transcribed, pass through time and take into themselves the meaning of the times.

The opening of "Agunot" with the words "It is said in the writings" is a gesture both essential and ceremonial: With this, the young Agnon announces that he is basing his artistic work upon the ancient Jewish structure of learning and demonstration, in which a new writing presents itself as subordinate to an earlier one and as deriving from it. But this is no simple opening. The story of the Holy One weaving a tallit that is steadily degraded on account of "some hindrance" does not appear in any "writings"! To be sure, it is formulated in a style derived from that of the midrash; it dresses itself up well as a traditional story, and its basic structure is that of the redemption story, but it is not a traditional story at all, and it also contains some odd gaps that are uncharacteristic of a midrashic story. It is in every way an Agnonic story. In a sense, it is a made-up quotation.[5] But that is not the point. Because this made-up quotation well preserves the spirit of the kabbalistic-hasidic redemption story. The point is that Agnon creates an autonomous structure that even contains its own ancient underpinnings as foundations internalized within itself. In this way Agnon changes the pose of a Hebrew author over against the ancient written authority, by claiming that this authority, too, is a contrivance that derives from within the writer no less than from "the writings." What had been an objective base standing outside the personal historical circumstances of the traditional Hebrew writer here becomes a living organ of creativity; its existence is absorbed into the "I" of the author.

In this way the overarching Jewish story, the redemption story, is comprehended as a narrative that can still be changed, as a story that is still being formed, and as sustaining some kind of "thread" linking this world, the human world, to the world of eternity and redemption; but, from another point of view, the concept of the "folk" itself has been seriously undermined. Who is this "folk"? Is it the same unified allegorical entity that is embodied in the figure of the beloved in the Song of Songs? Is anything tangible and comprehensible left of it by the end of the story?

II

In the short story "Three Sisters," Agnon constructs a converse situation to that underlying "Agunot": While "Agunot" rests upon the most constitutive and all-embracing narrative of the "folk" and melts back into the realm of "folktales," "Three Sisters" is presented as a folktale even though it is not one at all. Moreover, Agnon here presents a kind of folktale, or artistic story, whose progression contradicts the most vital foundations of a folktale:

> Three Sisters
> *To B. Katznelson, blessings!*
> Three sisters lived in a bleak house sewing white vestments for others. From dawn to dusk, from the end of Sabbath to Sabbath eve their fingers never strayed either from scissors or needle and sighing never left their hearts, neither in the season of sunshine nor in the season of the rains. But their efforts did not produce any benefit. When they found a dry crust of bread it failed to relieve their hunger. On one occasion they engaged in making a lovely wedding dress for a wealthy bride. Upon completing their handiwork they recalled their sorrows, for they had nothing on their flesh but frail skin, and that too was growing old.
> Their hearts overflowed with grief.

---

5. See Gershon Shaked, *Other Aspects of Agnon's Oeuvre* (Tel Aviv: Hakibbutz Hameuchad, 1989), Hebrew.

One sighed and said, All our lives we sit and toil for others while we lack even a piece of cloth to make burial shrouds for ourselves. The second one told her sister not to tempt Satan. She sighed as well and shed a tear. The third also wanted to say something, but when she opened her mouth to speak blood splattered out and stained the bride's garment.

When she brought the dress to the bride, her wealthy father came out of his hall. He saw the stain and rebuked the seamstress — it goes without saying he did not pay her.

Oh, if only the second sister had spat blood and the third had wept we could have laundered the garment with her tears, and the wealthy father would not have been enraged. But things don't occur beautifully, in their time. And even if everything did occur beautifully in its time, that is, if one had wept after the other spat blood, there would still be no true consolation.[6]

"Three Sisters" is not a folktale, nor is it based on a folk source. It is based on a Yiddish poem by Y.L. Peretz entitled "Three Seamstresses," which is written somewhat in the style of a folktale, or of an artistic folksong. But "Three Seamstresses," too, is not based on a folk source; it is a reworking or a somber parody of a very well known English song, "The Song of the Shirt," by Thomas Hood. In the second half of the nineteenth century, "The Song of the Shirt" was a kind of hymn of protest against the fate of the workers who were being oppressed and exploited by their wealthy capitalist employers. It was the most famous song in the western world on the subject of workers' rights — particularly those of women. After stirring up a storm when it was first published in the London magazine *Punch* in 1843, it was immediately translated into several European languages and gave rise to innumerable imitations, parodies and reworkings. It was adapted as a play and set to music, and it became an iconic motif in visual artwork. Peretz drew quite precisely upon the opening lines of "The Song of the Shirt," but he continued it in a direction of his own, giving it a tripartite course that leads to a tragic end. This continuation also makes use of various details from "The Song of the Shirt." Peretz changed the identity of the heroine — from one wretched seamstress (Mrs. Biddell of Lambeth, who is not mentioned in Hood's poem but was made known by it to the world) to three seamstresses — and he also added to it some distinctively Jewish traits and turns of phrase. Here is a translation from the Yiddish:

Three Seamstresses

Their eyes red, lips blue, cheeks bloodless, foreheads pale, covered with sweat, their breath short and hot, three girls sit and sew.

6. Translator's note: This rendering of "Three Sisters" is adapted from Shelly Lilker's English translation, in S.Y. Agnon, *Forevermore and Other Stories*, ed. Jeffrey Saks (New Milford, CT: Toby Press, 2016), 123–124. The translation has been revised to adjust it to the author's discussion, which is based on the Hebrew text.

The needle gleams, the linen is like snow. One girl thinks: I sew and sew by day and by night. But I have yet to sew my wedding dress. What's the point of my sewing? I neither sleep nor eat. If I could give alms for charity, perhaps I'd find a widower or an old man with children who'd marry me.

The second girl thinks: I sew and tread and tread till my braids turn gray. My head burns, my temples throb and the machine beats in rhythm. I understand that man's wink. Without a wedding, without a ring, it would be a game, a dance, a year-long affair. But what then?

The third girl coughs blood and sings: All I sew is illness and blindness. My breast is pierced with every stitch and he's getting married this week. I wish him no harm. Forget the past. The community elders will provide a shroud and bit of earth where I will rest undisturbed. I will finally sleep, sleep.[7]

"Three Sisters" continues in Peretz's path; it is a story that endeavors to sound like a folktale, and it rests upon one of the most widespread formulas in the folktale world: The Three Sisters. This formula plays a fascinating role in the story, and Agnon uses it to make some impressive moves. By virtue of this trinity, the whole exposition (up to "On one occasion") becomes an expansive, all-embracing symbol, turning the fate of the seamstresses into a grim depiction that is cast upon the fate of all humankind. Even so, the narrator in this story makes no effort to sound like an ordinary teller of folktales, and at a very early stage he pokes some striking holes into its quasi-folk aura. As it were, he stands beside the story as though it were a play being performed onstage, while he serves as a kind of narrator-mediator reporting upon it to his audience. Three times, he discloses his active presence. In the third sentence, "But their efforts did not produce any benefit," he reveals his awareness that his story up to now should have engendered an expectation that the sisters would reap great profit from their persistent, endless labor, and he intervenes to dash that expectation. In the next-to-last paragraph, he remarks: "it goes without saying he did not pay her," casting a sideways glance at his audience to confirm the absence of any hope of reward or profit, as if to say: "You and I of course know …," and adding a note of moral affirmation: The seamstresses have lost their wages because they damaged the cloth (which, as was customary, belonged to the man of wealth), and, more importantly, the garment's symbolic value; and that is how he concludes the first part of the story. The third time is in the final paragraph, which is the second part of the story and is entirely devoted to the narrator's observations about this world, which is the story of the three sisters: "Oh, if only the second sister had spat blood and the third had wept …" He stands over against the world, expressing his wish that the stained garment could have been laundered with tears, and understanding the impos-

7. Y.L. Peretz, "Dray Neytorins" (Warsaw: M. Kipnes, 1918). English translation in Eleanor Gordon Mlotek and Joseph Mlotek (eds.), *Pearls of Yiddish Song* (New York: Education Department of the Workmen's Circle, 1988).

sibility of changing the order of things. At a stroke, the closing words turn the foregoing narrative into a bleak symbol. This isn't about any real possibility of laundering a bloodstain with tears; it's about the possibility of still being able to weep, be purified and recover after the breakdown and destruction represented by the bloodstain — for that stain is the symptom of a terminal illness, or rather, of a breakdown and a fatal flaw of the greatest and most profound dimensions.

The narrator's inability to change the order of things is a fascinating meta-literary signpost, in that the narrator claims by this that he is not the omnipotent creator of the story. Even though he is its author, he is not at liberty to shape it according to his will. He is a witness to a truth greater than himself, to which he is obliged more than to himself or to the human expectations of those who cry "Oh, if only," yearning for things to occur "beautifully in their time,"[8] like the Holy One's work of creation and like the rains called down in the annual prayer recited at the conclusion of the festival of Sukkot. In this way Agnon creates a dimension of truth as an independent realm, stronger than the external pull of any desire or idea. This truth is also not identical with the supposed righteousness of God's deeds, as the narrator explicitly remarks: "But things don't occur beautifully, in their time." In his eyes, rather than creating a work of fiction or of the "imagination," writing and narrating involve close observation, which must be entirely faithful, of something that unfolds outside of the author's consciousness and exists objectively. The word "tale" here does not imply something tenuous from the point of view of its existence, as in "fairy tale"; it marks something that "happens in the world." It is therefore subject to the universe's most stringent and overpowering laws and as such is paradigmatic. It embodies an eternal law that supersedes all else.

*

Peretz's poem deals with poverty and disease, overtly and unambiguously setting out what it has to say about the sisters' spinsterhood, their poverty, and the disease of tuberculosis that is devouring the third sister's lungs. Notwithstanding an occasional trenchant statement, such as "All I sew is illness and blindness" (in the Yiddish: "Ikh ney mikh krank, ikh ney mir blind"), it does not endeavor to

---

8. Translator's note: Agnon's expression, *hakol 'asui yafeh be'ito*, derives from Eccles. 3:11, where it explicitly refers to the work of God: *et hakol 'asah yafeh be'ito*. Lilker (above, note 6) renders *yafeh be'ito* as "at the proper time," which arguably is closer to the sense of the Hebrew expression, both in the story and in the biblical context — as reflected, for example, in the rendering of the verse in the 1985 New JPS translation: "He brings everything to pass precisely at its time." However, *yafeh*, both in the biblical context and in rabbinic and modern Hebrew, can mean either "beautiful" or "nice, fitting, seemly, proper." In the concluding section, the author argues that Agnon uses this word to intimate something about the working of artistic beauty in human life. I have therefore rendered it in accord with the 1917 JPS translation of the verse: "He hath made everything beautiful in its time."

deliver a singular statement going beyond expressions of grievance that seek to unburden their load of sorrow and withdraw. These are emotive messages that do not seek to turn into any kind of discursive insight.

For all that, Agnon clearly did not disparage the poem or see in it only a source for the great symbol of the three sister seamstresses; he saw himself as obliged to the "tale" it embodied, as shown by his taking many details from it and treating them with great attentiveness: the impression created by the poem's rhythm and repetitions — as though the sisters work was never-ending (an element borrowed from Hood); the wedding of the wealthy man's daughter; the order of the sisters' speaking; the spitting of blood; and the sighs — all these find their place in Agnon's story. But Agnon locates these details within an entirely new framework, marvelously complex and quite different from the point of view of the mental and moral world embodied in it. He also eliminates from it all traces of the modern world (= the sewing machine) to create a world that is archaic and timeless. Above all, Agnon creates a powerful and constant tension between the folk symbol of the three sisters, with its all-encompassing dimensions, and the unique texture of the story, which, in every one of its details, declares itself not a folktale, or even the antithesis of a folktale. "Three Sisters" is what Linda Hutcheon has called a "narcissistic narrative,"[9] noting a long list of instruments (to be discussed below): the carefully molded shape of the speech; the subtle modulations of the tone and its emotional burden; and the multiple and fluctuating gaps between the "world" and the narrator. This is a classic example of what Robert Alter has called a "self-conscious genre."[10] Even so, as I shall ultimately argue, Agnon ultimately seeks not to eliminate the story's folk-mythic dimension entirely, but rather to create a literary situation that is stretched between the folk and the romantic modes.

"Three Sisters" commences with a series of general statements: five sentences that form the story's exposition, the sum of advance knowledge needed to construct the story in its entirety. The four sentences are laid out in two groups — two against two. The first two describe the sisters' toil, and the next two the "life" for which they toil. The first sentence functions almost as an axiom: It is the law that is imposed upon the whole story:

Three sisters lived in a bleak house sewing white vestments for others.

A longer look at this sentence reveals that its second half relates to the first in an extraordinarily sophisticated way: It presents it with a kind of opposition — between "a bleak house" and "white vestments." However, the opposition isn't a simple one — "white" is not the opposite of "bleak" — but rather is implied in

9. Linda Hutcheon, *Narcissistic Narrative: The Metafictional Paradox* (Waterloo, Ontario: Wildred Laurier University Press, 1980).
10. Robert Alter, *Partial Magic: The Novel as a Self-Conscious Genre* (Berkeley, CA: University of California Oress, 1975).

a cluster of oppositions that arises in its wake. "White vestments" are the vestments of marriage (linens, nightclothes and undergarments), highlighting the obvious fact that the sisters are unmarried, since they all live in the same house. Moreover, it seems that all the "others" are getting married, leaving the three spinster sisters to make their wedding vestments. Beyond that, the sentence's implied opposition emphasizes that the whole world, as it were, is engaged in getting married and is all drenched in light, while the three sisters are shut away in a house as bleak as a grave. This only emphasizes the additional implication of this opposition (not at all to be felt in Peretz's poem), that it is unmarried women who are tasked with preparing the bridal vestments. Upon this tension — the sexual tension between the spinster women and the acts of coupling embodied in the white vestments — will rise the Agnonic story.

The second sentence, long and complex as it is, puts together a very radical picture of time and labor. It is magnificently constructed as two time-worlds immersed one inside the other, each precisely ordered: The dimensions of external time expand — day, week and seasons of the year, "From dawn to dusk, from the end of Sabbath to Sabbath eve … neither in the season of sunshine nor in the season of the rains" — while the motion of labor is monotonous, painstaking and never-ending: "their fingers never strayed either from scissors or needle, and sighing never left their hearts." Moreover, external time, which passes during the time of laboring, is described such that its dimensions expand right up to the limits of the possible, whether from the perspective of bodily needs or from that of Jewish law, so that the time in which "life" happens, the time for which the sisters toil to make a living, shrinks to the point of disappearing altogether from the picture. Over against this, the labor is depicted as an almost involuntary motion, monotonous and mechanical, in which the scissors and needle acquire independence and move all by themselves, like the brooms in "The Sorcerer's Apprentice." The list that creates this monotonous impression is made up almost entirely of negations: "never … never … neither … nor" (Hebrew: *lo … lo … velo … velo … lo … velo*), and it is these negations that bind the picture of monotonous labor to the seasons of the year that surround it!

The complexity of this construction is worth a lingering glance. Not only does the accretion of negatives create a negative tension on its own, but the transition from the motion of needle and scissors to the seasons of the year, by means of the word "neither" (*lo*), creates an additional symbolic dimension: The three sisters are blind to the seasons of the year. "Season" (*'onah*[11]) in Hebrew signifies not only a period in the annual cycle, but also a woman's periods of fertility. It thus emerges that the sisters' toils cut them off entirely from the cycle of fertility, from the natural element of humanity. We may look as well at the list of chores,

---

11. Translator's note: This word does not actually appear in the story; instead, Agnon uses the word *yemot* — "days" or "time."

which, along with working with needle and scissors, includes the sighing that "never left their hearts." Even these cries of distress are objectified by being put on the list.

Over against the first two sentences come two brief, blunt statements. The story denies the sisters any satisfaction and almost any livelihood: no benefit (*berakhah*) and no bread. The picture is even more hyperbolic: not bread, but a "dry crust"; and they were not remunerated, but rather "found" it. Already here, it is keenly felt that the sentence structures and choice of words operate as they do in the poem: The complex structure of the long preceding sentence, the structures of its parts and its rhythm having created an overall impression — actually, a distortion — of the sisters' life, the short succeeding sentences now amplify and emphasize it all the more. The picture is bitter and stark: "life," the thing (*davar*) for which the sisters perform their Sisyphean labor, is tenuous, elusive and practically evaporates from their hands.

Here ends the exposition, without any special graphic indication (such as beginning a new paragraph) to indicate it, but only the disruption of all these general statements with the words "On one occasion." Everything stops, and instead of generalized, cyclical time and a distant, generalizing gaze come a focused gaze in a singular time. It is the lovely dress for the wealthy bride that stops the perpetual motion. Everything changes at once. The gaze captures the sisters at an entirely different moment from that with which the reader has been familiarized — at the moment of finishing a job. No longer are objects doing as they will, but the three sisters stop what they are doing and recall: "Upon completing their handiwork (*mel'akhtan*) they recalled their sorrows (*tsaratan*) for they had nothing on their flesh (*besaran*) but frail skin ('*oran*), and that too was growing old." It is enough to listen to this sentence, with its new rhythm, the quiet rhyming that enters it and its chilling conclusion, to sense all at once that the distancing irony of the opening has vanished, and a new attitude of intimate, empathetic listening has taken its place.

The relationship between the exposition and the "discourse" that begins with the words "On one occasion" will be clarified and develop into a complex frame, which is the story's center. I am using the word "discourse" (*davar*) as a calque of the Greek word *logos* (λόγος), as in the concept of a "prologue" (πρόλογος). The meaning of *logos* resembles the biblical meaning of *davar*: a statement or discourse that discloses a way or principle (as in *devar Elohim*, "the word of God"), and also an object, event or deed. The relationship of the exposition to the "discourse" in "Three Sisters" is that of a rule and the exception to the rule. The turning point that occurs with the words "on one occasion" eventually will utterly disrupt the rule described in the opening.

The sentence that concludes the first paragraph manifests the crucial role played in the story by intonation. Agnon deliberately sets a different tone against

Peretz's blunt onomatopoetic rhyming repetitions, which create a kind of dirge-like melody around the sisters' rememberings. The sentence's concluding phrase, "and that too was growing old," is crowned with a tone so full of feeling and so far from the intellectualizing world of the exposition that one cannot help but see what an extraordinarily important element in the continuous stream created up to now resides in the intonation. Not only the cadences varying from one sentence to the next, but also the shades of the vowel sounds and their rich associations with the meaning of the words.

And here, after the whole progression constructed up to now has taken up one long paragraph, the author devotes a whole paragraph to a single line: "Their hearts overflowed with grief" (*Nitmale liban tsa'ar*). This is an overtly poetic element: The use of the graphic shape of the text to enhance its power. These three Hebrew words stand suddenly on their own over against the opening, and in that instant the delicate drama to which Agnon is directing our gaze is revealed: Over against the phrase "and sighing never left their hearts" comes the statement "Their hearts overflowed with grief." What had been a kind of mechanical release, of the stuff of acquiescence and routine, is transformed and turned into a process of welling emotion, of feeling and comprehension. What had impressed us as small figures encased in puny, repetitively mechanical activities expand before our eyes into large, human figures, imbued with value. But the main thing is the change of focus: What had begun with ironic distance and continued with that pause to recall their sorrows now swells into a full stop of reflection upon their grief. This sentence, because of its location and the course that has led up to it, is not only about grief; it conveys its great and simple meaning with surprising power and bears it up to the reader in the fullness of its vulnerability and harshness. Suffice it to recall for another moment the sobbing lines of the poem to see the difference between the sentimental unburdening of feeling and its comprehension. It is here, on this spot, that Agnon turned his back upon the poem and utterly changed what it was about.

In the second part of the story, paralleling the structure of the poem, each sister has something to say — something else for each. From "three sisters" they turn into three individuals, each with something else to say. This is no mere technical transition from description to dialogue. In the flow of the movement generated up to now — in which we have seen a gradual closing in of gaze and perspective onto the sisters — this dialogue is keenly sensed as the climax of that closing in: What had been described from a great distance of space and time is now described from a proximity so intimate that it is immersed in the very circle of the sisters' voices, attuned to the distinctive character of each. Agnon, like Peretz in the poem, arranges their expressions by order of intensity, with the last of them coughing up blood: The first "sighs"; the second "sighs as well and sheds a tear"; while the third, "when she opens her mouth to speak, blood splatters out." But this order turns in the story into a complex, multi-toned structure that is unparalleled in the poem: Each one says two things, which may be defined, respectively, as intellectual utterances over against emotional ones — such as sighs. The emotional utterance escapes unmediated from the body; from the breast; from the heart.

The first sister begins with a sigh and then makes her statement, and her statement is the longest. The second sister begins by speaking, briefly, and then sighs, and she also weeps and sheds tears. As for the third sister, she prepares to speak, but what comes out of her mouth is not a sigh but a splattering of blood.

These are not mere pedantic details, but a tension-filled plot sequence. Each of the sisters presents a different character and a different set of relations between emotion, body and mind. The first sister prefaces her speech with a sigh as though to dispatch it, and her body, and she speaks at length. She is the wisest and most intellectual of the sisters. Her words may appear simple, but they are a very serious symbolic distillation of their situation: She stresses that they are women. She declares: "All our lives we sit and toil for others." What had seemed an arbitrary contrast at the beginning — "white vestments for others" — here becomes a pointed disparity between spinsters and married women. Only here, it seems, did their consciousness of themselves as women, and not just people in general, emerge. Instantly, the meaning of their "sorrows" is transformed. That they have "nothing on their flesh but frail skin" is now grasped not merely as material poverty, but as awareness of their solitary lives, of the absence of a companion or mate, the absence of affection, and above all — of active sexuality or motherhood. And she adds another thing that they lack: "a piece of cloth to make burial shrouds for ourselves." Here Agnon exploits the double meaning of the "white vestments" mentioned at the outset, a double meaning that has been dormant up to now. The two kinds of white vestments, notwithstanding the obvious contextual opposition of marriage and death, play a similar role: They are symbols of purity. They are symbols of value, holiness and ceremony, whether of marriage or of burial. The words of the first sister thus amount not to a complaint or a distraught cry, but to a statement of frank comprehension: We have missed out on the ceremony of espousal. We weren't there at the right time and season. And now the next ceremony that's in store for us — we're about to miss out on it as well. It is this that constructs the relationship between vestments of marriage and of death as one that is correct and inevitable.

The second sister not only speaks little, but what she says is that they ought to keep silent and refrain from speaking out. She expresses fear of speaking, as though death itself were bound up in it and in its protraction. But, on the other hand — she sighs and sobs, and here the story produces a new and fascinating regimen, governed by a kind of "principle of the conservation of energy" in the economy of emotions and the body: What is blocked in speech and thought builds up and bursts out by way of the body and its fluids. Here, for now, only in tears. The second sister is positioned between the first and the third not only as the median between them, but also as a turning point. The principle of silence, in which she puts her trust, turns out to "tempt Satan" in and of itself. Or the reverse: Her attempt to block the first sister's outburst missed its chance. Satan had already been tempted.

The third sister coughs blood: "Blood splattered out and stained the bride's garment." A bloodstain is the most inexcusable thing that could stain a bride's garment before her nuptials. From the garment and the blood erupts a terrifying picture: The sister, by way of the stain, has turned the garment into her own bridal garment. The splatter of blood, which appears in the poem as well, here entirely loses the melodramatic quality so characteristic of nineteenth-century stories of poverty and exploitation and of the great woman-centered operas of Verdi and Puccini, as it loses almost all connection with its pathological cause, the disease of tuberculosis. The blood-splatter in the story is above all emotional and psychosomatic. What is sprayed on the garment is the blood of virginity's loss, bursting out at the wrong time and from the wrong place — not from the womb, but from the mouth. This is no tear-jerker, but a grotesque picture, created not by the dimensions of the stain or even by its place on the garment, but by the full and unbroken course of the mouth being switched for sexuality and the womb. That switch is made fully manifest by the word "when" (*keivan*): "when she opened her mouth to speak blood splattered out." In other words — at the very moment that she opened her mouth to speak, blood spurted out of it. It turns out that the blood is her speech. It is the thing that is said in her speaking, because the body here has demanded the right to speak, and it has spoken in its own language. But the body's speech, after such long years of sorrow and suffering, is its demise. This is the conclusion of the process that had begun to manifest itself in the words of the second sister, but from here on it is clear that it had been building up for all of the sisters' lives: Their poverty is but a cover for their womanly loneliness and the terrible desperation born of a lack of sexual and emotional fulfillment. The "sorrow" that has grown up with them throughout their lives is a sorrow of body and soul that cannot be parted. The blood spurting from the mouth is the voice of womanliness, which should have burst forth in the blood of virginity's loss, when the girl reached maturity — when her "season" began. And by virtue of the "principle of the conservation of energy" at work here, the blockage of that blood, the blood of virginity, was a dam that broke and could not hold back the outburst, because what was blocked was no small thing, but a force of nature — motherhood.

Agnon makes use here of a rare Hebrew word, *tsinorah*, "a spurt." It appears in the Jerusalem Talmud (*Ḥagigah* 79:7), where it refers to a splash of spittle that pollutes the priestly garments. Even without knowing this, one is well aware here of the polluting force of that drop of blood, but discovering its source enhances and intensifies the exquisite precision of the word's use in this specific place. The choice of this precise word out of the range available in Hebrew offers a substantive lesson in Agnon's attentiveness to the Hebrew vocabulary. The story as a whole is written in very simple, straightforward language. Just once does Agnon use a rare form: *toshesh*, "frail"; and just once, a rare word: *tsinorah*. In both cases, one is keenly aware of how precise and pointed is his choice of words and, above all, how "self-aware" this narrative is of itself as a tale immersed in the timeless Hebrew textual ambit — an ambit quite distant from the linguistic world of folktales.

"Blood splattered out and stained the bride's garment": Clearly, the third sister has spoiled the garment. She has besmirched it with a stain that pollutes it and makes it unfit to play its role in the wedding ceremony of a rich bride. Worse: In so doing, she has taken the garment for herself — again, bearing in mind that the cloth for sewing was given to seamstresses by their clients. Thus, plainly, "it goes without saying he did not pay her." The wealthy man's hall (*teraqlin*), though unexceptional in the world of the story, hints, by the very use of the word *teraqlin*, at the well known metaphorical use of this word in *Pirkei avot* (*Ethics of the Fathers*) 4:16: "this world is like a vestibule before the world to come; prepare yourself in the vestibule, so that you may enter the banqueting-hall (*teraqlin*)." The word's very use instantly turns the story into a dark allegory about the course of a human life on the way to the world to come: The white cloth is one's life, given to the individual as a pledge — but they, by force of their suffering and the depth of their flaws, spoil it and sully its purity, ultimately facing their judgment wretched and ashamed, misunderstood and, above all, alone. What does the wealthy man know of spinsterhood and disease?

The story had pointed to an allegorical reading even before this, in its very use of the typological number of three sisters. But the number's allegorical nature is more open-ended and does not necessarily refer to the relationship between humans and the Creator; it refers, rather, to a more general human condition: the pattern of toil, suffering and misfortune that ultimately sully the value of the work and the suffering undergone for its sake. Herein lies the root of Agnon's interest in integrating the folkloric element of the motif of the three sisters into a new, "narcissistic" narrative framework, which creates so deep a disturbance in the narrative flow as to drive into it a dimension that utterly contradicts the conviction it purports to declare — that the sisters are victims of the evil that surrounds them. The verbal and symbolic associations that Agnon generates disclose another dimension — one in which the sisters appropriate the garment for themselves, turning it into a white vestment for a kind of ghostly wedding. This direction, which, in effect, justifies the wealthy man's refusal to pay them, comes from a place that contradicts any ethos bound up with the folktale.[12]

12. On elements that contradict the world of the folktale see B. Bettelheim, "Fairy Tales as Ways of Knowing," in M.M. Metzger and K. Mommsen (eds.), *Fairy Tales as Ways of*

The last paragraph is not an epilogue but a "metalogue": It is the narrator's statement regarding the story's open-ended allegorical conception. Without making it explicit, that statement nevertheless sharpens the reader's thinking about a "discourse" that is revealed to their eyes to a heightened degree of precision. The narrator sees in tears a symbol of mourning and weeping. His question discloses that he, too, is overwhelmed with questions and expectations upon reading the story: Fulfillment of the wish to go on weeping after the moment of catastrophe would signify that one might still live on and turn it into a dawning of insight, so that the moment of destruction would not be the final event in the fateful process — the critical event that spoiled everything. That, if it could have happened, would have been a thing "beautiful in its time." But "beautiful" is not the same as "lovely" (like the dress). "Beautiful" is a moment of value within its own negation; it is a human overcoming of the blow that makes an end of it. "Beautiful in its time" is perhaps more like the classic tragic endings, in which a "lesson" emerges from the suffering. But that is not the human situation in this place. Utter destruction is the final thing, so all-consuming that there can be no rising from it, and the person crumbles into their own flawed nature. The narrator does raise the heroic possibility that a person might rise up from the ruins and launder their life with tears, inasmuch as to say: Such a possibility exists in the world — but not in this story. This is a declaration by the narrator of faithfulness to, or rather dependence upon the existential, inexorable truth standing over against him. This is the story's truth claim. The narrator does not excuse himself from relating to the second, "beautiful" possibility from a higher perspective: Even if it were to exist, "there would still be no true consolation." The order of the world is flawed at the root, without any possibility of rectification, now or in the future.

We must still direct our gaze at the turning point in the sisters' lives, the crisis point in the story, the point at which "on one occasion they engaged in making a lovely wedding dress for a wealthy bride." Why is it precisely here that the repetitive continuum of their everyday routines, which continued for so many years, is broken? Why is it precisely here that the twinge of recollection occurred that suddenly brought them to look at themselves — at their "lives," their "sorrows" and their "grief"? Here, more than anywhere else in the story, we encounter Agnon's metaphysical world, by way of his construction of a disturbing causational gap. What "causes" the turning point? The reason for it lies in the "loveliness" of the dress. That loveliness has to do with the bride's wealth. With this dress, the sisters had to go beyond what was usually required for wedding ceremonies to create something especially appropriate. No mere white vestment was made here, but something exceptional that entered the realm of art. It was the need to create

Knowing: Essays on Märchen in Psychology, Society and Literature (German Studies in America, 41), (Bern: Peter Lang, 1981), 1–24.

beauty that elicited a different process, at the end of which the three sisters were faced with a work of art crafted by their own hands. The dress, as a thing of beauty, ceased to be a mere vestment and commenced being a symbol imbued with meaning. Moreover, the value of beauty derives from the force of the eros that passes into objects and words. The three sisters suddenly were exposed to the meaning of their deeds and to the erotic power passing into the dress and back to them like light reflected from a mirror. It was the sisters' "moment of art" that disrupted their life routines and faced them with their own death.

***

The "beautiful" is conditioned by material wealth. It has to do with abundance and surfeit. It can never have a place in the realm of poverty and need. The "beautiful" goes beyond the realm of labor and its reimbursement. It wrings the essence of their lives out of the seamstresses. That is the reason for the differentiation between the "lovely" in this section and the "beautiful" at the story's conclusion — the beauty draped in weeping. That is to say, in this story Agnon differentiated between two kinds of beauty. For the one, the beauty of a work of art, he uses the word *na'eh* ("lovely"), drawn from the language of the rabbinic texts; for the other, the beauty manifested in the sorrow of human existence, he uses the more elevated biblical word *yafeh* (beautiful). Here the story utterly contradicts the world of the poem. It is not poverty, exploitation and disease that have ravaged the lives of the poor seamstresses, but the advent of an external force that departs from any socio-historical comprehension. The "beautiful" is absolute cruelty. It may be conditioned by material wealth, but material wealth cannot explain it, and neither can the physical powers that generate it in the lives of its creators. Through this "beauty" the entire story is refracted.

The structure of "Three Sisters" rests upon the dialogue between the exposition and the "discourse." The nuanced reiteration of several of the elements mentioned in it — like the masculine "others" (*aherim*) in the first paragraph, which become feminine "others" (*aherot*) in the third, and the "sighing [that] never left their hearts" reflected in their "hearts overflowing with grief"; and the sense of a sharp and profound change that transpires with the onset of the "discourse" — all these construct a very organic framework, spare and tightly compact. That framework is structured by the tension between the "lovely" and the "beautiful." The "lovely" depends upon devastation. The "beautiful" remains outside of reality. This ideational agenda is clearly no concern for a folktale. What this story is concerned with is the touching of "high" art upon human life.

A final comment regarding the dedication: "To B. Katznelson, blessings." Berl Katznelson was a close friend of Agnon's and one of the few Zionist leaders whom Agnon respected and even admired. He saw him as one of the "four smiths":[13]

13. Cf. Zechariah 2:3.

When I look at the country and see how the *Yishuv* has arisen from clutches of emigrants and bands of dreamers, I see four smiths, who, it seems to me, have endowed it with shape and form, [...] These four men in whom the Almighty, I believe, vested the power to give shape to the *Yishuv* were Y.H. Brenner, Arthur Ruppin, our great rabbi R. Abraham Isaac Kook of blessed memory and Berl Katznelson.[14]

To define the force of Katznelson's leadership, Agnon quotes a laborer who belonged to the Second Aliyah:[15]

We would get up and do our plowing,[16] and each of us was sunk in his own troubles and didn't see himself as doing anything beyond toiling for his living. One day Berl Katznelson came and started talking with us, and he gave us a breath of life. We started to feel like this work that we were doing out of routine, for lack of choice, for the sake of getting by, was a service not to be excelled.

The dedication of "Three Sisters" to Berl Katznelson is surely a gift of love. However, it also seems to imply a solemn, somber statement addressed against Katznelson's optimistic-messianic attitude regarding the rationale of Zionist labor and the rectification it was meant to embody — a statement in the form of an allegory: The three penurious, unmarried sisters, laboring in toil and trouble, were the Jewish people in exile. The lovely garment that seems to herald some kind of way out, by virtue of the man of wealth — the Holy One, Blessed be He — or at least to speak to them of marriage, beauty and restoration, is the Zionist revolution, with its concept of labor as a way to remedy the people's situation and its fate. But the three sisters (the people) have languished for so long in the realms of decline and disease that the rectification, coming so late, will now lead only to destruction and ruin, and there is no healing in it — as in the words of the proverb: "Hope deferred sickens the heart" (Prov. 13:12). There is a limit to hope, beyond which comes the too late, overturning the restoration.

The folk element in "Three Sisters" imbues the story with a mythic dimension. The story's strange effect flows precisely from the irresolvable tension between its modernist progression, leading to the utter subversion of the balance of good and evil in it, and the naïve quality of the symbolism that underlies it. Agnon sought in this story to galvanize the full power of its folk element and even to "update" it, in sharp contrast to the place of the "folk" element in the ending of "Abandoned Wives," in which it is in effect identical with the loss of all

---

14. S.Y. Agnon, *Me'atsmi el 'atsmi*, 148. The translation of this sentence is taken from Orr Scharf, "The Double-Edged Sword of Criticism: Berl Katznelson and the Partition of Palestine," *Havruta* (Winter 2012), 68.
15. The wave of immigrants that arrived in Erets Yisra'el between 1904 and 1914, mainly from eastern Europe.
16. The word for plowing, *ḥoresh*, is homonymous with *ḥarash*, smith.

meaning. There, it is the depth of oblivion, into which the voice of the whole story vanishes. The "folk" element stands on both sides of the story's unfolding: It is its source and also its loss to oblivion.

Professor ARIEL HIRSCHFELD, a researcher and cultural critic, is a professor of Hebrew literature at the Hebrew University of Jerusalem, where he studied musicology and Hebrew literature, and serves on the faculty of the Mandel School for Educational Leadership. Among his Hebrew books are: *Aten yod'ot: Siaḥ ha'ahavah ba'operah shel Mozart*, 1994; *Reshimot 'al maqom*, 2000; *El aḥron ha'eilim: 'al mizrekot Roma*, 2003; *Rishumim shel hitgalut*, 2006; *Kinnor 'arukh: leshon haregesh beshirat Ḥ N. Bialik, 2011; Liqro et Agnon*, 2011; and with Dan Miron, *Hakokahvim lor rimu: Kri'ah meḥadash*, 2019.

18 *Agnon's* Yamim nora'im: *Then and Now*

James S. Diamond

It is at this writing 75 years since S.Y. Agnon's classic anthology of High Holy Day material and lore, *Yamim nora'im* (in English as *Days of Awe*), was first published.[1] This moment provides a good opportunity to raise sets of questions. The first should be asked of any work that has attained the status of a classic: is it as widely read today as its reputation warrants? Is *Yamim nora'im* as valuable and as potent a resource for 21st century Jews as it was for those in earlier generations? Is it still a standard work for rabbis or laypersons who want to prepare for Rosh Hashanah and Yom Kippur and who seek to enhance their experience and observance of those days? The second question concerns the origin and objective of the work. How did Agnon come to write it? Why did he write it? And what did he hope to accomplish by it? The two sets of questions are related, for in answering the second, we can hopefully make some headway with the first.

To some extent, to ask about the status and stature of *Yamim nora'im* in our time is a leading question. A strong case can be made that the principle of *dor dor vedorshav* (each generation requires its own interpreter) applies here. The cultural horizon under which Jews today live - not all Jews by any means, but many or even most Jews — and within which they read and interpret the texts and traditions they have inherited, is quite different from the pre-World War II, pre-Holocaust, pre-State of Israel, pre-postmodern, pre-cybernetic, pre-globalized horizon under which *Yamim nora'im* first appeared. In which case it would be quite understandable that it could not address the spiritual condition of those 21st century Jews who want to make Rosh Hashanah and Yom Kippur less an autumnal Jewish Gathering of the Clans and more an experience of three, or ten, days that are religiously meaningful.

[JAMES S. DIAMOND *z"l* was the director of Princeton University's Center for Jewish Life and a scholar of Hebrew literature. Jim was a collaborator with and dear friend of Alan Mintz *z"l*, together producing the annotated English editions of Agnon's *The Parable and Its Lesson* (Stanford, 2014) and, with Jeffrey Saks, *A City in Its Fullness* (Toby Press, 2016). Unfortunately, these books were only published after Jim's tragic death during Passover 2013; both volumes are dedicated to his memory. This essay was drafted a few months before the accident which claimed his life and we are grateful to Jim's widow, Judy Diamond, for permission to present it here and to Saks who helped prepare it for publication. *–Eds.*]
1. Originally published by Schocken in Germany in 1937. The English version, *Days of Awe*, trans. Maurice T. Galpert (New York: Schocken Books, 1948), omits some material in the original.

Building a City: Writings on Agnon's Buczacz in Memory of Alan Mintz (2022): 293–306
DOI: 10.2979/BuildingaCityWriting.o.o.19

On the other hand, the midrashim, parables, Hasidic vignettes, rituals, customs and teachings that Agnon painstakingly anthologized in *Yamim nora'im* are not costume jewelry or, as Kafka complained, intriguing souvenirs that belonged to our grandparents or great grandparents but spiritual assets created by significant Jewish minds and souls in the past and preserved in the vault of cultural and national memory. That, at least, is how Agnon perceived them, but with one other important assumption in mind: that these are liquid assets, available and usable by any Jew willing to claim and be enriched by them.

Although some may think so, it is not a foregone conclusion that these two perspectives are antithetical and mutually exclusive. It may not be a case of "either/or" but of "both/and." The disconnect between the present and the past is real and profound. And yet, at the same time, the received texts of our tradition and the values enshrined in them are no less available to us today than they were to our forebears, even as we do not — cannot — read them as they did and even as we appropriate them differently. I believe Agnon understood all this, understood it as well as anyone, and it is this realization that I think underwrites the whole laborious project he undertook of compiling *Yamim nora'im*.

*

Why did he undertake it? What was it that impelled Agnon in the mid-1930s to forego more than two years of literary creativity and dedicate his time, often for as much as 16 hours a day, to research, review and evaluate, thousands of texts from the Bible, Talmud, midrash, Zohar and other mystical, Hasidic and halachic lore, and then select and arrange them into an intelligible series and a coherent whole? It was a decision for which he was criticized by some literary critics, including his friend and colleague Dov Sadan. Sadan had heaped praise on Agnon's stunning novel of 1935 *Sippur pashut* (*A Simple Story*) and now, when *Yamim nora'im* was about to appear, he wrote to him complaining that he longed for more such wonders from Agnon's literary imagination but instead "you give me an anthology!"[2] Such rebuke was not something Agnon heard only from others. He had already heard it within himself. A year earlier, when he was already hard at work on *Yamim nora'im*, he wrote to Sadan that the manuscript had grown to about 1,000 pages and he was struggling to reduce it by half.

> But still my publisher [Schocken] is not satisfied, and I shall be unhappy if I have to cut another 50 pages. In the meantime I am working like a slave. The

2. Dov Sadan, letter to Agnon of Oct. 10, 1937 in *Missod ḥakhamim*, [Letters and correspondence between Agnon and Y. H. Brenner, Ḥ. N. Bialik, F. Lachover, B. Katznelson and Dov Sadan, 1909–1970 (Jerusalem & Tel Aviv: Schocken, 2002), 268. See also Dan Laor, *Ḥayyei Agnon* [S.Y. Agnon: A Biography] (Jerusalem & Tel Aviv, Schocken, 1998), 286–288.

project in itself "interests" me, so what can I do? In the meantime the desire to write a new story gnaws at me literally every day.[3]

Why did the project "interest" him (and why the quotation marks)? Several reasons can be adduced to answer this question. For one thing, anthologies and anthologizing were very much on the agenda of Hebrew writers at the end of the 19th century and in the early years of the 20th when the ideology of Ahad Ha'am's cultural Zionism was in the ascendancy and the project of *kinnus* [ingathering; anthologizing] was a major means of implementing it. *Kinnus* was

> the name that Bialik gave to the enterprise of "ingathering" important works of the Jewish past that appeared destined to be forgotten in the modern world. They were to be preserved and to reenter the bloodstream of modern Jewish culture by collecting them into well-structured and properly conceived anthologies.[4]

Bialik and Ravnitsky's *Sefer Ha'aggadah* and Berdichewski's parallel work *Mimeqor Yisra'el* are only the most well-known and monumental products of the anthologizing enterprise, which was by no means restricted to aggadic material. Peretz and others took folktales from the Yiddish tradition and retold them in a more modernist narrative style.

Agnon too was an eager and important participant in the project. Laor tells us that already in the first years of his fruitful stay in Germany (1912–1924) he had created three anthologies in German: a collection of folktales of Polish Jewry, and anthologies on Passover and Chanukah.[5] These were done during the time Agnon was working for the Jüdischer Verlag, the Jewish publishing house founded by Martin Buber and others with the purpose of bringing acculturated German Jews closer to their Jewish heritage. Another scion of German Jewry who was also deeply interested in using his publishing house to show German Jewry the beauty and the authenticity of Jewish life in the lands that lay to the east, and, along with this, to mediate to them the classic texts of Judaism and Jewish tradition, was Shlomo Zalman Schocken. In 1915 he became Agnon's patron. In Agnon Schocken knew he had a writer whose encyclopedic knowledge of almost all sources and genres of Hebrew literature equipped him superbly not only to write imaginative literature but also to advance the anthological project. Laor

---

3. Letter to Sadan of September 1936. *Missod ḥaḥamim,* 253.

4. Shahar Pinsker, *Literary Passports: The Making of Modernist Hebrew Fiction in Europe* (Stanford, CA, Stanford University Press, 2011), 279.

5. Laor, *Ḥayyei Agnon,* 280. Laor lists these respectively as: *Das Buch von den Polnischen Juden,* with Ahron Eliasberg, 1916; *Chad Gadja: ein Pessachbuch,* 1914, and *Moaus zur: Chanukkahbuch,* 1918. The latter two were done with Hugo Hermann; see Laor, 710. A collection on Purim was planned but did not materialize. The stories of Polish Jewry came out in Hebrew under the title *Polin: Sippurei aggadot* in 1925 just after Agnon returned to Palestine. It was later included in the volume *Eilu ve'eilu* of his collected works.

relates that "on Shocken's initiative, Agnon undertook, already in 1916, to prepare a comprehensive anthology on Jewish culture — the provisional title was 'On the Jew' — but for some reason he never carried out this commitment."[6]

Agnon's time in Germany also saw the germination of one of his most ambitious anthological initiatives: the idea of developing a definitive multi-volume collection of the stories and teachings of Hasidism. This was something he evidently conceived on his own, without prompting from his patron or anyone else, but one in which he sought the collaborative efforts of Martin Buber. Agnon knew and understood Buber's engagement with Hasidism, and enlisting perhaps the major spiritual figure of German Jewry in the project underscored its promise and significance. The two of them set to work with high hopes, but it never came to fruition. The manuscript of one volume was completed, mostly by Agnon, but, tragically, was lost, along with the rest of his library and papers, in the fire that engulfed Agnon's house in Bad Homburg in 1924, the event that precipitated his return to Palestine.[7]

But *Yamim nora'im* was not conceived solely out of the anthological impulse. By the mid-1930s, when Agnon started to work on it, its subject, or more precisely its content, had for a long time been a key topos in modern Hebrew literature, as described by Shachar Pinsker:

> [I]n the last two decades of the nineteenth century [Yom Kippur] appeared in stories such as David Frishman's *"Beyom hakippurim"* [On the Day of Atonement, 1880–1881], Ben Avigdor's *"Elyakim hameshuga'"* [Mad Elyakim, 1889], Mordecai Ze'ev Feierberg's novella *Le'an* [Whither, 1899], and Micha Yosef Berdichewski's story *"Me'ever lanahar"* [Beyond the River, 1899.]
>
> In spite of some differences in the ways the theme functions in all these texts, it is safe to say that Yom Kippur was employed in all of them as a background for recording the collapse of traditional Jewish institutions and for describing the tensions between fathers and sons, between tradition and the allure of modernity. These elements are the building blocks of the narrative of apostasy and loss of faith that is so common in the literature of the period.[8]

Pinsker goes on to show how the literary representation of Yom Kippur was modified in the 20th century in the fiction of such ostensibly secular writers as Brenner, Schofman and Gnessin. Yom Kippur figures in their works not so much as a marker for the alienation of their protagonists from the tradition but as a moment for a Joycean epiphany that enables them to reconfigure their inner world and reconstitute it into something more coherent and even joyful.

6. Dan Laor, "Agnon and Buber: The Story of a Friendship, or: The Rise and Fall of the 'Corpus Hasidicum' " in Paul Mendes-Flohr, ed., *Martin Buber: A Contemporary Perspective* (Syracuse & Jerusalem: Syracuse University Press & The Israel Academy of Sciences and Humanities, 2002), 62.
7. The full story of this ill-starred project is in Laor's essay. We learn there that years later both Buber and Agnon each succeeded in publishing respective anthologies of Hasidic lore: Buber's *Or haganuz* (1947) and Agnon's *Sippurei haBesht*, which was published posthumously in 1986 and contained material that Agnon had collected, some of which had appeared in his lifetime.
8. Pinsker, *Literary Passports*, 337.

Thus it was that in 1934, when Moritz (Moshe) Spitzer, who was then editor-in-chief of Schocken Verlag, floated to him the idea of doing an anthology on what we call in America the High Holy Days, Agnon responded positively and unhesitatingly.[9] He did so not only or merely for the historical reasons I have just noted, reasons that he, as a Hebrew literary artist, knew as well as any of his colleagues. He did so for reasons that were deeply personal and which take us to the wellspring of his literary imagination and from which much, if not all, of his astonishing and monumental corpus flows. A look into the origins and objectives of *Yamim nora'im* will help us understand not only why Agnon created it but will also point the way to answering the larger questions I posed at the outset.

*

During the time he was working on *Yamim nora'im* in the mid-1930s, Agnon, contrary to his remonstration that the project was keeping his creative muse at bay, was writing two significant works of fiction that are almost contemporaneous with the anthology: the story "Pi shenayim" ("Twofold") and the novel *Oreaḥ natah lalun* (*A Guest for the Night*). Both appeared in 1939, and both deal substantively with Yom Kippur. They deal with Yom Kippur by problematizing the day both as idea and as experience. Both story and novel turn on the notion that Yom Kippur is a touchstone of Jewish sensibility and that it does not come easily to many modern Jews. Both story and novel are written in the full awareness of how Yom Kippur functioned in the narratives of Feierberg, Berdichewski, Schofman and Gnessin. When we look at them together we get an idea of what Agnon intended to achieve with *Yamim nora'im*.

Yom Kippur takes up the first five chapters of the novel. The unnamed narrator, who had years earlier emigrated to Jerusalem, arrives back in his hometown of Shibush on a visit late in the afternoon on the eve of Yom Kippur. The town constitutes a microcosm of the reality that will be depicted in the 75 chapters that follow, and the impaired spiritual condition of its inhabitants serves to define that reality. A young man, Daniel Bach, accompanies the narrator to his hotel and when the two of them arrive there, Bach wishes him a full atonement.

> I took his hand and said to him, "The same to you, sir." Bach smiled and said, "If you mean me, it's a wasted greeting, for I don't believe the Day of Atonement has any power to make things better or make them worse. ... I'm a skeptic. ... I don't believe the Almighty cares about the welfare of His creatures. But why should I be clever with you at dusk on the eve of the Holy Day? I wish you a full atonement.[10]

---

9. Laor, *Ḥayyei Agnon*, 280f. Spitzer was reprising the project of creating anthologies for all the Jewish holidays that Agnon had done for the Jüdischer Verlag in Germany in 1914–15.
10. *A Guest for the Night*, trans. Misha Louvish (New York: Schocken Books, 1968), 4.

This exchange prepares us for what the narrator will soon encounter. At the hotel he finds that the fast is about to begin and it is too late to eat anything, much less a full pre-fast meal. So he takes his maḥzor and his tallit and goes to the Great Synagogue.

> In my childhood I thought that there was no bigger building in the world than the Great Synagogue, but now its area had dwindled and its height shrunk, for to eyes that have seen temples and mansions the synagogue appears even smaller than it is.
>
> There was not a man I knew in the synagogue. Most of the worshippers were recent arrivals ... . The radiance that is wont to shine on the heads of the sacred congregation on the Eve of Atonement did not shine . . . and their prayer shawls shed no light. In the past, when everyone would come to pray and each would bring a candle, in addition to those that burned in the candelabra, the synagogue was brightly lit, but now that the candelabra had been plundered in the war and not all came to pray, the candles were few and the light was scanty. In the past, when the prayer shawls were adorned with collars of silver, the light used to gleam from them upon the heads of the worshippers, but now that the adornments had been carried off the light was diminished. The cantor did not draw out the prayers — or perhaps he did, but that was my first prayer in my home town, and it was Atonement Eve, when the whole world stands in prayer, so I wanted to draw out the prayers even more and it seemed to me as if the cantor were cutting them shorter all the time. ...
>
> After the service they did not recite psalms, nor did they chant the Song of Unity or the Song of Glory, but locked the synagogue and went home.[11]

This experience of a less than satisfying Yom Kippur is reprised in the story "Pi shenayim," but in a more compressed way. When it originally appeared in the Hebrew literary periodical *Moznayim* it carried a subtitle: "Pi shenayim o meḥussar yom" ["Twofold: or The Day That Was Missed."][12] The subtitle encapsulates the whole story. The narrator here is situated in Jerusalem on Yom Kippur eve just as darkness is falling, and, as in the opening of the novel, he is late. In the story's opening sentence he declares: "At that hour I had not prepared myself for Yom Kippur." The consequences of his failure constitute the substance of the story. The narrator attends the Kol Nidrei service in his local shul and finds it insipid. He returns the next morning late and finds the service already underway but the seats empty. After sitting there for a short time he is uninspired and leaves. Outside he is put off by people standing and socializing. He falls into wistful reveries about past Yom Kippurs that were more meaningful, one from his boyhood when he was about seven or eight, and one from when he was older and living in

11. Ibid. 5.
12. *Moznayim* IX:5 (1939). In the collected works of Agnon the story is in the volume entitled *Samukh venir'eh*, 128–142.

a German city. These memories are particularly powerful as he recalls the sights, sounds and smells of the brilliantly illuminated synagogue of his boyhood:

> Countless large candles, one for each worshipper, were standing and burning, and the smell of wax and honey filled the synagogue and mixed with the smell of the straw covering the floor, and a new light sparkles from the candles. Wrapped in his tallit, father stands among the other worshippers, with a large, radiant tallit-crown of silver over his head. Frightened and flustered I stood gazing at father, and the doubly radiant light shining from his forehead.
>
> How I loved the night of Yom Kippur! The Gates of Heaven are open and God Himself, as it were, bows down to hear the prayers of Israel. He needn't bow, since He knows the heart of every man, but out of affection for the Jewish people, He bows down, like a father who inclines his ear to his little boy.[13]

But soon these reveries evaporate and the narrator finds himself again in the tawdry present, as he stands outside the synagogue he has left. As the day passes, he slowly musters up his strength to go back inside. But then the greenish Dome of the Rock[14] on the Temple Mount gleams in the distance, and this impels him to want to go the Western Wall for the remaining prayers. But first he must recover his tallit from the neighborhood synagogue where he had left it earlier that day. When he cannot do so — someone else seems to be sitting in his place and wearing it — he goes home, where he has two tallitot. But then he cannot decide which one to take, and as the day wanes, he decides he will go back to the neighborhood synagogue for the concluding services. Before he can set out he hears the Shofar and he realizes it's too late and the sacred day is over. Having not really had a fulfilling Yom Kippur, he takes upon himself the pious custom of observing a second day of Yom Kippur. He makes every effort to do this but during the day another problem arises. That year Yom Kippur fell on a Thursday, and so now it is Friday and he begins to think about putting up his Sukkah, in accordance with the custom of doing so immediately after Yom Kippur. But time rushes on and very soon Shabbat comes, and his break-the-fast meal becomes his Shabbat dinner. The story concludes with a reflection he has years later: though he has become more deliberate about his observance of Yom Kippur and now gets to shul early and sometimes stays there from sunset to sunset, "And yet, I am still restless because of the missing Yom Kippur which passed me by empty-handed."[15]

13. The translation by Jeffrey Saks appears as "Twofold" in S.Y. Agnon, *The Outcast & Other Tales* (New Milford, CT: Toby Press, 2017), 149–62.
14. In the 1930s the Dome was of copper, which turns green with oxidization. The gold leaf cover we see today overlies anodized aluminum and was added in 1994, a gift from King Hussein of Jordan to restore the original gold that was melted down in the middle ages to repay some caliph's debt.
15. See also the story "Tallit aheret" [Another Tallit, 1951] which is cut from the same fabulative cloth as "Pi shenayim." A translation by Jules Harlow appears as "Another Tallit" in *The Outcast*, 187–9.

What has happened here? Why did the narrator fail to have a fulfilling Yom Kippur? It is not for lack of knowledge; he knows what the day is about and what he must do on it. When he decides to observe a second day he consults the Shulḥan Arukh for the exact procedure. There is, furthermore, no indication that he has the same skeptical metaphysical perspective as that expressed by Daniel Bach in the novel; he is rather predisposed to having a good Yom Kippur experience.

*

So here we have two texts roughly contemporaneous with *Yamim nora'im* and in both of them Yom Kippur is problematical. To suggest a single or main reason why this is so would diminish the thick complex of issues that Agnon throws up in them. I see at least three interrelated issues that form the ideational substratum on which *Yamim nora'im* rests: time, solitude, and childhood.

We understand this more fully when we situate the three contemporaneous works in a larger context. From 1932–1945 Agnon wrote a score of stories that comprise the cycle *Sefer hama'asim* [The Book of Deeds]. "Pi shenayim" is part of that cycle. In most of these stories the narrators are variations of the same persona: an addled and hapless man who simply cannot get it together. The title "The Book of Deeds," as Baruch Hochman noted over 40 years ago

> is scathingly ironic. "Deeds" [*ma'asim*] suggests positive religious as well as profane action, and any kind of action seems virtually impossible here — most of all, acts of real piety … . The tales vary widely in detail, but they characteristically involve missions accomplished late, badly, or not at all. Many of the stories involve lapses in ritual observance — especially that connected with the Day of Atonement and the ritual cleansing of guilt.[16]

That is true enough, but there is more to it. The core issue in the stories of the *Sefer hama'asim* cycle, as Ariel Hirschfeld notes, is time — the press of time in general, and in some stories the more particular Jewish challenge to take leave of secular time so as to be ready to enter sacred time.[17] The narrators in almost all these stories are struggling either to complete a task before a deadline or to make the transition into sacred time and the observances it entails in the face of the unceasing and inexorable flow of minutes and hours.[18] These are difficult transitions, to be sure, for merely to be alive in this world is to live in time and its relentless impingements, and to be a Jew in this world requires an awareness that sacred time is qualitatively different from secular time; leaving the latter and

---

16. Baruch Hochman, *The Fiction of S.Y. Agnon* (Ithaca & London: Cornell University Press, 1970), 164.
17. Ariel Hirschfeld, *Liqro et Agnon* [Reading Agnon] (Tel Aviv: Aḥuzat Bayit Publishing House, 2011), 202.
18. See, e.g., the stories "Leveit Abba" [To Father's House], "Hanerot" [The Candles], "Habayit" [The Home].

entering the former involves entering into a different mode of being. It is not hard to see why these narrators are always late and why they often open their narration by admitting that they have not used time properly so as to prepare themselves for the deadlines they have either set or that the clock imposes on them. The opening of the celebrated story "Pat Sheleimah" [A Whole Loaf, 1933] is paradigmatic of the works of the period:

> I had not tasted anything all day long. I had made no preparations on Sabbath eve, so I had nothing to eat on the Sabbath. At that time I was on my own. My wife and children were abroad, and I had remained all by myself at home; the bother of attending to my food fell upon myself.[19]

We see in this opening a second feature of the existential situation of the narrators of *Oreaḥ natah lalun*, "Pi shenayim," and all the stories of that period: they all live in apparent solitude. The Guest in *Oreaḥ natah lalun* spends his year back in his much diminished hometown of Shibush as what Hochman calls an *isolado*. Though he meets and goes among people, with many of whom he establishes a relationship, he is essentially detached from them and from family. He is not at home in his permanent dwelling; he is on his own, a guest in a hotel, a temporary lodging. In Agnon's world "the free individual must define himself in solitude."[20] Likewise, the narrator of "Pi shenayim," goes through Yom Kippur utterly alone. While he does ask his two children to shine his shoes — he wears them even though he knows of the Yom Kippur prohibition of leather shoes — they do not seem to accompany him to the services.

No wonder that in the lonely aridity of the Yom Kippurs of the present the respective narrators are overtaken by memories of those of the past, when the power of the day was fully known to them. The memories go back to childhood but they are more, much more, than wistful reveries or a self-indulgent submission to a pleasant nostalgia. They are memories of precisely what the narrators of the two texts in question are *not* having: a real or authentic religious experience. The memories are not so much ideational as sensate: of radiant light coming from the candles and refracted off the silver neckbands of the worshippers' tallitot, and of the particular smell of the honey wax candles and the straw on the floor. What Shachar Pinsker writes of the depiction of Yom Kippur in Gnessin's novella *Beterem* [Beforehand, 1908] is surely operating in Agnon's:

> It is clear that Uriel's [the protagonist in *Beterem*] religious experience might be concealed and suppressed at the back of his consciousness, but there are some occasions when it comes to the fore. The numinous can be stimulated in different ways — by sensory sights, sounds, and smells

---

19. "A Whole Loaf" in S.Y. Agnon, *A Book that Was Lost and Other Stories*, ed. Alan Mintz and Anne Golomb Hoffman (New Milford, CT: Toby Press, 2008), 373.
20. Hochman, *The Fiction of S.Y. Agnon*, 161.

and by memory and introspection. In some cases, the religious experience or the sense of the numinous is attached to specific religious texts and formulations (Jewish and non-Jewish) that are activated and brought to new life within the act of narrative. In other cases it is attached to specific people and moments in time. Sometimes it affects the current life of the protagonist, and in other cases it can appear and disappear without any evident consequences. Most of all ... it seems to strike the protagonist especially in moments of great despair and calamity.[21]

This is the fictional milieu in which *Yamim nora'im* was written and against which it should be read. These are the issues I believe it was intended to address. It is true that the first rule of reading fiction is to separate the author from the narrators he or she creates. The protagonist in all the stories noted here is assuredly not Agnon. But there is no minimum distance an author must maintain from his characters, and sometimes it can be very close. In Agnon's case it is very close indeed. Laor's exquisitely detailed biography of Agnon tells about as much as can be known of his doings in the world of people and events. The narrators of these stories offer important clues about the author's inner world.

*

Most anthologists usually introduce their collections with prefatory remarks about the anthology — the material or items that were collected, the criteria by which they were selected, and the principles or order by which they were arranged. More often than not, there is also a personal note in which the anthologist explains his relationship to the material and why he compiled that particular anthology. Agnon's short preface to *Yamim nora'im* delivers on the former; it is conspicuously lacking in the latter. It begins with these words:

> For the benefit of my brethren and friends who seek to know about Rosh Hashanah and Yom Kippur and the days in between, I have collected some items from the Torah, the Prophets, and the Writings, from the Babylonian and Jerusalem Talmuds, from halachic and aggadic Midrash, and from the Zohar and other books written by the early and later Rabbis, of blessed memory; and I have arranged this material in three sections, according to the order of the days, each section and its issues.

Agnon then proceeds to explain his anthological methods and principles. It is all succinct and quite without affect. Other than the opening sentence, the preface to the first edition offers no indication of what impelled him to do the collection or what he personally hoped to accomplish by it. Dan Laor reports that the preface was more elaborate but it was condensed by a directive from Schocken, who wanted the introductory matter to be concise.[22]

21. Pinsker, *Literary Passports*, 353f.
22. Laor, 284f. Additionally he notes that when Agnon acknowledges the individuals who inspired and assisted him in his anthological endeavor, the name of Moritz Spitzer is not mentioned.

This changed in 1946 when *Yamim nora'im* came out in a third edition (a second was published in 1939) This edition was to be done by the New York branch of the Schocken operation and for it, Laor tells us, "Agnon arrogated to himself the right to publish a special introduction ... ."[23] That introduction supplies the missing personal detail that the original preface lacked and in the third edition it appears after that preface as a separate text under the title "Zikaron basefer." The words are from Exodus 17:14, which Robert Alter translates as "a remembrance in a record." In our parlance the title is best understood as a personal memory. I cite here the key portion of the text of the introduction because, as Barukh Kurzweil first noticed,[24] it furnishes the experiential background out of which *Yamim nora'im* sprang and also serves to bring all the texts mentioned here into their proper relation, as the reader will clearly see:

> The heavens were crystalline and the earth was at peace. All the streets were empty. A fresh wind wafted through the world. And there I am, a child of four, all dressed up in holiday clothes, taken by someone from my family to the synagogue, where I stand beside my father and my grandfather. The synagogue is full. The men are all in white, wrapped in prayer shawls, with their silver neckbands enfolding their heads, and books in their hands. A myriad of candles all planted in long rows of sandboxes give out a wondrous light and a lovely fragrance. And an old man stands bent before the podium. His prayer shawl drapes the whole top half of his body, and sweet and pleasant sounds issue from inside it. I stand by the window of the synagogue shivering in amazement at the lovely sounds and the gleaming silver neckbands and the wondrous light and the sweet smell of honey that the wax candles give off. It seemed to me then that the ground that I walked on and the streets that I walked through, indeed the whole world, were nothing but the entry way into this building. I was not yet able to conceptualize ideas and so the notion of the beauty of holiness was not known to me. But I had no doubt whatsoever that at that hour I felt the holiness of the place and the holiness of the day and the holiness of the people standing in the house of God in prayer and in song. And even though until that hour I had never seen anything like this, it did not occur to me that it could stop. And so there I stood looking around at the synagogue and at the people standing in it, and I could not differentiate between one person and another, for all of them and the whole building together with them appeared to me as one single organism. A deep joy suffused me and I was engulfed by a great love for that place and those people and those melodies. Gradually the melodies subsided, then they echoed faintly, and soon they stopped. My spirit constricted within me and suddenly I let out a great cry. My father and my grandfather were alarmed and everyone tried to calm me

23. Laor, 381.

24. In *Ḥavayat yom hakippurim bekhirvei 'Agnon* [The Yom Kippur Experience in the Writings of Agnon], *Ha'aretz*, September 28, 1958. Collected in his *Massot 'al sippurei Shai 'Agnon* [Essays on the Stories of Agnon] (Jerusalem & Tel Aviv: Schocken, 1970), 269–282. See especially 277ff.

down. But my tears kept streaming as people began asking each other what it was that made the child cry. No one knew.

Now I will tell what it was that made me cry. The moment when the service stopped, the enchanting wholeness that I had felt disintegrated. Some of the men had removed their prayer shawls from their heads and some began conversing with each other. The demeanor of those for whom I felt love had changed. Their stature and the stature of the place and the day were diminished. That is what made my heart sad and that is what made me cry.

Several years have passed and the amazement that I felt then still holds a place in my heart, as does that pain. And every Yom Kippur, when I see fellow Jews, "all garbed in white, glorifying You like winged seraphs," exchanging prayers of petition for purposeless prattle, my spirit constricts as on that day.

Many times I asked myself: are not the prayers and piyyutim the means by which Israel connects with their Heavenly Father? How can a holy people subvert the holiness of its sacred days with idle talk and trivial things? How can they sully the glory of days and hours that, once gone, are lost forever? Thoughtful people do not forget even for a moment how special those days are. But what is a simple person, one who cannot always be at that level when he stands facing his Creator, what is such a person to do? But God is our stronghold, and so one should always ponder how to find the way to Him, all the more so during the ten days when the Holy One, blessed be He, disposes Himself toward those who seek him. One should, therefore, not let those unique hours given for Israel's fulfillment pass fruitlessly.

Reflecting on all this gave me the idea of composing an epic work on the Days of Awe, one that a person could read for inspiration during the intervals between the different parts of the service. But who am I to come after the prayers and piyyutim composed by the great and holy ones of our people? Who would find anything substantial in a book written by one such as I? So I put the idea away. But each year, during the days of confession and seeking God's mercy, when I would look through the relevant sources to understand better what God asks of us, I would mark with my fingernail any edifying text I came upon. Eventually I was prompted to copy out those texts and weave them into a book for Rosh Hashanah, Yom Kippur and the days in between. I am grateful to God for turning my idea into actuality and enabling me to present this new work replete with ancient wisdom from the Written Torah and the Oral Tradition. It is a book to read and contemplate during the breaks in the service. Nothing in it was written by me. I have rather proceeded like an artisan who is given fine silk to make a garment. All he needs to add are the threads to hold it together.[25]

Anyone who has ever read Agnon knows that we should never take what his narrators tell us at face value. Very often they mean the exact opposite of what they are saying. Here, however, Agnon himself is addressing the reader in his own voice, without irony and the Galicianer shtick that are the hallmarks of his

---

25. *Yamim nora'im*, 3rd ed. (New York: Schocken Books, 1946), front matter. The English ediiton, *Days of Awe*, does not present this passage; the translation is mine, JSD.

style. In this deeply personal piece Agnon supplies the reason why the exhausting project of compiling *Yamim nora'im* was, as he told Dov Sadan, of "interest" to him. "Interest" in that letter was in quotation marks because, as we now see, his motivation was more and deeper than merely intellectual. The anthology represents his response to the spiritual condition of the narrators of the stories he created during the time he was working on it. The verbal connections between this specially written introduction and the synagogue scenes in *Oreaḥ natah lalun* and "Pi shenayim" make this clear. Those narrators live in an impaired reality when the dross of the world obscures and darkens the doors of perception, but their memories recover from their early years a more luminous reality. In "Pi shenayim" the narrator goes back to when he was a boy of seven or eight, but here, in this introduction, Agnon goes back much earlier, to when he was a child of four. This tells us that the cause of the clouded perception of the various narrators is not modernity per se but the simple and inescapable reality of being an adult in this unredeemed world, when the clouds of glory that Wordsworth invoked in the Immortality Ode have departed, or, in Buberian terms, when "the exalted melancholy of our fate [is] that every Thou in our world must become an It."[26] Bialik gave us the most exquisite explication of this sensibility in his classic memoir of childhood, *Safiaḥ* [Aftergrowth]:

> It has been said very truly that man sees and grasps only once in his life, during his childhood. Those first sights, virgin as when first they left the Creator's hands, are the embodiment of things, their very quintessence. What comes later is no more than a defective second edition. It is done after the fashion of the original, to be sure, and is faintly reminiscent of it, but it is not the same thing. I have found this to be true of myself. Whatever I have seen and deemed worthy of blessing in the skies above or on earth in the course of my life has been enjoyed only by virtue of that original, that primal seeing.[27]

Primal seeing. That is what Agnon experienced on Yom Kippur in the prayer-house of his childhood, when time and separateness were transcended in the splendor of the numinous. That is what he suggests we Jews need to recapture in our synagogues if we are to surmount the constrictions of time and the bleakness of individualism and experience the High Holidays as actual days of awe. To be sure, we cannot recapture true primal seeing, for were we to do so such perception would not be primal. What Agnon hopes to catalyze is "a defective second edition" of that consciousness, something akin to Paul Ricoeur's idea of "a second

---

26. Martin Buber, *I and Thou*, trans. Ronald Gregor Smith, in *The Writings of Martin Buber*, ed. Will Herberg (N.Y.: Meridian Books, 1956), 49.
27. *Aftergrowth and Other Stories*, trans. I.M. Lask (Philadelphia: The Jewish Publication Society, 1944), 43.

naiveté."[28] *Yamim nora'im* was intended to serve for contemporary Jews as a spur to attaining it, and the material he collected as a bridge to the Maḥzor. The midrashim and stories and homilies are meant to function as the textual equivalent of the madeleine that enabled Proust's narrator Marcel to recapture lost time.

Can they do so in our time and our place? The question is more easily asked than answered. Agnon compiled *Yamim nora'im* with certain assumptions, however tacit, about his readers and certain givens about their sociology. He presupposed a modicum of Jewish literacy and some familiarity with the material he collected. He wrote in a society that was much less open, fluid, mobile and individualistic than what has evolved in North America and less sectored than contemporary Israel. For those Jews today who attend services on the High Holidays primarily seeking a religious experience, *Yamim nora'im* is a necessary book, but it is not sufficient. There is still a need for some prior material and experiences, verbal and non-verbal, sensate and ideational, that could help us apprehend the world in child-like (not childish) freshness and thus begin to open us to the sublime discourse of the Maḥzor. For the original concern that led Agnon to compile *Yamim nora'im* is still very much relevant: Rosh Hashanah and Yom Kippur, and the days in between, are not to be squandered. Those "days and hours ... once gone, are lost forever. Thoughtful people do not forget even for a moment how special [they] are."[29]

JAMES S. DIAMOND (1939–2013) taught in the Program in Judaic Studies at Princeton University, where he also served as the Hillel rabbi. Rabbi Diamond was ordained by the Jewish Theological Seminary and held a PhD in Comparative Literature from Indiana University in Bloomington. Prior to coming to Princeton he served as Hillel rabbi and faculty member at Washington University in St. Louis. He was translator of S.Y, Agnon, *A Parable and Its Lesson*, published by Stanford University Press (2014).

---

28. See the final essay in Ricoeur's *The Symbolism of Evil*, trans. Emerson Buchanan (Boston: Beacon Press, 1969), 347ff.
29. In the years after *Yamin nora'im* was compiled Agnon seems to have modified or expanded his notion of what Yom Kippur and the Days of Awe can achieve. In such stories as "Baderekh" [On The Road, 1944] and "'Im kenisat hayom" [At the Outset of the Day, 1950] it is not the primal vision of childhood that is recaptured in the synagogue on Yom Kippur but a more generalized memorialization of and reconnection in the living present to the communal Jewish past. See Malka Shaked, *Haqemet shebe'or haraqia'* [Wrinkle in the Skin of the Sky] (Jerusalem: The Hebrew University Magnes Press, 2000), chapter 2, 28–48.

IV. Agnon Himself

19   *The Partners*

S.Y. Agnon

1

IN THE CITY HALL THERE IS A CELLAR, its length without measure, without end. It has been said that it goes on and on and on, all the way into another country, and that it was made this way because of the Tatars; if the city should fall, the city's leaders would not fall into their hands as captives. You descend on stone steps into the cellar, where four iron doors are set in place, two inside and two outside. The outer doors are closed and locked; the inner doors are left open. When the Tatars were no longer a threat to Poland, they stopped locking the cellar from inside.

The entrance to the cellar is lower than the height of a medium-size man, and it is open to the marketplace. At the top, a stone juts out from the threshold, and a high step leads up from the basement. On top of this step, which is as wide as a workbench, stands a statue of Naḥum Ber Wallach, the yeast merchant who inherited the cellar from his father, just as his father had received it from *his* father, going all the way back to their ancestor Naḥum Ze'ev the charcoal maker, who received it as a gift from Potocki the count of Buczacz, along with a commission for making and selling yeast.

This is exactly what galled the three brothers of the House of Potocki: not only had their ancestor brought in a partner to share the city hall, but that partner was a Jew. This was really too much to swallow. They had already offered Naḥum Ber Wallach an enormous sum—some say it amounted to thousands of gold dinars—to buy out his partnership and vacate the cellar. This is how he responded: If I have already gained the privilege of a partnership with the distinguished nobility of the House of Potocki in the city hall that is the glorious splendor of the city and an object of envy throughout Poland, could I possibly dissolve the partnership? I would not dissolve it for all the money in the world.

2

Why did the Potocki brothers' grandfather bring him in as a partner in the city hall, a man who was not only a Jew but a yeast merchant? Was it because

Building a City: Writings on Agnon's Buczacz in Memory of Alan Mintz (2022): 309–327
DOI: 10.2979/BuildingaCityWriting.0.0.20

he owed him money? Potocki was a wealthy man. Had he lost money at cards? He had many, many villages, forests, and farmlands with which he could pay his debts, aside from the city itself and its branches, and aside from distilleries that produced be'er and brandy. No, Potocki *gave* the cellar to Naḥum Ze'ev the Jew, and Naḥum Ber Wallach was his descendant. And why did Potocki give such a generous gift to a Jew? He did so on account of a certain incident. And here is an accounting of that incident.

Potocki had gone out on a hunt in the forests around the city, forests that extended on and on, endlessly, beyond measure, for at that time, all the suburbs that now surround the city were still forests. Potocki was accompanied by his hounds and his servants, as well as by the minor lords who ate at his table and accompanied him wherever he went. When he caught sight of an animal, he took aim with his rifle and shot. He missed, however, and then ran after the animal. This brought him to a spot far removed from his companions. So, suddenly, he found himself alone, without his servants and companions, without food or water, and even without his faithful hounds. He tried to return to them but could not find the way. He began wandering here and there, and this went on and on until his legs gave out and he fell down. Having fallen, he just lay there. And, once he had fallen down, sleep overtook him; he dozed off into slumber, and slept.

In that city, there was a Jew who at one time had the lease on a tavern, like his ancestors, and like their ancestors before them. After a few years went by, he was no longer able to pay the lord what was due on the lease. The lord warned him that if he did not pay, he would throw him into a pit. As long as no other Jew came along to rent the tavern, the official was content to let him stay there. But one year, when another Jew came along and leased the tavern, the lord threw him out. He lacked the funds to lease a tavern elsewhere. So he began wandering around from one place to another, in search of a place where he could earn a living. But he found none.

One day, he came to one of the forests owned by Potocki. There was an old man there who knew him from better times and had often benefited from his largesse.

The old man asked him, Nuhum Ze'yv, what are *you* doing here?

He responded, My sons and I are cutting down trees in the forest to make charcoal that we take to the city and sell to Jews.

How blessed you are, and how blessed your children, for you have something to do! So you certainly must have food to eat and a place to rest your heads. But I, my friend, have become homeless, a wanderer, and neither my wife nor I has anything to eat, or even a roof over our heads.

The old man said, Stay here with us, and the One who provides bread for all flesh will also provide for you and your wife. Hearing this, he stayed with the old man and his sons in the forest, passed the time with them, and learned how to cut down trees and make charcoal, which they sold in the city. Eventually, the old man died; one of his sons became a soldier, one indentured himself as a servant, and the other was arrested for brigandage. Naḥum Ze'ev was left to fell trees and make them into charcoal, which he sold in town.

At that time, he had already raised his sons and daughters and sent them out into the world. He was left alone with his wife, she busy with her goat and her chickens and her kettles and he with his trees and his charcoal. And so it went all week. But on Sabbaths and Holy Days, and on weekdays when the Torah is read, he would take leave of his trees and his charcoal and try to reach the synagogue before sunrise so that he could pray there at the proper hour. Nothing stopped him, neither rain in the summer nor snow and winds in the winter. During the week, he would walk along, carrying a bag of charcoal over his shoulder. He would sell the charcoal in order to buy those things that are sold in town but are not to be found in the village.

One day, he rose early, as was his wont, and went on his way. What occupied his thoughts at that hour? No one really knows what is on his neighbor's mind. One could assume, however, that he wanted what most villagers want, namely, to live in a city with other Jews so that he could pray every day with the community. This is especially so for the morning prayer, for at dawn, you can sense God's workings, restoring souls to lifeless bodies, and the heart seeks to acknowledge God in a house of prayer that has a holy ark and religious books and Jews.

And so Naḥum Ze'ev stepped along from wood to wood, and from thicket to thicket among the tall and lofty trees that cover the road with their thick branches, refusing to reveal even the hint of a path to anyone who spends most of his days in the city, hiding even a hint of a path from all except those who had spent most of their days in the woods. When rain in the summer and snow in the winter muddy up the path beyond recognition, the fragrance of the roadside trees serves to lead one along the right path, for every tree had its own fragrance. However, he also sensed a human smell, and that is the smell that drew him along, until he came to a thick oak tree. He saw a man lying there, beneath the oak. Was he drunk? Or was he just someone who had been walking along, decided to rest a bit, and fell asleep? Many, many people walk along that road, wandering from one place to another, and wherever they lie down they make the place their own. The moon rose, casting its light upon the man's clothes. Naḥum Ze'ev had the feeling that this was an important lord lying there. But if indeed he was so important, where were his servants and his bodyguards? How could they have left him alone in the forest in the dead of night in a place of danger?

When he bent over the man, he was amazed and astounded to realize that this man beneath the tree was none other than the lord of Buczacz. Why was the lord of Buczacz lying here in the forest? Naḥum Ze'ev actually had heard the sounds of carriages and the barking of hounds and the shouts of officials who had gone out with Potocki to hunt. If that is what he heard, where were his companions? And why had they left him alone in the forest in the dead of night? Had a wild animal attacked and bitten him? If that was so, he certainly must not be left alone there in the forest.

Looking closely, he saw no sign of a bruise, a discoloration, a fresh wound, or blood on his clothes. In any case, he could not leave him alone there because of the wild animals, and it was impossible to wait until he awoke, because it was already autumn and his blood could congeal.

He set down his bag of charcoal, placed his talit and tefilin on top of it, and tried to wake the man up. But he would not wake up. After some thought, he decided to carry him on his shoulders, and, taking his talit and tefilin in one hand, he returned to his hut with the man on his shoulders.

He took small steps so that he would not wake up before they reached the hut. Potocki was not a heavy man and not too much of a burden. However, he was a short-tempered man, and whenever he lost his temper, no one was able to bear it.

At dawn, the birds began to chirp, all the trees of the forest awoke, and each and every branch and leaf and shrub gave off its own fragrance, the fragrance of an autumn morning covered in dew.

3

When Naḥum Ze'ev brought Potocki to his hut, his wife, Ḥayyah Sarah, was about to set pots over the fire to boil. Even before he entered, she could hear the heavy tread of his feet. She was surprised that he was returning home, because it was impossible that he already had recited the entire service that morning, including the Torah reading and the long petitionary prayers for Monday or Thursday. When he entered, she saw that he was carrying on his shoulders one of the great lords, who appeared to be dead, and she thought that her soul would take flight. Naḥum Ze'ev lifted up his burden and put him down on his bed; then he took his sheepskin coat off its hook and covered him with it. His bed, near the wall, was made of stones, soil, and mud covered over with plaster. Spread over that was a straw mattress and a pillow stuffed with feathers. A wider bed jutted out from the opposite wall, with a straw mattress and a bundle of clothes. This wider bed was Ḥayyah Sarah's; the narrow one belonged to Naḥum Ze'ev.

When Ḥayyah Sarah recovered from the shock, she wanted to ask her husband what was going on but could not find the words. Standing there, she just stared ahead without any expression in her eyes. Finally, she leaned over her husband. Naḥum Ze'ev told her, Set your questions aside for a bit, add some logs to the fire, and heat up some water.

Ḥayyah Sarah shouted, Are you going to tell me what this is all about? The lord, shaken by the sound of her shouting, opened his eyes. His eyes did not reflect the slightest bit of amazement, but they glared with a kind of indignation that cannot be expressed in words. Perhaps this was because she had awakened him, or perhaps his anger had preceded his sleep. Whatever the reason, he closed his eyes again and fell asleep again.

Naḥum Ze'ev, who had seen the lord opening his eyes and was unaware that he had closed them again, raised his arms heavenward and said, Blessed be the One who has restored the breath of life to this exalted lord! I will not try to hide from my master my fear that his blood had congealed and that he would not regain consciousness again so quickly.

Potocki opened his eyes again and asked, What did you say? Then, almost at one and the same time, he shouted: Where am I and who are you?

Naḥum Ze'ev bowed down to him, in fear and trembling, and told him that at night, near dawn, he had gone out to walk to the city, to pray at the synagogue there. On the way, in the forest, he saw a man lying beneath one of the trees. As he drew near, he realized that this was the great lord of Buczacz, who had decided to take a rest on the ground in the forest beneath a tree. The Holy One's kindnesses had kept the cold at bay. Nevertheless, he was very concerned lest the exalted lord should suffer a chill because it was no longer summer and the forest was covered with dew. Therefore, he boldly took courage and lifted up the exalted lord in his arms, brought him to his hut, and laid him down on the bed. He added, And if the master so desires, we shall bring him something warm to drink.

When Ḥayyah Sarah heard this, she brought an earthen pot of water boiling with licorice root. Naḥum Ze'ev took the pot and brought it to Potocki's lips. Potocki was silent and amazed.

Naḥum Ze'ev said to Potocki, If the master would be kind enough to drink until he is no longer chilled.

Potocki took one swallow and asked, What have you given me to drink? Don't you have a little wine, or mead? Naḥum Ze'ev answered, There is neither wine nor mead in the house. If the master would like some brandy, I shall bring it to him.

He poured it into his kiddush cup, filling it to the brim. Potocki drank it, and asked for another. Naḥum Ze'ev said, Praise the living God! Indeed, my master lives, and thus may he continue forever!

Potocki said, Take me home.

I am at my master's command.

Said Potocki, So, what are you waiting for?

I cannot conceal from my master the fact that I have not yet prayed the morning service. So I will do so now while my wife goes to the village to bring back a horse and a carriage.

Said Potocki, Go, pray to your God, and pray for me, too.

The hut consisted of one room, with two beds of stone and soil jutting out from the walls; these beds faced each other and were used for sitting by day and for lying down at night. In the middle of the room, a barrel turned upside-down served as a table. Opposite the barrel, near the door, was a stove with an oven. Near the hut stood a sukkah for use during the Sukkot festival. Naḥum Ze'ev thought about praying in the sukkah, as was his custom in the summer. However, it would be awkward to leave the lord there by himself, since Ḥayyah Sarah had gone to the village to find horses and a carriage. So he made up his mind to pray in the hut. Then he rinsed his hands, wrapped himself in talit and tefilin, picked up a prayer book, and was ready to say his prayers.

Approximately eighteen hundred Jews lived on Count Potocki's estates. Among them were leaseholders of farmland and taverns, grain merchants, and businessmen who handled financial transactions, not to mention shopkeepers and artisans. But when it came to the customs of the Jews, he had not the least notion, and their prayers he had never heard, except for parodies of them by the banquet jesters who were a constant presence at his table. Now that fate had placed him in the home of a Jew who was preparing himself for prayer, he lay there with eyes wide open, waiting to see a Jew at prayer. But fatigue and the brandy overcame him, and he fell asleep.

Naḥum Ze'ev completed his prayers, wrapped up his talit and tefilin, put them into a bag with his prayer book, and hung it on a hook in the wall. The loud noise made by the carriage wheels woke up Potocki, who asked Naḥum Ze'ev, Why aren't you praying?

I have already prayed, he responded.

The lord replied in amazement, You prayed already?

Yes, my enlightened, generous, exalted, and distinguished lord. And now that my wife has brought up the horse and the carriage, if my lord so desires, I shall bring him to his city, to his castle. Listen! The horse is neighing in joy, just to hear that! Then, turning to Ḥayyah Sarah, Naḥum Ze'ev said, Take the mattresses and spread them out in the carriage. Then, with our lord's permission, we shall lift him up into the carriage for the trip to his city and his palace.

Potocki realized that there was no longer any sign of danger, but his strength had left him. He was just lying down and looking at the man and the woman as they took him down from the bed and out of the hut, lifted him up to the carriage, lay him down there, and covered him with the woolen cloak, placing a pillow beneath his back. Potocki realized that they were taking care of him, yet he was confused. *Who* was taking care of him, Potocki wanted to know. He did not understand what was happening. He was keenly aware of everything that was being done for him but did not recognize who was doing it.

4

Potocki was lying down in a carriage harnessed to a horse. He just lay there in amazement, for never in his life had he seen such an appalling sight. Is it possible that anyone could be making use of such broken-down things, like the ones this Jew and his wife were using to take care of him?

Naḥum Ze'ev rubbed his hands and said, Thank God, we are on our way!

The lord awoke and realized where he was, traveling with this Jew in that same carriage with that same horse. He went over the Jew's words in his mind and gave them some thought: We are on our way!

Then he continued, to himself, I really should offer a prayer, but what would a prayer do for us? When I went out to hunt, didn't the priest offer a prayer, and at the end… well, what about the end? What did I intend to say? Well, I really did not intend to say anything. But I will speak with the Jew.

Potocki asked Naḥum Ze'ev, Is this horse yours and is this carriage yours?

He replied, With your permission, esteemed lord of great compassion, I am a poor man, with neither a horse nor a carriage.

Potocki continued his questioning, So how do you come to have them?

He replied, My wife borrowed them from our neighbor in the village. The horse belongs to Nekiti, and I don't know who owns the carriage. Maybe it belongs to Nikolai and maybe it belongs to Nekiti. Both of them have been boasting that they were about to purchase a carriage, so it clearly belongs to one of them.

Potocki nodded in agreement, and then, resting his head on his shoulder, he dozed off.

Naḥum Ze'ev led Potocki along the same path that he used to bring his charcoal to town. He took the charcoal by horse, whereas he took Potocki by horse and carriage. When they reached the thickets of the forest, there was no way for a carriage to pass. He stopped the horse and looked at the lord.

Are we there?

He replied, We have not reached the city, but we have reached a place where the carriage cannot pass.

Potocki shouted in anger, Why?

Naḥum Ze'ev responded humbly, Because there is no road here.

Potocki said, Tell my servant to put me up on the carriage. Why are you silent?

While this one was thinking about how to answer, the other one reached a decision and said, I will give it a try, and maybe I will be able to ride on the horse.

Potocki came down from the carriage and tried to mount the horse. As soon as he got on, he felt dizzy and thought he would fall. Naḥum Ze'ev came to his aid and helped him to sit down on a fallen tree trunk. He then began talking to himself, Let's leave the carriage here in the forest, but let's hide it to keep it from thieves, and when we return safely from town we will give it back to Nikolai or Nekiti, but the horse we shall take along with us, we shall take the horse with us.

Potocki asked him, What was the prayer that you offered?

He replied, I was not praying. I was thinking about the path that I should take.

And what conclusion did you reach?

What conclusion did I reach? With the permission of my exalted lord, I reached the following conclusion: If my lord desires to go by foot, he will reach his castle at sunset. Should it be too difficult for him to proceed on foot, I will carry him on my shoulder, just as I did on the road from the forest to my house, when my lord showed us his kind favor by resting there.

Naḥum Ze'ev hid the carriage among the trees, whistled for the horse to follow him, took hold of Potocki by the arm, and they were on their way. At times, Naḥum Ze'ev stopped to give Potocki a rest; and at times, he stopped because Potocki was leaning so heavily against him.

It was close to sunset when they neared Buczacz.

5

The entire city was lit up with torches, and its streets hummed with the tumult of search parties gone out to look for their lord, who was lost in the forest. What was the cause of all this celebration? Potocki angrily asked Naḥum Ze'ev that question, and then demanded, Go and ask! Look! There is a reckless drunkard dancing around. Ask him.

Naḥum Ze'ev asked him, Why is the whole city lit up?

The drunkard answered him rudely with a vulgar word and said, Shut your mouth, Jew, and get out of the way of esteemed lords.

Potocki asked Naḥum Ze'ev, What did he say to you?

Naḥum Ze'ev said, I could not understand his language.

Potocki replied, You don't understand Polish? When will I get to my castle?

Naḥum Ze'ev said, We are not far from town. If the torch carriers don't cause us any delay, my lord will reach his castle in a short while.

Night had just begun when they neared the castle, with Naḥum Ze'ev holding Potocki by the arm, drawing the horse along behind him. Because of all the noise and the press of the crowd, no one noticed Potocki or his companion or the horse that was being drawn along behind them.

As the horse and the lord and the Jew were being drawn along in the crowd, one of the torch carriers saw a Jew being pushed along. He kicked him in the legs. Naḥum Ze'ev faltered, and Potocki fell down with him. Startled, Naḥum Ze'ev asked Potocki, Have you been hurt?

Potocki asked angrily, What happened?

Naḥum Ze'ev lacked the strength to answer. The rope with which he had been holding the horse had been pulled out of his weakened hands and fell near the horse's hooves. Sensing that the rope had come loose, the horse picked up his hooves and went on his way. The two of them, Naḥum Ze'ev and the lord, lay down there, without any sense of time or of pain. But they were too weak to get up. Potocki lay there with eyes wide open. Looking around, he could see groups of people walking along, and he thought that he heard them mention his name. Little by little, he began to recognize them. Some were nobles who ate at his table. He knew who they were, but their names he could not recall.

Once again, he heard them mention his name. He recognized two of them. The names by which they were known were really indecent; so even now, when he was in such trouble, he had to laugh.

He said, Please hear me out gentlemen. What are these torches all about?

One of those he asked did not respond, but one of them did respond, At this time tomorrow, I'll give you an answer.

There were so many torches that their faces were not recognizable. Naḥum Ze'ev, with great effort, managed to stand. He examined his legs and said, It's nothing.

Then he said to Potocki, Is our lord close to his castle? Then Naḥum Ze'ev let the lord lean against his shoulder, and the two of them walked along together. A little while later, they reached the castle. Everything was wide open. There was no one in the castle. All the lord's servants and all the other officials who had been with Potocki on the hunt had gone out to look for him. All the rooms in the castle were lit up, and the tables were laden with platters and dishes, cups and goblets, bottles and jars and remnants of food and drink as if there had been a great banquet there.

Potocki was weary and did not utter a word. He realized that the palace had been left unguarded. He looked at the remains of the meal, but his weariness outweighed his anger. He closed his eyes and said, Help me lie down on my bed.

Now, Naḥum Ze'ev had never been in Potocki's palace and did not know where Potocki's bed was located, and it was impossible to ask Potocki because he was asleep. He caught sight of a couch at the end of the hall and went over to it. Potocki thought that he had brought him to his bed and said, Put me down there.

The nobles returned and sat down at the table. They had dispatched their servants and the lesser nobles to look for their master. The food and drink that was left over from the big banquet was not enough to satisfy their appetite. They had been scouring the countryside in search of their lord and were starving. They clapped their hands and rattled the silverware to arouse the household servants. However, the servants who had already returned to the castle had not returned to their duties.

One of the lords saw the master of the house lying on the couch. He roused the others with the cry, Long may he live! The others arose and began to dance. Potocki paid no attention to them and did not say a word. They approached his couch, babbling in confusion, telling him how upset they had been when they realized that he had disappeared and how they had left the catch from their hunt in order to scatter about looking for him, and finally, when they still had not found him, how they had gone out with torches in search of him.

Potocki asked derisively, And did you find him? Where is the Jew? Where is my rescuer?

The officials did not know whom Potocki was talking about, for Naḥum Ze'ev had already slipped away out of dread of being caught in the company of Potocki's men.

Potocki said, Go after him, and bring him here to me. And let no one do him any harm.

Potocki lay down with open eyes and waited impatiently for the Jew. The head of his household came to ask, What is my lord's desire, and what may I bring him?

Potocki shouted angrily, You can bring me my rescuer! Why are you just standing there? Why have you not brought him here?

The head of the household bowed and said, They have already gone out to look for him. They surely will bring him here very soon.

Potocki shouted, And you? Why did you let him go?

I? I did not see him.

Why *didn't* you see him? You didn't see him? What do you have eyes for? Anyway, here he is!

Naḥum Ze'ev was standing in front of Potocki, being held up by two of his men, one at each side.

Potocki shouted at them, Let him go! Take your hands off of him and get out of here!

And to Naḥum Ze'ev, he said, You have gone to a great deal of trouble for me, you and your wife. You gave me bread to eat and liquor to drink, a bed to lie down on, and you have looked after me all day, from nightfall to nightfall.

Everyone in Potocki's house stood there listening. Some who heard him imagined that Potocki was feverish, and some who heard him imagined that Potocki said what he said only to let the officials know that they had not acted as the Jew had acted, and still others did not understand what they heard.

Potocki spoke again, What can I give you as a reward for your trouble?

Naḥum Ze'ev was silent.

Potocki said, What is your answer to my question?

Naḥum Ze'ev said, What can I say? I had the opportunity to perform a mitzvah, so I am not asking for any reward.

One official said to Potocki, Give him *something*, give him whatever you want, so he won't have the opportunity to boast about doing you a favor.

Potocki continued speaking to Naḥum Ze'ev, If you want to return home, go there, and if you want to have two or three drops of wine, have a drink. And to his servants Potocki said, Two or three of you should see that he gets home.

Naḥum Ze'ev said, With my lord's kind permission, please allow me to go by myself.

By yourself? Why?

Naḥum Ze'ev said, Since I find myself in town, I would like to go the synagogue for the evening prayer.

Potocki nodded his head, giving permission, and Naḥum Ze'ev went on his way.

6

Lying in his bed at night, Potocki recalled the day's events. In all his life, nothing like this had ever happened to him. Were it not for that Jew, Potocki thought to himself, I would be dead, and all the lords who had gone out on the hunt would be making decisions now about the funeral arrangements. They said that they had gone out to look for me. Undoubtedly, they indeed had gone out to look for me. And what was the result? They looked, and they did not find me. However, I am amazed about my dogs. They also went in search of me and did not find me. How could that have happened?

Potocki lay in his bed and thought about several of his dogs, each one by name, and also thought about each one's traits. One of them jumped up on him, and then another and another, each one expecting its master to pat its head, stroke its neck, say a kind word. Potocki did not move a hand or utter a word. At that moment, all his wonderful dogs were no more important to him than a pack of friends. He twisted his lips, stretched his hands out, and scattered the group of dogs that had gathered quietly around him as he shut his eyes tight to fall asleep. He already had fallen asleep about half an hour earlier, but in his dream he had imagined that he was awake, unable to sleep.

The next morning, when his elderly servant came to dress him, Potocki told him, I'm going to sleep all day, so do not let anyone bother me. And tell me now what I should give to the Jew who saved my life. Why are you silent? Why don't you answer me?

He said, I'm thinking about it.

What are your thoughts telling you?

With my lord's kind permission I will tell him what happened to me with that Jew.

Potocki said, Tell me.

He said, Several days ago, I was invited to that Jew's place. I was able to take note of his poverty and his labors, as well as what he had to eat, which could not have been satisfying. When I asked if he was being supported by charity, he replied, Thank God, I have enough to eat.

I asked him, What are your heart's desires?

He repeated my question: What are my heart's desires? One thing that I do ask for is to be worthy before God in His service.

I said, That really was not the purpose of my question. What do you need to have a chance to rest from your labors, to make life better for you?

He answered, What do I ask for? I ask that God will enable me to be satisfied with whatever He gives to me and my wife.

I told him, *Everyone* has something special to ask for, and that must apply to you as well. However, you prefer to hide that from me, and you don't want to tell me.

He said, I did have a special request, but I put it out of my mind.

Why?

Because I have seen that if a man asks for more than he has, they take away from what he has already.

I said, What did you have, and what did they take away? From what I can see, you had nothing that could be taken away from you.

He said, Don't say that. I had something, and I still have it. But it just is not the same now as it was before. All my life, I regretted that I could not pray every day with other Jews in a synagogue, for I lived in a village and the synagogue was in town. But I tried, and even now I try to go to town at fixed times. However, now that I am getting older, this has become difficult. Look, a man must be satisfied with what he has been given, and he should not ask for what he has not been given.

Potocki was lying down with his pipe between his lips, looking at his servant, who was waiting for the opportunity to say something to his master.

Potocki held out his pipe and said, Take it. But let me know why you've told me this whole story. I asked you for some advice, not for stories. Not only have you failed to give me advice; you stand there telling me things I know nothing about.

The servant said, With my lord's permission, I have something to add to what I have said already.

Potocki said, Well, what do you have to say? Are you looking for an excuse, you scoundrel? I ask you for advice and you try to get out of it by telling me stories.

The servant said, In my opinion, with my lord's kind permission, if he is allowed to pray daily at the synagogue in town, he could have no better reward.

Potocki shouted at him, And who is preventing him from praying in town? Did the Jew tell you that I prevent him from praying wherever he wants? Do you mean to say that if I, who gave my own architect to the Jews in my town to build their house of prayer, allowed him to pray in the synagogue in town that this would be a reward?

The servant said, In order to pray every day in town, he would have to *live* in town, and in order to live in town, he would have to rent a place in town, and in order to rent a place, he would have to pay rent. And even if he had the money, he would not be able to find a place because most of the Jews' houses have been destroyed since the days of the great fire, and anything that even resembles a house is filled with tenants.

Potocki said, So there is no place to live in the entire town?

The servant answered, With my lord's permission, there is not one available place in town.

Potocki said, In that event, I will be pleased to offer him the cellar of the city hall. Why are you silent? What is this? Does my gift not please you?

The servant said, I have been silent because I have been doing some thinking.

Potocki said, And what have you been thinking about?

He replied, Actually, I really have not been doing that much thinking, but I have been saying to myself that my lord's advice is quite good—very, very good. However, upon further consideration, I do not know how a Jew could support himself and his wife here. In the forest, there is always charcoal to be made. But what could he do in town? Nonetheless, my lord's advice is good, very, very good. If my lord would make the cellar available, there would then be a place where one could live. And God would also provide a livelihood, as people say: just as a master is good to his servants, so God the Master will be good to His creatures.

Potocki and his servant had no advice to offer. But a Jew who had dealings with Potocki's servant had some advice to give. What was it? To sell yeast.

I shall explain this is in some detail. Because most communities are small and unable to support their rabbis and because it has been said that one should not use the Torah "as a spade to dig with," the yeast concession was given to rabbis' wives. That is how it was in most small communities, and so it was in Buczacz as well. However, the rabbi's wife was ill and therefore unable to take on the business. It was announced that anyone who wants to have the concession to the yeast trade should come forward and take out a lease. Potocki contacted the town's leaders and purchased for himself the right to sell yeast in perpetuity.

Potocki arranged to meet Naḥum Ze'ev, to transfer the city-hall cellar to him with all its keys, and he gave him a bill of sale for the cellar stamped with his name and official seals. The document stated that from this time forth, the cellar is his in perpetuity and that Potocki's heirs, and *their* heirs, and anyone officially representing him or them for any reason whatsoever have no legal right to eject the Jew Naḥum Ze'ev from the cellar. And Potocki also transferred to him the communal document that grants the holder permission to sell yeast. This satisfies the amazement of people who wonder why the yeast trade in Buczacz is in the hands of a family of laymen rather than in the hands of the rabbi's wife.

7

Naḥum Ze'ev left his forest, his trees, his charcoal, and his hut to come with his wife to live in town. They set up house in the cellar of the Buczacz city hall that extended on and on into another country. But Naḥum Ze'ev and his wife made do with only a small part of the cellar, which was adequate for their needs. They cleared out their part of the cellar of rodents and insects that had been swarming there forever. Many people were envious of Naḥum Ze'ev, who had found a spacious place to live, for which he paid nothing, and because they were so jealous, they said to him, We are surprised that you can live in such a place, a place full of demons and evil spirits, a place where you can often hear weird noises coming up from the cellar because of the rats that are dancing around there.

Naḥum Ze'ev, however, had no fear of demons; indeed, he had no reason to fear them because before he took up residence in the cellar, he affixed a kosher mezuzah on each doorway that required one. So from then on, one heard no shrieks or mocking laughter coming from the cellar but only the sound of chapters of Psalms being recited, for it was Naḥum Ze'ev's practice to recite each day the psalm designated for that day.

David, king of Israel, has already expounded the matter in the Book of Psalms: *The wicked may lay it up, but the righteous will wear it.* When a ruthless person builds a house, he thinks that it is for himself and for his children and their children. In truth, however, he is building it for the righteous person who will appear in the future. This cellar, built by ruthless people out of fear of those who are even more ruthless, as a refuge in times of disaster, was given as an outright gift to that poor Jew for a place to live where he could serve his Creator and pray every day with all his fellow Jews.

We have something further to say about this matter. The Holy One makes use of everyone in order to accomplish His purposes. For example, a lord goes out on a hunt, and an animal crosses his path. The bullet that he shoots does not reach its target. He is drawn in pursuit of the animal and, after a time, finds that he is far away from his group and does not know how to get back. He begins to wander and then lies down and falls asleep. After he is discovered by a righteous person, he is returned to his castle. The point of all this is nothing other than to reward a Jew who yearns to pray together with others.

Thus, what that righteous man yearned for is given to him. Morning and evening, he would go to the synagogue and pray with the community. And between one service and another, he would sit in the cellar and sell yeast. Potocki had purchased this business for him from the community. Truth to tell, this is a story that we have told before. So why are we repeating it? We are repeating it in order to add the fact that the yeast made by Naḥum Ze'ev was of superior quality. The merchants therefore no longer had to purchase yeast from other locations to sell in Buczacz. Naḥum Ze'ev took pains to make his yeast so well that everyone could enjoy their daily bread and their Sabbath loaves. In this, he differed from other yeast sellers, whose only concern was profit and who caused anguish and shame for Jewish women when their bread did not rise and their hallot were not beautiful, but had collapsed, just like the flat noses of the gentile soldiers who had attacked Buczacz. For a man's wife is his equal and Ḥayyah Sarah was his true helpmate, just as Rashi had explained about Adam, first man: if he was deserving, she would be his helpmate.

From the first day that Naḥum Ze'ev and his wife had come to live in town, their sons and daughters would come to visit them, for the city of Buczacz was a metropolis, a center of trade. In addition to the market day that the founding fathers had established on Thursdays, Buczacz boasted a large fair every year. People came to it from a variety of places, some to sell and some to buy, including the sons and daughters of Naḥum Ze'ev and Ḥayyah Sarah, who were pleased to see that their children were following God's ways. To tell the truth, all Jews followed God's ways, but some do so out of habit because that is the custom, and some do so simply out of love of God, even though they had grown up in the forest without the good fortune of studying Torah. The integrity of their father and the modesty of their mother stood them in good stead.

8

It is customary for someone who owns a home or a courtyard to see that all of it is being utilized as a source of income. He rents out a room here or a large corner there or a bit of space elsewhere to store his merchandise according to his needs. This Naḥum Ze'ev did not do, but he kept the interests of others in mind. This was also the case for his children, and their children and *their* children, too. And this was true of Naḥum Ber, with whom I began this story.

What does it mean to be benevolent? There are small traders in town who do not have the money to rent a shop. They find small spots in the market where they spread out their merchandise. This takes a great deal of effort and entails the loss of a great deal of time because in the morning they bring their wares to the market, and at evening, they haul them back. There are certain kinds of merchandise too heavy for one man to handle. This necessitates an enormous amount of exhausting work. And if their merchandise is food, dogs and pigs can be an annoyance. And where do these small traders live? Far, far away from the market. It is only the wealthy who can afford to live nearby either because they inherited their homes or can afford the high rents. The poor and the needy are forced to live far from the market, far away from the source of their income.

Naḥum Ze'ev told them, There is space in my cellar for all the merchandise in Buczacz. Bring your merchandise to my cellar, and when you come for it in the morning, you will find it where you left it, and I am not asking for rent or for any kind of fee.

You can imagine the degree of help this afforded these small traders. He lightened the burden they bore in eking out their meager livelihood. This was truer still on Thursday, market day, when they were in a rush to set up in the morning and returned home late at night because of the people from villages who had come to town to purchase what they needed.

The traders, men and women alike, came every day between the afternoon and the evening prayers, or a little earlier or a little later, bringing their merchandise to the cellar, where it was safe from thieves, dogs and pigs, and fire. For the doors to the cellar were stronger than the doors of the stalls in the market, and this merchandise was safer than all the other merchandise in the market. How so? Because sometimes when the night watchman in the market would doze and the thieves heard his snores, they would open the doors and take out all the merchandise. Or perhaps the watchman and the thieves were in cahoots, and he let them make off with the merchandise. But the goods in the cellar were safe from thieves, for the cellar had double doors of iron so that if the inner doors were unlocked, the locked outer doors could be opened only by someone in possession of the key. This was the large key of the long cellar of the great city hall of Buczacz, given by the lord of Buczacz to that elder on the same day when he handed him the deed of title for the cellar. If you know how much the Poles feared the Tatars, you can imagine how fortified the cellar was, for it was there that the leaders of Buczacz sought protection from the Tatars. And if you know that this cellar is part of that great city hall that was the envy of all the cities of Poland, you can begin to imagine the pain that this caused the descendants of the noble house of Potocki, whose great-grandfather had brought them into partnership with none other than a Jew.

Those descendants had already made attempts to buy back the lease in perpetuity from Naḥum Ber Wallach, who had wisely responded, If I have attained the merit of being a partner to distinguished leaders from the House of Potocki, is it possible that I would withdraw my partnership?

Why am I repeating all of this since I have already told the entire story? It is to let you know how praiseworthy is Naḥum Ber, for he knew that the inheritance of a Jew, which was bequeathed to him by his ancestors, is more valuable than thousands and thousands of gold coins.

And so it was that Naḥum Ber Wallach did not sell his rights but continued to occupy the cellar and sell yeast, just like all his ancestors, in a chain of lineage stretching back to Naḥum Ze'ev the charcoal maker, who had received the cellar as a gift from Potocki.

At this point, I will leave the story of the generations between Naḥum Ze'ev and Naḥum Ber, to concentrate solely on Naḥum Ber.

Naḥum Ber was the last of his family to live in the cellar, for the Great War uprooted the people who lived in Buczacz and destroyed the town. When the war ended, and a few of the people of Buczacz were able to return, Buczacz was no longer ruled by Austria but by Poland, and Poland did not recall the kindnesses of ancestors, did not maintain the agreements forged by their predecessors with the Jews, and oppressed the Jews in every way possible. So the cellar was never returned to the heirs of Naḥum Ber, who was the last of those who had a stake in the cellar.

Naḥum Ber Wallach did not have the privilege of having sons, though he had two daughters. The name of the eldest I have forgotten; the name of the youngest was Nechi. The eldest did not have any good fortune. She was married to a difficult man who squandered her dowry and sent her away penniless. She returned to her father, bringing with her only the bad habits that she had learned from the man who had divorced her. She desecrated the Sabbath in public. One Sabbath, she was observed knitting while sitting on a bench near the River Strypa. Neither the pleas of her father nor his promises to buy her a sweater lovelier than the one she was making were of any avail. People said that she had gone mad and that she wanted to irritate the God-fearing, who thought that the world should be governed by their standards. God-fearing people paid her no attention, but she caused her father pain when he saw his own daughter desecrating the Sabbath and leading a life that would lead her to Gehinnom.

People would ask, Why is Naḥum Ber being punished by having a daughter who transgresses Jewish law and religion? And they did not realize that in the future, their own children and grandchildren would be asking why *they* were being punished, being killed just because they were Jews.

We shall now set aside the questions that sages greater than we have asked without finding an answer, and we shall set aside Naḥum Ber's eldest daughter, who atoned for her sin through her suffering, and we shall say something about the youngest daughter Nechi, who was a source of comfort for her father all his life. I knew her when I was a youngster because my mother, my teacher of blessed memory, acted as her guardian after her mother died and left her without any relatives living in town.

It was because of changes in the nature of people and in the temperament of the generations that Nechi's mother died. People said that she died because of the unhealthy air in the cellar. Naḥum Ber left the home that he had made in the cellar and rented a place elsewhere. Because his Nechi was so attached to my mother, of blessed memory, he rented a place that was near our home. Thus Nechi could be close to her guardian and visit her whenever she wanted, rather than spend the entire day isolated and lonely. When Naḥum Ber was on his way home from evening prayers on winter evenings, he would visit us to drink a cup of tea. He did so for his health because people of that generation were not yet accustomed to drinking tea as a beverage. They considered it to be medicinal; in fact, in Polish, tea is called *herbata*, the name of a medicinal herb.

Nechi was married to a relative of ours, an upright man who was a grain merchant, Feivush Ringelblum by name. They lived together in contentment and had a brilliant son named Monyo. This was Menahem Emanuel, who was Emanuel Ringelblum, murdered by the filthy, accursed agents of the wretched abomination, in the Warsaw Ghetto.

I do not know whether any of Nahum Ber's family are still alive, or whether they shared the fate of most of the people in Buczacz, who were wiped out by the accursed filthy mobs. Whatever their fate was, I want to retain the memory of Nahum Ber Wallach, the last of the family of Nahum Ze'ev the charcoal maker, who received as a gift the large cellar in the great city hall of Buczacz because of his desire to pray with a congregation. And Nahum Ber likewise would spend morning and evening in the study house, praying with the community.

Nahum Ber was not among those who spent time in Torah studies; however, he had great esteem for those who studied Torah. In spite of all his troubles, he was a happy man who made other people happy as well. I remember that when I was studying Torah in the old study house with my father, my teacher, a righteous man whose memory is a blessing, the shop owners in the market would come to the study house in the winter several times a day to warm up and escape the cold because in the old study house there was a stove that was very well attended to; it was kept burning throughout the winter, day and night. And even Nahum Ber Wallach would come to spend time there.

Whenever he came in, he would look around, with eyes that shone with joy, at the students sitting there in groups studying Torah. He would stand there and clap his hands while chanting one of the old melodies that inspire one with the love of Torah.

Many melodies have I heard and forgotten. But there is one that remains with me. When I remember days of the past, when our town was filled with Jews and our old study house was filled with the study of Torah, my mind goes back to that melody that Nahum Ber would be humming as he came in to the study house. I am unable to repeat that melody, but its words were in Aramaic, and here is their translation:

> God, who is exalted, unending and boundless,
> The Torah, with favor, bestowed He upon us.

Translated by Jules Harlow

The Partners

"Hashutafim"; orig. pub. in *Ma'ariv* (September 9, 1963), and in *Ir umelo'ah* (Tel Aviv: Schocken, 1973), 239–255.

Two of them walked along together / Echoing Genesis 22:6.

A spade to dig with / Avot 4:5; that is, as the rabbi should not profit from his holy work in the rabbinate, the yeast business was given to him to generate income to live by.

The wicked may lay it up, but the righteous will wear it / The verse is actually taken from Job 27:17 rather than Psalms.

As Rashi had explained about the first man / Rashi to Genesis 2:18.

Emanuel Ringelblum / (1900–1944) was a historian, politician, and social worker, known for his *Notes from the Warsaw Ghetto*, and the *Oyneg Shabbes* (Ringelblum) Archives of the Warsaw Ghetto, an immensely important cache of documentary evidence (stored in milk cans) on life inside the Ghetto. In fact, Agnon's tale of his cousin's demise is inaccurate: Ringelblum escaped the Ghetto, but his hiding place was discovered by the Gestapo, and he was killed along with his family and those who were hiding them.

Figure 9: Buczacz Town Hall. (Credit, Wendy Zierler).

20 *From* The Parable and Its Lesson
Editor's Introductory Note

S.Y. Agnon

Fɪʀsᴛ ᴘᴜʙʟɪsʜᴇᴅ ɪɴ *Ha'aretz* in 1958, *The Parable and Its Lesson* is set in seven-teenth- century Buczacz. It is narrated on two levels, first by an omniscient, self-reflexive narrator who walks us through his process of storytelling, identifying his own tangents and engaging the reader. The second narrator is the shamash (sexton) of the Great Synagogue of Buczacz, on trial for shaming an important member of the community by escorting him out of the synagogue because he wouldn't stop talking during the Torah service.

The shamash defends himself by telling a fantastic tale about his descent into Gehinnom fifty-four years earlier with Reb Moshe, the town rabbi at that time. In the story, the rabbi and the shamash go down to Gehinnom in order to locate a missing man, Aaron, married to Zlateh, Reb Moshe's adopted daughter, a survivor of the Chmielnicki massacres. Aaron has vanished, leaving Zlateh, not even twenty years old, an Agunah. Reb Moshe suspects that Aaron has died so he decides to take the shamash down to Gehinnom with him in order to find Aaron and ascertain his death. They find Aaron, but more importantly, they witness the strange suffering of righteous men in Gehinnom, who could not stop talking during the reading of the Torah portion. Granted, they discussed the Torah itself, but the shamash points out that under no circumstances are the words of men to supersede the words of God. In Gehinnom Reb Moshe and the sexton see illustri-ous men aching to share their Torah insights with their peers, but unable to do so because of various grotesque and disturbing impediments. Thus, the shamash defends his actions toward the member of the community that he escorted out of synagogue, saying that he was trying to protect him from the fate of his forebears who had to live throughout eternity in a state of frustration and silence.

The excerpt from *The Parable and Its Lesson* from sections 5–7 of the novella that we have chosen to republish here presents Aaron's story as told to the shamash. It gives a good sense of the Agnonian narrator's method of parsing his own narrative style. Alan Mintz discusses this particular novella at length in the UCLA lecture we have transcribed and published in this volume, as well as in several places in *Ancestral Tales*.

Agnon's narrator, as Alan Mintz notes, "is fully aware of the Holocaust in gen-eral and the gruesome manner in which the Jews of Buczcacz died in particular."[1] Instead of steeping himself in outrage and lament, however, he commits himself

1. Alan Mintz, *Ancestral Tales*, 73.

Building a City: Writings on Agnon's Buczacz in Memory of Alan Mintz (2022): 328–338
DOI: 10.2979/BuildingaCityWriting.0.0.21

to recreating the shamash's story (which had been previously recorded in the city's *pinkas* that had been destroyed along with the community), thereby building with words a former, Jewishly sanctified place and time:

> So now, since that *pinkas* went up in the flames and Buczacz has been destroyed, and the deeds of the former generations have been forgotten in the recent suffering, I pondered the possibility that the Gehinnom of our time would make us forget the Gehinnom that the shamash saw, and the story about it, and all we can learn from that story. So I said to myself, Let me put it all down in a book and thus create a memorial to a holy community that sanctified its life in its death as its ancestors sanctified their lives with Torah, which is our life.[2]

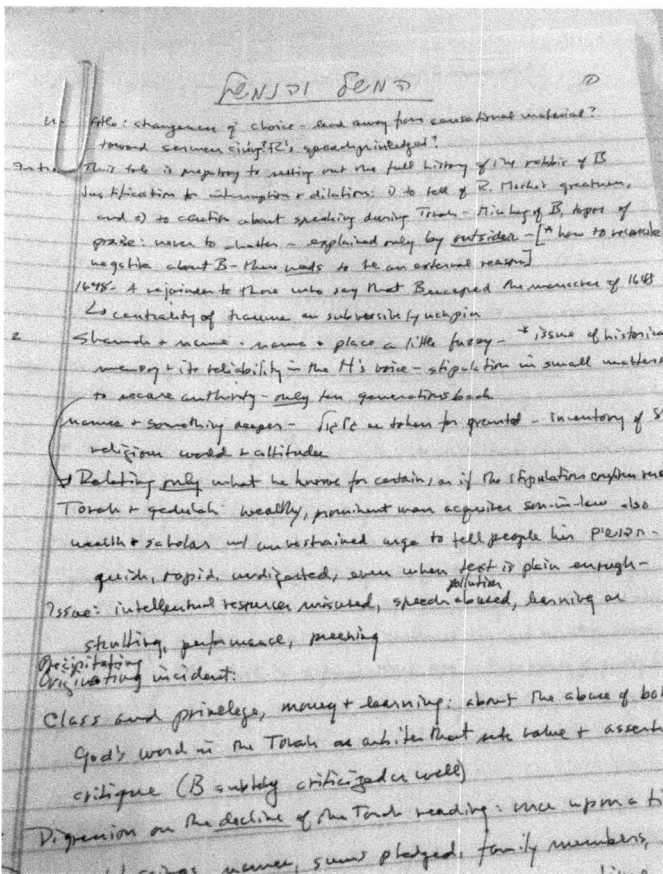

Figure 10: Alan Mintz's Notes on *Hamashal vehanimshal*. (Credit, Beverly Bailis)

2. S.Y. Agnon, *The Parable and Its Lesson: A Novella*, translated and annotated by James S. Diamond, with an Introduction and Critical Essay by Alan Mintz (Stanford: Stanford University Press, 2014), 68.

5

On the Friday evening of the Sabbath of Repentance I went to our Master to ask him when he would give his discourse on repentance so that I could announce it. Truth be told, there really was no need to inquire. The normal order of things was that on the Sabbath of Repentance right after the midday meal, everyone would gather in the synagogue and recite psalms until the rabbi would get up to speak. But in those days nothing was done in our town without first asking our Master. I used to think that this was simply out of respect for him, until he once told me that all things require preparation in advance, especially repentance. A discourse on repentance certainly requires preparation of the heart. Our Master set the time. But right after I left him he called me back. I thought he was calling me back to tell me when we were departing for that place, I mean going to visit Gehinnom. He looked at me and said, "When you announce the time of my address, say in my name that people should be careful not to put up their Sukkah in an impure place."

This was a brand new directive that no rabbi had ever issued before, and he could see that it puzzled me. The rabbis of our town had never been concerned about this issue; nor for that matter had the rabbis of other communities. Our Master continued, "Our many sins compel us to live where we live and go where we go, and no one can be sure on what ground his feet are treading or where exactly he is standing. But a Sukkah, which epitomizes the mystery of the clouds of glory that God spread over Israel in the desert, requires a taintless spot on which to be erected, and we have to be very, very careful about that." When our Master said, "and go where we go" I had the feeling that we were already on the way to the place where the young agunah's husband was. Our Master gave me an approving look and indicated that our conversation was over.

On the way home I went over every word I had heard. How good it is to know that we have leaders whose words keep us on the straight path and sustain us in this Exile.

I came home and began making preparations for the Sabbath. Not only what was needed in the synagogue but at home as well, for my wife, may she rest in peace, was quite weak and could hardly stand on her feet. After the Sabbath I turned to Yom Kippur preparations. God's mercies were with us, because the holy day passed without incident. No one fainted from the fast, those who led the service did not stray from the proper melodies, the Torah reader made no mistakes in chanting the text. Not a single candle went out, neither those lit for the living nor those lit for the dead. There were so many candles that they all melted together. A great many people had perished in the slaughter and their surviving relatives lit candles in their memory. Our Master lit many for his own family. The only one left was that little girl now in limbo because of the sin her husband committed.

The next day I brought over to our Master the silver case in which he kept his etrog. Every year my first wife, may she rest in peace, would polish it in honor of the approaching festival. She always did this between Rosh Hashanah and Yom Kippur. That year, because she was not well, she waited until the day after Yom Kippur. This meant a change in our Master's routine, for it was his custom in the evening, at the end of Yom Kippur after havdalah, to take out his etrog and put it in its case. Our Master did not even notice the change.

I entered to find him in the company of two men, the venerable magnate Reb Akiva Shas, so named because he was fortunate to own a complete set of the Talmud, and, like him distinguished in stature and character but not in wealth, Reb Meshullam, a Jew from Germany who was a descendant of the composer of the Akdamut hymn read on the festival of Shavuot. Old age had kept them from visiting the evening before, right after Yom Kippur, so they came the next day.

I put the etrog case down in front of our Master. He looked at it and remarked, "I understand your wife is in need of mercy from on high." "Yes," I said, "she is sick. And, thank God, we have a houseful of little children." I expected our Master to make some kind of blessing for her recovery, but he did not. Only later did I understand why. He knew what we did not: that her end had already been ordained. She died that year. Our Master then placed the etrog in the case and left the case open.

The etrog gave off its fragrance as our Master resumed reminiscing with his two elderly visitors about bygone days, and in due course he told a story that, in the particular context, was disconcerting. There was a time when for many years etrogs were scarce and people began to worry that Jews would soon forget what an etrog was. One year, between Rosh Hashanah and Yom Kippur, two Jews from a distant country showed up with etrogs for sale. The community bought one at a very steep price. No one seemed to care that the community was mired in debt, having borrowed money from the local priests to ransom prisoners. Many doubted that the etrog was kosher or if one could even make the blessing over it. Nevertheless, everyone did, even the doubters, because the commandment to bless the etrog was very dear to them. After the Sukkot festival someone got the idea that the etrog should be examined. Everyone came to see. They cut it open and discovered that it was in fact a lemon, which meant that all the blessings made over it were in vain. Around Passover time, when the snow was melting, two corpses were found in the forest. Wolves had eaten them and nothing was left but bones and clothing. The clothing was examined and found to be that of the men who had sold the etrog. Whom to suspect of their murder? Not Jews, for even if they had known that the men had sold them a lemon instead of an etrog they would not have committed murder. Not God, for God does not execute judgment unjustly. They convened a beit din to look into the legal status of the wives of the dead men. Were they agunot or did the clothing found prove them to be widows? The question became moot when the wicked Khmelnitski's pogroms erupted and many women were taken into captivity, including the widows of the etrog sellers.

Once his two visitors had gone, our Master showed me the passage in the talmudic tractate ʿEruvin where it says that Gehinnom has three openings: one in the desert, one in the sea, and one in Jerusalem. He also showed me another passage there that says that Gehinnom has seven names, and he explained to me the fine points of the differences between them. He concluded by telling me that since the destruction of Jerusalem not every wicked person has the merit of going down to Gehinnom from the opening that is in Jerusalem. For the majority of the wicked, Gehinnom opens right at their feet, under their very feet. He then taught me some laws relating to Gehinnom. But there was no mention of a visit there.

That night after the evening service I could see that our Master was staring at me. I went over to him but he said nothing. I stood and looked at him and saw that his face was burning and his white curls were glistening with sweat. Because of headaches that resulted from a sword wound, our Master never cut his hair, not even for Yom Kippur.

I stood before him but he paid no attention to me. I did not move. I thought to myself, he is not looking at me like that for no reason. He continued staring at me, when he said, "Take the lantern and let us set out. Even though he did not say where we were going, I knew. Of course, when he said "let us set out" his actual words were "In the name of God, let us go." I do not quote his exact words because any intelligent person knows that nothing is done without asking for God's help first. Happy is he who asks and happy is he who is answered.

I now return to the main story.

I had with me candles made from the wax that dripped from the ones lit in the synagogue on Yom Kippur. I normally used them on Hoshanah Rabbah and on the twentieth of Sivan. In our Master's time people did not run to catch the wax drippings from the Yom Kippur candles right after the concluding evening prayer. They were too intent on greeting our Master and getting a blessing from him. So the wax was mine for the taking. I took all the candles I had with me so that darkness would not engulf us if the journey would prove to be a long one. When a person is alive he cannot see that the pit of Gehinnom is open right in front of him. I put the candle into the lantern but had no need to light it, for all this happened between Yom Kippur and Sukkot and it was a bright night.

We went out to the courtyard of the synagogue. Our Master stood and checked the direction of the wind. He sniffed the breeze, got his bearings, and said, "Let us go."

We passed the synagogues and came out behind the Strypa at the Butchers Street. From there we got to Ox Gore Street, so named because an ox once gored a woman and her children there. Today it is called King Street. From there we headed northwest.

As long as we were in the town our Master would take one step and stop, one step and stop. It seemed as if it was hard for him, as if he had almost forgotten how to walk. He never went outside more than twice a year, once to draw the water for making matzot and once on Rosh Hashanah to perform the tashlikh ritual. And if the first day of Shavuot was clear, he would go out to the surrounding hills to commemorate the giving of the Torah at Mt. Sinai. You can still see the rock on which he would sit and rest.

The moon shone and all was still. In the silence every so often we could hear the sound of hammering. People were putting up their sukkot. Once or twice our Master stopped to whisper the words "Hark! My beloved knocks." I knew that his whole reason for stopping was to take in the sight of all those sukkot. He remembered the terrible years when people were hiding from Khmelnitski's hordes and no one could observe the commandment of dwelling in the sukkah.

Once we got beyond town the moon disappeared and the road became rugged. I quickly lit the candle and held on to the lantern tightly. It felt as if someone were trying to grab it away from me. At times I thought I heard someone trying to blow out the candle though there was no wind. And it seemed as if someone was whispering in my ear, though I could not hear what it was. I got an earache from those murmurings. My fingers were shaking from holding on to the lantern so tightly.

We walked on in silence. When our Master was quiet, I was too. No one ever dared speak in his presence unless he gave them permission-----that is how much respect we had for him. How far we walked I cannot say. Once we left the town I lost all track of time. I became numb with fear. If our Master had not motioned for me to take hold of the hem of his cloak, I would have died of fright. At first I thought he had some amulets with him, but when I heard him whispering, "Though I walk through the valley of the shadow of death, I fear no evil, for Thou art with me," then I knew that he put his trust in the Eternal One, in Him alone, may He be blessed.

6

Were I to tell of all the difficulties our Master and I had on the way, 1 would never finish. Were I to recount all the places we passed, I would never get to the site of this story. Our Master extracted me from the domain of space just as he had taken me out of the flow of time. Much later, when I got back from where we had gone, all the places we passed through came back to me. They swirl before me even now, sometimes all jumbled together, sometimes hovering dimly on the ravines of hills and mountains, the sky above them lowering. The space between heaven and earth is as thin as an eggshell. Sometimes the earth rears itself up and presses against the sky, and sometimes the blue dome of the heavens takes on the dark color of the earth below. When I stand here, down below, it feels as though I am there, up above, and when I stand there, up above, it feels like I am here, down below. But enough of this.

The shamash proceeded:

Those who think that a wicked person who dies goes down to Gehinnom do not know that there is a punishment even more severe. It is known as "being hurled from the hollow of the sling." This sling punishment is not a place, as the treatises have it, but a bloody brawl, so named because of what is done to the sinners. They are so battered by the embroilments of their sins that they try to seek refuge in Gehinnom. But no sooner do they approach its gates than they are flung back to all the places where they sinned and where they thought about sinning. But now they cannot find those places because the sins committed there have disfigured them, and the ones that are still recognizable crumble underfoot, and sharp spikes spring up and impale their soles. Snarling dogs appear and nip at their heels. Some of these sinners are encrusted with soil, and when they are flung the soil is hurled and they remain suspended in midair. Some return to the gates of Gehinnom, while others never arrive there again.

A sinner's punishment, then, is hard, but even worse is what happens to someone who wants to sin but does so only in thought and not in deed. Someone who has actually sinned is to some extent cleansed by the remorse, suffering and heartbreak he will feel. But one who wanted to sin and never had the chance to do so will be undone by the prideful illusion that he knows how to control himself even as the fires of temptation still burn within him. Worst of all are those contemptible people who feel false pangs of conscience and fancy that they have repented, yet all the while they are consumed by sinful thoughts and their illusory pleasures. No one can accuse me of loving sinners, but when I see them flung around like that, I am quite ready to hire myself out as the doorkeeper of Gehinnom so I can personally let them in.

The shamash proceeded:

There are distinguished people who think that after they die they will go straight to Gan Eden. But when I visited Gehinnom with our Master I saw that it was filled with such people. Let me be more precise about this. Those who fill the ranks of Gehinnom are people who have already attained considerable merit. Those who have not descend to the nethermost parts of Sheol, which is to Gehinnom as Gehinnom is to Gan Eden. I mention no names here out of respect for their families. In this regard I try to emulate a practice our Master instituted after he came back from Gehinnom. Before he went, his study was focused on the Zohar and the writings of the Ari, aside from the regular classes he gave in halakhah. When he came back he devoted himself to studying Mishnah. The Mishnah study was for the purpose of raising up the souls of those who went down to Gehinnom, even though everyone thought they were righteous while they were alive. I try to do likewise. Though I am poor, whenever I get penny from the children and grandchildren of such people, I light a candle in their memory.

7

When the shamash finished these digressions, he resumed his story, first telling about the husband who abandoned his wife, then recounting all the twists and turns of the journey, then relating all the extraordinary things he had seen—everything that led up to and resulted from the fact that he had thrown a scholar from a prominent family out of the beit midrash for talking during the Torah reading.

I remove myself from the narrative and take on the character of the shamash so he can speak in his own voice. But lest you start thinking that this story is about me, I intrude periodically with the words "the shamash said."

And so he did, as follows:

Look how modest our Master was, may the memory of the righteous be for a blessing: he had taken me with him to serve as his spotter, yet it was he who recognized the wicked one first. When Aaron realized he had been seen, he ran over to our Master and said, "Rebbe, you are here! I always knew you would come to me. When a scholar goes into exile, his master is exiled with him." Our Master nodded. "Tractate Makkot Folio 10a, a little below the middle of the page!" Our Master, may the memory of the righteous be for a blessing, always did that. Whenever someone quoted a passage from the Talmud he would think for a moment and then cite the tractate, the folio, the precise side of the folio—a or b—and sometimes even the exact line and whether it was on the top half of the page or the bottom half of the page. The two of them began to converse quietly.

Our Master said to Aaron, "How could you leave your wife, the woman you married according to the laws of Moses and Israel? You transgressed, but what about your wife? What was her sin that you made not the least effort to release her from the shackles of her chained state? How terrible it is that your sin has wiped out your capacity for mercy, which is the hallmark of a Jewish person."

At this Aaron let out a wail and began crying loudly and bitterly. "They never let me! They never let me to go to her! They buried me in their cemetery, a Gentile cemetery with a cross on my grave! Two sticks, vertical and horizontal. They cut me off from Jews, and I had no way to get to a Jewish home. When I wanted to leave my grave to visit my wife in a dream and tell her that I was dead and that she was free to remarry, the cross would bar my way, and I could not get to her. Rebbe, Gehinnom is terrible, but the torment of knowing that I left my wife to be an agunah is much, much worse."

I could see tears in our Master's eyes. I heard him ask, "My son, how did you get here? For what sin did you die?" I heard Aaron's answers and got the gist of what he said, but I was so terror-stricken that I do not remember his exact words. But I do remember the gist of it. If there is a difference here between what he said and what I report, it is not in the content. He spoke in the first person, the technical term for which is "indirect speech." I give over his words in the third person.

He spoke, he cried, he spoke, he groaned, he sighed, and I was as one who heard it all from afar.

When Aaron saw the troubles that had overtaken Israel, he began to wonder about what God had done to this people and what lay behind this great and terrible anger. He started to probe the matter deeply but found no answers. He immersed himself in volumes of theosophical speculation, the great texts of the Kabbalah, the *Kanah* and the *Peli'ah*. Now a man who is righteous and along in years will read such texts and attain an even deeper sense of awe. But a young man wet behind the ears who starts delving into Kabbalah will bring upon himself only inner turmoil, all the more so when he fills his head with metaphysical investigations. He will not only fail to grow in piety, he will fall into the depths of the qelipot. That is what happened to Aaron. He not only failed to resolve his doubts, he reached the dire conclusion that the God of Israel had disengaged Himself from Israel, Heaven forbid, and had become, Heaven forbid, an enemy.

As the saying goes, "One who seeks to purify himself will get help from above, just as one who seeks to pollute himself will find the door open to him." Foolishly, Aaron decided to find out what the Gentile scholars say. He took the trouble to learn Latin and picked up in one year what the priests could not learn in seven. He buried his nose in their books and pored over their words, but the ideas he found there brought him no satisfaction. And sure enough, when a person loses his way, Satan comes and leads him on.

Satan showed him the way to a priest. Those priests have books that deal with what is above and what is below and what came before and what will be in the end, and they put forth ridiculous ideas that do nothing to resolve doubts about those matters. They say, for example, that when the different languages originated after the Tower of Babel, God created strange creatures with swordlike hands with which they incised letters in their books. Some of those books were written under the sign of Mars, and their guardian angel was Gabriel. That is totally false. Gabriel loves the Jews and champions their cause. Some of those books were written under the sign of Venus and were protected by the daughters of humans who were corrupted by the superhuman sons of God. That is a bit closer to the truth but needs to be qualified, because one of the maidens separated herself from transgression and ascended to the firmament to become one of the stars of the Pleiades. The priests bind all their books in pigskin, and as they read them the light in their soul darkens until eventually they fall into tehom, the abyss which is hinted at in the verse *and darkness was over the surface of the deep.* And note: the word tehom is made up of the same four Hebrew letters as the word hamavet (Death), and the two are one and the same, which is why tehom is the domain of the qelipot.

Aaron borrowed a few books from the priest and secreted himself away with them as one would with an adulterous woman. He drank of the bitter water, and the bitter water induced its curse within him. A person possesses two souls, an outer one that encompasses him about, and an inner one. When a person sins, God forbid, his inner soul descends below while he is still in this life.

One Friday night Aaron was at home alone. Zlateh had gone off to search for her father's grave. As you know, her father disappeared just after the murder of his father-in-law Reb Naftali. Both deaths occurred right before the pogroms of 1648–49 and were forgotten in the ensuing carnage.

It so happened that a Jewish butcher from our town made a trip to a certain place to buy cattle. A Gentile there started bragging about his cows, which, he said, were of superior quality because they grazed in a field where Jews were buried. On hearing this, the butcher pretended not to believe him. So the Gentile called his mother, who related how she had worked in the home of Naftali the wine merchant and how his son-in-law worked with him in the business. One day Naftali came to the estate in a wagon loaded with casks of wine. When night fell he slept in the open next to his wagon. Now the lord of the estate had some young noblemen who regularly dined with him. They caught the scent of the wine, went out and opened all the casks, and proceeded to get good and drunk. When they sobered up they became fearful that the lord would punish them, because he had promised the authorities that no harm would come to merchants passing through his estates. Besides, they knew that with a nobleman of his stature no actions were to be taken without his orders. After debating what to do, they killed the wine merchant. They knew it was likely that some nobleman would inform on them. After all, noblemen informed on Jews and were just as likely to inform on them. So they took the body and buried it in a field where there were Jewish graves from long ago. When Zlateh heard about all this she went with the butcher's wife to find her father's grave. But she got delayed and could not get back before the Sabbath.

That night Aaron dined with our Master. After dinner he went home and forgot that it is forbidden to sleep in one's house all alone. Why, you may ask, did our Master not remind him about that? He assumed that Aaron had arranged for a Yeshiva student to come over and stay with him overnight. So Aaron went home, sat down, and read through the weekly Torah portion. When he finished and then reviewed the prophetic reading, he found a verse in it that troubled him. He reviewed the commentaries but found no explanation that satisfied him. He then went to see what the Christian exegetes had to say. From under his bed he took out one of the books the priest had loaned him and started reading but could not make out a single letter. He thought that this was because the candle was set down too low. He did not know that on the holy Sabbath Jewish eyes cannot take in anything written in Gentile script.

One whose punishment already awaits him will forget that it is Sabbath, as Aaron did that night. He got up and took the candle and placed it on top of one of the Christian books and sat and read. Satan then did his work and Aaron's eyes did theirs. He went on reading until the candle burned down without his noticing. The candle burned through the book it was sitting on, leaving a round hole in the middle. When Aaron later returned the book, the priest took one look at it and promptly accused him of deliberately setting fire to it. He threatened to have Aaron drawn and quartered and thrown to the dogs, but if he accepted the Christian faith he could be saved. Furthermore, they would spare him all the suffering the Jews were facing, and if he feared retribution from them, the priest would arrange for him to be taken to a place where there were no Jews and no fear of Jews. Aaron chose life over death and thus bartered eternal life for this transient one. In his heart he fantasized escaping to another country, returning to the God of Israel, and getting word to his wife to come and join him. Fearing that the Gentiles would somehow discover his designs, he redoubled his violations of Jewish practice so as to show them that he accepted their god with a perfect faith. But he was torn up inside. He began to afflict his body by fasting, even though he knew that fasting without repentance is of no avail. His body shriveled and the volume of his blood shrank, not only from the fasting but also from the agony he suffered. At length he took sick and died. They buried him in a Gentile cemetery and put a cross on his grave, thereby setting up a permanent barrier between him and the Jews and preventing him from visiting his wife in a dream to inform her that he was dead and she could remarry. When a Jew engages in idolatry it is as if the idolatry itself is empowered to do him harm.

That is the story of Aaron. But I must add here something that I really should have stated earlier. That year, on the Sabbath of Repentance before we went on the journey to Gehinnom, our Master began his discourse with these words: "Preachers who chastise their congregations customarily begin with a verse from the weekly Torah portion and conclude with the verse *And a redeemer shall come to Zion and to those in Jacob who turn from transgression, says the Lord.* I, however, shall begin with that verse. *And a redeemer shall come to Zion* summarizes the foundation of our faith and the basis of repentance, for when we see year after year the same tribulations, and we continue to wait for the End of Days, and we are not destroyed by the Gentiles—all that gives us the strength and the courage to turn in complete repentance." That is what I mean when I say that our Master possessed the power of prophesy. Because even before he spoke with Aaron in Gehinnom, he already knew that his sin consisted in his having questioned the very idea of an End of Days.

That is the story of Aaron, husband of Zlateh, and it is through his fate that I came to see how severe is the punishment for all who talk during the service and the Torah reading.

If this introduction is longer than the story, more severe still is the story itself. I wish I were not telling it, and now that I am telling it, I hope it will not be taken as just a story but rather that you will learn from it how very careful we must be not to talk in the synagogue during the prayers and especially during the reading of the Torah.

V. List of Publications

21 *Alan Mintz: List of Publications*

Compiled by Menachem Butler

Books

1. *George Eliot and the Novel of Vocation in England* (PhD dissertation, Columbia University, 1975).
2. *George Eliot & The Novel of Vocation* (Cambridge, Mass.: Harvard University Press, 1978).
3. *Ḥurban: Responses to Catastrophe in Hebrew Literature* (New York: Columbia University Press, 1984).
4. *Banished From Their Father's Table: Loss of Faith and Hebrew Autobiography* (Bloomington: Indiana University Press, 1989).
5. *Hebrew in America: Perspectives and Prospects,* ed. Alan Mintz (Detroit: Wayne State University Press, 1993).
6. S.Y. Agnon, *A Book That Was Lost and Other Stories*, eds. Alan Mintz and Anne Golomb Hoffman (New York: Schocken, 1995).
7. *The Boom in Contemporary Israeli Fiction*, ed. Alan Mintz (Hanover, NH: Brandeis University Press and University Press of New England, 1997).
8. *Popular Culture and the Shaping of Holocaust Memory in America* (Seattle: University of Washington Press, 2001).
9. *Translating Israel: Contemporary Hebrew Literature and Its Reception in America* (Syracuse, NY: Syracuse University Press, 2001).
10. *Popular Culture and the Shaping of Holocaust Memory in America* (Seattle: University of Washington [Stroum Lectures], 2001).
11. *Translating Israel: Contemporary Hebrew Literature and Its Reception in America* (Syracuse University Press, 2001).
12. *Ḥurban: Responses to Catastrophe in Hebrew Literature* (Jerusalem: Mosad Bialik, 2003) (Hebrew).
13. *Reading Hebrew Literature: Critical Discussions of Six Modern Texts*, ed. Alan Mintz (Hanover, NH: Brandeis University Press, 2003).
14. S.Y. Agnon, *A Book That Was Lost: Thirty-Five Stories*, eds. Alan Mintz and Anne Golomb Hoffman, expanded edition (New Milford, CT: The Toby Press, 2008).
15. *Sanctuary in the Wilderness: A Critical Introduction to American Hebrew Poetry* (Stanford: Stanford University Press, 2012).
16. S.Y. Agnon, *A City in Its Fullness*, eds. Alan Mintz and Jeffrey Saks (New Milford, CT: The Toby Press, 2014).

Building a City: Writings on Agnon's Buczacz in Memory of Alan Mintz (2022): 341–349
DOI: 10.2979/BuildingaCityWriting.0.0.22

17. *Ancestral Tales: Reading the Buczacz Stories of S.Y. Agnon* (Stanford: Stanford University Press, 2017).
18. *American Hebraist: Essays on Agnon and Modern Jewish Literature* ed. Beverly Bailis and David Stern (College Station, PA: Penn State University Press, 2022).

Articles and Reviews:

1. "Fear and Trembling: A Retrospective Critique of United Synagogue Youth," *Response: A Contemporary Jewish Review, vol. 1, no. 1* (Summer 1967): 16–20.
2. "Agnon on the Individual and the Community," *Response: A Contemporary Jewish Review,* vol. 1, no. 1 (Summer 1967): 28–31.
3. "Jewish Students and the War: A Strategy," *Response: A Contemporary Jewish Review,* vol. 2, no. 2 (Fall 1968): 32–35.
4. "New Metaphors: Jewish Prayers and Our Situation," *Response: A Contemporary Jewish Review,* vol. 3, no. 1 (Spring 1969): 7–13.
5. "Notes on a Point of Departure," *Midstream,* vol. 16, no. 3 (March 1970): 45–50.
6. "Response to Daniel Bell," *Response: A Contemporary Jewish Review,* vol. 3, no. 2 (Fall 1969): 36–37.
7. "Along the Path to Religious Community," in James A. Sleeper and eds., *The New Jews* (New York: Vintage Books, 1971), 25–34.
8. "New Metaphors: Jewish Prayers and Our Situation," in James A. Sleeper and eds., *The New Jews* (New York: Vintage Books, 1971), 205–213.
9. "Epilogue," in James A. Sleeper and eds., *The New Jews* (New York: Vintage Books, 1971), 244–246.
10. "Contribution to Symposium," *Response: A Contemporary Jewish Review,* vol. 4, no. 4 (Winter 1970–1971): 103–104.
11. "Our Old Seem Very Blind," *Sh'ma* 2/23 (31 December 1971): 22–24.
12. "Creation: Theses in Preparation for a Theology of Growth," *Response: A Contemporary Jewish Review,* vol. 6, no. 1 (Spring 1972): 25–40.
13. "Is Our Schizophrenia Historically Important?" *Response: A Contemporary Jewish Review,* vol. 6, no. 3 (Fall 1972): 54–62.
14. "Along the Path to Religious Community," in Jacob Neusner, ed., *Contemporary Judaic Fellowship in Theory and in Practice* (New York: Ktav, 1972), 167–174.
15. "Religion and Modern Man: Review of 'Unsecular Man: The Persistence of Religion', by Andrew M. Greeley," *Commentary Magazine,* vol. 56, no. 2 (August 1973): 83–86.
16. "Toward An Integrated Jewish Theology," *Response: A Contemporary Jewish Review,* vol. 7, no. 3 (Fall 1973): 73–80.
17. "Encounter Groups and Other Panaceas," *Commentary Magazine,* vol. 56, no. 1 (July 1973): 42–49.
18. "Letter," *Commentary Magazine,* vol. 56, no. 4 (October 1973): 30–31.
19. "Participatory Theology – Review of *The Seduction of the Spirit: The Uses and Misuses of People's Religion* by Harvey Cox," *Commentary Magazine,* vol. 57, no. 3 (March 1974): 94–97.

20. "American Jews – Review of 'The Future of the Jewish Community in America', by David Sidorsky," *Commentary Magazine*, vol. 58, no. 2 (August 1974): 73–75.
21. "Mothers and Daughters: Review of *Anya* by Susan Fromberg Shaeffer," *Commentary Magazine*, vol. 59, no. 3 (March 1975): 88–90.
22. "Daniel Deronda and the Messianic Vocation," in Alice Shalvi, ed., *Daniel Deronda: A Centenary Symposium* (Jerusalem: Jerusalem Academic Press, 1976), 137–156.
23. "The People's Choice: A Demurral on Breira," *Response: A Contemporary Jewish Review*, vol. 10, no. 4 (Winter 1976–1977): 5–10.
24. "A Reply To My Critics," *Response: A Contemporary Jewish Review*, vol. 11, no. 2 (Fall 1977): 108–118.
25. "Mordecai Zev Feierberg and the Reveries of Redemption," *AJS Review*, vol. 2 (1977): 171–199.
26. "Negating the Diaspora – Review of *Letter to an American Jewish Friend* by Hillel Halkin," *Response: A Contemporary Jewish Review*, vol. 11, no. 3 (Summer 1978): 93–100.
27. "A Series of Sojourns: Review of 'History of the Jews', by Chaim Potok," *The New York Times Book Review* (17 December 1978): 3,34.
28. "Demanding Like the Land – Review of *The Story of Young Shlomzion the Great* by Yoram Kaniuk," *The New York Times Book Review* (21 January 1979): 8,27.
29. "Guenzburg, Lilienblum, and the Shape of Haskalah Autobiography," *AJS Review*, vol. 4 (1979): 71–110.
30. "Agnon in Jaffa: The Myth of the Artist as a Young Man," *Prooftexts*, vol. 1, no. 1 (January 1981): 62–83.
31. "The Song at the Sea and the Question of Doubling in Midrash," *Prooftexts*, vol. 1, no. 2 (May 1981): 185–192.
32. "Seeing It Whole – Review of *By Words Alone: The Holocaust in Literature* by Sidra DeKoven Ezrahi," *The Jerusalem Post Magazine* (19 June 1981): 16.
33. "The Rhetoric of Lamentations and the Representation of Catastrophe," *Prooftexts*, vol. 2, no. 1 (January 1982): 1–17.
34. "On the Question of Hebrew," *Forum*, no. 46–47 (Fall-Winter 1982): 73–76.
35. "The Russian Pogroms in Hebrew Literature and the Subversion of the Martyrological Ideal," *AJS Review*, vol. 7–8 (1982–1983): 263–300.
36. "Ahad Ha'am and the Essay: The Vicissitudes of Reason," in Jacques Kornberg, ed., *At the Crossroads: Essays on Ahad Ha'am* (Albany: State University of New York, 1983), 3–11.
37. "Plain and Philosophical – Review of *The Static Element: Selected Poems of Natan Zach*" *The New Republic* (31 October 1983): 34–35.
38. "Prayer and the Prayerbook," in Barry W. Holtz, ed., *Back to the Sources: Reading the Classical Jewish Texts* (New York: Summit Books, 1984), 403–429.
39. "On the Tel Aviv School of Poetics," *Prooftexts*, vol. 4, no. 3 (September 1984): 215–235.
40. "Under Hitler's Spell – Review of 'Reflections of Nazism: An Essay on Kitsch and Death,' by Saul Friedlander," *The New Republic* (1 October 1984): 40–41.

41. "Matzoh Ball Soup – Review of *Origins of the Seder: The Passover Rite and Early Rabbinic Judaism* by Baruch M. Bokser'," *The New Republic* (22 April 1985): 40–42.

42. "Berdichevsky and Erotic Shame: A Study of the Story 'Urva Paraḥ'," *Jerusalem Studies in Hebrew Literature*, vol. 9 (1986): 77–101 (Hebrew).

43. "Review of '*Parables in Midrash: Narrative and Exegesis in Rabbinic Literature*', by David Stern," *Jewish Studies*, vol. 33 (1986): 75–80.

44. "Review of *Midrash and Literature* eds. Geoffrey H. Hartman and Sanford Budick," *Shofar*, vol. 4, no. 4 (Summer 1986): 46–47.

45. Judith Bar-El, 'The National Poet: The Emergence of a Concept in Hebrew Literary Criticism (1885–1905)," *Prooftexts*, vol. 6, no. 3 (September 1986): 205–220, trans. Alan Mintz.

46. "Catastrophe," in Arthur A. Cohen and Paul Mendes-Flohr, eds., *Contemporary Jewish Religious Thought* (New York: Scribner's, 1987), 41–45.

47. "Modern Hebrew Literature and Jewish Theology: Repositioning the Question," *Orim*, vol. 3, no. 1 (Autumn 1987): 93–109.

48. "Feldman's Gabriel Preil," *The Jewish Quarterly Review*, vol. 78, no. 3–4 (January-April 1988): 316–318.

49. "Review of 'Imagining Hitler,' by Alvin H. Rosenfeld," Studies in Contemporary Jewry, vol. 4 (1988): 399–400.

50. "Review of 'Cunning Innocence: On S.Y. Agnon's Irony,' by Esther Fuchs," *AJS Review*, vol. 14, no. 1 (Spring 1989): 78–80.

51. "Fiction: A Major Israeli Novel," *Commentary Magazine*, vol. 88, no. 1 (July 1989): 56–60.

52. "A Major Israeli Novel," *Hado'ar*, vol. 69, no. 8 (1990): 13–18 (Hebrew).

53. "Agnon Without End," *Commentary Magazine*, vol. 89, no. 2 (February 1990): 57–59.

54. "A Sanctuary in the Wilderness: The Beginnings of the Hebrew Movement in America in the Pages of Hatoren," *Prooftexts*, vol. 10, no. 3 (September 1990): 389–412.

55. "Echoes of the 'Event' – Review of *From the Kingdom of Memory: Reminiscences* by Elie Wiesel," *The Jerusalem Report*, vol. 1, no. 2 (25 October 1990): 57.

56. "Brenner's 'Baḥoref' and the Hebrew Autobiographical Tradition," *Dappim: Research in Literature*, vol. 8 (1991): 221–236 (Hebrew).

57. "Review of *Shmuel Yosef Agnon: A Revolutionary Traditionalist* by Gershon Shaked," *Hebrew Studies*, vol. 32 (1991): 61–66.

58. "The Erosion of the Tarbut Ivrit Ideology in America and the Consequences for the Teaching of Hebrew in the University," *Shofar*, vol. 9, no. 3 (Spring 1991): 50–54.

59. "Tellers of the Soil – Review of *The Blue Mountain* by Meir Shalev," *The New Republic* (9 September 1991): 39–42.

60. "Hebrew Literature," in Barry W. Holtz, ed., *The Schocken Guide to Jewish Books* (New York: Schocken, 1992), 244–258.

61. "Manners, Morals, and the Academy – Review of *Jews in the American Academy, 1900–1940* by Susanne Klingenstein," *The New Republic* (9 March 1992): 41–44.

62. "Response to Mrs. Diana Trilling," *The New Republic* (6 April 1992): 4.

63. "Introduction," in ed., *Hebrew in America: Perspectives and Prospects* (Detroit: Wayne State University Press, 1993), 13–26.

64. "A Sanctuary in the Wilderness: The Beginnings of the Hebrew Movement in America in the Pages of *Hatoren*," in ed., *Hebrew in America: Perspective and Prospects* (Detroit: Wayne State University Press, 1993), 29–67.

65. "Catastrophe," in Arthur A. Cohen and Paul Mendes-Flohr, eds., *Contemporary Jewish Religious Thought* (Tel- Aviv: Am Oved, 1993), 185–187 (Hebrew).

66. "A.B. Yehoshua, Mr. Mani," *Tikkun*, vol. 8, no. 2 (March-April 1993): 60.

67. "The Future of Hebrew in America," *Gesher*, no. 127–128 (Fall-Winter 1993): 70–79 (Hebrew).

68. "The Collapse of the Poet's Self-Myth in 'The Streets of the River'," *Jerusalem Studies in Hebrew Literature*, vol. 14 (1993): 335–341 (Hebrew).

69. "The Counterlives – Review of 'Mr. Mani', by A.B. Yehoshua," *The New Republic* (29 June 1992): 41–45.

70. "Hebrew in America," *Commentary Magazine*, vol. 96, no. 1 (July 1993): 42–46.

71. "The Prophet of Tikkun: Can Michael Lerner Heal Himself?" *The Forward* (16 September 1994): 1–10.

72. "One of the People – Review of *Elusive Prophet: Ahad Ha'am and the Origins of Zionism* by Steven J. Zipperstein," *Commentary Magazine*, vol. 98, no. 4 (October 1994): 66–68.

73. Alan Mintz and Anne Golomb Hoffman, "Introduction," in S.Y. Agnon, *A Book That Was Lost and Other Stories*, eds. Alan L. Mintz and Anne Golomb Hoffman (New York: Schocken, 1995), 9–34.

74. "Review of *Between Exile and Return: S.Y. Agnon and the Drama of Writing* by Anne Golomb Hoffman," *The Jewish Quarterly* Review, vol. 86, no. 1–2 (July-October 1995): 239–240.

75. "A Passage to India – Review of 'Open Heart', by A.B. Yehoshua," *The New York Times Book Review* (2 June 1996): 15–16.

76. "Dark Passages," *Partisan Review*, vol. 63, no. 4 (Fall 1996): 691–704.

77. "What Lasts – Review of *The Book and the Sword: A Life of Learning in the Shadow of Destruction* by David Weiss Halivni," *Commentary Magazine*, vol. 103, no. 3 (March 1997): 65–67.

78. "The Divided Fate of Hebrew and Hebrew Culture at the Seminary," in Jack Wertheimer, ed., *Tradition Renewed: A History of the Jewish Theological Seminary*, vol. 2 (New York: Jewish Theological Seminary of America, 1997), 83–112.

79. "Introduction," in Alan Mintz, ed., *The Boom in Contemporary Israeli Fiction* (Hanover, NH: Brandeis University Press and University Press of New England, 1997), 1–16.

80. "Israeli Literature and the American Reader," *The American Jewish Year Book*, vol. 97 (1997): 93–114.
81. "Israel Comes of Middle Age: Hebrew Blooms Beyond Zionists' Dreams," *Newsday* (13 May 1998): A40.
82. "Sushi and Other Jewish Foods," *Commentary Magazine, vol.* 106, no. 4 (October 1998): 43–47.
83. "Going for 'the Gold Medal in the Victimization Olympics' – Two Books Look at the History of America's Ever-Growing Fascination With the Holocaust," *The Forward* (14 May 1999): 11–12.
84. "999 – Review of *A Journey to the End of the Millennium: A Novel of the Middle Ages* by A.B. Yehoshua," *Commentary Magazine*, vol. 108, no. 1 (July–August 1999): 84–86.
85. Vardit Ringvald and Alan Mintz, "Introduction: Which Hebrew? Policy and Strategy in the Teaching of Hebrew in America," *Journal of Jewish Education*, vol. 65, no. 3 (1999): 8.
86. "Fracturing the Zionist Narrative," *Judaism*, vol. 48, no. 4 (Fall 1999): 407–415.
87. "A 'Crazy' Dog Has His Say in Agnon's Surreal Epic: Translating a Masterpiece of the Second Aliya; Only Yesterday," *The Forward* (19 May 2000): 11–12.
88. "Between Holocaust and Homeland: Agnon's Ha-Siman," in Anita Shapira, Jehuda Reinharz, Jay M. Harris, eds., *The Age of Zionism* (Jerusalem: Shazar, 2000), 317–335 (Hebrew).
89. "Two Models in the Study of Holocaust Literature," in Michael A. Signer, ed., *Humanity at the Limit: The Impact of the Holocaust Experience on Jews and Christians* (Bloomington: Indiana University Press, 2000), 400–428.
90. "In The Seas of Youth," *Prooftexts*, vol. 21, no. 1 (Winter 2001): 57–70.
91. "Sefer ha'aggadah: Triumph or Tragedy?" in William Cutter and David C. Jacobson, eds., *History and Literature: New Readings of Jewish Texts in Honor of Arnold J. Band* (Providence, RI: Brown University, 2002), 17–26.
92. "Hebrew Literature in America," in Hana Wirth-Nesher and Michael P. Kramer, eds., *The Cambridge Companion to Jewish American Literature* (Cambridge: Cambridge University Press, 2003), 92–109.
93. "Introduction," in ed., *Reading Hebrew Literature: Critical Discussions of Six Modern Texts* (Hanover, NH: Brandeis University Press, 2003), 1–20.
94. "'The Sense of Smell' by S.Y. Agnon," in ed., *Reading Hebrew Literature: Critical Discussions of Six Modern Texts* (Hanover, NH: Brandeis University Press, 2003), 126–134.
95. "Hebrew Culture in America: The Second Act," in Zvia Ben-Yosef Ginor, ed., *Essays on Hebrew Literature in Honor of Avraham Holtz* (New York: Jewish Theological Seminary of America, 2003), 177–182 (Hebrew).
96. "Review of *Modern Hebrew Fiction* by Gershon Shaked," *AJS Review*, vol. 27, no. 1 (April 2003): 161–165.
97. "You're in the Army Now – Yehoshua Kenaz Gives Readers a Glimpse into Israeli Society's Holy of Holies," *The Forward* (19 September 2003): 14.

98. "In Memoriam – Edward Said: Inclusive Mind, Exclusive Idea," *The Forward* (10 October 2003): 11.

99. "Foreword," to Haim Gouri, *Facing the Glass Booth: The Jerusalem Trial of Adolf Eichmann* (Detroit: Wayne State University Press, 2004), ix–xiv.

100. "Editing As Intellectual Community: A Retrospective Manifesto," *Prooftexts*, vol. 24, no. 3 (Fall 2004): 273–276.

101. "Group Therapy – Review of 'Jews and the American Soul', by Andrew R. Heinze," *The New Republic* (21 February 2005): 31–33.

102. "From Silence to Prominence: The Holocaust in American Culture," in Dan Michman, ed., *The Holocaust in Jewish History: Historiography, Historical Consciousness and Interpretations* (Jerusalem: Yad Vashem, 2005), 463–489 (Hebrew).

103. "Kishinev and the Twentieth Century: Introduction," *Prooftexts*, vol. 25, no. 1–2 (Winter-Spring 2005): 1–7.

104. "Is Teaching Ivrit B'ivrit Worth The Trouble?" *ha-Yedion* (2006): 4–5.

105. Alan Mintz and Anne Golomb Hoffman, "Introduction," in S.Y. Agnon, *A Book That Was Lost: Thirty-Five Stories*, eds. Alan L. Mintz and Anne Golomb Hoffman, expanded edition (New Milford, CT: The Toby Press, 2008), 9–34.

106. "Writing about Ourselves: Jewish Autobiography, Modern and Premodern," *The Jewish Quarterly Review*, vol. 98, no. 2 (Spring 2008): 272–285.

107. "Knocking on Heaven's Gate: Hebrew Literature and Wisse's Canon," in Justin Cammy, Dara Horn, Alyssa Quint, and Rachel Rubinstein, eds., *Arguing the Modern Jewish Canon: Essays on Literature and Culture in Honor of Ruth R. Wisse* (Cambridge, Mass.: Center for Jewish Studies, Harvard University, 2008), 23–34.

108. "Du silence a l'evidence interpretation de la Shoah dans la culture americaine," in Francoise S. Ouzan and Dan Michman, eds. *De la mémoire de la Shoah dans le monde juif* (Paris: CNRS Éditions, 2008), 253–281 (French).

109. "Reb Gershon and Reb Yudl: Thoughts on the Achievement of Gershon Shaked on the First Anniversary of his Death," *Hebrew Studies*, vol. 49 (2008): 299–305.

110. "Seven Theses on Hebrew and Jewish Peoplehood," *Contact*, vol. 10, no. 3 (Spring 2008): 9..

111. "Eisig Silberschlag and the Persistence of the Erotic in American Hebrew Poetry," in Sheila E. Jelen, Michael P. Kramer, and L. Scott Lerner, eds., *Modern Jewish Literatures: Intersections and Boundaries* (Philadelphia: University of Pennsylvania Press, 2010), 169–188.

112. "Abraham Regelson and the Apotheosis of Hebrew," *Prooftexts*, vol. 30, no. 1 (Winter 2010): 6–34 .

113. "Love and War – Review of *To the End of the Land*, by David Grossman," The *Jewish Review of Books, vol. 1, no.* 3 (Fall 2010): 9–11.

114. "The Hebraist Moment in American Jewish Culture and What it has to Say to us Today," *Contact*, vol. 13, no. 2 (Spring 2011): 11.

115. "Foreword," in Michael Weingrad, *American Hebrew Literature: Writing Jewish National Identity in the United States* (Syracuse, N.Y.: Syracuse University Press, 2011), xi–xii.

116. "The Rebbe and the Yak – Review of 'Back From Heavenly Lake', by Haim Be'er," The Jewish Review of Books, vol. 2, no. 3 (Fall 2011): 10–12.

117. "Reading 'HaHazanim'," *'Ayin Gimel: A Journal of Agnon Studies*, vol. 2 (2012): 93–107.

118. "Israel's Arab Sholem Aleichem – Review of 'Second Person Singular', by Sayed Kashua, trans. Mitch Ginsburg," *The Jewish Review of Books*, vol. 3, no. 2 (Summer 2012): 24–26.

119. "Symposium: Why Did You Go Into Jewish Studies?" *AJS Perspectives* (Spring 2012): 55–56.

120. "Introduction to *To the End of the Land* by David Grossman: A Symposium," *Hebrew Studies*, vol. 54 (2013): 285–286.

121. "Spanish Charity – Review of *The Retrospective* by A.B. Yehoshua," *The Jewish Review of Books*, vol. 4, no. 2 (Summer 2013): 30–32.

122. "Ora's Tale: The Narrative Ambitions of David Grossman's *To The End of the Land*," *Hebrew Studies*, vol. 54 (2013): 335–344.

123. "Introduction," in S.Y. Agnon, *A Parable and Its Lesson* (Stanford: Stanford University Press, 2014), ix–xiv.

124. "Nation and Narrative – Review of *Like Dreamers – The Story of the Israeli Paratroopers Who Reunited Jerusalem and Divided a Nation* by Yossi Klein Halevi," The Jewish Review of Books, vol. 5, no. 1 (Spring 2014): 28–30.

125. "Haim Gouri at 90," *The Jewish Review of Books*, vol. 5, no. 2 (Summer 2014): 36–39.

126. "Essay on The Parable and Its Lesson: HaMashal VeHaNimshal," in S.Y. Agnon, *A Parable and Its Lesson* (Stanford: Stanford University Press, 2014), 79–158.

127. "The Life of the Flying Apercu – Review of *Why Not Say What Happened: A Sentimental Education* by Morris Dickstein," The *Jewish Review of Books*, vol. 6, no. 2 (Summer 2015): 19–20.

128. "Reader, I Adopted Him – Review of Maya Arad, *Land of Kazan*" The *Jewish Review of Books*, vol. 6, no. 4 (Winter 2016): 14–17.

129. "The Brief Moment Between Assimilationism and Nationalism," *Mosaic online Magazine* (9 May 2016).

130. "My Life with Hebrew," *Mosaic online Magazine* (13 April 2017).

131. "What's Yichus Got to Do With It? – Review of *The Marriage Plot: Or, How Jews Fell in Love with Love, and with Literature?* by Naomi Seidman," The *Jewish Review of Books*, vol. 7, no. 4 (Winter 2017): 16–17.

132. "Adventure Story – Review of 'The Story of Hebrew', by Lewis Glinert," The *Jewish Review of Books*, vol. 8, no. 1 (Spring 2017): 10–12.

133. "Review of 'Indebted: Capitalism and Religion in the Writings of S.Y. Agnon', by Yonatan Sagiv," *AJS Review*, vol. 41, no. 2 (November 2017): 510–511.

134. "The Future of Jewish American Literature: Notes from a Recovering Snob," *Studies in American Jewish Literature*, vol. 37, no. 1 (2018): 101–104..

135. "Hebrew in America: A Memoir," in Naomi B. Sokoloff and Nancy E. Berg, eds., *What We Talk about When We Talk about Hebrew* (and What It Means to Americans) (Seattle: University of Washington Press, 2018), 211–226.

136. "Viva Voce: Vicissitudes of the Spoken Word in Hebrew Literature," *In geveb: A Journal of Yiddish Studies* (June 2020).

137. "Cooking for Others: Fancy and Plain," *Sephardic Horizons* (2020) https://www.sephardichorizons.org/Volume8/Issue3&4/Mintz.html

MENACHEM BUTLER is Program Fellow for Jewish Legal Studies at the Julis-Rabinowitz Program on Jewish and Israeli Law at Harvard Law School, and Contributing Editor at *Tablet Magazine*.

Index

www.ingramcontent.com/pod-product-compliance
Lightning Source LLC
Chambersburg PA
CBHW032342280326
41935CB00008B/420